The

Mouth

That Begs

Post-Contemporary Interventions

Series Editors: Stanley Fish and Fredric Jameson

Gang Yue

The Mouth That Begs

Hunger, Cannibalism, and the Politics of Eating in Modern China

Duke University Press

Durham and London

1999

Printed in the United States of America

on acid-free paper ∞

Designed by C.H. Westmoreland

Typeset in Quadraat with Post Antiqua display

by Tseng Information Systems, Inc.

Library of Congress Cataloguing-in-Publication

Data appear on the last printed page of

this book.

For my parents

Yue Guangxi and Yuan Guangyou

Contents

Acknowledgments

This book originated from the dissertation I completed at the University of Oregon in 1993. I remain deeply indebted to the vigilant and compassionate readers of that dissertation: Wendy Larson, Rey Chow, the late Alan Wolfe, Stephane Durrant, and Forest Pyle. To my colleagues at the University of North Carolina at Chapel Hill—Judith Farquhar, Eric Henry, James Hevia, and Jerome Seaton—I have many thanks to give for their useful comments on various portions of the book during different periods and especially for their support and guidance that have sustained my intellectual growth in the past six years. I thank my friends Allen Carey-Webb, Li Tuo, Lydia Liu, Jing Wang, and Xudong Zhang for suggesting sources, raising touchy questions, providing scholarly advice, or otherwise sharing in this endeavor. I am grateful to the anonymous readers of Duke University Press for their suggestions of new sources and their inspiring critiques that challenged me to rethink some key issues and restructure the chapters. I thank my editor, Reynolds Smith, for his warm encouragement.

Portions of chapter 5 were originally published under the title "Surviving (in) the 'Chess King': Toward a Postrevolutionary Nation-Narration" in *positions* 3, no. 2 (fall 1995) by Duke University Press. A spring 1996 fellowship at the Institute for the Arts and Humanities at the University of North Carolina at Chapel Hill gave me time to complete the first version of the book. The College of Arts and Sciences and the Curriculum in Asian Studies provided a semester of teaching relief in fall 1997 and made the timely revision of the book possible. Nothing can compare, of course, to the love of those who have fed me in my life, especially the good tastes of Wenling Guo and Selene Yue, who have to endure my voracious appetite for wasting time.

Introduction

A Modern Saga of "Eating"

The "people revere food as if it were Heaven" (*minyishi weitian*), goes a Chinese adage. If food is Heaven, paradise can be reached with a smack of the lips, tasted in the twist of the tongue, and digested through the movement of the bowels. A common form of Chinese greeting epitomizes this earthy attitude: "Have you eaten?" In this way the everyday is lived with a touch of religious piety, and religion melts into the rituals of the everyday.

The millennial history of Chinese culinary culture has nurtured a vast and ever growing territory of meaning. The ancient Chinese chef-politician carries on a dialogue with the solitary drunken poet, the Confucian gourmet-sage converses with the "hunger artist," and the modern writer sets out to overthrow the old cannibalistic feast. Political deliberation, economic calculation, philosophical speculation, moral education, and artistic imagination all draw inspiration from food and the experience of eating. Eating and talking are not the same, of course, but the latter does reflect the cultural preoccupation with the former by wrapping up the experience of the mouth around a double orality. An old joke provides a telling example: "Anything with two legs is edible except your parents; so is anything with four legs, except the bed" (qtd. in Xia 1992, 9). In the same vein, a more recent Chinese gourmet makes fun of his and the culture's fabulous appetite: "I want to eat! / Anything that flies in the sky but kites, / Anything that has four legs on the earth but stools" (qtd. in Zha 1995, 121).

In North America, the most successful sino-original business is none other than the mushrooming eateries serving half-baked Chinese dishes. Yes, these are "original" and "half-baked" at the same time: the fortune cookie best showcases the point. Mysteriously invented overseas, this little mass-produced goody packages simulations of "Chinese wisdom" in fortune-cookie English, the Charlie Chan style of "Chinglish," which was invented by Hollywood and is in turn a vestige of earlier Western fantasies of Chinoiserie. What really lasts in time and fascinates us, then, is this imaginary culture of cooking and eating, as the box-office success of such movies as *The Wedding Banquet* and *Eat Drink Man Woman* illustrate. Above all, one can eat just so much or, in our diet-conscious age, just so little. In the end, the distinction between where the mouth of eating ends and where the mouth of talking begins becomes blurred.

Thus, we should not be surprised to find that the history of twentieth-century China can be conceived as a saga of "eating." In the grand narrative of revolution, as I will show, the old China was a monstrous human-eating feast; only through revolution could the oppressed masses free themselves of that devouring system and transform it into egalitarian revelry. But the revolutionary struggle was not a civic banquet; the masses had to be prepared to tighten their belts, swallow bitterness, and sacrifice their flesh and blood. Tragically, the utopian carnival fell through the broken iron rice bowl, as the "big pot of socialism" became too depleted to sustain the belly for the promised feast yet to come. In a matter of a decade, however, the saga took another turn. The haunting memory of the hungry past quickly faded away in the dazzling emergence of plenty when the sudden arrival of consumerism sharpened the cultural appetite for instant gratification. The new era saw, once again, the return of insatiable voracity.

The past two decades have seen the publication in English of a dozen scholarly books on food and eating in Western literatures (e.g., J. Brown 1984; Kilgour 1990; Jeanneret 1991; Ellmann 1993). A number of scholarly works have also been published that approach Chinese food and food culture from historical and anthropological perspectives (K. Chang 1977; E. Anderson 1988; Simmons 1991). To my best knowledge, however, there has not yet been a book-length study of alimentary discourse in Chinese literature. Given the fact that Chinese literature is one of the oldest textual traditions developed from one of the oldest cultures with the largest agricultural population in the world, and that the most frequent contact of the average American with "Chinese culture" is through Chinese food, a book of this kind is long overdue.

With various semantic, symbolic, and structural ramifications, "eating" is underscored by a broad concern and anxiety expressed by writers about the material and social conditions of collective survival. If eating is one of the most biologically determined acts, in what ways is it also shaped by cultural values and social relations? To what extent has a culture's experience with food molded its outlook on the world? How does alimentary discourse simultaneously reflect lived realities and cultural arrangements and motivate historical changes? These questions all point to the problematic relationship between our animal instinct and our human spirit, between the stomach and the head, so to speak. The relationship between food and words lays bare the compensatory *and* pathological nature of alimentary writing. In a utopian state of lasting abundance, peace, and harmony, food perhaps would contain little compensatory or surplus value for the artistic imagination. Conversely, given that modern China has suffered so much from war, political oppression, social devastation, ecological degradation, and moral degeneration, nothing can better capture its cultural pathology than the themes of hunger and cannibalism. It is this paradox of pathology and imagination that provides a critical pathway to the dialectic of the body politic and the body corporeal.

Setting out with a brief account of alimentary themes and tropes in ancient Chinese writings, this book has its main body focused on delineating a historical trilogy from cannibalism to hunger to cannibalism: from Lu Xun's allegory of the old human-eating China and Shen Congwen's "modest proposal" through the hunger narrative in the revolutionary and postrevolutionary writings to the post-1989 works on cannibalism and carnivorism. Women writers historically did not participate in this alimentary saga. To address this gender imbalance and complicate the linear trilogy from a comparative perspective, six women writers are grouped together in the last part of the book, including three Chinese and three Chinese American authors. While I treat hunger and cannibalism as symptomatic revelations of distorted realities of material and moral "lack," in the conclusion I bring up the issues of indigestion and overconsumption and suggest that "eating" must be broadened to take account of historical changes and environmental implications in this era of mass consumerism.

Chapter 1 provides a preliminary sketch of four motifs in ancient Chinese writings that have continued to shape the modern saga: (1) hunger/fulfillment as the principle that defines the relationship between the peasantry and the state, (2) cooking as a metaphoric model for governance that blends oral experience with political and philosophical persuasion, (3) fasting as a gesture of moral sagehood and social protest, and (4) the ritual of social coercion that recycles hatred in the form of "revenge cannibalism" and the allegorization of the human condition conceived on the negative paradigm of being eaten. If ancient China was an orality-centered culture that treated food in a quasi-religious fashion, this collective cultural unconscious was molded in the historical experience of hunger and reinforced by the ancestry-oriented, this-worldly attitude toward food. Alimentary discourse, then, cannot be narrowly defined in terms of rhetorical device or figurative speech. It serves as a contested site for social negotiation and cultural embodiment, where the survival of the physical body exemplifies the struggle of the body politic.

Among the major writers active from the May Fourth period to the 1930s, Lu Xun and Shen Congwen stand out for their alimentary writing for cultural embodiment. Chapters 2 and 3 discuss their works respectively. I read these two writers in terms of dialogism in order to explore their distinctive, and sometimes opposite, subject positions, moral postures, and formal strategies. Looked at from the angle of cultural history, their "dialogue" maps out the parameters of a discursive field in which younger generations of Chinese writers participate through what David Wang calls "reciprocal invocation" (1992, 292). While recognizing the profound complexity of Lu Xun as a historical figure, I relocate this "fatherly" personae at the intersection where his early personal experience is reenacted in the colonial context of Chinese modernity. Lu Xun's memory of the past is fraught with the fear of being devoured, traceable to his traumatic childhood and his fascination with the ancient Chinese imaginary world of the grotesque. Consistently acted out in his historical odyssey is a journey from oral-libidinal anxiety to visual-symbolic solution. This deep-seated anxiety comes into play with the modern discourse of cannibalism as the personal is constituted, through reading and writing, in the political. Cannibalism accords him a powerful trope of negative totality in interpreting traditional Chinese culture and society. But Lu Xun's border crossing is only a microcosmic effect of the larger pattern of colonial travel dating back to the Great Voyage, when the term *canibales* was coined in Columbus's accidental misreading of what has since been called the "Caribbean" in his search for the old Cathay. Derived from that "original" moment of international travel and cartography, Lu Xun's allegorical embodiment of history reveals the ideological configuration of the third world intellectual and the teleology of world history.

Caught in the same social contradiction and intellectual predicament, Shen Congwen "regresses" from visuality to orality by internalizing social misery in order to digest and spit out the ugly truth. His alimentary presentation of Chinese society emerges from an agrarian understanding of the materiality of food and is ingrained in his own experience of hunger. Writing about eating, he evokes the lost idyllic homeland through a ravenous nostalgia and translates that hungry desire into a utopian fulfillment. In Shen's works, food is closely associated with the image of the mother and the warmth of the hearth, and oral experience stakes out a minor territory of the imaginary at the margin of the symbolic. He reciprocates Lu Xun's outcry, "save the children," by putting forward a "modest proposal" in the spirit of Swift's Irish model, thereby reorienting the national body downward toward diseased social conditions. Ironically, the "reactionary" Shen Congwen comes closer to, and anticipates, the hunger narrative in the literature of the Communist revolution. As a writer, Shen is clear about the limited power of literature in transforming society yet insists on the formal integrity of the text. Emphasizing the primacy of the carnal body but skeptical about the political function of the textual body at the same time, Shen created a phantasmagoric world-in-text that would have to wait five decades to become a major source of inspiration for post-Mao writers.

Hunger is the central theme in the next episode of the saga, which I present in chapters 4 and 5. The texts are chosen according to their thematic affinity rather than the historical periodization of modern (pre-1949) and contemporary (post-1949) China. Working in the post–Cold War environment, I take it as an important task to revisit the dialectic of materialism and utopianism embedded in the revolutionary narrative. The Communist revolution, though inspired by Marxism-Leninism, should be understood as a third world peasant rebellion motivated by fundamental economic destitution. The path to fulfillment is forged around a metaphorical transformation of Lu Xun's human-eating old society into a futuristic carnival of socialism. To the extent that "hungry revolution" describes the historical transformation, "revolutionary hunger" breeds the collective consciousness in an open-ended narrative of desire. The tragedy of the revolution lies in its ideological mystification and narrative closure, which fixates the hungry desire on a newly constructed transcendental signified: the great savior of Mao and the Party. The first section of chapter 4 discusses the interplay of "hungry revolution" and "revolutionary hunger" in Yan'an literature. The second section explores how the critical power of "revolutionary hunger" is revitalized from the tragic end of the revolution in Wang Ruowang's autobiographical novel *Hunger Trilogy* (1980) and Lu Wenfu's novella "The Gourmet" (1983).

Chapter 5 carries the topic of hunger into the postrevolutionary rewriting of the metanarrative in Zhang Xianliang's "Mimosa" (1984) and Ah Cheng's "The Chess King" (1984). Both texts reappropriate the irreducible materiality of food and its metaphoric power, opening new possibilities for articulating desire. In "Mimosa," the critical thrust cuts deeply into the fixed meaning of "Marx" and "the People," turning the two major icons in the revolutionary narrative into a verbal feast. Particularly important is Zhang's bibliophagy of Marx, which stands the head on the stomach and ideology on materiality. "The Chess King," on the other hand, bypasses the metanarrative altogether and zeroes in on food and chess so that food consumption and chess playing are reconnected with the carnal body. By foregrounding the rewriting of the grand narrative of revolution (especially in "Mimosa") and the contextual reconstruction of a nativist imagination (mainly around "The Chess King" and the movement of "searching for roots"), this chapter approaches the postrevolutionary condition from a global postmodern and postcolonial perspective.

Perhaps the most ironic episode in the saga is the recurrence of cannibalism in the early 1990s. Chapter 6 features Zheng Yi's *Red Monument* (1993) and Liu Zhenyun's "Revisiting 1942" (1993), while the whole of chapter 7 is devoted to Mo Yan's *Liquorland* (1992). Because all three texts were written in the immediate aftermath of the mass protest movement of 1989, the resurfacing of cannibalism completes a trilogy that seems to end where it began. There is no question that June Fourth resonates with May Fourth as the two most devastating moments of intellectual crisis in twentieth-century China. Nowhere is the traumatic shock better dramatized than in the haunting images of cannibalism and madness. While such an allegorical interpretation of history may provide a convenient framework for theorization and periodization, I chose these texts also to show the radical differences among the authors, which enables us to rethink the most entrenched trope in constructing historical totality since Lu Xun.

Sharing the same premise already applied to the topic of cannibalism, the three "grandchildren" continue to either reproduce Lu Xun's legacy or rewrite it through parody and pastiche. Zheng Yi's "journalistic" investigation of a 1968 incident of real cannibalism in a remote region of southern China at once enlarges the Madman's journey and reinscribes the madness of the Cultural Revolution. In his ferocious attack on Maoism and its presumed roots in Marxism and Confucianism, Zheng Yi recycles the very rhetoric of "class hatred" and "revolutionary revenge" that fired up that brutal event of cannibalism in the first place, reaffirming the logic and power of ideological appellation and reproduction. Likewise, Liu Zhenyun's fictional visit to the 1942 mass famine in the war-torn province of Henan shows the ideological and epistemological resiliency of the master trope when he becomes caught up in some flesh-eating anecdotes despite his professed experiment with historiographical writing. Mo Yan's novel, on the other hand, shifts the critical focus from the human(istic) order to the carnivorous nature of the human animal, thus dissolving the high-handed moralistic discourse of cannibalism in the messy material world of meat consumption. Through Mo Yan's low-angle, Gothic depiction of the predatory "meat-market" in the post-1989 era, the moral authority of the Madman is also liquidated in the intoxicating liquor. Placed side by side, the three texts form a dialogical counterpoint that can be traced to Lu Xun and Shen Congwen.

The last part of this book provides a sample of feminine and cross-cultural perspectives. Chapter 8 examines the "art of hunger" in Xiao Hong's personal essays collected in *Market Street* (1936), the postrevolutionary reconstruction of an alternative social history around the stove in Wang Anyi's novel *Melody of Lasting Regret* (1996), and the violent connection of meat consumption and female abuse in Li Ang's *The Butcher's Wife* (1983). Three writers, representing pre-1949 China, the People's Republic (PRC), and Taiwan respectively, thus map out a territory on the margin of the male-dominated trilogy as much as their distinctive personal and geo-historical positions play out the paradox of intra-gender difference.

This gender perspective from Chinese-language literature is complemented, in chapter 9, by a cross-cultural reading of alimentary themes and tropes from three Chinese American women writers, namely, Jade Snow Wong, Maxine Hong Kingston, and Amy Tan. The inclusion of

American texts is meant not so much as an abstracted comparison of differences and similarities as it is a way of highlighting the problems of cross-cultural encounters in concrete experience. My reading of these texts begins with an account of my own American experience, played out around the ethnic epithet "banana," the notorious monkey brain feast from Kingston's *The Woman Warrior* (1975), and the circulation of the fortune cookie in several unexpected events of public and pedagogical significance. In analyzing two of the most fortune cookie–like texts, Wong's autobiography, *Fifth Chinese Daughter* (1945), and Tan's *The Joy Luck Club* (1989), I argue that the "desire" of the fortune cookie for survival must be recognized and reappropriated from the melting pot. In the end, Tan's unquestioning use of an ancient Chinese ritual of flesh slicing reorients our journey back to where modern Chinese literature set out: the question of cannibalism and Lu Xun's national allegory.

The inclusion of certain authors and texts to the exclusion of others is perhaps a perennial headache for scholars, especially considering the scope of this book, which addresses a number of historical periods and geographical locations. Yet, because the topic has rarely been explored in a systematic fashion, I have to map an uncharted course of history by selecting the most salient signposts. As far as the trilogy from cannibalism to hunger to cannibalism is concerned, this is not too difficult a task. The selected texts speak for the alimentary saga in such a meaningful way that they speak to one another with cultural-historical awareness of the discursive field of eating, sometimes with intertextual reference to a particular predecessor. What may be problematic and in need of justification is the apparently arbitrary choice of six women writers who do not fit in the main body of the book. Nevertheless, this choice is made by default as well as design.

In my survey of twentieth-century Chinese literature, I find that major women writers in modern China seem to be rather "fed up" or find alimentary writing uninteresting. Of the few relevant texts, the three I have chosen provide alternative views of the alimentary saga while a few others are omitted because they do not quite fit the framework of this study and merit separate treatment.[1] In the following chapters, I will provide a more detailed explanation of this gender imbalance. It suffices to say here that the preoccupation with "eating" is mainly a male phenomenon in modern Chinese literature, not to mention the ancient tradition. This suggests to me that the alimentary trilogy is arguably a male version of history. This gender imbalance does not make our study less relevant by itself, of course. But it does raise some questions, the most obvious of which is why Chinese women writers lack the appetite for a crucial area of culture that has attracted much attention, say, from American women writers (e.g., the late M. F. K. Fisher) and feminist scholars (see C. Kim 1985). The trouble is that we cannot adequately address such a question because the actual absence of sufficient textual evidence lies at the very root of that question.

The relatively low profile of women writers nevertheless has important implications, so I would like to offer a few speculative notes. Perhaps it has to do with the traditional role of the domestic kitchen servant played by housewives: liberation begins with steps to free women from the shackles of domestic labor. Perhaps high culinary culture in traditional China was largely a male domain and the prototype is the master chef Yi Yin (discussed in the next chapter). Even today the master chef remains a male image, about which the second daughter in *Eat Drink Man Woman* voices much resentment. Perhaps hunger means a different kind of "lack" to men and women since girls are the first to be traded for food to feed a starving family. The exchange of women for food is a central theme of Li Ang's *The Butcher's Wife.* Although women are said to hold up half the sky in revolutionary China, they—especially working-class women—continue to attend to the bulk of the domestic groundwork. In addition to these sociohistorical factors, the "woman writer" is very much a modern product and a revolutionary image. When pushed to the extreme, the portraits of revolutionary women in the PRC are the mostly idealized and degendered superwomen who "don't eat human food," as the Chinese expression *bushi renjian yanhuo* puts it. The ideological inflation of the "iron girl" leaves little room for the artistic imagination of gustatory pleasure, and the boredom of the daily routine is only worthy of some passing reference, as in Shen Rong's novella "At Middle Age" (1980). Class privilege and the benefit of being well educated—at least before 1949 in comparison to working-class women—may be another reason for female writers' lack of interest in cooking. What is known, from Xiao Hong's essays and Wang Anyi's novel, is that women writers are more concerned about the libidinal economy of the body when they write about eating. Most intriguing is that, unlike their male counterparts, they do not evoke the image of the mother or the return to the "oral stage."

The same is not true for Chinese American women writers. By no means do I want to imply that women writers are less liberated if they write extensively about food and domestic scenes. Rather, gender constructs are intertwined with ethnicity for Chinese American writers, and the symbolic space in which Chinese food signifies "Chineseness" is informed in the larger American cultural imagination that simultaneously *ethnicizes* and *feminizes* "China"—the "Chinaman" included (see Chin et al. 1972; Chin 1991; also see Chow 1991, chap. 1 for a similar but more complex mode of "feminizing China"). The disproportionate concentration of Chinese Americans in the restaurant and other cheap-labor service "industries" before the immigration reforms of 1965 and the civil rights movement has certainly reinforced that cultural image. At the same time, Chinese Americans' memory of the old country is often preserved and disseminated through alimentary practice and food lore. As a matter of fact, an impressionistic look at the cultural landscape and food imagery in North American Chinatowns (as well as in much of Chinese American literature) often evokes the memory of an older and more "authentic" China, as "exotic" to visitors brought up in Mao's China as they are to non-Chinese tourists. Food customs and food-related rituals are a mainstay in the development of ethnic self-awareness. Growing up in such an environment and educated by their parents to survive on the principle of necessity (see S. Wong 1993), American writers of Chinese ancestry inevitably have to appropriate this legacy in their cultural negotiation and literary representation. While many other "native" symbolic resources are not readily accessible to their American readers, they utilize the simple but rich signs of food and cooking simultaneously to stimulate and alter the cultural appetite of the reading public.

It must be noted that male writers in the Chinese American tradition take as much interest in alimentary writing as their female counterparts. Louis Chu's 1941 novel, *Eat a Bowl of Tea*, and many of Frank Chin's stories organize their narratives around food and eating. But American ethnic politics has worked to the disadvantage of male writers such as Chu and Chin, who refuse to play into the feminized fantasy of China. I choose three women writers because their texts participate in the historical narrative of "assimilation" as a metaphoric process from the "melting pot" to the "salad bowl." Textual construction of self-identity revolves around orality in its dynamic process of eating and storytelling and operates on a special mode of "double-tongued" signification. Their use of Chinese food lore, culinary procedures, and gustatory symbols is not only akin to their Chinese heritage. It also transforms "Chinese food" into a hybrid, gender-specific mode of signification and thematizes the children's relationship with their immigrant parents around "oral" conflict and bonding. Thus, the inclusion of Chinese American women writers in this study is meant to examine issues related to cultural incorporation and hybridity as much as to present a gender-specific point of view. Due to the content and scope of this project, I can only sample its most significant aspects, leaving much to be explored in some later work.

Toward a Theory of Consumption and Double Orality

In this volume, I often put "eating" in quotation marks for several reasons. First, the primary emphasis of this book is on the politics of alimentary representation and imagination. By definition, language is already removed from the primordial experience. Second, the themes of cannibalism and hunger are twice removed from the ideal situation of material abundance and social harmony. Most important, though, *chi*, the Chinese term for "eating," encompasses a far broader semantic and discursive field and possesses more generative and transformative capacities than its English counterpart. Thus, the interaction between the mouth and the world is always mediated by specific semiotic systems and historically situated modes of cultural embodiment. Because "eating" is inscribed in various economic, political, social, and cultural codes, its semantic and symbolic field cuts across the disciplinary and discursive boundaries. The principle that governs my reading is a dialectic between the physical body and the body politic, with "eating" posing as the central locus on which the natural body and the social body join and shape each other in their dynamic interplay. This conceptual model is formulated in figure 1, where "eating" is foregrounded as an epistemological concept much as a trope that organizes various textual practices. Let me elaborate on some of the theoretical implications of this model.

From Nature to Culture

Acquisition of food through organized production is perhaps the single most important practice in human history as a whole. Only in the post-food as object of fulfillment

---

production	distribution	preparation (material *practice*)	consumption	
political economic		sociocultural codes (*discursive* practice)		←Symbolic
			ingestion digestion elimination	←presymbolic
			hunger as lack	←desire or libidinal drive

Figure 1

World War II era has the capacity of food production surpassed the demands of consumption. Much of this accomplishment can be attributed to scientific and technological advancement. Paradoxically, the more advanced our technological intervention in nature the closer we come to surpassing the earth's food-carrying capacity and the further the body is removed from the ecosystems of nature. The simple fact is that modern advancement in agriculture and health care has provided the basic material condition for the world's population explosion. Given the fact of limited natural resources, an infinite increase in food supply is not possible. While I am not in a position to deal with the ecological question, the earth's food-carrying capacity should always lurk in the background when we discuss "eating" as a metaphor for the human condition.[2]

In mainstream economic theory, a sufficient food supply often figures as a triumphant footnote to the classical narrative of the development of capitalism. The struggle for survival—still articulated as a struggle of "putting food on the table" in the affluent society of the United States—is narrated as a success story of humanity's climb up the food chain. Although of late a health-conscious minority, mainly in the developed world, has been moving "down" the food chain, their dietary "regression" is counteracted by the increased production costs of organic food. Our success story in modern times tells an anthropocentric epic simplified as "you are what you eat" in the scheme of the "natural law." The trouble is that this post–World War II window of plenty may soon disappear if current rates of growth in population and consumption continue. But even with this unprecedented level of food supply hunger has persisted in much of the world. Sufficient production does not by itself lead to adequate consumption. The culprit is uneven distribution, which can be attributed to various factors.

In Marxist political economics, the uneven distribution of wealth is both a reflection of and a necessary condition for the unequal relations of production under capitalism. Meanwhile, natural resources for food production, such as arable land and fresh water, have never been equally distributed. This inherent disparity is further aggravated in modern times by uneven development of the world. Capitalism goes hand in hand with imperialism in creating and perpetuating international disparity through territorial expansion, colonial conquest, and exploitative trade. In proposing a different path than capitalism and imperialism, Marxism has insisted that international socialism will eliminate inequality and unleash productive forces to the highest potential. The ultimate goal is to liberate the human race from the shackles of necessity. At the same time, Marxism has reappropriated the narrative of material advancement measured against the progress of production and the increase in productivity. In combating socioeconomic injustice, Marxism has also inherited the very logic of modern productivism.[3]

Classical Marxism does not propose an elaborated theory of consumption. The shift from production and distribution to consumption took place as the USSR was undertaking a rapid, massive industrialization made possible only by a high rate of accumulation and at the expense of consumption. The policy of rationing food and other necessities in the societies of state socialism, originally devised in response to domestic scarcity and international embargoes, has become a yardstick for the imbalance between production and consumption. But the critique of consumption, best known through Georg Lukács's work, has strengthened the moral overtone when the critique of political economy shifts the focal point to expose "bourgeois decadence" and its most visible symptoms of greed and excess. More recent neo-Marxist critiques of late capitalism, represented by Fredric Jameson's work, enlarge the critical scope beyond political economy and morality. Jameson's major contribution lies in his analysis of the cultural logic of consumer capitalism, on which contemporary international capital circulates and expands. Sharing the same critical ethos in opposition to capitalistic exploitation, the political economics of classical Marxism and the cultural critique in neo-Marxist thought together delineate a full conceptual spectrum from production to consumption. To historicize this critical shift, one may well hold that Marx's work belongs to a time of material scarcity whereas Jameson's arises from an era of cultural excess.

Marxism is not without its historical limitations and theoretical blind spots, with the latter largely a function of the former. Above all, Western Marxist thinkers are both historical products of, and oppositional figures in, existing capitalist societies. Questions concerning how to *construct* a socialist economy and society cannot be fully addressed from a fundamentally *critical* stance, especially when socialist construction takes place in a predominantly agrarian society like that of China. It certainly makes sense to attack, say, the schizophrenic mode of mass consumption in the United States, where less than 5 percent of the world's population gobbles up a third of its natural resources. The story of consumption in China comes almost at the other extreme, though the economic modernization launched since the late 1970s is narrowing the gap. While Chinese socialism has reinscribed the classical Marxist narrative of production, it has also refashioned it by injecting the moral critique of bourgeois decadence traceable to Lukács and the Soviet experience. In this way, a cogent critique of capitalism is misplaced in a different society to the neglect of the basic needs of the population, turning historical materialism into "asceto-Marxism."[4] The uncritical subordination of basic material needs to some "higher cause" was theoretically misconceived and historically disastrous.

While Marxism offers a conceptually useful but historically limited account of economic and social activities from production to consumption, both its usefulness and its limitations also reflect its cultural roots in European and North American conditions. This is particularly so when we recognize that eating is not just another form of consumption. The palate is much less mutable and adaptable than, say, one's appetite for automobiles or clothing: pushed too hard, one would simply vomit. Moreover, cooking and eating are governed by other social and cultural rules, which often operate on their own terms regardless of whether a particular item is edible or not. Hindus do not eat beef; Muslims do not touch pork; and, in a similar vein, dogs are not part of the American diet. In examining food preparation and consumption as cultural activities, anthropological studies (e.g., those of Lévi-Strauss, Mary Douglas, K. C. Chang, and E. N. Anderson) have developed some epistemologically relativist methods that allow us to understand a culture and its material practice through its intrinsic foodways. What is most interesting, though, is that the culturalist approach sometimes subverts the linear narrative of civilization and its analogy to the food chain. Lévi-Strauss's "culinary triangle" is such a case in point.

Horizontally along the sociological axis, the mode of consumption defines the ways in which the physical body partakes in, and is shaped by, the political economy and cultural practice of the social body. Central to the sociological locus of consumption is its intersection with the physiological axis, which is particularly significant in the study of literary representations of eating as a form of cultural embodiment. In her recent studies on the clinical experience of traditional Chinese medicine in post-Mao China, Judith Farquhar points out that the cultural practice of "eating Chinese medicine," though still located "within the reach of language and the play of instituted power," reveals a social process that should not be rigidly "differentiated into the ideal and the material aspects." "Politics speaks history," she argues, but it is not necessarily true that "food and medicine can only dumbly figure it" (1994, 473). Cultural embodiment, in other words, must be understood in terms of specific historical configurations of the body. At this nodal point, where Marx intersects with Freud, the boundaries of the political and the personal become blurred. Because the historical configuration of the body in twentieth-century China has been largely constructed in favor of Marx over Freud, I will emphasize the Freudian notion of desire in order to foreground a different kind of discourse regarding the body. While the food people eat and the ways people eat may already be coded in the symbolic, the physiological mechanism of eating is presymbolic, that is, presocialism, precapitalism, and pre- any other philosophical and political "ism." The figure of desire defines eating, like sexuality, as an act conditioned by various forces according to a certain society's value and belief systems and material resources. But eating is also one of the most natural acts by which the physical body survives and reproduces itself. The bodily zone that "speaks" for the nodal point of the two axes is the oral space where desire, always caught in the symbolic, constantly invests its libidinal energy by transgressing the symbolic. Conversely, transgression also manifests itself as a symptom of repression.

The repressed desire is revealed in a variety of textual strategies. As a narrative figure, hunger is what motivates the signifying process to move from lack to fulfillment. Here, hunger is as much a physical reality as a trope. Its symbolic power derives from but also surpasses the primordial materiality of food as the desired object—just as the sexualized libido works in the Freudian interpretation. The same structure of incorporation and approximation is embedded in the other oral activity: speech. Drawing on Freudian theory, James Brown argues that "[t]he journey from remoteness to intimacy is none other than the paradigm of orality imposed on all communicative acts." As a result, "eating and speaking share the same motivational structure; language is nothing other than the praxis of eating transposed to the semiosis of speaking: both are fundamentally communicative acts by which man appropriates and incorporates the world" (1984, 12–13). Eating and speaking are thus entwined in a twofold manifestation of the desire for approximation and fulfillment. Amplified through metaphoric transformation and metonymic displacement, hunger is as nostalgic as it is futuristic. It is nostalgic because human beings become hungry only for something they have already tasted or learned to desire in the past. It is futuristic because each and every moment of hunger can be fulfilled only after it is felt. Disseminated in the narrative of hunger is the eternal desire to return to the open-ended utopia of the oral stage.

It should be clear from the above description that this book is about the *discursive practice* of literary alimentation. The theoretical model I adopt is meant to approach the subject from a multisided perspective that does not fit into any single existing narrative of consumption. Because the underlying assumptions of this model belong largely to the contemporary discourse of what has simply been called "theory" in the American academy, it cannot be overemphasized that we need to balance that universalizing tendency by heeding the specific cultural and historical conditions in which the texts in question were written and received. Just as the desiring subject in the text can speak only in and through a sign system, the eater's preference for food must be taken as an effect of the lived material and symbolic realities that cultivated his or her taste. If ancient China had a food-centered culture that invested in food an absolute value, this cultural attitude has permeated the Chinese sign system and shaped its discursive practice.

Linguistic Mediation: Two Key Terms

As a verb, *chi* (eating) signifies the most elementary act of life by connecting the body to the life-supporting world; primarily a noun, *wei* (flavor) enables the eater to make sense of the world through sensuous correlatives of the palate. Both characters are composed with the mouth radical, and together they provide the basic syntactic structure for alimentary narrative. Through their numerous compounds and configurations, we "figure out" our existential experience and establish sense through the senses.

The character *chi* can be read as an ideograph: a "mouth" is followed by "beg." This ideographic reading has more to do with its reinterpretation in modern times because a more common word for "eating" in classical Chinese is *shi*, which is also a noun meaning "food." In "Wangbuliao chi" (Can't forget about eating), for instance, Mo Yan alerts his readers to such an ideographic exegesis. Like many mainland Chinese educated to use the simplified script of *jianti*, Mo Yan originally mistook *chi* as the *jianti* version of the traditional *fanti* character (which shares the same mouth radical but uses a different phonetic component). Looking it up in the dictionary of *Cihai*, he notes that the *fanti* character is actually a variation of the *jianti* word in classical Chinese, the opposite of the popular impression. In light of this discovery, he writes: "The begging of the mouth, the begging mouth—how accurate it is! This character embodies the meaning of craving and starving, and signifies the lowly social status [of the one who begs food]. I guess the person who coined it must have been very poor and hungry. If it had been created by Miss Lin Daiyu [from the *Dream of the Red Chamber*] or Lord Liu Wencai [a rich and cruel landlord and a notorious icon of the class enemy in the PRC], it wouldn't look like this. Since their stomachs were filled up to the point of indigestion all the time, 'food begging for the mouth' would be more fitting. . . . It is self-evident that language embeds class consciousness, not just an abstract system of signs" (1997, 92). Mo Yan's reference to class is as much a confirmation of historical materialism as a part of his consistent pastiche of the images that give lip service to the official ideology. What is significant at this point is his exegesis, which simultaneously literalizes and reinterprets *chi* by limiting its meaning to hunger. Such an interpretative strategy is emblematic of the thematic focus on the politics of eating in modern China. If the model of consumption I propose can be viewed as a universal structure of abstraction, *chi* adds a linguistic-specific illustration to that discursive field.

Perhaps because *chi* graphically embeds in itself a basic narrative move from lack to fulfillment, in constructing compounds it traverses a much broader semantic field than its English counterpart and is more flexible in generating rhetorical tropes and crisscrossing thematic terrains. For example, after a baby is born, one of the first instincts he or she follows is *chinai* (eat milk or suck the breast). If the mother doesn't nurse her or him well, the baby has to *chili* (eat strength or make an effort). When he or she still cannot suck some milk, the baby may *chijing* (eat shock or be startled). He or she may then fall ill and in that case has to *chiyao* (eat medicine). If the baby is the only son in the traditional household, the grandma might scold the mother for making him *chiku* (eat bitterness or suffer). Even if the mother has good reasons, say, she didn't yield much milk, she was normally not supposed to retort but instead *chiyabakui* (eat the mute's loss or keep quiet despite ill treatment). Suppose the mother is a concubine, while the first wife of the family doesn't have a son; then she will be able to *chilaoben* (eat old capital or rest on the fact that it was she who gave life to the only son, the sole heir in the patriarchal genealogy). The first wife, without the grace of having a son, might then *chicu* (eat vinegar or become jealous).

I made up this crude narrative simply to show the generative and transformative power inherent in *chi*. As far as this literary study is concerned, the role that *chi* plays in the sign system aptly demonstrates the relationship between the *chi* that constitutes a primary realm of human existence and the *chi* that partakes in metaphoric transformation. This returns us to the notion of double orality. Alimentary configuration of the body with textuality is a transfiguration of food into food signs. In Chinese cuisine, for example, the criteria by which the quality of a dish is judged come in order of color, fragrance, and flavor, known as *se xiang wei*. A meal well served must offer the pleasure of reading, smelling, and tasting. The act of *chi*, like that of reading, requires a knowledge of decoding a déjà vu. If a banquet is encoded by the host as a text, to eat it first entails interpretation. This is also true of the *chi* of the ordinary people. For example, in northern inland rural areas, where fish is not usually available, a wooden fish, "cooked" or carved and decorated as if real, is served at the New Year's banquet as a substitute. It is set in the center of the table as the main "dish" to signify *yü* (surplus), derived from the expression of the wish that every year there should be surplus food, known as *niannian youyü*. Both "fish" and "surplus" are pronounced *yü*. If a guest fails to decode the "text" by poking his chopsticks at the "fish," it would at least confuse him and embarrass his host.[5]

If the meaning of the wooden fish is determined by the phonetic interchangeability of the signifier and the signified, the "surplus" meaning of the "fish" is generated through metaphoric transformation for imaginary compensation motivated by what is lacking in reality. Once our discussion enters the realm of signification, we may well subject *chi* to another ideographic reinterpretation. As in another usage of *chi*, one that means "stammer," expressed as *kouchi*, it signifies "a mouth [that] begs for [words]." This usage is exclusively assigned to the "mouth-begging" *chi* and is not shared by its *fanti* form. The linguistic economy of *chi* is such that a single character means "the mouth that begs for food and words." Because food and words share the same verb in thematic motivation and syntactic structuration, they overlap in establishing a discursive symbiosis of gustatory and aesthetic experience. Correspondingly, a single noun, *wei*, both describes our sensibility and designates sensuous qualities to food and words.

Stephen Owen explains that *wei* is "an important master metaphor in describing the aesthetic experience of the text" (1992, 593). As in the case of *chi*, *wei* generates more surplus meaning than its English counterpart, "flavor." Following Mo Yan's exegesis of *chi*, let me take some liberty and offer a similar ideographic reinterpretation of *wei*: it shows a "mouth" followed by "not yet," signaling the potential for open-endedness of meaning. Distinct flavors are registered on the taste buds when food has not yet reached its destination in the stomach. This is a position of betweenness that signifies the tangible attributes of the object and the subjective feeling of gustatory-aesthetic taste, awaiting both digestion and assimilation. Through a series of compounds of incremental abstraction, *wei* stands for the ultimate limitation under which meaning can be established only as an effect of indeterminacy and ambiguity.

Four compounds illustrate the scale from the most tangible to the most abstract, namely, *weidao*, *ziwei*, *quwei*, and *yiwei*. On the material end, *weidao*, the "Dao of flavors," indicates the carnal ontology of taste.

Various *wei* are summed up in the five flavors of sweet, sour, bitter, pungent, and salty. Blending the five flavors in harmony is a central principle in ancient Chinese culinary art and political philosophy, known as *tiaohe wuwei*. Similar to *weidao* but descriptive of a wider spectrum of nuanced sentiment is the term *ziwei*, "flavors bred and multiplied [by saliva]"—if we take a liberal reading of the water radical of *zi* as denoting "mouth water." Life experience is assimilated through the palate, ranging from *bushi ziwei*, "unsavory," to *wanzhong ziwei*, "full of flavors." Moving toward the next stage of aesthetic abstraction, *ziwei* is succeeded by *quwei*, "flavors of interest," or simply "taste." Unlike the five flavors that are descriptive of objective experience, *quwei* is normative in evaluating subjective taste, judged in accordance with socially constructed hierarchy and relative to trends, fashions, styles, and ideologies. In high culture, the less one's taste is removed from the "interest" of the body, the lower one's *quwei* becomes. The highest *quwei* is invested in refined poetic and intellectual exercise.

Yet because the finest taste is still contained within the semiosis of the mouth, the meaning of art and poetry hinges on this oral basis and often is called *yiwei* or "flavors of meaning." Unlike its closest synonyms, such as *yisi*, "meaning," and *yiyi*, "significance," *yiwei* connotes implication and indeterminacy, often too elusive to classify or too subtle to grasp in words. While *yiwei* may apply to an everyday speech act as well as a fine poem, to a real event as well as a text, it is one of the few expressions that is not applied to negation. We can add the negative particle *mei* to *yisi* and *yiyi* to make up words meaning "meaningless" or "uninteresting" and "insignificant" (and many more negative compounds), but the same rule is not applicable to *yiwei*. Because *yiwei* usually implies abstract flavors to be ruminated, as in the phrase *yiwei shenchang*, to say the opposite one cannot use antonyms to replace the adjectives, as one would in the case of *yisi* or *yiyi*. Instead, the idiom *weitong jiaola* is most fitting to dismiss something that "tastes like chewing wax." The alimentary origin of *yiwei* seems to be persistent enough even in underpinning the most nuanced of aesthetic and intellectual experience. Meanwhile, the temporal structure of "not yet" keeps implied meanings of *yiwei* as open-ended as our gustatory-cum-aesthetic adventure will allow.

When *chi* enters the realm of *wei*, alimentary themes intersect with, and are regulated by, generic and stylistic flavors or rules. If the poetics of eating tends to underscore the personal aspect, the politics of eating highlights the public domain, even though *writing* is always invested with both and politics and poetics always crisscross in the text. In modern Chinese literature, there are three major thematic and generic configurations. In the most political, hunger and realism join hands, mostly in narrative fiction, in attempting to reflect and rectify social reality. Cannibalism contains a strong political edge, yet the style of writing cannibalism is tinged with surrealism. The most aesthetic of all is the presentation of the refined taste of the scholar-gourmet in forms of poetic prose such as the personal essay and lyric fiction. There are of course many examples of overlap and crossover. It suffices here to say that these three sets of thematic features and generic attributes outline the spectrum of alimentary discourse in modern China, with the first two being the dominant force in shaping its grand narrative. Since the chapters are focused on the politics of eating, let me expend a little more ink on the poetics of eating.

The ancient tradition of the literatus-gourmet is exemplified by the Song poet and essayist Su Shi. His modern heirs include Zhou Zuoren, Lin Yutang, and Wang Zengqi among others. By purely aesthetic standards, these modern gastronomists' works epitomize the highest achievement in modern Chinese prose writing. Apart from brush painting and traditional theater, the personal essay is perhaps the best preserved of all ancient Chinese arts. For a modern literature advanced by breaking away from traditional culture to promote revolutionary change, the realization of artistic value cannot but be sidelined and postponed. The poetics of eating remains, as always, a marginal cause of individuated taste and pleasure at a time when the masses are starving. This historical condition underscores the irreconcilable tension, crystallized on the linguistic level, between the material reality of *chi* and the aesthetic ideal of *wei*. If the realism of *chi* requires the writer to feed words, as food, to the mouth that begs, the poetics of *wei* figures in the open-ended pursuit of an illusive dream. In a utopian situation, the two would not be mutually exclusive. In historical reality, the former exists at the expense of the latter and the latter can only establish itself in reaction to the former.

Zhou Zuoren's life best embodies this dilemma. Although Zhou shared the same goals of cultural enlightenment with his brother, Lu Xun, during the May Fourth period, they parted politically at about the same time that their personal relationship became strained. Zhou's reluctance to commit himself to the political cause is enunciated as an aesthetic distance. The gesture of disinterested aestheticism, however, paradoxically points to the very reality to be distanced, and the ghost of the irreducible tension constantly emerges between the lines of his writing. In reading a collection of essays by the Song poet Lu You, for instance, Zhou sets out to renounce the ideological zeal devoted to this patriotic poet of ancient China. He distinguishes Lu You's more socially oriented poems from his personal essays, stressing his preference for the latter as a counterpoint to the call for a literature of national defense in the mid-1930s. One of the autobiographical accounts in Lu You's work relates his encounter with a master chef known for his unsurpassable art in frying chestnuts. Yet the more Zhou ruminates over the beauty of Lu You's prose and the marvel of the chestnuts, the less possible it becomes that the ghost of history can be erased. It turns out that the chef was forced into exile by the invading troops of the Jin, against which Lu You strikes the theme of the tragic loss of homeland. And Zhou Zuoren expressed his preference for the personal essay and fine food over patriotic literature at the very moment of the all-out war against the Japanese invasion in 1937.[6] In the end, the scholar-gourmet Zhou would have to trade his fine taste in art for the crass feed of dogs by turning himself into a "running dog" of the Japanese aggressors. Though an extreme case, Zhou's life story is an apt illustration of the incompatible flavors of the aesthetic ideal of *wei* and the brutal reality of *chi* when the writing of food (the legend of chestnuts) and taste ("apolitical" essay) proves the pathology of history.

In sum, if the mouth that begs for food and words keeps telling the story of the "always already" of hunger, the words of food that project the "not yet" feed on the narrative of the "never ever" to add spice to the drama of life. *Chi* generates alimentary narratives only to see them transformed into the varieties of *wei* that are rooted in, yet transcend, our immediate concerns with food. The sign system is a projection of the cultural unconscious molded in the collective historical experience. In a schematic way, the almost all-encompassing linguistic capacity of *chi* alone may be taken as a sign for the value system. While historical change may alter the use to which food is put and the context in which its meaning is created and circulated, the preoccupation with eating on the part of many Chinese writers, even Americans of Chinese ancestry, has not changed. For this reason, a culture-specific reading must be emphasized when such a reading is informed in a universal theory of consumption.

Some Notes on Cannibalism

At first glance, cannibalism might not seem to fit in the framework of consumption outlined above. Indeed, the mere mention of the word evokes anything but our experience with food. A broad range of images from the most Gothic to the most exotic come to mind, all about the "other" and unrelated to "us." This underlying structure of binary opposition has recently come under critical scrutiny (e.g., in Kilgour 1990; Hulme 1986; and Harris 1985). In modern times, the problem of cannibalism is concerned less with actual practice than with the construction of the "other." Hulme suggests that " '[c]annibalism' is a term that has no application outside the discourse of European colonialism: it is never available as a 'neutral' word." For cannibalism means "the image of ferocious consumption of human flesh frequently used to mark the boundary between one community and its others," and thus "no other word, except perhaps 'sex,' is so fraught with our fears and desires" (1986, 78–87). Hulme's conclusion needs to be qualified, of course. The term does have a profound application to the colonized when the discourse of colonialism travels to modern China and is internalized by Lu Xun as a master metaphor for the old China. With Kilgour, this colonial legacy would be just one form of imperialism among many others that have evolved through the millennial process of incorporating what lies outside the body and, by extension, what lies outside the political and moral order of Western civilization (1990, 226-27).

A postcolonial critique of the modern myth of cannibalism is a theoretical focus of this study. This approach is particularly relevant to the use of cannibalism in constructing the "national allegory" of modern China. Although allegorical writing has been established since the time of Lu Xun, long before Jameson's theorization of it, its specific method of interpretation enters our academic discourse through Jameson's encounter with third-world texts—Lu Xun's "Diary of a Madman" being a major episode. To situate my own reading, I would like to highlight the theoretical and institutional context of that encounter.

Jameson's "third world" project is part of his "cognitive mapping," a term he coined in the essay "Postmodernism, or the Cultural Logic of Late Capitalism" (1984a). In a note at the end of his "Third-World Literature in the Era of Multinational Capitalism" (1986, 88), he makes it clear that "[w]hat is here called 'national allegory' is clearly a form of just such mapping of the totality, so that the present essay—which sketches a theory of the cognitive aesthetics of third-world literature—forms a pendant to the essay which describes the logic of the cultural imperialism of the first world and above all of the United States." During this same period, when he was entertaining the idea of using a numeral game for his global cartography, Jameson offered an even fuller global map by configuring the literature of another China—China under Mao—as "missing second numeral," meaning the literatures and cultures of socialist countries (1984b). This missing second numeral is described later as a hidden agenda in the global postmodern or late capitalist context (1987b, 24). In theoretical cartography, China alternates between the third and the second worlds in serving up a pendant to Jameson's global mapping. In historiography, Lu Xun and Mao represent the "stages" of a China neatly fit in a Hegelian-Marxist teleology of history. Such a syntax of narrating world history is nothing new to Chinese Communism. And as far as global mapping is descriptive of the geopolitical totality of the contemporary world there is little we can do to change that grand narrative except by historicizing the meaning of "national allegory" in its contemporary American academic context before we connect it to the allegorical writing of cannibalism in modern China.

Jameson's alignment of the third-world national allegory with his critique of first-world aestheticism can be situated in the shifting boundaries of comparative literature, a "field" of humanistic scholarship that has never felt secure about its shaky institutional status nor been content with the disciplinary and departmental divisions of labor in teaching national cultures and literatures. In a little-known paper discussing the paradigmatic changes in comparative literature, Jameson was among the first leading scholars of Euro-American literature to articulate a vision beyond the self-proclaimed cosmopolitan yet strictly Eurocentric field map of comparative literature (1987b). After he described four stages the field has undergone (namely, the "influence" approach, the approach of "international movements and period styles," "historical area studies," and "modern studies"), he sketched the emergence of a new approach: "I do not know that anything like a 'postmodern studies' has emerged today; but feminism . . . certainly projects an 'interdisciplinary' coherence. . . . Black or Afro-American studies . . . falls largely open to the fourth central topic of American intellectual life today, namely the interest in what has come to be called, for better or for worse, Third World culture" (18). What characterizes this postmodern discourse of the "third world" is a set of issues clustered under such key terms as *race* and *gender*. The notion is indicative of a more local (American) and theoretical consciousness in dealing with issues related to, but not confined by, the geographical and cultural space of the non-West.

Jameson's cognitive mapping thus must be situated against this broad backdrop. This was a time when new approaches or paradigms were being shaped, inspired by a group of "third-world" scholars within the American academy (e.g., Edward Said, Gayatri Spivak, Stuart Hall, Cornel West, and Henry Louis Gates Jr.) as well as "first-world" intellectuals like Jameson. This was also the time when many mainland Chinese students, like me, were beginning graduate studies in the United States. Although the prefix *post-* requires more nuanced methods of inquiry when applied to China (it being in both the third and the second worlds), my postcolonial approach to the national allegory of cannibalism is indeed "educated" and informed by the paradigm changes of the time. This educational experience is as much academic as it is personal, as I will show in the last chapter, which demonstrates the convergence of a postcolonial critical consciousness and cultural ethnicization.

To return to the seeming irrelevance of cannibalism to the model of consumption, the notion of incorporation is crucial to the thematic configuration of eating and being eaten. In the chapter on Lu Xun, I will detail the process in which his allegorical reading of the old cannibalistic China is based on his incorporation and assimilation of colonial discourse, which ethnicizes his writing in the form of national allegory. What makes the problem of cannibalism much more complex and ambivalent is that the incorporation of the outside goes hand in hand with a strong sense of repulsion. This is because the image of the cannibal is constructed as being simultaneously neither inhuman nor fully human. Epistemologically, the subhuman cannibal occupies a liminal site that belongs to neither the inside nor the outside: it constantly threatens the binary opposition on which the stability of the self hinges. In the end, the threatened collapse of the self is reflected by an abyssal sense of madness when the self finds that the cannibal actually exists in his own dark heart. This is exactly what happened to the "third-world" subject of colonial modernity (Lu Xun's Madman) as well as to the "first-world" hero of colonialism (Conrad's Kurtz, for example). As far as cannibalism and madness are entangled in writing, only language (understood in the poststructural sense) can reestablish the order of sanity. Here, the narratives of hunger and cannibalism both function as a kind of therapeutic writing, though the former proceeds to fill a lack and the latter attempts to prevent the self's collapse into a void.

Cannibalism in China is a doubly ambivalent topic. On one hand, Confucianism in ancient China provided the foundation for a civilizing order against barbarism, flesh-eating included. Yet in modern times Confucianism has served as the primary scapegoat for revolutionary intellectuals. On the other hand, there is a traditional genre of the grotesque that began with the ancient *Book of Hills and Seas* and culminated in the sixteenth-century epic *The Journey to the West.* A central feature of this genre is the fantastic image of the human-eating monsters and demons that at once stands for the insatiable hunger of the outside world and stimulates artistic imagination. This tradition has fascinated Chinese writers, ancient and modern alike, and left its surrealist imprint on works about cannibalism regardless of whether it is unrecognized (as in the case of Lu Xun) or is activated into narrative consciousness (as in Mo Yan's work). In examining cannibalism in ancient China, we always need to bear in mind this distinction between an actual flesh-eating practice and an imaginary incorporation of the grotesque. Since the writing of cannibalism defies reductionist clarity and ahistorical conceptualization, I will address its theoretical implications through concrete readings in the following chapters. At this point, I would like to introduce two issues related to real cannibalism in history before I move to a brief reference to the linguistic feature of *chiren* (eating humans).

One way to disentangle us from the colonial discourse is to distinguish two kinds of flesh eating in history. While both can be tied to the notion of consumption, they differ in whether the act is motivated mainly by material need or is performed for extramaterial reasons. The first type is represented by the so-called *hunger cannibalism* or *cannibalism of desperation*, terms used by Sanday (1986, 4–5) and Mote (1977, 234), respectively, to describe the kind of flesh eating that results from lack of food during famines, wars, and other emergencies. Until recently, this type of anthropophagy was a universal phenomenon of major civilizations, and its causes had little to do with any specific cultural formation. For Harris, "the practice of people eating [people] when the only food available is human flesh . . . occurs the world over from time to time regardless of whether the eaters and the eaten come from societies that approve or disapprove of the practice" (1985, 199). Tannahill provides a broad picture of this kind of cannibalism in Europe and Asia during the first millennium and points out that "[i]n Europe the situation seems to have been as bad as in China" (1975, 46).[7] Looked at from the angle of food consumption, this type of flesh eating must be treated as just another tragic episode in our collective history of survival. There is nothing inherently repulsive about it.

The problem of material survival, however, has become completely mixed up with the question of morality as we have moved up the food chain. One wonders why the teleology of civilization always goes hand in hand with the narrative of evolution: even humans who are left behind in the food chain for various reasons are by definition "underdeveloped." Historically, the moralization of survival under material scarcity is complicated by the fact that many occurrences of hunger cannibalism may not have been documented and some of the extant records may not be true. In the latter case, recent findings invalidate some results of previous research. In *The Food of China*, for instance, E. N. Anderson points out that there is no evidence to support the popular attribution of cannibalism to the Stone Age Peking Man (1988, 8). For Anderson, William Arens in his controversial *The Man-Eating Myth* "overstates his case" that most tales about Aztec cannibalism are fabricated myth, "but for China he is nearer the truth than are the histories" (1988, 85). Anderson's view is echoed by other scholars on Chinese food culture. Mote argues that the cannibal tales in the Ming novel *Water Margin* "become a cliché, a symbol of heinous crime" and that "cannibalism of desperation accompanying times of famine and disaster is sometimes reported, again somewhat symbolically, as the measure of calamity" (1977, 243). According to Jonathan Spence, the most familiar "litany of the phrase in the local gazetteers, 'In this year people ate each other' " (*xiangshi*), sometimes "was meant as metaphor" (1977, 261). Myth, symbol, or metaphor may not reflect facts, but they are not necessarily false either, in the sense that they register cultural responses to material conditions that are cross-cultural in scope. A student of literature and culture, then, must recognize the complexity of the historical picture while examining how a given culture responds to the experience of anthropophagy, historical or otherwise, in a way that is culturally meaningful.

The second type of anthropophagy is concerned with institutionalized "ritual cannibalism," which largely existed in some aboriginal communities and indigenous societies in Oceania and the Americas. Ritual cannibalism is an act performed in a broader cultural framework within which consumption of flesh is not the sole purpose. Rather, it is a symbolic response to the believed relationship between members of the society, between one society and another, and between the human world and the world of the god(s). It has been an area of debate in cultural anthropology (see Sanday 1986; and Brown and Tuzin 1983). While some cases of cannibalism other than those of "hunger cannibalism" in ancient China may not be strictly part of the "ritual" in the religious sense of the word, as used elsewhere, they are "ritualistic" in the sense that the very Confucian term *li* is translated as "ritual." My analysis of the culturally motivated practice of cannibalism does not strictly fall into the category of "ritual cannibalism" but treats it as "ritualistic" nevertheless.

The general problem of cannibalism as presented in anthropological and historical studies delineates a contour for my textual analysis. However, as I propose to locate "eating" in the *episteme* and rhetoric of *chi*, textual inscription and figurative use of *chiren* in China need to be approached with particular attention to linguistic features concerning the tissue and texture of the human body. For a point of departure, "flesh" and "meat" in Chinese share the same word, *rou*. This term occupies a vast field of signification from human flesh to all different kinds of animal and fruit meat, modified only by the animal or plant's name as a descriptive attribute. The compounds of *rou* include *renrou* (human flesh), *gourou* (dog meat), *zhurou* (pork), *niurou* (beef), *jirou* (chicken meat), *niaorou* (bird meat), *yurou* (fish meat), *sherou* (snake meat), *chongrou* (bug meat), *hetaorou* (walnut meat), just to name a few. Like *chi* and *wei*, *rou* is much more powerful in generating ambiguity than "flesh" and "meat" combined. The above list of compounds and their English translations illustrates such linguistic capacity and flexibility.

When *rou* is combined with *chi* in the verb-object structure of *chirou*, it literally locates human consumption of *rou* and the human body itself in the order of *carnivora*. Once the human animal—its carnivorous propensity as well as its physical substance and tissue—is thus conceived, the body becomes a decentered piece of *rou* as well. Figuratively, *chirou* may be used as a syntactic protocol to generate a vast terrain of semantic and narrative crossover through the overlapping of "flesh" and "meat," that is, between cannibalism and carnivorism. In this case, textualization of the body and cultural embodiment must be understood in terms of multiplicity, reciprocity, and dispersal. Only in the order of anthropocentric civilization—whose eating trope is the triumphant human omnivore standing at the top of the food chain—can the meaning of cannibalism be established by separating flesh eating from carnivorism. The separation of the human body from the realm of meat consumption narrates the "stages" of social evolution and historical progress. I will discuss at length the theoretical implications of *rou* and *chirou* in my analysis of Mo Yan's novel *Liquorland*, in which the legacy of cannibalism since Lu Xun is placed side by side with Mo Yan's phantasmagoric universe of carnivorism.

In summary, to the extent that cannibalism is the central theme and trope in the national allegory of modern China, the allegorical text is invested with at least three major "flavors," namely, the colonialist incorporation of various localities of the world into the symbolic order of Eurocentric civilization, the historical memory of ancient flesh eating and its modern residues, and the artistic imagination of the grotesque world and its discursive recycling of *rou*, human and nonhuman alike. All these forces converge in the metaphor of *chiren* to stage one of the most mystified dramas of modern China. It is time to "spit out" what has been so uncritically assimilated.

1. Discoursing Food

Some Notes toward a Semiotic of Eating in Ancient China

This chapter serves as a footnote, historical and cultural, to those that follow. Without this footnote, my reading of modern texts would stand on sand; yet to describe what came prior to modernity with sinological rigor would require lifelong research and result in a huge separate project. As a footnote, this chapter allows me to do the necessary without being drowned in the bottomless.

A footnote also allows me to isolate and highlight a few examples that make sense to my own reading without pretending to claim comprehensive expertise. To borrow a phrase from the traditional exegesis of the classics, it is the classics that "annotate" me rather than the other way around. By no means will these examples describe a complete picture of "Chinese eating." There are rules, for sure, that govern social behaviors, as minor as etiquette and table manners and as major as food taboos and sacrificial rituals. There also are many unwritten rules that prescribe who should produce and cook what kind of food for whom and under what circumstances. These rules in turn delineate the power structure whereby eating becomes not only a part of human regeneration but also part of the reproduction of social relations and institutions. And, much as our experience of food is diverse and open-ended, my reading of these instances is inconclusive and suggestive.

Semiotics, like any mode of thinking that claims to be scientific, could provide a bit of rigor for analytical intervention into such an "illogical" experience as that with food if—and only if—it gave up its claim to some kind of universal syntax and signifying structure. The poststructural shift from syntax to semantics and pragmatics that reemphasizes contextual production of meaning and culture-specific signification has raised the possibility that "[s]emiotics is mainly concerned with signs as social forces" (Eco 1979, 65). Without plunging into a general theory of semiotics here—and even less so in using its arcane terminology in my reading—I would simply define the title of this chapter as "a semiotic of eating in ancient China," meaning a culture-specific reading of food signs and symbols and alimentary discourse as social forces. These social forces have organized the Chinese experience with food and eating on the one hand and constituted a particular way of interpreting general cultural experience in accordance with the very principles of these social forces on the other. Or, to borrow a definition from James Brown and slightly alter it for the sake of simplification: "Semiotic . . . refers to the relationship between the literary [and cultural] sign (here designated as fictional [and any textual] meal complex) and the cultural context wherein the sign is born and which invests it with meaning(s)" (1984, 9).

As for "discoursing food," Roland Barthes's description of "discourse" and "figures" is analogous to the way I will analyze the alimentary discourse of China in terms of figures: "*Dis-cursus*—originally the action of running here and there, comings and goings, measures taken, 'plots' and 'plans': the lover, in fact, cannot keep his mind from racing, taking new measures and plotting against himself. His discourse exists only in outbursts of language. These fragments of discourse can be called *figures*" (1978, 3).

Metaphorically, Chinese food is not served as "course" but as "dish." Symbolic of the "running to and fro" and "conversing" that occur between the East and the West—as exemplified by my writing of Chinese food and eating in English at the present moment—the "discourse" in which such writing is engaged cannot be better described than as "dis(h)-coursing" (food). As a result, the "figures" or textual fragments are carved out of the whole to serve up four thematic items: (1) the mythological figure of the Red Emperor/Noble Farmer and agri/cultural initiation and critique, (2) the rhetorical figure of cooking as a metaphor for government, (3) the mythological-historical figure of Bo Yi and moral-political fasting, (4) and the historical and fictional figure of the

"Chinese cannibal." The central figure that "configures" these is the material body and its historical embodiment.

The Ancestral God of Agri/Culture and the Absolute Value of Food

Various versions of the inception of agri/culture[1] in ancient China attribute the discovery of grains and the introduction of farming to one of the two legendary ancestral gods, the Red Emperor (Yandi), while the other, the Yellow Emperor (Huangdi), is believed to be the one who invented the stove meant for cooking.[2] The Red Emperor, whose name, *yan*, symbolizes the sun, is also called Shen Nong, the "Noble Farmer."[3] From various written fragments about the Red Emperor/Noble Farmer, there are three significant roles he has played in the agri/cultural initiation of China. First, he introduced the farming of the "five grains," which is synonymous with all staple food, invented the plow and other tools, and taught the primitive people how to cultivate the land.[4] God as he is, he is once described as having "a human body with the head of an ox" (Yuan 1979, 79), the latter being a folk cult belief because of the major role it played in farming until modern mechanization. Second, as god of agriculture, the Red Emperor/Noble Farmer also discovered hundreds of medicinal herbs by actually tasting them to gauge their effects, and according to some folk tales he eventually was killed by a poisonous plant.[5] Third, the Red Emperor/Noble Farmer not only provides the source of energy (food) and health (herbal medicine) but as the "heliogod" he embodies the primitive measurement of time.[6]

This "creation" myth is significant in four respects. Ontologically, eating occupies the core of a prehistoric belief system. In contrast to the biblical source or Greek mythology, it is the ancestor-creator who eats, not out of "sinful temptation" but to satisfy a primordial human need. Nor are the food and drink he "creates" such celestial stuff as the ambrosia and nectar served to the Olympian pantheon; they are the kinds of food and drink his descendants are still consuming today. This secular and "humanist" myth has nurtured Chinese culture with an element of rationality: food and eating must be taken as a matter of fact in this, the only world.

This earthly attitude toward food found expression in the early classics and survives in modern writings. In *The Analects*, when asked by Duke Ling of Wei for his advice about military affairs, Confucius says: "I have indeed heard about matters pertaining to *tsu* (meat stand) and *dou* (meat platter), but I have not learned military matters" (15.1; K. Chang 1977, 11).[7] Such a novel cross-reference by the sage shows his contempt for the immorality of war on the one hand and the importance he attaches to food as a fundamental human concern on the other. In *Mencius*, the philosopher Guo Zi contends: "Appetite for food and sex is nature" (5.a.4; Mengzi 1970, 161). While such a permissive attitude toward sex has rarely been the norm in Chinese society, especially for women, the appetite for food has been treated as a matter of fact. "If there is anything we are serious about," writes Lin Yutang, "it is neither religion nor learning, but food" (1935, 337).[8] In his introduction to the pioneering work *Food in Chinese Culture*, K. C. Chang's somewhat tautological remark drives this point home: "[P]erhaps the most important aspect of the Chinese food culture is the importance of food itself in Chinese culture" (1977, 11). What is foregrounded here, to borrow a phrase from Ted Huters's reading of a contemporary text, is "food as an absolute value" (1985, 397).

Epistemologically, the Red Emperor did not exactly "create" food but "discovered" hundreds of herbs through his mouth. Eating thus also functions as the primary mode of knowing. His attempt to experience the "tree of knowledge" led to the birth of an old agri/culture rather than the downfall of the human race. This "eating epistemology" is not so much theological and transcendent as it is grounded in the practices of everyday life. The fact that Chinese cuisine utilizes as many "exotic" material resources as possible seems to be partly due to this ancestral god's pragmatic boldness. The priority of practice over speculation, or knowing as the result of doing, seems to anticipate the Confucian system that dictates that all action begins with *gewu zhizhi* (differentiation of things leads to knowledge).

Perhaps in every traditional culture food habits function as a means of cultural and class differentiation. Food and cooking have served as a cultural marker in ancient China to establish its cultural superiority. Chapter "Wangzhi" of *The Classic of Rituals* records such a piece:

> The people of those five regions had all their several natures, which could not be made to alter. The tribes on the east were called Yi. They had their hair unbound, and tattooed their bodies. Some of them ate their food

> without its being cooked with fire. Those on the south were called *Man*. They tattooed their foreheads, and had their feet turned in toward each other. Some of them ate their food without it being cooked with fire. Those on the west were called *Jung*. They had their hair unbound, wore skins. Some of them did not eat grain-food. Those on the north were called *Ti*. They wore skins of animals and birds, and dwelt in caves. Some of them did not eat grain-food. (qtd. in K. Chang 1977, 42)

What is remarkable in this passage is that cultural differentiation hinges on an apparent distinction in appearance and food rather than social activities, religious practices, and cultural icons such as written language or the lack of it, all of which are commonplace in writings of the modern world.

The third aspect of the myth addresses a morality of eating. Because the Red Emperor/Noble Farmer's eating as a practical mode of knowing involves risking his life, he sets an ideal model of what I would call "divine sacrifice for mundane need." This mythological figure became a popular ancestral god most probably due to his sacrifice for the common good of the populace. Perhaps it might be more accurate to say that the high moral demand on the ruling elite in later Confucian culture calls for mythological creation and transformation of this highly worshiped ancestral god into an ideal moral example to be followed by all emperors and officials. Because this kind of sacrifice is rare in reality, the Red Emperor/Noble Farmer not only must serve food to his people but must sacrifice himself as spiritual nourishment for the hungry imagination of the hardworking but poverty-stricken peasants. The ruling elite is thus constantly reminded of the well-being of the ordinary peasants as their *yishi fumu* (parents who provide clothing and food).

Yuan Ke, a leading scholar of Chinese mythology, wrote in the context of the PRC: "The emperor Shen Nong tasted hundreds of herbs until he sacrificed his life for the people, poisoned to death by the last herb he tried. . . . This spirit of loyalty to the people is unforgettable" (1960, 71). Obviously, the popularity of the myth lies in the god's "first bite," which "discovers" as much as his "last bite," which "sacrifices" him as ancestral-spiritual nourishment. The theme of "divine sacrifice" or, according to the Chinese tradition, "noble sacrifice"—"noble" in both the moral and the sociological senses of the word—has served as the mythological foundation for a quasi-religious moral philosophy. Modern revolutionary discourse, developed from scientific socialism, requires this sort of powerful (re)mystification to mobilize the masses for revolutionary sacrifice. Yuan's reinterpretation of the myth in terms of noble sacrifice is only part of the construction of the grand narrative of revolution in modern China.

The last but not the least important aspect of the "creation" myth is the ancestral god's power, which unifies both the "Chinese race" and, being the "creator" of time, Chinese history. Nothing could be more effective for cultural identification than the invocation of a shared ancestry, along with the idea of a great tradition that constructs the collective cultural consciousness and connects it to that ancestry. Since the dawn of modernity when the Middle Kingdom began its metamorphosis into a modern nation-state, the term *yanhuang zisun* (sons and grandsons of the Red and the Yellow Emperors) has been invoked whenever a national crisis is perceived.

The sense of a shared history rests on real or imagined shared historical experiences. Yet ironically it is one of the most devastating experiences shared by all humankind in the past—hunger, famine, and mass starvation—that has haunted the rulers of China throughout its history. If the myth of the Red Emperor/Noble Farmer has any historical value apart from its mythical power, it would seem to support the simple truth that the rulers of China must take food seriously or be devoured in the hungry waves of peasant revolt. It is in this real history that eating has served as a powerful weapon of social criticism.

The remark by Confucius quoted previously points to this critical implication. In *Mencius*, the term *shi* (food, to eat, to feed) is used 106 times, including once for "eclipse" (even an astronomical phenomenon is described as "being eaten"; see Mengzi 1984, 409). Many times where the word appears Mencius lectures his audience of kings and dukes on the importance of food and their mistakes concerning it. His attack on King Hui of Liang is a well-known passage, part of which reads:

> There is fat meat in your kitchen and there are well-fed horses in your stables, yet the people look hungry and in the outskirts of cities men drop dead from starvation. This is to show animals the way to devour men. Even the devouring of animals by animals is repugnant to men. If, then, one

who is father and mother to the people cannot, in ruling over them, avoid showing animals the way to devour men, wherein is he father and mother to the people? (1.a.4; Mengzi 1970, 52)

A couplet by the Tang poet Du Fu, which is part of the primer of classical Chinese from which schoolchildren in the PRC learn about their "feudal" past, reads: "[W]hile the wine and the meat have spoiled behind the red doors [of rich households], / on the road there are skeletons of those who died of exposure" (qtd. in K. Chang 1977, 15). The contrast of class difference shows the important function of food in signifying the wide disparity between the rich and the poor and the critical power of food signs in attacking such disparities. And it is this tradition of critical consciousness, traceable to the early Confucian sages, that would provide a meaningful, indigenous framework for the adaptation of historical materialism to Chinese soil in modern times.

The Red Emperor/Noble Farmer thus is a dual-faced cultural icon. It signifies two basic social forces whose contradiction and conflict have governed the operation of Chinese political culture. On the one hand, the (Red) Emperor represents the imperial state. The ideological legitimacy of the state depends on the believed mythological/historical authority and continuity of the mandate of the ancestral gods. On the other hand, the (Noble) Farmer represents the ideal and interest of the peasantry as the opposite of the imperial state. They share the same ancestry-orientated belief system, but the peasants demand that the mandate of the ancestral gods must be executed according to their own interpretation of the myth. In other words, it is not the (Red) Emperor but the (Noble) Farmer who justifies the very existence of the state, and thus the state must act like him. The fact that in Chinese history peasant revolts could topple one empire after another but the terms of ideological legitimation for such dynastic changes never changed testifies to this logic.

Such contradictory duality embedded in the formation of an ancestral god can be traced to the composition of a key term in the sign system: *mu*, meaning "to 'ox-herd,' " "herdsman," and, in classical political terminology, "governance."[9] Its metaphoric structure appears similar to that in the Christian tradition except that the former emphasizes worldly governance and the latter spiritual nurturing. But the two are different in terms of animal symbolism and cultural implications: *mu* is derived etymologically from "ox," which corresponds to the mystical image of the Red Emperor/Noble Farmer, and adds to "ox" "a hand that holds a whip." The two halves of the character *mu* vividly describe the dual "face" of the ancestral god. The "ox," probably a sediment carried over from a primitive totem, symbolizes its intimate relation to a culture centered on grain production and was used by the peasantry to create their collective ancestor in the Noble Farmer. The "whip" represents the imperial power once that cultural icon was attached and transferred to the ancestral god in the Red Emperor. Thus, from the "egalitarianism" of the ancestral god as both the provisioner and the ox developed a symbolic and social division between the ruler and the ruled. Their relationship has never been stable in history precisely because *mu* requires that the ruler does not "crack his whip" but "herds" and, in times of hardship, makes "noble sacrifices." Much of the social tension between the state and the peasantry can be understood as the struggle between the two major conflicting forces embodied in the dual-faced god.

Guanzi, a book named after and partly attributable to the Spring and Autumn statesman Guan Zhong (d. 645 B.C.E.), describes the relationship between the state and the citizenry in these terms. The first chapter is titled "Mumin," meaning " 'ox-herding' people" or "governing" (them). Guan Zhong begins with his lecture this way:

> All those who possess territory and "ox-herd" people must pay heed to the four seasons and watch over the granaries. If the state has an abundance of wealth, people will come from afar; if the land has been opened for cultivation, they will settle down. When the granaries are full, they will know propriety and moderation; when their clothing and food is adequate, they will know [the distinction between] honor and shame. (Rickett 1985, 22)[10]

Guan Zhong's model of government is based on the ideal of the unity of the (Red) Emperor and the (Noble) Farmer. One also notices that his political wisdom is quite close to modern utilitarianism: "economics" comes first (*yishi zu*) and "morality" ensues (*zhi rongru*).

The ox as a popular cultural icon symbolic of noble sacrifice has been carried into modern China. In a couplet in his famous poem "In Mockery of Myself," Lu Xun likens himself to the ox in terms of his relationship with the ordinary people: "Fierce-browed, I coolly defy a thousand pointing fingers, / Head-bowed, like a willing ox I serve the children." Both a member of the cultural elite and an iconoclast, Lu Xun certainly understands the symbolic power of the "ox" and would feel guilty if he did not "humble" himself to defy the "whip." In his "Talks at the Yan'an Forum on Literature and Art," Mao quoted Lu Xun's couplet, urging that "all Communists, all revolutionaries, all revolutionary literary and art workers should learn from the example of Lu Xun and be 'oxen' for the proletariat and the masses, bending their backs to the task until their dying day" (1961, 3:878; 1965, 3:96). If we compare Mao's call with Yuan's interpretation of the myth, cited previously, we find the very trace of the "ox" that connects the mythical god with the revolutionaries. Even Mao's life, however complicated and tragic, can be seen in this light. Taken as a whole, his life path has seen his metamorphosis from an "ox" or a "noble farmer" (considering his peasant background and the loss of his wife Yang Kaihui, two sons, two brothers, and many more for the Communist revolution) to a "whip" or "red emperor" in his last years. Lu Xun and Mao, two major figures of modern Chinese revolution, projected themselves as the very model of the collective cultural consciousness along the trajectory of the ancient myth.

In sum, the myth of the Red Emperor/Noble Farmer suggests that food has been a primary concern and an absolute value, and its signification reflects its importance as such. Ontologically, food signifies the omnipresence, since the time the ancestral god discovered it, of the god who stands for those unknown prehistorical cultivators of the land. Epistemologically, the discovery of food and its production are grounded in, and requires, a practical mode of knowing and differentiating the surrounding world and social relations. Morally, food is coded with laws that stipulate how members of the society relate to each other in terms of sharing (food and other things) rather than with concerns about what kind of food is allowed or prohibited according to certain religious beliefs. The moral meaning of food is not imposed from "above" but is construed among the eaters. Historically, the "first bite" signifies the lack and the constant need to fill it. But as long as the lack results from social disparity rather than natural disaster, or the latter worsens the former, the mouth that swallows food is turned into the mouth that devours the ruler and the privileged. To study food and eating is thus to study the mouth's struggles: to eat or not eat—this is the ultimate concern.

Well-Cooked Words: Alimentary Metaphors in Political and Philosophical Discourse

In "Food in Early Chinese Literature," David R. Knechtges observes that "[o]ne of the most pervasive uses of food in ancient Chinese literature is as metaphor in political or philosophical discourse." The examples from various ancient texts he cites all show that "the proper seasoning of food is a common analogy for good government" (1986, 51). In *The Classic of Documents*, King Wu Ding of the Yi requests his minister Fu Yue to offer advice in such a way that "[a]s if making wine and must, you be Our yeast and barm; [a]s if making blended stew, you be Our salt and plum" (12.9a; Knechtges 1986, 51). The metaphor of the blended stew is also used by the statesman Yanzi in the *Zuo Commentary*:

> Harmony (*he*) may be compared to a stew. Water, fire, vinegar, meat pickles, salt, and plums are used to cook the fish filets. It is heated by means of the firewood. The cook blends (*he*) the ingredients and equalizes them by taste, adding whatever is deficient and decreasing whatever is excessive. His master then eats it and thereby composes his mind. The relationship between lord and vassal also is like this. Whenever there is something objectionable in what the lord deems acceptable, the vassal presents his objection in order that he may make it acceptable. Whenever there is something acceptable in what the lord deems objectionable, the vassal presents his approval so that he may remove his objection. Thus, when the administration is composed and inobtrusive [*sic*], there are no contentious hearts among the people. (49.14a-b; Knechtges 1986, 51)

The early Daoist philosophers also employ cooking metaphors to express their ideas. The first line of chapter 60 of *Laozi* (a.k.a. *The Tao Te Ching*) reads like this: "Governing a large state is like boiling a small fish" (1963, 121). Too much control leads to chaos much as overhandling the fish ruins it. In *Zhuangzi* (a.k.a. *Chuang Tzu*), there is a famous parable about the master cook Ding. After nineteen years of carving more than a thousand oxen with the cleaver never being sharpened once, the blade shines as though it had been freshly honed. This is achieved because he always follows the principle of adjusting his cleaver to the natural way. But such a marvel, Cook Ding explains, is not what skill itself can achieve.

What I care is about the Way, which goes beyond skill. When I first began cutting up oxen, all I could see was the ox itself. After three years I no longer saw the whole ox. And now—now I go at it by spirit and don't look with my eyes. Perception and understanding have come to a stop and spirit moves where it wants. I go along with the natural makeup, strike in the big hollows, guide the knife through the big openings, and follow things as they are. So I never touch the smallest ligament or tendon, much less a main point. (Zhuangzi 1968, 50–51)

The way of "nurturing life" (*yangsheng*, which also is the subtitle of the chapter) is just like that: do not contrive, evade man-made confrontations, simply follow the Way, or the way life is.

The same kind of metaphor that conveys Daoist pacifism, ironically, is used by the early Han statesman and essayist Jia Yi (ca. 200–168 B.C.E.) for the purpose of realpolitik:

The ox butcher Tan could carve twelve oxen in one day, yet his pointed blade never became dull: the reason was that wherever he thrust and hacked, skinned and sliced, it was always along the various natural lines and joints. But when he came to the thigh bones and buttocks, if he didn't use a hatchet, then he used an axe. Benevolence, charity, grace, and generosity are the pointed blades of a ruler of men; authority, power, laws, and regulations are the hatchets and axes. (Knechtges 1986, 52–53)

The analogy between cooking and governing has formed, in Knechtges's view, a topos. This topos, I want to add, can be used to describe the genre of the ancient philosophical and political writing in which the eloquent officer feeds symbolic nourishment to his "hungry" but dumb lord. And all this can be traced to the mythological story of Yi Yin. Although Knechtges rightly points out that *Lüshi chunqiu* (Annals of Master Lü), the earliest extant text (third century B.C.E.), which provides a full biographical account of Yi Yin, "is usually treated as a handbook of political philosophy, not a work of literature" (1986, 52), the story nevertheless offers one of the most palatable anecdotes of Chinese mythology because of the rare "literary" flavor it produces in our modern imaginations. In the modern world, a head of state or a chief of a government cabinet may well make a good cook, but the opposite is hardly believable. Moreover, what makes this story so interesting is not simply the way in which a cook becomes the highest-ranking official but how cooking generates a rich conception of politics. Because of Yi Yin, King Tang (the founder of the Shang and one of the benevolent emperors in the imperial genealogy) defeated Emperor Jie of the Xia, an archetypical tyrant along the lines of the imperial villains of ancient times.[11] But due to the absence of any authentic contemporary documents, the prominent prime minister and his great achievement is constructed in hindsight around his master-handed manipulation of orality in its interplay between speech and eating.

Benwei, the subtitle of the chapter, means "essential taste."[12] Yi Yin's articulation of the "essential taste" is aimed at persuading King Tang to carry out the mandate of the ancestral gods. He manages to convince the king by "sharpening the king's [gastronomical and philosophical] imagination to its utmost (*shuitang yizhiwei*)." He argues that the art of cooking, simple as it may appear, signifies a harmonizing process toward the great way of the sage. This is because a good cook must uphold the highest principle of balance between water and fire, pungency and mildness, rawness and artificiality. As he contends:

> The transformations in the cauldron are so utterly marvelous and of such subtle delicacy, the mouth cannot put them into words, and the mind cannot comprehend them. They are like the subtlety of archery and charioteering, the transformations of the *yin* and *yang*, and the circle of the four seasons. Thus, the food is cooked for a long time but is not ruined, well-done but not over-done, sweet but not sugary, sour but not bitter, salty but not briny, hot but not biting, bland but not insipid, fat but not lardy. (Knechtges 1986, 53)

The process of going from the raw materials to the artifact is thus a "subtle transformation" that eliminates stinks, purifies odors, refines flavors and yet still preserves the material basis on which the "essential taste" is crystallized.

But how, in practice, can the cook achieve all this? The material resources of cooking are as inexhaustible as anything the world can offer and yet the fineness of taste is as inexplicable as the mystery of the cosmos. To demonstrate that he is the master cook, Yi Yin lists a whole body of mystical plants, mythological animals, and esoteric game animals and fish, showing that the great cook's wisdom, much like the sage's, derives from the broadest knowledge of the cosmos. And only by establishing oneself as a sage can one establish one's empire, which represents the emperor's "ultimate taste" (*zhiwei*) exactly as the finest item represents the cook's. Hence, the kitchen exemplifies the throne, cuisine epitomizes politics, and the master chef embodies the great sage. In short, Yi Yin single-handedly serves himself up as the "essential taste," just right for the king's political hunger and philosophical appetite.

The text not only is based on and developed from a trope that transfers the gastronomical into the political discourse, but, more importantly, it constitutes a "trope"—or a "turn." In the text, Yi Yin turns his tongue around, switches it between the mouth that eats and the one that speaks, and stimulates the king's gastronomical imagination and political ambition—all by means of well-wrought words. The tongue itself becomes a kind of topos that seems to occupy a large semantic field and possess a strong generative capacity in the Chinese sign system. Besides its function of distinguishing flavors, the tongue often stands for the entire mouth as the organ of speech. Many idioms in modern Chinese still carry this function of the word. In a way, it is Yi Yin's tongue that "tropes" cooking into politics, much as the trope "turns" his tongue that tastes into the one that speaks. It should be noted that Yi Yin's primary role in the text is neither that of a cook nor that of a prime minister (yet) but that of a *shuike* (the ancient shuttling persuader-mediator between the great powers). He, as the idiom puts it, turns around his "three-inch manipulative tongue" (*sancun bulan zhishe*). He is the man who can put into words things "so utterly marvelous and of such subtle delicacy [that] the mouth cannot put [them] into words, and the mind cannot comprehend [them]" (Knechtges 1986, 53). This paradox brings the sagelike image of Yi Yin into sharp contrast with that of King Tang. The latter, like the "dummy" ("pacifier" in American English for the second sense of the word as used here), merely stays "fed."

The *Lüshi chunqiu* was written and compiled under the auspices of Lü Buwei, himself a prime minister of the state of Qin during the later Zhou period. To the extent that Lü controls the text's writing and interpretation, the chapter "Essential Taste" epitomizes the genre of ancient political writing wherein the eloquent *shuike* feeds (his advice) and the "hungry" king or duke consumes (it). In other words, their dialogues hinge on a textual trope. This trope not only metaphorizes political and philosophical discourse but establishes itself as the rhetorical model of that discourse.

This interesting resonance between the theme and its "narrative strategy" was discovered by Mozi, the founder of the classical philosophical school named after him. In "Guiyi" (Esteem for Righteousness), the forty-seventh chapter of *Mozi* (parts of it date to the fifth century B.C.E.), he advocates the ancient version of "meritocracy" via a similar metaphorical reinterpretation of the relationship between Yi Yin and King Tang:

> Anciently, [King] Tang was going to see Yi Yin and let a son of Peng be the driver. On the way, the son of Peng inquired where the lord was going. Tang told him that he was going to see Yi Yin. The son of Peng said: "Yi Yin is but a humble man of the world. If you want to see him just send for him and he will feel quite flattered." Tang said: "This is not what you can understand. Here is some medicine. When taken (*shizhi* or "eaten"), it will sharpen the ears and brighten the eyes. Then I will be pleased and endeavor to take it. Now, Yi Yin to me is like a good physician and an effective medicine. Yet you don't think I should see him. It means you do not want to see me become good." (Mozi 1929, 223)

Here King Tang is not only "hungry" but "sick." Yi Yin is turned into the "physician" who will feed and cure him with well-wrought words. His are words of wisdom, which must be swallowed like food and medicine. The figural equation of words with food and medicine—and they are inseparable here—reveals a "holistic" understanding of life anchored on the ontology of orality.

The topos of well-cooked/wrought words that nurture a specific genre of writing was to be developed to an even more fantastic degree in "Qifa" (Seven stimuli) by Mei Cheng (ob. 140 B.C.E.). In this text, a prince and his eloquent guest, both fictional, are engaged in a series of conversations in which the latter single-handedly cures the former's illness with nothing but words. After the guest's diagnosis of the symptoms and cause of the prince's illness—overindulgence—he tells him: "Your illness has now reached the point that neither plant nor mineral medicines, acupuncture nor cauterization can cure you. Only through the exposition of essential apothegms and marvelous maxims may you be rid of it" (Mair 1988, 33). These "essential apothegms and marvelous maxims" (*yaoyan miaodao*) consist of "seven stimuli," each exciting a sensual pleasure. The second one stimulates the prince's gastronomical appetite:

The fat underbelly of a young ox,
With bamboo shoots and bulrush sprouts;
A blended stew of plump dog,
Smothered in mountain rind.
Boiled rice from Miao Mountain in Chu,
Boiled cereal from wild rice—
Rolled into balls they do not crumble,
But once sucked into the mouth they dissolve.
And then, have
Yi Yin to fry and boil,
Yi-ya to season and blend:
Well-done servings of bear paws,
A sauce of savory seasoning;
A roast of thin tenderloin;
Autumn-yellowed perilla;
Legumes soaked in white dew;
Thoroughwort blossom wine,
Poured to rinse the mouth;
A course of hen pheasant;
The fetus of a tamed leopard.
Eat little or drink much,
It's like boiling water poured over snow.
(Knechtges 1986, 57; also see Mair 1988, 43–45)

It is a small wonder that if these items were ever realistically available at all the prince, who lived in such extravagance, as described early in the text, should have access to them. Yet it is not these actual foodstuffs but the well-cooked words that lead to his recovery. Yi Yin's "essential taste" is perfectly realized in Mei Cheng's "essential apothegm." And the reference to Yi Yin himself rightly situates the text in that thematic and stylistic tradition.

Some later texts about Yi Yin continue to play on the trope and the theme it has engendered. In Sima Qian's *Shiji* (Records of the historian, first century B.C.E.), chapter "Yinbenji" (The basic annals of the Yin), it is said that Yi Yin "carried his *ding* (cooking tripod) and *zu* (meat stand) along to see the king, fed rich flavors and delicate tastes to the fancy of the King, and persuaded him to execute the mandate of ancestral gods (*fudingzu, yiziwei shuitang, zhiyu wangdao*)" (Yuan 1979, 394). In another

Han text, *Huainanzi*, the image of the cook as an eloquent persuader is further Confucianized: "Yi Yin was greatly concerned about the turbulence and disorder of the world. Blending the five flavors and carrying his *ding* and *zu*, he shuttled between Emperor Jie and King Tang to offer his advice five times each" (394). The Confucianization of Yi Yin in the above texts, however, puts the king in an awkward position as a mere consumer. In book 397 of *Taiping yülan* (1199), an encyclopedic collection of early classics edited and annotated for the imperial court of the Song, the story is rehearsed from the side of King Tang:

> When King Tang was eager for virtuous advisers he had a dream of seeing a man smile at him. That man carried a cooking vessel *ding* and shouldered a chopping block *zu*. Waking up, the king sought for divination, which goes as follows: "Since *ding* is used for blending a variety of flavors and *zu* for chopping and carving, they may well mean blending forces of different interests and rearranging the world order respectively (*dingwei hewei, zuzhe gecai tianxia*). Who could that man be but my prime minister!" (391)

Interpreting the trope by himself, the king turns himself, the consumer, into the cook and the feeder. But the figural structure remains unchanged and actually is reinforced because this time it is the king who "envisions" the intimate tie between cooking and governing.

The mystical figure of the master cook and the rhetorical figure of eating and cooking are configured with, and transfigured into, the figure of the prime minister and that of governance. Without a "sophisticated," "rationalized" language of government such as that of modern political science, abstraction and theorization naturally tend to resort to expressions of concrete experience. But why do eating and cooking assume this important responsibility? To ask the question differently: Why were these enriched alimentary and gastronomical metaphors mainly channeled into a political function?

Recent findings could lead to some sociological answers to this question. In his introduction to *Food in Chinese Culture*, K. C. Chang points out the importance of the kitchen in ancient China:

> The importance of the kitchen in the king's palace is amply shown in the personnel roster recorded in *Zhouli*. Out of the almost four thousand persons who have the responsibility of running the king's residential quarters, 2,271, or almost 60 percent, of them handled food and wine. These

included 162 master "dieticians" in charge of the daily menus of the king, his queen, and the crown prince; 70 meat specialists; 128 chefs for "internal" (family) consumption; 128 chefs for "external" (guest) consumption; 62 assistant chefs; 335 specialists in grains, vegetables, and fruits; 62 specialists of game; 342 fish specialists; 24 turtle and shellfish specialists; 28 meat dryers; 110 wine officers; 340 wine servers; 170 specialists in the "six drinks"; 94 ice men; 31 bamboo-tray servers; 61 meat-platter servers; 62 pickle and sauce specialists; and 62 salt men." (1977, 11)[13]

From this perspective, the wisdom and knowledge of Yi Yin as represented in the *Lüshi chunqiu* cannot be attributed to just one legendary figure much as the text itself must not be attributed to Lü Buwei. The whole food culture and its discourse in ancient China were created collectively over a long time. The highly organized nature of the kitchen bureaucracy indicates that "eating" has been "contaminated" with politics and loaded with heavy worldly concerns from the beginning of China's written history. The opposite is likewise true: precisely because eating is the primary concern and can generate very rich experiences and expressions, it must be utilized to serve the ultimate Dao of governance. Yet metaphors, alimentary and political alike, are not merely rhetorical devices; as social forces metaphors constitute the "texture" that weaves fragmentary threads of human experience into meaningful form. They register the forces that mold our mind and frame our interpretation of the human condition. What this interesting kinship between eating and politics reveals is close to what recent feminist theory has discovered and advanced: the personal is the political. The ancient Chinese experience simply confirms that to understand the political one needs to examine the "fabric" of the "mouth." To turn the idealist structure upside down: we eat, and therefore we are.

Between the Stomach and the Heart/Mind: Politics of Fasting and Morality of the Sage

One of the curious behaviors that exclusively belongs to the human race is its culturally motivated "negative eating." While we do not know whether modern "diseases" such as anorexia and bulimia existed in ancient times, there is no lack of documents about the ancient version of the "hunger strike." The earliest recorded story of a hunger strike in China concerns the two aristocratic brothers Bo Yi and Shu Qi. According to "Bo Yi liezhuan" (The biographical account of Bo Yi) in Sima Qian's *Records of the Historian*, the two brothers abdicated the throne. It was first handed over by their father to the younger brother Shu Qi, who in turn yielded in favor of Bo Yi, the older brother, after the death of their father. The latter could not accept the rulership because he felt a responsibility to comply with his father's wish. Thus, both brothers left their homeland to pursue the benevolent King Wen. On their way, Bo Yi and Shu Qi found out that King Wen had just died. They met his son King Wu marching against Emperor Zhou of the Yin, a tyrant like Emperor Jie of Yi Yin's time. They attempted to stop King Wu by accusing him of being unfilial toward his father, waging war while still in mourning, and acting as an immoral subject by attacking his lord. Despite their objections, King Wu went on and won the war. After the founding of the Zhou Dynasty, Bo Yi and Shu Qi, to quote Sima Qian:

> were filled with outrage and considered it unrighteous to eat the grain of Zhou. They fled and hid on Shou-yang Mountain, where they tried to live by gathering ferns to eat. When they were on the point of starvation, they composed a song: "We climb this western hill / and pick its ferns; / replacing violence with violence, / he [King Wu] will not see his own fault. / Shen Nong, Yu, and Xia, / great men gone so long ago— / whom shall we turn to now? / Ah—let us be off, / for our fate has run out." They died of starvation on Shou-yang Mountain. (5.2123; 1969, 13)

Two other versions of the legend add that the brothers even refused to eat ferns because a peasant woman told them that the ferns they gathered for food also grew in the land of the Zhou.[14]

This story is not exactly one about a hunger strike of the modern kind. The hunger strike is, in semiotics at least, a "public show"—very "serious" in most cases though—which stages itself so that it might generate a tragic effect upon its audience. It is a mortgage of death as a credit for a better life or lives. "To be or not to be" is acted out as "to eat or not to eat." But the fasting of Bo Yi and Shu Qi failed to affect the tragic and violent cycle of dynastic changes throughout Chinese history. Their principle of "nonviolence" has never been (received as) a theme of their fasting, as in the case of, say, Mahatma Gandhi.[15] The story would evolve into a kind of "postmortem" drama whose historical development and unraveling up to our time strikes the thematic chord not of nonviolence but of "no humiliation even if one has to die (*shi kesi er buke-ru*)." This is because their political fasting has been depoliticized through a moralistic discourse that is itself entangled with its interpreters' political concerns.

This moralistic tone was set by Confucius. In *The Analects*, he refers to Bo Yi and Shu Qi as setting moral examples. "Not to lower their purpose or to allow themselves to be humiliated describes, perhaps, Bo Yi and Shu Qi" (18.8; Kongzi 1979, 187). This moral standard is set against greed and material wealth: "Duke Jing of Qi had a thousand teams of four horses each, but on his death the common people were unable to find anything for which to praise him, whereas Bo Yi and Shu Qi starved under Mount Shou Yang and yet to this day the common people still sing their praises" (16.12; 1979, 167). Sima Qian echoes Confucius's praise of Bo Yi and Shu Qi, but his account is tinged with irony. The sense of irony reflects his resentment of his own situation as a castrated prisoner of the imperial court. This forces him to elevate his reading of the two to an even higher moral ground in order to symbolically solve his own predicament. Before he tells the story, Sima points out that the song is "very strange" and forecloses its authenticity by quoting Confucius as saying that "Bo Yi and Shu Qi never bore old ills in mind and seldom had any feelings of rancor" and "[t]hey sought to act virtuously and they did so; what was there for them to feel rancor about?" (5.2122; Sima 1969, 12). After he recounts the story along with the song, Sima asks again: "Do we find any rancor or not [in this song]?" This question is raised in a seemingly rhetorical way, since he has already discredited its authenticity. But by including this song in his account and raising the question of its authenticity, which solely hinges on the presence or absence of "rancor" in it and Confucius's comment, Sima has prepared a way of developing a theme relevant to his own situation and sentiment. This theme is about the highest moral standard by which great men of virtue should be judged.

He asks whether Heaven rewards goodness, with references to eating and cannibalism:

> Can we say then that Bo Yi and Shu Qi were good men or not? They piled up a record for goodness and were pure in deed . . . and yet they starved to death.
>
> Of his seventy disciples, Confucius singled out Yan Hui for praise because of his diligence in learning, yet Yan Hui was often in want, never

getting his fill of even the poorest food, and in the end he suffered an untimely death. Is this the way Heaven rewards the good man?

Robber Zhi day after day killed innocent men, making mincemeat of their flesh . . . but in the end he lived to a ripe old age. For what virtue did he deserve this? (5.2124–25; Sima 1969, 13)

Since even Heaven does not appear to be fair, who should be the judge of the highest moral standard? The judge cannot be anyone but an upright sage like himself. Sima continues, quoting a motto of Confucius and then rewording a maxim by Laozi, both with highly coded imagery depicting the great sage: "When the year becomes cold, then we know that the pine and cypress are the last to lose their leaves. When the whole world is in muddy confusion, then is the man of true purity seen" (5.2125; 1969, 14). Without any reference to their nonviolence principle, Bo Yi and Shu Qi's self-starvation is thus conceptualized as an action of moral ideals. As historians themselves, Confucius and Sima helped create the myth of King Wu as a benevolent ruler and his overthrow of the Yin Empire as a great emancipation. This makes the specific message and context of the two brothers' reaction to King Wu irrelevant not only to Chinese history but to Confucius and Sima Qian. On the other hand, Bo Yi and Shu Qi embody for Confucius and Sima frustrated but unyielding men of great integrity and commitment. This moral aspect of their action is all that remains meaningful in the experience of the alienated Confucius and Sima. As men who regarded themselves as possessing great virtue, they had to suppress their own bitterness by moralizing a political act and portraying its actors in an absolute moralistic light. That is probably one of the reasons why Confucius did not include the song attributed to Bo Yi and Shu Qi in *The Book of Songs*[16] and Sima Qian used it as a negative reference to set off the positive solution of his own dilemma. This is an excellent example of how a myth is re-created and its meaning reinterpreted by two of the great historians according to their own historical circumstances, individual sentiments, and moral ideals.

In his "Bo Yi Song" (Eulogy of Bo Yi), Han Yu (768–824) elevated Bo Yi to the highest sagehood. He describes Bo Yi as the lone scholar who swims upstream against the tide of history. "There are only a few," writes Han Yu,

who can press forward persistently and are not beset by doubts despite the objections of a family. There is only one in the whole empire who can press forward persistently and is not beset by doubts despite the objections of a whole state or prefecture. There is only one in a hundred or thousand years who can press forward persistently and is not beset by doubts despite the objections of the whole world.

> But a man like Bo Yi, who went so far as to disregard even the eternal Heaven and Earth and the judgement of generations yet to come in order to uphold his principle, eclipses the sun and the moon, dwarfs Mount Tai, and dwindles the cosmos. (1957, 36–37; cf. Han Yu 1979, 39)

More than a thousand years after Han Yu's "Eulogy," this historical myth reasserted its mystical power in a completely different context. In his "Farewell, Leighton Stuart" (1949), a declaration of the end of the American presence on the Chinese mainland symbolized by the departure of the last U.S. ambassador, Mao Zedong writes:

> The Americans have sprinkled some relief flour in Beiping, Tianjin, and Shanghai to see who will stoop to pick it up. . . . But he who swallows food handed out in contempt will get a bellyache.
>
> We Chinese have backbone. Many who were once liberals or democratic individualists have stood up to the U.S. imperialists and their running dogs, the Kuomintang reactionaries. Wen Yiduo rose to his full height and smote the table, angrily faced the Kuomintang pistols and died rather than submit. Zhu Ziqing, though seriously ill, starved to death rather than accept U.S. "relief food."[17] Han Yu of the Tang Dynasty wrote a "Eulogy of Bo Yi," praising a man with quite a few "democratic individualist" ideas, who shirked his duty towards the people of his own country, deserted his post and opposed the people's war and liberation of that time, led by King Wu. He lauded the wrong man. We should write eulogies of Wen Yiduo and Zhu Ziqing who demonstrated the heroic spirit of our nation. (1961, 4:1499–1500; 1975, 4:437–38)

To Mao, Bo Yi was wrong because he was a "counterrevolutionary" against the great leader King Wu and his war of liberation (and Mao and the Communist revolution by implication). Han Yu was therefore wrong to praise Bo Yi. And the grain of the Zhou became American flour. What remains unchanged and reappropriated after a mythological time is an act of fasting that organizes a moral discourse for specific ideological purposes.

With all this dramatic unfolding and development of mythological fasting, eating again is reaffirmed as an absolute value and the highest measure of human behavior. Yet this time the symbolic power of eating operates as an absolutely negative paradigm. As a primal mode of connecting the human body to the world, refusal to eat existentially signifies one's rejection of the body as well as its material relationship with the world. Thus, the absolute rejection of food also signifies something absolute: the will and power to kill oneself, a social behavior unique to the human species.

From the "oral stage" to "oceanic feeling" is the path from the human animal to the great sage, and yet at the same time it is a subordination of the body to the symbolic.[18] The regime of this system, established on the model of eating, has in turn "eaten" many human beings under the name of morality. Such is the most notorious code of conduct imposed on Chinese women: "To die of hunger is a trifling matter, to lose chastity is a grave matter" (qtd. in Chow 1991, 60). The issue is not the moral value of noble fasting per se but the relativity of the political and ideological function of that absolute moral value and the human body that embodies it. Put differently, despite the fact that fasting is sublimated to the highest moral ground, its historical and ideological function reveals that its meaning is never fixed but is relative to historical contingencies and political needs. What has been canceled out in the dissemination of noble fasting is not only its original theme of "nonviolence" as a principle of social change but also a fundamental attitude toward the human body and its nonviolent existence. The theme of this story and its dissemination read: I don't eat, and therefore I am.

To Eat and Be Eaten: About Cannibalism

If culturally motivated self-starvation is a unique human experience, cannibalism has drawn a borderline between "civilized man" and his "barbarous other." Yet the image of human eaters has haunted the "civilized" as indefinable monsters neither inhuman nor truly human. Moreover, many members of civilized societies have certain cannibalistic experiences of their own in dreams, nightmares, or other psychic formations that still puzzle psychologists and psychiatrists. The ancient hero Odysseus had no doubt in his mind as to what he should do to the cannibal Cyclops, but Marlow in Conrad's *Heart of Darkness* is much more confused and frightened by the fact that the anthropophagic Africans are "not inhuman"; their "humanity is like yours"—"Ugly" (1988, 37–38). The more civilized we become, the more difficult we find it to cope with our memory of such a "Horror." But in either case it is the representative of the civilized world—Odysseus or Marlow—who has traveled to the "other" land and "discovered" the cannibals. To discuss cannibalism in the late twentieth century, therefore, involves the risk of plunging into a nightmare that comes back to haunt us as our own "other" image—that is, in Conrad's case Europe's own "heart of darkness" mirrored in the "dark continent" of Africa.

The problem is further complicated when it comes to cannibalism in China. As one of the world's oldest civilizations, China by definition long since should have seen the departure of institutionalized anthropophagy. In the early classics, "[e]ven the devouring of animals by animals is repugnant to men," as Mencius was previously quoted as saying. Sima Qian, also quoted earlier, contrasts Confucius's most diligent disciple Yan Hui with Robber Zhi to establish the fundamental distinction between the sage and the flesh-eating barbarian. But throughout Chinese history the eating of human flesh has been more than isolated cases occurring during wars and massive famines. At the same time, traditional Chinese culture has been condemned as cannibalistic by Lu Xun. The old cannibalistic China as modern China's historical other is constructed, as I will discuss in detail later, precisely in the way Marlow creates his African "other"—but without the kind of ironical distance inserted between Conrad and the narrator.

Anthropologist Marvin Harris addresses the disproportionate emotional investment of modern humans in cannibalism as follows:

> It is one of the great ironies of history that for the last five thousand years the people who fought the bloodiest battles with the most combatants and the highest levels of destruction—who fought wars so staggering in scope and ferocity as to be unimaginable to any poor cannibal—are to this day horrified by the very thought of consuming the remains of even a single human being. . . .
>
> I regret to have to say that human flesh became bad to eat for essentially the same reasons that the Brahmans stopped eating beef and Americans won't eat dogs: the costs and benefits changed. (1985, 218–20)

Harris's comment defamiliarizes us from our emotional and educated attachment to this "lurid" topic, though his "materialistic approach" has been rejoined by a representative of the "culturalist approach," Marshall Sahlins. The latter "sees the 'Western business mentality' at the heart of Harris's view of Aztec cannibalism" (see Sanday 1986, 18–20).

What interests me here are historical occurrences and fictional references (some used by Lu Xun's in his "Diary of a Madman") that have specific cultural meaning for "Chinese eating." I choose them partly because they warrant detailed analysis and partly because I will link these examples to latter discussions of Lu Xun, Zheng Yi, and Mo Yan. In Lu Xun's "Diary of a Madman," there are two allusions to the *Zuozhuan*, the oldest work of narrative history covering the period 722 to 468 B.C.E. But the sources of these allusions are not depictions of cannibalism as such, and their contexts and textual inscriptions reveal social formations and ideological constraints that seem to be quite paradigmatic of the discourse of cannibalism in ancient China.

The first idiom is *shirou qinpi*, literally "eating [one's] flesh and sleeping on [one's] hides," which appears in the section "Duke Xiang 21st Year" (552 B.C.E.).[19] Zhou Chuo, formerly a warrior of the Jin who had just surrendered to the Qi, was engaged in an argument with Duke Zhuang of the Qi. The reason was that Duke Zhuang had called two of his generals, Zhi Chou and Guo Zui, "my heroes," even though they had been defeated by Zhou Chuo in a recent battle. Zhou Chuo resented the honor the two whom he beat had received from the duke and contemptuously remarked that they were unworthy of being called heroes. Zhou Chuo told the duke: "As to those two, they are like beasts; I will eat their flesh and sleep upon their hide" (Zuo 1960, 492). This classical source about man-eating, if taken on its own, has little to do with the practice of cannibalism as such, and Zhou Chuo's remark cannot be characterized as a speech act about cannibalism. Rather, it reflects hatred and contempt for one's enemy through a simile ("like beasts") that equates humans to beasts. Such a rhetorical device is commonplace in many cultures. What is "Chinese" here is the consequence of the figural equation: the destruction of the enemy's body does not end with his killing but should be carried further by dissolving the enemy's physical being into one's own mouth and guts. As a fundamental way of joining others and the world, eating is inverted to the function of denying or devouring the other's very existence. In rhetoric, "eating the other" is a common metaphor signifying a disturbed state of emotion such as "fury" in the popular saying "I really want to eat you" (*henbude bani chile*) and its variation "You look as if you wanted to eat me." Zhou Chuo's speech is symptomatic of a regression to the brute human-beast at an oral stage where he or she, if frustrated, is desperate to devour another.

This symbolic gesture, however, may well be a residue of what anthropologists call the "revenge cannibalism" practiced during tribal wars prior to China's written history—considering the fact that the text is the first work of narrative history and the *parole* or speech act is only meaningful within the *langue* or discursive system. While there is little information available to us about that practice in prehistory, this speech act reveals a cultural belief about the relationship between the eater and the eaten, an attitude toward the enemy adopted and manifested in historical ramifications of "revenge cannibalism." Edward Schafer describes its practice during the Tang dynasty with examples taken from the *Zizhitongjian*.[20] He writes:

> A very special kind of ritual food was human flesh. It was by no means an uncommon occurrence for outraged Tang citizenry to chop up the body of a corrupt or tyrannical official and eat him. . . . In 739 an officer of the court, who enjoyed the monarch's favor, accepted a bribe to cover up the crime of a colleague; the affair came to light, and the ruler had the offender beaten severely, after which the official supervising the punishment cut out the culprit's heart and ate a piece of his flesh (214, 7a). Again, in 767 a man murdered his rival, who had accused him of misdeeds, and having sliced his body into gobbets, he partook of them (224, 5a). In 803 a military officer led a mutiny against his commander, killed him, and devoured him, presumably with the help of his associates (226, 5b). (1977, 135)

The case of the revolutionary Xu Xilin (1873–1907) in Lu Xun's "Diary of a Madman" also falls into this category.[21]

While the political meaning of "revenge cannibalism" varies, the ritualistic performance has remained basically unchanged throughout history—be it to "show one's teeth" to a personal enemy, a tyrannical official, or a modern revolutionary. Again, eating as the primal mode of human existence also functions as the utmost means of eliminating the enemy. The ritualistic performance, via consumption of human flesh, thus completes a ritual of life circle from orality to orality.

The other source from the *Zuozhuan* reads *yizi ershi*, meaning "exchanging sons to eat." The idiom appears in the section "Duke Ai Eighth Year" (487 B.C.E.), where the army of the Wu was invading the Lu and a Lu official persuaded his lord to resist the aggression rather than humiliating themselves by signing a truce at their own capital when it was under siege.

The army of Wu offered to make peace, and a covenant was about to be made. Jing Bo said: "When the army of Chu besieged [the capital] of Song [in 604 B.C.E.], the men exchanged their sons[22] for food and claved their bones for fuel; and still they would not submit to a covenant at the foot of their walls. For us, who have sustained no [great] loss, to do so, is to cast our State away." (Zuo 1960, 817)

The speaker, and perhaps the author, apparently are not interested in this case of "hunger cannibalism" as such but in its practice as the utmost limit of the war's ferocity and the warriors' unyielding spirit. One also notes that there are more than a hundred years between the actual occurrence and the time it was reported in the context of another war. This may work two ways for the modern reader. Perhaps the fact that the text does not give account of the incident until more than a century afterward reveals the moral unconcern of the author and his time in regard to what we would deem to be a gruesome and atrocious act. Conversely, perhaps it is just too gruesome and atrocious to record in historiography unless and until it must be invoked to fight another war. In either case, its "rareness" might suggest, historically, that approval of cannibalism under extreme circumstances was rather rare even in the earliest period of China's written history. But precisely because of its "rarity" and its inclusion in what was to become a Confucian classic, the idiom is indicative of the relationship between the father and the son in ancient China.

We do not have to go into the familiar topic of the family structure of ancient China to understand the importance of the son in the family and the importance of the family in its relationship with the state. The "sacrifice" of the son, even though it was not so much conducted for the purpose of following certain rituals as out of desperation or hunger, is rather "ritualistic." I am even tempted to argue that the sacrifice of the son is symbolic of the very discourse of war, in which it is always the son who is called upon to fight and sacrifice for his "fatherland" (*zu* in the term *zuguo* is composed of "ritual" and "phallus" even though the semantic meaning of the term has become feminine or motherly). Suffice it to say here that however important the son is to the father for reproducing the institution of the family under extreme circumstances he must be exchanged for food, as food, and submitted for the good of political power.

At the same time, due to his importance the son's sacrifice as food for the father must not be taken lightly. It must be condemned when no extreme circumstance justifies it. This is the case of *Yi Ya xianzi*, the third reference in Lu Xun's text to ancient Chinese cannibalism. The story of Yi Ya's cooking of his son is recorded in the *Guanzi*. Guan Zhong single-handedly established the state of the Qi as one of the five powers of the Spring and Autumn period. After illness in his senior years confined him to bed, he was asked by Duke Huan for advice in case he should leave the world soon. The first advice he offered was concerned with personnel arrangements, and the first person he singled out was Yi Ya:

> I want you to send Yi Ya . . . far away. Now, Yi Ya harmonizes tastes to serve Your Grace, and when you said that the only thing you had never tasted was steamed child, he thereupon cooked up his son's head and presented it to you. It is human nature to love one's children. If he does not love his son, how can he have any love for you? (Rickett 1985, 428)

It might be useful to compare this comment with another one he made about "exchanging sons for food." When discussing the futility of using force and waging war, Guan Zhong says:

> Now, if swords are crossed and armed forces engaged so that afterward one must continue to provide for them, this is to vanquish oneself. If one attacks a city or lays siege to a town so its occupants [are forced to] exchange their sons for food and crack their bones for cooking, such an attack is merely to uproot oneself. (Rickett 1985, 394)

Guan Zhong, as a statesman, indulged less in speculation about moral philosophy than in a utilitarian philosophy of government. Yet precisely because of his focus on utility instead of morality his condemnation of Yi Ya's "special menu" fails to implicate the cannibal "gourmet," his lord Duke Huan, and his criticism of the political and economic consequences of forcing people to exchange their sons for food falls short of a religious or moral concern over social misery. This comes into sharp contrast with the Confucian tradition exemplified by Mencius's moral lecture cited earlier.

The same passage in the *Guanzi* reappeared almost unaltered in the *Hanfeizi*, a book named after the legalist philosopher Han Fei (d. 233 B.C.E.).[23] Not surprisingly, Han Fei presents Yi Ya's case in a larger historical context Guan Zhong could never have known. After Guan Zhong's death, Duke Huan did not follow his advice to get rid of Yi Ya and other disloyal officials. He paid the high price of his own death for employing people about whom he had been warned. The use to which Han Fei puts the case is also slightly different: it is the mistake made by Duke Huan of not following the wisdom of the sage, rather than the evil nature embodied in Yi Ya's cooking of his son, that is the focus of his argument in the chapter entitled "Ten Mistakes" (Shiguo). This reinforces the already established theme of political utility rather than moral concern—even though the latter is used in their argument for the former.

Compared with the earlier historical sources, literary representations of flesh eating in vernacular fiction are more diverse and distanced, ranging from the most dispassionate to the most fantastic. In the Ming novel *Sanguo yanyi* (Romance of the Three Kingdoms), Liu Bei is offered in his desperation a dish of game by the hunter Liu An, only to find out later that the meat was cut from the arm of the hunter's wife. She was killed by her husband because he was out of game to provide for the imperial uncle Liu Bei, who was to become the emperor of the Shu. The text describes Liu Bei's departure like this: "He was deeply affected at this proof of his host's regard and the tears rained down as he mounted his steed at the gate. 'I wish I could go with you,' said Liu An, 'but as my mother still lives I cannot go so far from home.' Liu Bei thanked him and went his way" (Luo 1972, 151–52; 1959, 194). What Liu Bei's tears cannot wash away—and what the filial piety in Liu An's reference to his mother fails to hide—is a gender-specific reenactment of the theme of sacrificing the son by the father, only changed to the wife's sacrificing by the husband. As always, the victim is offered as food to the political "phallus."

Like this fictional episode, the "black deeds inns" that sell steamed dumplings filled with minced human flesh in the Ming novel *Shuihuzhuan* (Water margin) must be read allegorically. E. N. Anderson has pointed out that "[p]erhaps someone, somewhere, tried this dubious means of making money, but such a business could not have been viewed with the cheerful moral indifference of the *Shuihuzhuan*—a book whose astonishing unconcern with murder and mayhem is comprehensible only in terms of the totalitarian, brutal society of late Yuan and Ming" (1988,

226, n. 3). Conversely, I would like to add, by representing the collapse of the mandate of Heaven most vividly epitomized through such heinous crimes, the author(s) of the *Shuihuzhuan* were able to legitimize the rebels' cause of "taking over the mandate of Heaven to execute it."

So far my inquiry basically has been limited to the mainstream of the imperial and Confucian traditions without touching the marginal but important traditions of popular religions. Largely due to Buddhism and the Daoist-Buddhist convergence, and especially their adaptation to popular religions of certain shamanistic nature, food symbolism and alimentary discourse in ancient China became enriched with mystical flavors.[24] Deposited in this mythical tradition is a timeless imagination of the ghost world, a world of the unknown depicted in grotesque and fantastic images and invested with much ambivalence. On the popular religious side, the fear of the ghost world is eased by providing hungry spirits with food in cultural rituals such as ancestor worship and seasonal festivals. We may even find some residues of such semishamanistic beliefs and practices in early Chinese American communities, as presented in Kingston's *The Woman Warrior.* In written texts, the fascination with a world beyond the human realm is a repeated theme in the strange tales of the Tang, the ghost stories of the Ming and Qing, and, most importantly, in *Xiyouji* (The journey to the west), an outstanding Ming epic novel. Their thematic and generic attributes are traceable to the ancient text of *Shanhaijing* (Book of hills and seas) and continue to surface in the work of modern writers such as Lu Xun and Mo Yan. A common feature shared by both popular religious rituals and written texts is the human-eating ghost world, which frightens humans yet attracts their imaginations at the same time.

So we should not be surprised that *The Journey to the West*, though based on the religious tenet that prohibits consumption of animal meat[25]—let alone human flesh—is structured allegorically on a narrative of being eaten. For the Tang monk Tripitika (his pilgrimage to India to obtain the Buddhist canon in the early Tang is the novel's main historical narrative line), his path to immortality is a breathtaking process of overcoming the eighty-one menaces, most of which involve the risk of his body being devoured for the longevity of the eaters. One may downplay the text as some kind of fantastic joke or, in Hu Shih's word, "profound nonsense"[26] since those "cannibals" assume the form and shape of beasts or monsters. As such, the meaning or the "nonsense" of the tale hinges on the dialectical interplay between the brutal human order, in which the body is treated as flesh to be devoured, and the redeeming divine order, in which the flesh must be cast away nonetheless. In other words, whether nonsense or allegory, it is the narrative of being eaten that has played out the fundamental dilemma of human life. This dilemma is described paradoxically as a redeeming journey toward *wukong*, the "enlightenment of emptiness," which is the heroic monkey's given name and illustrates a central concept of Buddhist philosophy.

"Revenge cannibalism" of hatred, moral and political considerations in prohibiting anthropophagy, and religious-artistic imagination of the human-eating world—these are three major semantic layers laid down like sediment in a symbolic culture of incorporation. The recurrence of cannibalism in modern Chinese literature is incomprehensible apart from the age-old ambivalence toward the "other," human and nonhuman alike. But the semantic scope of cannibalism in modern literature is limited to a political narrative of social evolution and cultural nationalism. The proliferation of "cannibalism" in modern writings is based on a political metaphor that informs the foundation of the revolutionary consciousness. Since revolution itself—whether the Nationalist or the Communist—is borrowed from the modern West, what James Brown says about the French Revolution (1984) may well apply to modern China. I quote his inspiring book to conclude this section. About eating and the French Revolution, Brown writes:

> Social disparities under the Old Regime were often transformed into gastronomical metaphors and were later used by novelists. . . . Figuratively speaking, the aristocracy devoured the people under the *ancien régime*; hence the metaphor of social and economic consumption which could be nullified only by reversing the social structure of the nation by means of revolution and thus producing a shift in identity from "eaten" to "eater." In many respects the Revolution of 1789 was an endeavor of the lower classes to become equals at the table and to partake fully of earthly bounty. (5)

Brown concludes his book in an emphatic way that I want to use to finish this chapter: "To eat or be eaten—that is the question!" (186).

 1

The Social Embodiment of Modernity

So much has been written on Lu Xun that it would be difficult to add to that formidable body of scholarship. In the Anglo-American academy alone, a half dozen book-length studies and more than a hundred book chapters and journal articles have been published in the past three decades, exhausting almost every aspect of Lu Xun's life and work with perhaps most existing methodological approaches. His name also has entered the reading list of scholars and writers outside the field and generated unexpected (mis)readings, much to the dismay of many specialists and the pleasant surprise of others.[1] Yet two recent, influential works on other authors or topics still introduce themselves via the "father," framing their respective theses as "After Lu Xun" (D. Wang 1992) and "An Old Tale Retold" (Chow 1995). I devote this chapter to Lu Xun for the same reason but with two questions as simple as these: why is it Lu Xun (as opposed to other writers), and why is it cannibalism (rather than other metaphors of social pathology)?

The first question grew out of an innocent curiosity. I was initially interested in tracing the literary development of *chirende jiushehui* (the human-eating old society), a household phrase in Mao's China and a pivotal figure in the grand narrative of revolution since the May Fourth Movement of the late 1910s. My assumption was that since the canonical history of modern Chinese literature started with Lu Xun's outcry to "save the children" from being devoured it would be meaningful to reconstruct a cultural genealogy by examining how his "children" have received, revised, reinscribed, or rejected his thesis. In my survey of major writers active from the May Fourth period to the early 1930s, I was frustrated that virtually no one really bothered to respond to the "father" by writing on cannibalism as a literary topos. Much as in Lu Xun's "Zhufu" (New Year's sacrifice), cannibalism is an "absent presence" in many works attacking the old China; it is present as an organizing trope for oppression yet absent in its lack of descriptive details. Above all, one would be hard put to believe that real cannibalism has been a systematic social practice since the dawn of Chinese civilization, and the topic is more suitable for tall tales than serious literature. In fact, the generic features of cannibalism and Lu Xun's "modernist" treatment contain a dense layer of allegorical surrealism and require sophisticated interpretation. This literary model is based on a rather elitist attitude and exercise (as Lu Xun himself came to recognize later), and thus it is too demanding for the ordinary reader, not to mention the majority of the society, who did not read in the first place. It is hunger, not cannibalism, that captured the material reality of the destitute masses. Consequently, "the human-eating old society" either remained an allegorical trope that had nothing to do with real cannibalism or was played out as a metonymic cliché.

My survey of modern Chinese fiction, however, had an important by-product: many socially committed writers during that period were not even interested in the topic of "eating," let alone cannibalism. Those writers did not display much appetite for writing about it at all. This finding was rather surprising to me at the beginning. How could a literary and cultural revolution, launched out of the ethos of national salvation and social emancipation with the promise to reflect and rectify the real world, ignore the serious problem of hunger? As I became attracted to feminist questions about domestic space, especially after I was drawn to the ubiquitous presence of food signs and eating scenes in the works by many Chinese American woman writers, I looked into the representative works by Bing Xin, Lu Yin, Ling Shuhua, and Ding Ling—four important woman writers in May Fourth literature. The result was disappointing initially but revealing in retrospect. It would appear as though educated women were so "fed up" with their repressive domestic space that they simply developed a distaste for food, exemplified by Sophia in Ding Ling's "Miss Sophia's Diary" (1928). The best-known and most controversial image of the "new woman," Sophia performs the tedious act of boiling milk three or four times a day but never drinks it.[2] She does so as if mischievously responding to her doctor's advice that she rest and eat more. Even though she no longer is confined to the old familial institution, her role in the public sphere is yet to be negotiated. Sophia's lack of appetite can be seen as an apt metaphor for the empty routine of the everyday in which she is mired and from which she struggles to break free.

If Sophia's cultural anorexia is gender specific, however, the symptom does not manifest itself in some other woman writers of the same period. In Bing Xin's sentimental and romantic world, for example, the young woman's golden voice chanting for pantheistic love and the beauty of nature is rarely aware of the other, more earthly function of the mouth. It does not follow that Bing Xin and her women characters fail to enjoy food. The nurse or the maid is a domestic fixture in her stories and occasionally shows up to take meal orders or serve tea and snacks. Food, or the lack of it, obviously was not a problem for a writer who was fortunate enough to attend Wellesley College in the 1920s. For both Ding Ling and Bing Xin, the absence of the hunger motif in their works suggests the distance between their artistic taste at the time and the social reality of poverty.

Having in my mind the big picture of hunger from the revolutionary writings of the Yan'an period and in post-Mao literature, I then turned to more "class-conscious" writers such as Mao Dun, a leading advocate for a "literature for life." But even in his most realistic writings on rural China and the devastated socioeconomic life of the peasantry, he made virtually no reference to food or the lack thereof. I do not mean that eating should rank high on every writer's agenda. But it does elude me how a leading advocate and practitioner of social (and later socialist) realism chose not to bother with the politics of hunger and eating, not even in passing. In the work of other male writers such as Ye Shengtao and Ba Jin, alimentary images are used at times to set domestic scenes only for decorative functions. Ironically, between the May Fourth literary revolution and the revolutionary literature of Chinese Communism, the "reactionary" Shen Congwen stands out for his versatile alimentary writing. He stands not only between two periods of literary history but also at the intersection where the politics and poetics of eating converge.

My survey is far from exhaustive. For one thing, I did not touch the vast body of popular fiction, since limited space only allows me to present the most salient signposts in cultural history. The brief account of my survey foregrounds a number of questions to be addressed, questions that also underline my own method of analysis. If most May Fourth writers were not interested in the politics of eating, why were Lu Xun and Shen Congwen so fascinated with it? This simple question demands a search for explanations beyond "cultural essence" or shared historical experience. One must look for the ways in which eating has shaped the writer's personal experience and quintessential sensibility. From this personal perspective, alimentary writing reveals the libidinal realm of the body. As such, my readings of Lu Xun and Shen Congwen often adopt a psychological approach informed by Freudian-Lacanian psychoanalysis.

The question "why Lu Xun?" cannot be fully addressed apart from the question about the topical, that is, "why cannibalism?" The personal body always has to act out to acquire its meaning in a historical context, and the libidinal becomes accessible only when it "speaks" in language. Lu Xun's alimentary writing is by and large limited to the ritualistic and symbolic dimension of eating and is short of serious attention paid to the materiality of food. This probably is a refraction of his view that the deformed physical body of China could not be reformed before revolutionary surgery is conducted on the diseased "head." Cannibalism easily lends itself to his cultural diagnosis and prescription. Still, why did cannibalism, among so many other symptoms of cultural disease and social misery, single-handedly touch off his grand repudiation of traditional culture?

The immediate answer is found in his reading, at about the same time, of two kinds of texts that contain some graphic depictions of flesh-eating practice: *Zizhitongjian* from ancient China and the writings of George Grey (1812–92), a British governor by way of New Zealand and South Africa and an ethnographer of Polynesian mythology and society. The practice of cannibalism described in *Zizhitongjian* resurfaces in the postexecution feasting of the anti-Qing rebel Xu Xilin's heart and liver, which serves as one of the five examples of cannibalism in "Diary of a Madman" (1918). Through Xu's case, Lu Xun links the mythical tale of Yi Ya's sacrifice of his son to the folk practice of curing tuberculosis with human blood, the latter to be further developed in "Medicine" (1919). Meanwhile, Grey's report on Polynesian cannibalism is implicitly reinscribed in Lu Xun's investigation of Chinese cannibalism. In the end, Lu Xun concludes that "China is still a cannibalistic nation" just as the two sources from ancient China and Grey caught his eye, so to speak, in his reading list (see 11:353).[3] While this kind of cross-reading generates much ambivalence and self-hatred, the political construct of the national body borrowed from colonial discourse supersedes the meaning of the personal body. In a short essay he wrote in 1919, for instance, he bitterly accepts the term *natives*, which is what one British missionary calls the local Chinese. Highlighting the term's association with the word *savages*, he compares Chinese "natives" with the Polynesian "savages" described by Grey. In his painful comparison, cannibalism once again tops his list of Chinese and Polynesian barbarism (1:327–28).[4]

This mode of intertextual making of the diseased national body is quite a standard practice in Lu Xun's early works. It lays bare the traces of "translingual practice" (L. Liu 1995) exactly at the point where Grey's colonialist model of historiographical writing translates the "native" body into a half-human object. The lens with which Lu Xun views the cannibalistic "natives" is literally filtered through the colonialist mapping of the world. Thus, more than his personal "palate" was implicated in his representation of cannibalism. To answer the question "why cannibalism?" one has to examine how his writing reinscribes and disseminates the meaning and form of cannibalism in a way that legitimates the ideological authority of modern historiography and ethnography. When we put the two questions together, *Lu Xun* and *cannibalism* signify the point of a historical configuration whereby the politics of reading and the politics of eating are mixed up in a symbolic incorporation of the "outside."

The "outside" is not monolithic, of course, and the so-called West is diverse enough to allow Shen Congwen to approach the national body of China from a different angle. Based on his assimilation of Jonathan Swift's "modest proposal," Shen Congwen ties the diseased social body to the depleted stomach, offering a more materialistic understanding of the world than most of his contemporaries. This striking difference from the early Lu Xun would make Shen a close ally with the later revolutionary "hunger artists." But the passage from satire to revolution demands that the writer translate words into action, subsume art under politics, and sacrifice diverse tastes for a unified vision. The generic boundary of satire turns out to be the symbolic limit of Shen Congwen's political excursion into the public realm. His "modest proposal" is not just a thematic counterpoint to the Madman's outcry but is characteristic of his modest view regarding the limited power of literary writing in instituting social change. It is Shen's modest view toward the word that has left us a corpus of alimentary writing poetically alluring and intimately private.

The concurrent presence of both the politics and poetics of eating in

Shen Congwen's works indicates that the public and the private body is inseparable in cultural embodiment. But there is a generic distinction in his works that exists largely between the more publicly oriented fictional writing and the personal essay or autobiographical prose. From a purely aesthetic viewpoint, the best literary works in modern China are found in the less politically engaged genres—the personal essay and lyric poetry being perhaps the two most distinctive. In considering the various factors that determine an author's topical and thematic options, we thus need to take account of generic attributes in addition to questions about his or her ideological orientation and artistic sensibility. If Lu Xun's totalization of tradition can be attributed to his cross-reading of *Zizhitongjian* and Grey's ethnography, the generic traits of historiography and fiction are mixed up in his "national allegory." By the same token, if satire allows Shen Congwen to launch a rare political critique, the personal prose is what formally enables his poetics of eating to surface. When politics and poetics become mutually exclusive, Shen Congwen chose silence, as he did after 1949, to protect himself from "decapitation": hence, the stories of the body and alimentary embodiment.

2. Lu Xun and Cannibalism

In this chapter, I first analyze the modern discourse of cannibalism, focusing on the ambivalent entanglement of orality and visuality in setting the boundary between the self and the other. Next I reconstruct a "pathological" road map to Lu Xun's "cannibal complex" by locating his fear of being devoured in his autobiographical accounts of his childhood experience. I will show how his oral-libidinal fixation is displaced into a visual narrative of self-reduplication and transformed into a recurrent spectacle of the body politic. What is disseminated visually is also inscribed around the tension of a double orality that juxtaposes silence and outcry, suffocation and consumption. Through this configuration of taste, vision, and voice, the final section concludes with his allegorical embodiment of the diseased and the deceased.

The complexity of the problem involving a complicated author at a difficult historical juncture, compounded by the "lurid" topic of cannibalism, defies any systematic closure and leaves this chapter as fragmented as perhaps the fragments of Lu Xun's writing on this topic would invite. Unlike our positively oralized experience of food and speech, cannibalism, especially its literary deployment, is by its ambivalent nature figured in negativity. On the other hand, the use of cannibalism in colonial modernity for establishing power relations and moral superiority is as unequivocal as the repulsive feeling toward cannibalism is ingrained in the modern human(ist) psyche. However, as Kilgour has demonstrated, the self-other relationship—a binary opposition that organizes our fundamental experience of the "inside" and the "outside"—is "constructed not by essential differences but by position" and is thus "infinitely reversible" (1990, 4). The reversal, just to repeat what is common sense, does not imply a regression to the "Dark Ages." Nor would I even fully embrace the return to the now highly reified "oral stage." Rather, the route of Lu Xun's "Chinese cannibal" reveals the historical trace of a powerful dehumanizing figure whose meaning can and must be renegotiated. Precisely because cannibalism has generated such an outcry of "Horror" in colonial encounters and has been exploited as a master metaphor for the self-hatred of the colonized, the absolute moralistic position vis-à-vis this intractable other must be re-*viewed*.

In a more reverent note to the "father," Lu Xun's body is like the cow's, an ideal example of self-sacrifice he sets for himself and his "children." As the cow eats only grass but produces milk for the world, so Lu Xun offers his "corpus" as nourishment to "save the children" and cure the ailment of the national spirit. The "corpus" thus must be taken as sustenance, squeezed out of the texture of his flesh and circulated in the blood of the body politic. It is truly tragic and ironic that the mouth cannot simply feed on the word. As his own body was consumed as a result of his excessive labor in words, the "milk" he produced for the world eventually drained his own blood. In this sense, Lu Xun died an autophagic death, a self-made victim of "auto-eating" who nevertheless has been recycled and redeemed as a martyr of modern China.

Orality and Visuality in the Discourse of Cannibalism

In a tear-jerking scene in Amy Tan's *The Joy Luck Club* (1989), which is dramatized in Wayne Wang's film version (1993) of the novel in an even more sentimental fashion, a disavowed daughter carves a piece of flesh from her arm, cooks it in a soup, and then feeds it to her dying mother. The mother dies anyway, but her soul is supposedly reconciled with the daughter's through this ritual of filial piety. The significance of this "communion," construed around the image of the "Chinese family," would be completely altered if, say, a member of the audience were to interrupt the film's indulgence by shouting: "But this is cannibalism!" This familial ritual, called *gegouliaoqin* in Chinese, is cited as one of the five examples of cannibalism in Lu Xun's "Diary of a Madman." Seventy years after Lu Xun, the "father," cried out to save the children, it seems as though a daughter of China has responded across the Pacific by serving up her flesh and blood to save the mother.

Tan's use of a traditional ritual to flesh out the novel's central theme of mother-daughter conflict and bonding will be analyzed in the last chapter. What I want to emphasize here is the different positions of enunciation or narrative points of view in relation to the eating of human flesh, symbolic or otherwise. The scene of *gegouliaoqin* in Tan's novel is not intended to be a case of cannibalism, and so far it has not provoked any outcry. The reason is simple: the narrator is positioned within the discursive field of orality, relating the story of the soup that channels the circulation of blood in the larger body of the ancestry-oriented kinship. This orality-centered viewpoint can be traced to the "oral stage," where the self and the m/other are yet to be separated. If we disentangle the Freudian metaphor from the teleology of historical progress, the "regression" to orality can be defined as a symbolic act that attempts to blur, if not completely demolish, the boundary between the self and the other. Although the real physical body is involved in the act of *gegouliaoqin*,[1] its mode of enunciation is similar to that in Communion in that the eater is connected with the *community*, and eating is congruent with the doubly oralized *communication*. Conversely, the modern representation of cannibalism hinges on the outside gaze that distances the self from the other in the sacrament of the viewing subject.

Looked upon from the reverse perspective, Communion and cannibalism are correlative to a semantic uncertainty of what is sacred. The ingestion of the Eucharist can easily shift to an act of barbarism. But if the modern discourse of cannibalism is in itself based on the assumption that the human life is sacred, the logic behind that assumption fails to explain why cannibalism elicits the deepest feeling of repulsion among all forms of "consumptions" of the human body, many of which are much more outrageous. Acts of inhumanity as deliberate as the massive destruction of human lives in wars and genocides may generate strong moral indignation but not the kind of physical repulsion induced by a mere mention of "eating one's own kind." Figured in the modern discourse of cannibalism is the threshold between the "inside" and the "outside." It is rooted in the fear of anything alien and unknown but has been conceptualized in a moralism that allies humanity with the self and attributes barbarism to the other. The epistemological and semantic shift from Communion to cannibalism can be attributed to the sacrament of the autonomous subject. It is that individuated embodiment of the sacred that shapes the dreadful image of the cannibal. And this binary construct, incidentally, can be found in the very making of the word *cannibal* in Columbus's encounter with what is today called the Caribbean.

History tells us, of course, that Columbus sailed off to old Cathay only to land in the "New World" by chance. His coinage of the term *cannibal* reveals a different trail, however. In his *Colonial Encounters*, Peter Hulme describes it as follows (here much condensed):

> [W]hat a symptomatic reading of [Columbus's] *Journal* reveals is the presence of two distinct discursive networks. In bold outline each discourse can be identified by the presence of key words: in one case "gold," "Cathay," "Grand Khan," "intelligent soldiers," "large buildings," "merchant ships"; in the other "gold," "savagery," "monstrosity," "anthropophagy." . . . The relationship between them is expressed as that between present and future: this is a world of savagery, over there we will find Cathay. But . . . "the soldiers of the Grand Khan" from the discourse of Marco Polo and "the man-eating savages" from the discourse of Herodotus are competing for a single signifier—the word "canibales." Columbus's wavering on 23 November belongs to a larger pattern of references in which "canibal" [*sic*] is consistently glossed by his native hosts as "man-eater" while it ineluctably calls to his mind "el Gran Can." In various entries the phonemes echo each other from several lines' distance until on 11 December 1492 they finally coincide: ". . . the Caniba are nothing else than the people of the Grand Khan." (1986, 20–22)

Hulme's description foregrounds several important issues in cross-cultural analysis that are often hidden beneath the rationality of instrumental communication. First, the making of the sign was a result of Columbus's imaginary reading of an unknown referent, a geographical location and its inhabitants that did not make sense to him. He interpreted what was available to him according to the two historical narratives of Herodotus and Marco Polo, remote from each other but both major figures in shaping Europe's view of its other, one dehumanized and the other idealized. Reading here, as the primary meaning-producing act, is at the same time an act of writing. There is no clear boundary between these two acts, and the production of the sign and its meaning hinges only on the intertextual glossing of preceding discursive systems upon a new place.

Second, as a metaphor condensed from two unrelated phonemes, *cannibal* also displaces two geographical locations into what has since become world history. In fact, this is a new but unexpected product of the ongoing narrative that propelled the great voyage in the first place. The irony of history resembles the historical making of *cannibal* itself: by sheer chance, a signifier was not only coined but was necessarily made meaningful. Temporally, it has constructed a narrative from a past (Marco Polo and Herodotus) via a present (the Caribs through an equation of the above two) to a future, the course of which was to be charted through violence. Spatially, it signifies the journey of modern man and his consequent mapping of the world in terms of "home" (Europe), "here" (the native land of the Caribs), and "over there" (Cathay). The historical meaning of *cannibal* has become as substantial as the making of the word appears to have been accidental. *Cannibal* is, in the realm of sign production, what colonialism is in the making of Manifest Destiny.

The third but not the least important aspect of Columbus's making of the new signifier has much to do with the position of the subject. It cannot be overemphasized that the modern representation of cannibalism is in its origin and nature constructed by the civilized self who "sees" and "reports" the other. Seeing and reporting constitute the predominant practice that characterizes the writing of travelogues, missionary journals, and even some anthropological accounts. As such, the self-other relationship is defined as an absolute moral difference according to a dualist totality.

Lu Xun's simultaneous reinscription of *Zizhitongjian* and George Grey in his writing reveal a pattern similar to Columbus's cross-referenced glossing. Modernity, with its specular opposition between the West and China, furnished an epistemological distance that allowed Lu Xun and his generation of intellectuals to take up a position as spectators of the old China. In its drive to modernize, the May Fourth new culture movement inherited a colonial legacy that was infused with the teleology and ideology embedded in historiographical writing since the Enlightenment. This can be found in the reader response to "Diary of a Madman" immediately after its publication. In a 1919 article entitled "The Tragedy of 'the Enlightened in a Cannibalistic Nation,'" the author declares that China is "uncivilized," "barbarous," and "a race of low quality" that exists only at the "medieval" or even "prehistoric" stage, "lagging behind the advanced Western nations for one to two thousand years" (S. Du 1989, 50–51). In Lu Xun's story "Diary of a Madman," as radical as the Madman's posture was to the Confucian classics, his practice was quite a standard one in the global cannibalizing of the "third world." What changed between Columbus and Lu Xun was a reversal: Marco Polo's romantic image of old Cathay had been transformed into its opposite. The specular structure of orientalist discursive practice remained unchanged, however.

The positional shift from the "eater" to the "spectator" signals the "discovery" and "capture" of the other, completed in the process of colonization and conquest. It characterizes an interior "travel" externalized for the constructing the borders. Yet because of the uncertain and ambivalent nature of the sign system, as in the case of Columbus's making of the word, the semantic and moral borders tend to undermine their own apparent stability, manifested in the simultaneous "assimilation" and "elimination" of the cannibal. On the one hand, cannibalism as such implies that the cannibal is not just an animal of another species that must be incorporated into the civilizing order; on the other hand, the civilized self cannot fully establish his or her moral superiority except by excluding the cannibal from the human race and subsuming him or her under the realm of the sub- or half-human. Between the self and the other thus stands the very contradiction of civilization whose nightmarish memory threatens to shatter its own order and moral authority. This ambivalence often surfaces on the edge of madness, whether in Lu Xun's Madman or Conrad's Kurtz in his *Heart of Darkness.* As a result, the narrative ambivalence constitutes the liminal site on which the ideology of the sacred subject simultaneously conceals and reveals its political unconscious. To foreground the narrative ambivalence and the encoded historical contradiction, one has to examine what strategy is adopted to formally contain the political unconscious and symbolically solve the contradiction.

Take Conrad's *Heart of Darkness*, for example. Cannibalism is not treated in a clear-cut bifurcation in the text, and its inherent ambivalence is mobilized to flesh out the ambiguous journey of European colonialism. Marlow's reflection on the African cannibals is figured in a destabilizing uncertainty. The double negativity in "not inhuman" and the mirror reflection in "like yours" are what collapse the symbolic and social order, leaving Marlow in a heart-wrenching limbo and driving Kurtz to his desperate recognition that he himself is the source of "Horror." However, the narrative as a symbolic act also formally contains the political unconsciousness of the irreducible negativity. It is contained by Marlow's embedding of Kurtz's story in his personal "adventure." The critical thrust of Marlow's recounting is further watered down through his choice of audience: he conceals the truth (the very function of ideology) from Kurtz's Intended and only divulges it to a selected few. The story of a personal adventure is finally retold to us by the anonymous I-narrator, among Marlow's audience, who reconstructs the entire narrative by pondering, on the Thames, Western civilization and its recent colonialist history. What we read in the final text is a highly aestheticized personal story, twice removed from the social reality of "Horror." In other words, Western civilization must be kept from going totally mad in its own "heart of darkness"; the narrative forms of personal "adventure" and historical-philosophical "speculation" only serve to symbolically resolve historical contradictions. In this way, "Horror" is repressed as the "missing content," to borrow a term from François Lyotard on high modernism. What triumphs in the end is the aesthetic coherence of the form.

The crux of the matter is that the novella's symbolic solution through narrative containment has little to do with the author's intended critique of colonialism, for Conrad's anticolonialist stance was among the strongest of his contemporaries. Rather, the text's formal strategy must be treated as a *parole* or symbolic act molded in the *langue* of colonialism. Translated in the historical narration of cannibalism, the enunciated subject of being "not inhuman" and "like yours" is disseminated through the enunciating practice of "seeing" and "reporting" and is reinscribed in the articulation of civilization. Because the text is formally contained in an outside traveler's narrative, the way in which the cannibal story is told remains unchanged from Columbus to Conrad.

Lu Xun's journey is more complicated. He is positioned as the traveler and the native at the same time: a native who "travels" to the outside world only to find himself ineluctably split on the "border." This subject position is obviously different from Marlow's. Yet Lu Xun is not unlike Kurtz because both become "othered," unable to cross the border back to their respective "native lands." They share the same symptom of madness and the same urge to "save" the native. In the sense that Lu Xun embodies the classic figure of split consciousness in the "third-world" intellectual, his works can be read as a kind of interior monologue that "travels" between different positions. On its pages is written the ambiguous journey of a divided self displaced to embody the historical path of Chinese modernity, a positional shift that has nevertheless been reified as an essential difference.

Furthermore, Lu Xun's writing, insofar as it is situated against what he believes Confucianism is, is intended in its own terms to articulate the political unconscious rather than contain it, whether it is articulated through the Mara Poet, the Niezschean Superman, or the ancient Chinese concept of *kuang* or "ecstatic madness." For him, the liminal site of the political unconscious is not simply "discovered," as it is in the case of Conrad or Marlow, but is a given condition on all the existential, epistemological, and historical levels. Consequently, we must study the phenomenology of his articulated political unconscious while also maintaining a critical-hermeneutic investigation of the inherent narrative ambivalence. And the traces of Lu Xun's unconscious must be first located in the two most sensuous and conspicuous zones of the "face": the mouth and the eye.

From the Mouth to the Eye

According to various biographical and autobiographical accounts, the young boy Lu Xun cherished a passionate fascination with the fantastic world of ancient Chinese myth, legends, and folktales. This fascination persisted into adulthood in his pioneering scholarly work on ancient Chinese mythology and in his rewriting of some prehistoric legends. Now, many of these tales and legends have at least one major topic in common: they are about ghosts, monsters, demons, goblins, and beasts that come out deep in the night to devour humans, especially children. Like *The Journey to the West*, a childhood favorite of his, these fantastic tales are told on the narrative paradigm of being "eaten."[2]

Lu Xun once recalled his old nurse Ah Chang in his reminiscence "From Hundred-Plant Garden to Three-Flavor Study" (1926), and what he remembered had a lot to do with "cannibalistic" stories she told him. When he was very young, she related a tale about a "beauty-woman snake." This snake would come out in the night to eat anyone who responded to her call. The meaning of this little parable, the author suggests, is that "if a strange voice calls your name, on no account answer." Its chilling effect, he admits, is that the "story brought home to me the perils with which human life is fraught" (2:279; 1:390–91). In the memoir "Ah Chang and *The Book of Hills and Seas*" (1926), troops of the Taiping Rebellion invaded his hometown and forced the whole family to flee, leaving only a gatekeeper and an old female cook to take care of the house. When a rebel entered the house and appeared in front of the woman, as Lu Xun describes, "she complained that she was starving. 'In that case,' said the Long Hair with a grin, 'you can have this to eat!' And he tossed over something round with a small queue still attached to it—it was the gatekeeper's head." This episode took place before his birth, and the cook was said to have never regained her senses. It was retold by Ah Chang and, as the title suggests, is juxtaposed with, and embedded in, his memory of the classical book of the fantastic, a book with illustrations of "man-faced beasts, nine-headed snakes, three-footed birds, winged men and headless monsters who used their teats as eyes" (2:245; 1:369).

The most distressing experience in Lu Xun's formative years was his father's prolonged illness and death. In his view, expressed in the preface to *Outcry* (1922) and in the memoir "Father's Illness" (1926), his father was literally consumed by traditional medicine. It bears repeating here that herbs and other "exotic" drugs used in Chinese medicine are blended either in decoction or in large, soft, round pills to be swallowed. In these two pieces, some of the drugs are depicted with names and looks that evoke the grotesque images of the ancient world. Part of the teenager Lu Xun's daily routine for four years was to acquire all kinds of unusual medications and then watch his father swallow them bit by bit, only to be "swallowed" himself day by day. The pain of seeing his father eat to be "eaten" gnawed away at the boy's mental health.

These fantastic tales and personal stories describe a childhood experience with the grotesque and the uncanny, and their meaning is beyond the little boy's comprehension. Yet precisely because they project a mythical shadow of life, death, and nature, these images belong to the "archetype" that has shaped the little Lu Xun's sensibility and molded his perception of the world. Looking at life from this dreadful yet fantastic angle, the child no doubt in his heart harbored the fear of being devoured. As these images were in fact remembered by the adult Lu Xun and retold in his writings, they punctuate the very surface of his remembering and reviewing things past.

Lu Xun is well known for his meticulous detailing and satirical depiction of the cultural surface of Chinese society. Under his scrutiny were distorted images ranging from hair to beard and moustache, from eyes to teeth, from facial makeup to fingernails, often depicted in repulsive forms and shapes. When his early memory resurfaces with the imagery of the mouth, the mouth sometimes "gazes" back in a language of the eye. What takes place in his writing is a reciprocal shift of the eye between the self and the "cannibal," who stares back and threatens to eat him. In the essay "On Photography" (*Lunzhaoxiang zhilei*, 1924), for instance, he recalls a childhood story about pickled fish eyes. In his hometown, he heard people talking about Westerners digging out the eyes of some local Chinese. A maid working in a missionary's home is said to have seen a "large vat of pickled eyes piled like carp fry, layer upon layer, right to the edge of the vat." To the author, that macabre picture reflects the villagers' xenophobic ignorance. As they stored up pickled cabbage for the winter, so the foreigner must have learned from them to preserve human eyes. The eyes look like little carps because the "goddess of sight" who was worshipped in the local shrine had fishlike eyes. With no access to anatomical illustrations of the eyeball in modern medicine, the local storytellers could not help imagining the pickled eyes in the distorted shape of little fish rather than the real round organ. These eyes were preserved, as some villagers believed, not for food; the foreigner used them for taking photographs. Why would they have anything to do with photography? It is because the villagers, who had no idea how photography worked, thought that photographs were produced in the same way a person sees his or her own image mirrored in the pupils of another person (1:181–82; cf. Denton 1996, 196–98). The story dramatizes how a premodern culture makes sense of its encounter with, and entry into, the modern era of image production.

Lu Xun's "deconstruction" of the folk imagination notwithstanding, it is worth noting that a purely fictional image would be so indelibly imprinted on his mind and be called back after decades in all its "fishy" details. It is only natural that this image would resurface in a table scene in "Diary of a Madman" that is no less macabre than the "real" story: "The eyes of the fish were white and hard, and its mouth was open just like those people who want to eat human beings. After a few mouthfuls I could not tell whether the slippery morsels were fish or human flesh, so I brought it all up" (1:425; 1:42). In *Lu Xun's Vision of Reality*, William Lyell locates Lu Xun's "vision" in what Lyell calls the "eye theme" prevalent in his works. To borrow Lyell's phrase, we can see that in the table scene the "eye theme" evolves first around the "white and hard" eyes of the fish, which in turn stare back at the narrator's pathetic gaze. Through a visual simile that links the fish to cannibalism, the normal process of ingestion is inverted: food is vomited, not eaten. By oralizing the experiential world around the mouth and then visualizing it through the eye, the Madman's nightmare plays out a corrupted circle from the physiological-psychological to the social orders. In this way, the text appeals to the abstract through the corporeal, the political through the libidinal, and transforms a childhood horror story into a ruined setting of history.

At the same time, the "eye theme," which activates the visualized dissemination of the oral-libidinal fixation, also serves as the organizing trope around which the Madman's story unfolds. The writing of the diary strictly follows a visual dichotomy between darkness and light that heightens the tension of the human-eating underworld and the Madman's enlightenment. Darkness is the predominant image employed to indicate the "heart of darkness" of traditional culture. Out of the thirteen "entries" or fragments of the diary, seven contain references to the physical time of day. In these seven fragments, four describe the night, and even in the three daytime entries there is no sunlight. The first section defines the Madman's relationship with the moon, which enables his journey out of the dark underworld: "Tonight the moon is very bright. I have not seen it for over thirty years, so today when I saw it I felt in unusually high spirits. I begin to realize that during the past thirty years I have been in the dark" (1:422; 1:40).

In the dark world, the narrator lived for thirty-odd years in his "normal" state of mind, and now he is traveling in a new world under the "lunatic" light of the moon. To the extent that the new world is in effect the same old one but only changed by moonlight, the reader's entry into the text entails a positional shift, a reinterpretation of the familiar from the moonlit viewpoint. As long as this mode of reinterpretation informs the textual experience, the reader, immediately following the first fragment, will encounter darkness in each and every moment of its presence when the second section begins with "Tonight there is no moon at all." This impression of darkness is reinforced in the third section, which begins with "I can't sleep at night," and in the sixth, which begins with "Pitch dark. I don't know whether it is day or night." Operating on three modes of signification, the moon symbolically distinguishes good from evil; metaphorically plays on a figural irony of sanity and insanity; and structurally (i.e., in terms of "plot making") anticipates the dramatic reversal that occurs when the protagonist "sees light" toward the end of the tale: the dark truth of his own unwitting participation in human eating.

Since the Madman's experience is figured in the visual-moonlight/oral-darkness opposition, "no matter what people say to him, the Madman is able to see through the smoke-screen of their words to the real cannibalistic intent in their hearts revealed by the expression in their eyes" (Lyell 1976, 271). Throughout the diary, the Madman reports what he sees, whether it is experienced in his delusion or results from his paranoiac association stimulated by real objects. This highly individuated narrative is semantically corporeal, logically inconsistent, figuratively condensed, and psychologically illusive. It culminates in his seeing through the book of "Confucian Virtue and Morality." As the text describes it: "Since I could not sleep anyway, I read intently half the night until I began to see words between the lines. The whole book was filled with the two words—'Eat people' " (1:424–25; 1:42).

The above examples suggest to me a unique phenomenology of taste and sight, a dramatic working out of his oral anxiety through visual dissemination. The fish eyes returning the Madman's gaze, the fishlike human eyes piled up in the vat—these images are some of the best preserved "fish eyes" in his memory, so uncanny that they may well be called the "fish-eye lens" through which his remembrance of the past and his perception of the present take shape. Deeply entangled in the psychic formation is a differentiating process from the "oral phase" to the "mirror stage," a traumatic experience rooted in the personal as well as cultural unconscious. This little journey from the mouth to the eye coheres with, and vividly metaphorizes, the historical travel from Communion to cannibalism. Once interwoven into the modern discourse of cannibalism, these "fish eyes" mold a narrative of Chinese modernity, immersing the libidinal in the political for the allegorical embodiment of history. To further examine how the personal is metaphorically transformed into the historical, I will turn to some of the familiar spectacles in which Lu Xun continues to struggle with his own specter of the past.

The "Fish-Eye Lens" of Colonial Nationalism

Many visual spectacles in Lu Xun's writings are staged as if they were shot through the "fish-eye lens" of a camera, always implicating and reduplicating the viewing subject. In the famous "iron house" scene in the preface to *Outcry*, for example, the narrator sees himself both as the subject who watches and as the object who is consumed in suffocation. Often, the split self hides behind another spectacle. In the essay "What Happens After Nora Leaves Home" (1923), Lu Xun writes:

> The Masses, especially in China, are always spectators at a drama. If the victim on the stage acts heroically, they are watching a tragedy; if he shivers and shakes they are watching a comedy. Before the mutton shops in Beijing a few people often gather to gape, with evident enjoyment, at the skinning of the sheep. And this is all they get out of it if a man lays down his life. . . . There is nothing you can do with such people; the only way to save them is to give them no drama to watch. (1:163–64; 2:91–92)

Under the gaze of the narrator as the superspectator, fear is projected onto the "devoured": the victim on-stage and the sheep being skinned. Through his identification with the victim, the inner spectacle of "enjoyment" is reframed in a larger spectacle of contempt and hatred. By staging this double spectacle under his own gaze while also calling for its cancellation to save the masses, the narrator-spectator establishes himself as the savior who, ironically, must also "gape." Through his reading and writing, which is configured as his viewing and reporting, the subject-position of a savior is constructed and received as the authentic vision of reality.

Almost identical to the above "show" is the spectacle that changed his life: the execution scene presented in a newsreel slide he saw in Japan. Viewing and reporting, he comments on the bystanders:

> It was a long time since I had seen any compatriots, but one day I saw a news-reel slide of a number of Chinese, one of them bound and the rest standing around him. They were all sturdy fellows but appeared *completely apathetic. According to the commentary*, the one with his hands bound was a spy working for the Russians who was to be beheaded by the Japanese military as a warning to others, while the Chinese beside him had come to *enjoy* the spectacle. . . . Before the term was over I had left for Tokyo,

because this slide convinced me that medical science was not so important after all. The people of a weak and backward country, however strong and healthy they might be, could only serve to be made examples of or as witness of such futile spectacles; and *it is not necessarily deplorable no matter how many of them die of illness.*[3] The most important thing, therefore, was to change their spirit; and since at that time I felt that literature was the best means to this end, I decided to promote a literary movement. (1:416–17; 1:35–36; emphasis added)

About this familiar episode there is a question as simple as this: how could the narrator tell from their "blank countenances" that the crowd also "enjoyed the spectacle," especially considering that they were present, above all, to be intimidated? We must note that the term *mamu* in *mamu de shenqing* denotes literally "blank" and morally or politically "apathetic." Lu Xun stages this spectacle as though those bystanders were simultaneously wearing two incompatible masks: "enjoying" a macabre scene with a "blank look."[4] It seems as if the "inscrutable Chinese" had finally put on a straight face. Whether this incident is factual or fictional is an important distinction, but let's accept it as "truth," since it is an authentic record of a crucial moment in the author's subject formation.

Roland Barthes has argued that photography "cannot signify (aim at a generality) except by assuming a mask." The mask "designate[s] what makes a face into a product of a society and of history" (1981, 34). What Barthes calls a "mask" here reminds us of Lu Xun's highly celebrated skill at creating "character types." His portrayal of the crowd in this show has been hailed as an exemplary "typification" of the Chinese masses. It unmasks, so to speak, the truth that the masses are blind to the misery of their situation under imperialism. It is the slide that designates the crowd with a "typical look" or "generality."[5]

These two masks, however, are made up of two words (*shangjian* and *mamu*) and, as such, are visualized as two distinct voices. This passage exists in both verbal and discursive mediums—which perhaps suggests why it is much more difficult to recognize the incompatibility of the two masks in a written text than it would be to see their distinctions in visual images—and thus requires a dialogic decoding. But the "dialogue" turns out not to be one between the narrator and the crowd but between him and someone hidden from the scene. For the term *shangjian* means more than just "enjoy": its social-linguistic usage belongs to the traditional literati and the modern cultural elite. As an aesthetic term, it semantically evokes the "fine taste" of a connoisseur, who "judges" an artwork such as a piece of brush painting or calligraphy, or that of a poet who "appreciates" a well-wrought verse. Between the lines, there is a typical Lu Xunian sense of mockery, where the term *shangjian* is superimposed upon the "blank look" of the bystanders (e.g., in the original, the "spectacle" [*shizhong de shengju*] approximates "a pompous show of public execution"). These hapless fellows, bland and apathetic as they might look, could come from any group in society except the well educated, which would be entirely too self-conscious and broken-hearted to "enjoy it with a blank look." So "appreciation" of the "pompous show" by the bystanders is not only imagined but projected as the interior monologue of a split self.

The obvious source of this projection is the jingoist gaze: the eye behind the camera and the voice of the "commentary." But what is obscure—obscured by the camera, that is—is the narrator's identification with that gaze and voice. In fact, he is virtually indistinguishable from the commentator. This narrator could not help but see himself among the crowd. He abhorred it because he could not do anything to change the situation depicted, while he saw, through that gaze, his own tarnished self-image. So he identifies himself at once with the gaze and its narrative commentary and with the crowd under that gaze. But his moral sense of self forces him to reject any identification with either entity in the scene (except the third entity in the actual center of the spectacle: death).[6] Caught in a web of double identification and double rejection, the narrator can cope with such a dreadful schizophrenia only by projecting a self-duplicated mask upon those apathetic faces. This mask is duplicated not simply in the sense of *dédoublement* but more so in terms of the semantic binary the former entails: "enjoy" versus "abhor." "Enjoy," inconsistent with "blank" if put on the same face, is rather more resonant with "abhor," its displaced opposite. Thus *shangjian*, a sign proper to the discourse of high culture but displaced upon the face of its social other, reveals the symptom of the speaking subject who is trying to make sense of his schizophrenia through intersubjective differentiation.

This psychodrama was recounted in the memoir "Mr. Fujino" (1926) in an even more personal as well as more strongly nationalistic mood. It is restaged immediately after the narrator has been wrongly accused of receiving special favors from his teacher, Mr. Fujino, in order to pass the exam. "No wonder they [his Japanese fellow students] suspected me," Lu Xun writes,

> But soon after this it was my fate to watch the execution of some Chinese. . . . And there was I, too, in the classroom.
>
> "*Banzai!*" the students clapped their hands and cheered.
>
> They cheered everything we saw; but to me the cheering that day was unusually jarring to my ear. . . . At that time and in that place, however, it made me change my mind. (2:306; 1:409)

What is represented in this piece is again a double spectacle. Added to but hidden behind the first scene is a second in which he dramatizes his viewing.

Barthes organizes his reading of photography through three categories, which describe the intersubjective construction in the above scene: the "operator" or photographer, the "spectator" or viewer, and the spectacle or what he calls the "spectrum," a term in etymology traceable to "the return of death" (1981, 9). In terms of the narrator's relationship with the operator, he is at one with the gaze insofar as his perspective is shaped; alarmingly, he has even failed to implicate the actual operator of the murder. Instead he focuses upon his uneasy relationship with the spectators. But there are three groups of spectators: the Chinese crowd in the slide, his fellow Japanese students viewing the slide, and the narrator himself watching both. He is the one located at the end of the viewing chain, a position defined in relation to the first two groups that determines the meaning of his viewing. This intersubjective connection is imagined both in terms of spatial (China and Japan) and temporal (past and present) distance and in the sense that Benedict Anderson has invoked in coining the term "imagined community" as the ideological foundation of modern nationalism. Yet this imagined linkage is superseded, and only made possible by the second group of viewers among whom the narrator existentially lived that moment of reality and history. It is the psychodrama of the second scene that mediates between the real world Lu Xun lives and the image world he sees in the slide. In this psychodrama, as the Japanese critic Hirakawa suggests: "Lu Xun points the camera at himself" and "the 'hidden topic' of the piece is that Lu Xun discovers he is Chinese and can't avoid being so, but does not like it" (qtd. in Larson 1991, 99). This formation of Lu Xun's perceptual and interpretive pattern, Larson points out, "pushes him toward a recognition of nation and race as ontological categories unavoidable in the interpretation of experience" (98). Returning to Barthes's distinctions, this photograph in its taking, viewing, and re-viewing captures, instead of unmasked truth, the mask of truth that turns those human faces into a particular product of colonial modernity.

It must be noted that the real center of the "show"—the murder—is obscured; the historical experience plays itself into a battle between the wounded self and his fellow viewers; this battle in turn has to transpose itself as the battlefield between nations; consequently the "victims" are "com-posed" with the "villains" as their accomplices. One would not be surprised at the remark, ironical as it is, that Lu Xun has made about the crowd: "it is not necessarily deplorable [i.e., somewhat "enjoyable"?] no matter how many of them die of illness" (1:416; 1:35). For him the physical well-being of the body is not as important as, if it is at all comparable to, the health of the national soul.

What is unmasked is the violent reality of power relations, located in the broader historical backdrop of modernity but superseded by the intersubjective relationship between the cultural producer and what he produces. In his attempt to save the masses, Lu Xun did have a specific problem. Once the colonial gaze has produced the dehumanized other, it "stares" back at him and forces him to scrutinize himself. It is true that Lu Xun's self-critique has separated him from his more self-indulgent contemporaries. But there are two kinds of self-scrutiny in his fictional works. One is directed at himself or the "dramatized narrator" in later and more successful stories such as "The New Year's Sacrifice," and the other aims at the nameless crowd in many early works published before and around May Fourth. In the latter case, the author condemns the old social system by ridiculing the victims of that system. In "The True Story of Ah Q," for example, the narrative authority and the truth of history are established in the end precisely by restaging a spectacle of execution under the "othering" gaze.[7]

The typical spectacle thus can be viewed as the enlarged projection of the phenomenology of the eye. From fish eyes to the camera lens, his visual discourse reenacts his oral fixation. If the dramatic theme is characterized as fear, hatred, and self-hatred, the specular form transcribes the "mouthed" fear and repulsion into the "eyed" hatred and contempt. Just as the spectacle shows the positional shift from orality to visuality, it also reveals another intrinsic tension existing in a negative form of double orality. As always, the construction of power and knowledge, authority and authenticity, and vision and reality is inseparable from the *telling* of truth. In Lu Xun's visual narrative of the human-eating old society, the silence of the "devoured" is often juxtaposed with the voice of the savior, resonating with his "outcry." The tension built around orality between being eaten and speaking is dramatized as another battlefield for the split self.

To Speak or to Be Consumed

Like the newsreel slide, the "iron house" has been hailed as an example of Lu Xun's typification of Chinese society. In the author's view, it contextualizes his writing and thus can be read as a "pre-text" for "Diary of a Madman." After the failure of the newly founded Republic to liberate China from imperialism and develop it into a strong modern nation-state, Lu Xun withdrew into the old literati type of scholarship. One day, a friend dropped in and urged him to write for the Marxist-inspired magazine *New Youth*. Lu Xun replied:

> Imagine an iron house having not a single window and virtually indestructible, with all its inmates sound asleep and about to die of suffocation. Dying in their sleep, they won't feel the pain of death. Now if you raise a shout to wake a few of the lighter sleepers, making these unfortunate few suffer the agony of irrevocable death, do you really think you are doing them a good turn?
>
> [The visitor] But if a few wake up, you can't say there is no hope of destroying the iron house.
>
> True, in spite of my own conviction, I could not blot out hope, for hope belongs to the future. . . . So I finally agreed to write, and the result was my first story "A Madman's Diary." (1:419; 1:37–38)

Apart from the failure of the Republican revolution, let's recall the theme of cannibalism in his first story, derived from *Zizhitongjian* and George Grey. If the iron house scene shows the same apathy of the crowd, their apathy now is oralized as lack of voice. Since silence perpetuates suffocation, the shouting voice is called upon to exhale the air of hope at one's last gasp. Cannibalism, symbolic of the breakdown of the human order, also signifies the collapse of communication. Once the civilized order of food and speech is shattered, emerging from its pieces is once again the divided self displaced now to embody the split voice in narrating the nation's cultural rupture. To speak or to be consumed, this is the question the split voice cries out in the iron house of silence.

I find Paul de Man's notion of irony, based on his reading of Baudelaire's "On the Essence of Laughter" (De l'essence du rire), useful in capturing the interior space of the split self in Lu Xun's early works, especially in "Diary of a Madman." First, the notion of *dédoublement*, "self-duplication" or "self-multiplication," is characteristic of "a relationship, within consciousness, between two selves" that is not an "intersubjective relationship." Second, this relationship obtains by "the *distance* constitutive of all acts of reflection." Being intrasubjective rather than intersubjective, the distanced Baudelairian irony constitutes a specific act of self-reflection. Third, the ironical act of self-reflection via self-duplication "belongs specifically to those who, like artists or philosophers, deal in language." Self-duplication for self-reflection is only a function or effect of the ironical mode of linguistic consciousness. When this self-splitting but inescapable power of ironic language is recognized, its dead end is reached. As a result, as in the case of Baudelaire, "[i]rony is unrelieved *vertige*, dizziness to the point of madness" (1983, 212–15), the fourth concept immediately applicable to "Diary of a Madman."

"[A]bsolute irony," argues de Man, "is a consciousness of madness, itself the end of all consciousness . . . a reflection on madness from inside madness itself. But this reflection is made possible only by the double structure of ironic language: the ironist invents a form of himself that is 'mad' but that does not know its own madness; he then proceeds to reflect on his madness thus objectified" (1983, 213). Although Baudelaire's notion of "madness" is associated with "those lunatics in asylums who have an illusion of superiority" (les fous des hôpitaux ont l'idée de leur supériorité), apparently contrary to the "persecution complex" of Lu Xun's Madman, the latter does metamorphosize under the "lunatic" moonlight into the savior.

Formally, "Diary of a Madman" has two narratives told by the same split voice. The relationship between the recovered "hero" who names the very title of the story in the prologue and the diarist himself is one between the same personage who is "a self and its other at once" (étre à la fois soi et un autre). This self-duplication produces a self-reflective distance between an empirical self who eats human flesh and a linguistic self who is afraid of being eaten, the former recuperated to the sanity of "normal" life while the latter experiences his "dizziness of madness." The textual self-duplication is voiced by means of juxtaposing two modes of linguistic signification, one in classical prose and the other in the modern vernacular. As the first text written in the modern vernacular, the diary is literally "invented" and the diarist necessarily "mad." The power of irony, then, resides in the double structure of the story, which defines the split subject and its "attempt at differentiation and self-definition."

This brief attempt to dovetail Lu Xun's story into de Man's theoretical framework could lend itself to a further comparison between Lu Xun and Baudelaire along the lines of literary modernism.[8] Yet there is a twist in Lu Xun's story, a turn of the trope toward what de Man calls "irony of irony," embodied by the "self-conscious narrator," who stands in for the "author's intrusion that disrupts the fictional illusion." Its effect, de Man contends, "serves to prevent the all too readily mystified reader from confusing that fact and fiction and from forgetting the essential negativity of the fiction" (1983, 218–19). The authorial intrusion in Lu Xun's text, however, is so "self-conscious" that he has to redouble himself in the form of negation of negation for his sense of irony of irony. That is, the author intervenes by assuming the role of his opposite and demanding reflection upon the Madman as the objectified ironical self.

The irony of irony is positioned as the narrative voice in the prologue, which is told by an omniscient narrator typical of the traditional fictional form of *xiaoshuo*. What we receive via him are three important messages. First, the protagonist has recovered from his insanity and gone somewhere to resume his "normal" official role in the imperial bureaucratic system. This diegetic foreclosure of the mimetic text (the diary itself) entangles the two subtexts and their two endings into a direct confrontation and imposes an interpretive quandary. Related to this foreclosure is that the very title of the story, so named not by the author-narrator but by the Madman himself after his recovery. Differentiating each from the other and defining each against the other, two linguistic systems and two narrative modes are valorized for the historical clash. Furthermore, by making the protagonist prefigure his own recovery in, and his relapse into, the empirical reality, the text foregrounds the overwhelming forces of the empirical world to ultimately set off the ironic negativity of the fictional diary yet to be disclosed. This irony of irony, therefore, does not come out at the end of the narrative but predetermines the historical conflict.

The third message is that the diary is to be disclosed for medical research and diagnosis. Here we recall that psychology and psychoanalysis, just like the whole body of modern Western medical science, was then largely new to China and that modern medical science was one of Lu Xuns two major tools in his literary diagnosis of Chinese society. Considering also that the diary yet to be disclosed is literally the first text written in the modern vernacular and the first use of diary writing as a fictional form, this message provides a crucial clue for the intended reader. Only the new reader, with the modern consciousness formed in the modern vernacular, can decode the diary. Meanwhile, the decoding of the Madman's outcry to "save the children" is contradicted by the disclosure in advance of the diarist's "happy ending"—his recuperation in the old social system. Thus, the ideal reader is forewarned of the danger of being "recuperated." If the text simply represents a bipolar world in two opposite narrative paradigms, any attempt to work out a "unified meaning," an understanding of the text's totality, will force the reader to readjust his or her measurement of what *sanity* means. In this sense, the reader must become "mad" and immersed in the world of fiction as the necessary form of negativity while remaining acutely aware of its fictional nature.

As a narrative strategy, the juxtaposition of the two subtexts simultaneously "tells" and "shows" the contradiction between two individuated experiences within the split subject, who, in turn, embodies the historical conflict of two systems of signification. The prologue, written in classical Chinese, stands for the entire symbolic system of the old Confucian tradition. By contrast, the inscription of the diary form presumes and guarantees the authentic voice of the self. It is around this authenticated voice that the linguistic materialization of modern China is established. If modern European nation-states emerged from the destruction of the "language of God"—Latin—and the establishment of "human language"—the vernacular—Lu Xun's text stands in for that moment in Chinese history when the "new"—the modern—must create itself out of the old.

The textual self-duplication presents itself as a meaningful form and a necessary condition for thinking about history. Since in the Chinese symbolic system the "transcendental signified" of "Communion" is not a religious god but the mythical-ancestral genealogy, Lu Xun's construction of Chinese modernity must stand in for the historical rupture of the old sacred language. This formal aspect of the story captures the radical discontinuity of tradition and modernity and the impossibility of genuine communication between them. The ironical distance at the communicative level corresponds to the social distance figured in cannibalism. Given the intractable entanglement of representational and historical contradictions, the only method proposed by Lu Xun to break loose from the hell of cannibalism is to shout in the iron house of language. It is this shouting voice that violates the central principle of textual negativity and transforms a powerful critique into an ideological edifice.

Since the publication of "Diary," questions have been raised around the Madman's plea to "save the children." The official canon in the PRC celebrates it because the cry delivered the promise of "hope" and thus made Lu Xun a writer not only critical of the old but anticipatory of the new. Many critics, including members in the early left-wing Creation Society, have questioned its narrative logic because the cry not only sounds ostentatious on the part of the narrator but constitutes an anticlimax in the overall development of the text. The aesthetic flaw of the story can be summed up in C. T. Hsia's comment that Lu Xun fails "to provide a realistic plot for the madman's fantasies . . . [he] merely garnishes his story with miscellaneous items relating to the practice of cannibalism in China and fails to present his case in dramatic terms" (1961, 33). These different views register the diverse and conflictive intellectual environment of the times and project the changing historical horizon of interpretation. One thing most critics and historians seem to agree upon is that Lu Xun was in fact "forced" under the circumstances to add this desperate plea against his own (more pessimistic) convictions.[9]

In discussing the "dead end" of the ironic mode, de Man points out a similar pattern in Western thought:

> The rhetorical mode of irony takes us back to the predicament of the conscious subject; this consciousness is clearly an unhappy one that strives to move beyond and outside itself. Schlegel's rhetorical question "What gods will be able to rescue us from all these ironies?" can also be taken literally. For the later Friedrich Schlegel, as for Kierkegaard, the solution could only be a *leap out of language into faith*. (1983, 222–23; emphasis added)

Earlier in his essay, de Man holds that "[i]rony divides the flow of temporal experience into a past that is pure mystification and a future that remains harassed forever by a relapse within the inauthentic" (1983, 222). So irony can only survive by repeating itself in each and every linguistic "now," that is, an empirical "void." To move out of irony without relapsing to the inauthentic is the choice between "faith" and "allegory." The former, in the case of Schlegel and Kierkegaard, refers to religion, the latter, as exemplified by Wordsworth, to "wisdom" (about death). The difference between the two lies in that the "faithful" leaps out of language whereas the "allegorist" "remain[s] housed within language, refuse[s] to escape out of time into apocalyptic conceptions of human temporality, but nevertheless [is] not ironic" (223).

The Madman's plea is clearly a leap out of language into faith. It stems from an overt authorial intrusion and violation of the textual logic. I have noted already that the moonlight-darkness antithesis furnishes a narrative tension that culminates in the narrator's recognition of the dark truth of his own unwitting participation in human eating. His "seeing the truth" plays itself out through several instances that build to a dramatic climax and tragic reversal. As early as the end of section 6 the diarist comes to realize that his brother is also a cannibal. He persists in investigating his family history and the history of cannibalism in China, all the while haunted by his delusion of being devoured. When he finally recognizes that he "may have eaten several pieces of [his] sister's flesh unwittingly," the Madman undergoes, amazingly, a "catharsis" himself, crying out, in Ted Huters's words, "the celebrated, if rather pathetic, call to 'save the children'" (1984, 61). Instead of tragic downfall, his recognition of himself as a personification of "four thousand years of man-eating history" has elevated him to sagehood. The "pathetic" outcry reveals a desperate self-sublimation by self-displacement. It simultaneously assimilates the conscious to a divine voice in the name of faith and eliminates the shattered pieces of its own unconscious from the entire culture of ancient China.

Let it not be understood that the Madman's call is in poor taste because it has violated some false "universal" principle of poetics. What I emphasize here is a serious epistemological and ethical question foregrounded by the aesthetic problem. His attempt to force the text out of its poetic orbit alone is not the primary issue at hand. Rather, the contrived plea erases the irreducible negativity figured in the discourse of *différance* and elevates a historical-specific subject to a "sacred" *identity*. This quasi-religious solution has since generated a metanarrative of "apotheosis," so to speak, which reminds us of the "demigod" status that traditional intelligentsia claimed for themselves.[10] To be Madman, in other words, he has metamorphosed from a madness of "persecution complex" to a madness of "absolute superiority"—which recalls the Baudelairian definition of *madness* without evoking the Baudelairian irony. By forcing the Madman to voice the message of the author-savior, this divine calling cancels out the critical thrust set in motion by the split voice and the narrative rupture and reestablishes the authorial relationship with the world quite against the author's antitraditional stance. If we place the endings of the two subtexts side by side, the political and moral choice between the old and the new intellectuals becomes conspicuously complementary rather than contradictory: a bureaucrat involved in governing the world (as in the prologue) or a priest committed to saving the soul.

As David Wang has observed: "Modern Chinese history has borne witness to the way the Madman's final outcry . . . can be realized in the most ironic and brutal ways. . . . In order to save a generation of Chinese children, millions of Chinese children would have to die for the Revolution; and in order to save China again, millions of Red Guard children would know how to brutalize their parents and themselves" (1992, 9–10). To speak or to be consumed may well be a real dilemma for Lu Xun and his generation of radical intellectuals. But to speak in a divine voice has foreclosed the articulation of other subject positions and historical possibilities. In hindsight, the first piece of fiction in modern Chinese literature already anticipated the later development of an all-powerful monolithic voice that, in the name of the Great Savior, speaks for the masses.

The Allegorical Embodiment of the Diseased and the Deceased

I have tried so far to delineate the route of the "cannibal" by reconstructing a phenomenological road map of taste, vision, and voice in Lu Xun's early journey. These sensuous zones, rooted in the personal, are intimately connected with the representation of cannibalism in the cultural cartography of the modern world. At various points, I have referred to that connection in terms of metaphorical transformation and narrative displacement. The last section attempts to piece these bodily fragments around the concept of allegorical embodiment, which I define as the ways the body corporeal is made to circumscribe the contour of the body politic according to the principle of allegorical totality. What brings the two bodies into an analogous configuration is the "corpus," understood equally in its conventional meaning of a self-contained body of written words proper to the author (as his "property") and in the poststructuralist sense of *écriture*, or writing constitutive of the texture of the authorial body in words. These two modes of writing are concurrent in Lu Xun's works, and their interplay embodies the totality of the interlaced fabric of the body corporeal and body politic.

The difference between the two modes of writing can be seen as one between two types of allegory, one constructive and the other deconstructive. The constructive allegory has been a familiar model in the West since the time of medieval hermeneutics.[11] In Anglo-American sinology, its application to the studies of ancient Chinese narrative literature has also yielded "constructive" fruit, represented by Andrew Plaks's groundbreaking analysis of allegorical structure in the *Dream of the Red Chamber*.[12] Fredric Jameson's narrative theory exemplifies a neo-Marxist reappropriation of the age-old hermeneutic tradition (1981, 29–33), and his notion of "national allegory" as a mapping tool to appropriate Lu Xun for his pedagogical intervention has reaffirmed the actual existence of the national allegory (though not stated as such in Chinese studies). It cannot be overemphasized that the metaphor of "the human-eating old society" initiated by Lu Xun and crystallized in the Communist discourse of revolution is the central, organizing trope for modern China's self-articulation. Lu Xun's fatherly status in modern Chinese literature simply reflects his allegorical embodiment of history in the "constructive" sense.

The deconstructive allegory indicates a negative dialectic of reading and writing. Its representational and hermeneutic features have been elaborated by Paul de Man and Walter Benjamin. In de Man's view, irony and allegory "are the two faces of the same fundamental experience of time." They differ in that the ironic subject experiences time in "an instantaneous process" and thus reveals "a synchronic structure," whereas "the structure of allegory" exists "in the tendency of the language toward narrative, the spreading out along the axis of an imaginary time in order to give duration to what is, in fact, simultaneous within the subject" (1983, 225–26). What irony is to the divided subject corresponds to what allegory is to the discontinued duration. In this sense, the Madman's leap out of language into faith is a "temporal" escape from death as well as a "spatial" solution to his existential predicament. To this temporal-narrative tendency, Benjamin's concept of allegory adds a more dialectic dimension. It is summed up in his famous aphorism: "Allegories are, in the realm of thoughts, what ruins are in the realm of things" (1977, 178). As ruins are signs that lay bare nature's decay, allegories are symptoms that manifest the decay of human history and the absence of teleological progress. Unlike Jameson's descriptive "national allegory," the Benjaminian allegory is "deconstructive."[13]

It is interesting to note that the symbiosis of the two modes of allegorical writing is also registered in Jameson's reading of Lu Xun, even though the theoretical concept of "national allegory" dictates that "the story of the private individual destiny is always an allegory of the embattled situation of the public third-world culture and society" (1986, 69). Jameson's approach to "the libidinal dimension" in "Diary of a Madman" foregrounds the entanglement of the two bodies in Lu Xun's allegorical embodiment. The public and private divide reified in the then interpretative enterprise of Anglo-American literary studies is blurred by his reading of the otherwise extremely "private" text: a diary. He rightly locates the crucial linkage of the libidinal and the political in a single verb "eat," the conjuncture centered not on "sexuality, but rather [on] the oral stage, the whole bodily questions of eating, of ingestion, devoration, incorporation" (72). I find Jameson's concrete analysis of the text illuminating because he fully recognizes the site of orality at the intersection of the public and private realms, and his engaged reading in fact defies his theoretical model, which is lodged on the Marx versus Freud binary. It is more illuminating to note how easily his engagement with the "third-world" text can be incorporated across the borders to his "first-worldist" mapping of history, tailoring a multifaced text into a one-dimensional aesthetics of third-world literature and reducing the Marx *and* Freud oral experience to a Marx *versus* Freud global theory.

The point of an allegorical double, then, is not to cancel out the Marx in Lu Xun, nor even to just restore the Freud. Lu Xun's allegorical embodiment of modern China can and must be situated right where the "body" is *displayed*: the site at which the private enters the public in a dynamic process of subject formation and historical constitution. Since the meaning of that body has long been allegorized to articulate totality, it is necessary to retrieve the pieces that have been eliminated in the constructive process of allegorical incorporation. In Lu Xun's own "corpus," once again, the semiotic-cum-physical site of the writing self and self-writing is centrally figured in the ideal body of the cow. As the cow eats only grass but produces milk for the world, so Lu Xun offers his own "milk"—the words squeezed out of his flesh and blood—to nurture his "children." The cow recalls the ox, the prototypical image of noble sacrifice (see chapter 1). In spite of the semantic distinctions of the image in different historical and cultural contexts, the narrative syntax on the sacrificed body continues to circulate the flesh and blood for the corporeal embodiment of the political. Placed in this mythical system, Lu Xun has made his own body a sacrificial offering just like the daughter's flesh in Amy Tan's novel. This syntactic recycling of the body even bears on a similar motif. Above all, the cow's milk, the word, is meant to cure the diseased nation much like the believed medicinal function of the flesh and blood in the ritual of *geguliaoqin*.

Yet at the moment he feeds his "milk" to the pen over a scene of execution and writes his flesh and blood into the texture of the corpus for national salvation Lu Xun cuts the physical body into two halves by separating the head from the body and turning the latter into a corpse. Just as Lu Xun's "cannibal complex" is at the tip of his tongue in his outcry, his "anxiety over decapitation and headlessness serves as the secret fountainhead of his literary inspirations" (D. Wang 1992, 215). The corpse is left unheeded as a dirty chunk of flesh ("it is not necessarily deplorable no matter how many of them die of illness"); the head is "capitalized" to reinvigorate the national spirit. The leap out of language into faith is again the escape of the soul from existential death, retaining the head to witness the decay of its own corpse. Lu Xun's allegorical embodiment, then, signifies a specific double: the allegorical assimilation of the head conditioned on the allegorical elimination of the "pound of flesh." As always, the myth has a double structure of self-signification. The head proper to the national spirit must be rejuvenated for the construction of a conscious self-identity at the expense of the corpse, dumped at the site of the "headless" other. The immortalized head, the transcendental signified of the national allegory, is cut loose from its own body.

What "decapitates" the sick and the dead body is the language of *différance*, the discourse of scientific knowledge, medical science in particular, that differentiates head from flesh or spirituality from carnality so as to defer the former's demise. In the story "Medicine" and the author's narrative accounts of his father's illness and death, the scalpel cuts both ways: traditional culture is cannibalistic because traditional medicine is literally eaten and figuratively eats, while the cultural diagnosis dissects the physical body by a hierarchical structure analogous to the signifying system of civilization. The construction of national allegory, in the sense of being "constructive," is only made possible by introducing itself as a hierarchical system against which traditional medicine comes to be seen as "human eating."

Compared with the "Diary of a Madman," "Medicine" is a much more powerful tale of autophagy or "self-eating." The experiential world is made to correspond to the allegorical level of meaning through an explicit code of nomenclature. The surnames of the two "heroes" or victims, Hua and Xia, are synonymous with "China." Another allegorical encoding by means of nominalism correlates the executed rebel Xia Yu with the historical figure Qiu Jin, a heroine and martyr for the anti-Manchu Republican Revolution (see Hsia 1961, 34; and Lyell 1976, 252). Just as Hua Xiaoshuan's disease symbolizes China's aliment, the two youngsters' deaths signify the fate of the young in the old cannibalistic society.

"Medicine" reinscribes the theme of "Diary of a Madman" in a strictly alimentary narrative. The horror is not just the disease of tuberculosis, which consumes Hua Xiaoshuan's body, but the contagiousness of consumption. Hua eats the steamed roll of *mantou* soaked with Xia's blood to "cure" his disease, only to be consumed himself. His body eventually winds up in the cemetery where Xia Yu is buried, where "the serried ranks of grave mounds . . . looked like *mantou* laid out for a rich man's birthday." The old society is such a huge cannibalistic feast that the children are not only consumed but, as Hua's fate indicates, are devoured by sucking other children's blood. Any special medicine or remedy intended to cure the diseased body would end up perpetuating the grisly feast.

As in the iron house, the consumed also is marked with the lack of voice. Hua Xiaoshuan never speaks but only coughs; the young rebel Xia Yu does not even show up, let alone speak, in the story. It is through the distorted voice of the villagers that the reader comes to hear about him. Imprisoned, he persists in propagating his revolutionary ideas, which lead to his torture and execution. A voiceless prisoner, he is considered by those whom his action was supposed to benefit to be *feng*, or "crazy," a distortion of the Madman's *kuang* (1:446; 1:64). *Feng*, though synonymous with *kuang*, as in the modern compound *fengkuang*, is different in terms of etymology and historical semantics. The basic contrast is that, while the Madman is a *kuangren* representing a critical consciousness to the author and the intended reader, he is a *fengzi*, clinically insane in the eyes of the "normal minded" such as his brother and the villagers. So Xia Yu as a *fengzi* in the eyes of the townsfolk implies its opposite, *kuangren*.[14] Amid the madness of the world, the disease of self-consumption in silence has been so normalized that the only cure is to turn the tables upside down.

The social conflicts between the old and the new in "Medicine" are also embedded in a narrative of seasonal, emotional, and visual changes. The last section, like the last call in "Diary," has been a focal point of discussion. In his preface to *Outcry*, the author makes it clear that he was indeed "forced" to make "a wreath appear from nowhere at the son's [Xia's] grave." This signifier of hope, however, is already anticipated in the narrative encoding of temporal progress. As Delezelova-Velingerova has pointed out (1977), the first three sections form the first unit of the story and operate mainly under the "principle of information manipulation." The story is told from the points of view of the characters in a series of actions, so information about the two young victims is divulged to the reader only through the villagers' voices. The last section, in contrast, is basically "a static episode permeated by a lyrical and reflective mood" and is told by a "hidden narrator." What is "concealed" by the hidden narrator is the symbolic meaning of highly encoded signs. The story begins in the deep night of fall, a pitch-dark moment "after the moon disappeared" and "before the sun rises." The last section is set in the spring morning of the Qing-Ming, the "clear and bright" day of commemorating the dead. Such a seasonal and visual change "transforms the victim of the darkness into a hero" and signals a hope for rebirth (221–31). Contrast is further drawn between the "naturally growing spring flowers" on Hua Xiaoshuan's grave and the artificially arranged flowers of the wreath set on Xia Yu's resting place, that is, between the naturally grown, "homemade" emblem and the human-made, imported symbol (the wreath was introduced to China). The story's ending is also symbolic: the flight of a raven, not toward Xia Yu's grave as his mother wished it to confirm her prayers, but "toward the far horizon," like a harbinger of impending revolution. Since the cemetery is filled with *mantou* soaked in the blood of the young and symbolizes the moral death of the old system, children can only be saved beyond the "far horizon."

We can see more clearly now than in "Diary of a Madman" the metaphorical transformation of discontinuity into teleology. The former inscribes the graveyard as a ruined setting of history on the face of the old China; the latter shifts to the deciphering of the secret meaning of a future, a meaning "missing" in the present, but promises its realization only if the reader participates in rewriting history by means of revolution. The genesis of revolution would be laid out even more clearly in the 1925 essay titled "Jottings by Lamplight": "Since the dawn of civilization countless feasts . . . of human flesh have been spread, and those at these feasts eat others and are eaten themselves. Feasts of human flesh are still being spread even now, and many people want them to continue. To sweep away these man-eaters, overturn these feasts and destroy this kitchen is the task of the young folk today!" (1:217; 2:157).

Conversely, the assimilation of the two youngsters into the symbol of Huaxia, or "China," is inseparable from the elimination of the diseased body. Social misery is subjected to a twofold allegorical abstraction that appropriates the "proper" nouns to the sublimation of nationhood while it buries the corpse "underground" at the same time. The narrative tendency of the constructive allegory toward a futuristic hope takes off, with the raven, precisely from the ruins of decay and death, the graveyard. The two allegorical elements are crystallized in a visual hierarchy, with the imported and artificial wreath "speaking" on the "head" of the *mantou*-like grave mound. Spirituality and carnality are thus frozen in the allegorical space of the nation to allow its narrative to unfold from the past to the future. This double structure of allegorical embodiment is consistent with the image of the halved body.

Yet the wreath and the *mantou*, though opposite symbols in "Medicine," belong to a larger pattern of "remembering the consumed." The imagery of the diseased and the deceased also permeates the first two pages in the preface to *Outcry*, where Lu Xun's "re-membering" of the consumed father is juxtaposed with his diagnosis of the diseased society. In a way, his medical discourse invites a reading of his anxiety over the national aliment vis-à-vis his own "dis-ease" with his father's death. Thus, "Medicine" can be read just as another dramatic reenactment of the author's early traumatic experience.

In the preface to *Outcry*, the author begins this short piece by telling the reader why he wrote the stories collected in the volume and what the stories mean in relation to the reason why he wrote them in the first place. As we are told, there were things he could not "forget completely," and these stories then "stemmed from those things" he was "unable to forget." What is it that he cannot forget or is fixed upon, still haunting his memory of the past? The answer is provided in the second paragraph: his father's illness and death and his daily routine in four years of dealing with pawnshop, pharmacy, doctors, and various unusual drugs. As the father was "swallowed" by swallowing traditional medicine, his body must be buried in those pages.

Immediately following his account of the father's illness and death, the author brings up another thing he is unable to forget: the fall of his family as a result of the death and the true face of the cold society he saw as a fatherless teenager. Then comes his encounter with modern science, which lands him in a Japanese medical school only to be interrupted by the slide show that redirects his eye to the decapitated head of the sick nation. By recalling two moments of his life history in two pages that span more than twenty years, the author links the diseased father and medicine to the sick China and literature. The connection of the sick and dead father with the diseased and dying China symptomatically reveals a Freudian condensation, that is, a metaphor, whereby all the stories in his first collection ought to be read. This incorporation of the father's body into the narrative of the body politic is quite a visible "absent presence" in the story of "Medicine." The fact that Lu Xun hated traditional medicine so much that he wrote "Medicine" to show its "cannibalistic" nature can be traced to his traumatic experience with the "devoured" father.

Meanwhile, his hatred is also magnified by a sense of guilt and self-hatred, as manifested in his memoir "Father's Illness." This piece consists of two units, each written in distinct narrative modes. In the first unit, which makes up the bulk of the text, the narrator portrays with disgust and disdain a caricature of a quack doctor, punctuated with his mockery of traditional medical lore. He then describes his father's illness and various treatments in a more controlled but still sarcastic mood. In the second unit, the narrative takes an intensely emotional turn by dramatizing his father's death with his own cry. This scene, according to Lu Xun's brother Zhou Zuoren, is fabricated.[15] Just before he describes the father's death, the narrator, the adult Lu Xun, comments on the traditional ritual performed by the wailing son at the deathbed of the father. Contrasting this ritual of filial fidelity with modern medical ethics and scientific knowledge, the author stages his father's departure and his own response as a spectacle of cruelty. Compelled by traditional custom, the boy assumes the role of the pious son by trying to call back the dying father. Lu Xun recalls the last moment in this way: " 'Father!' I kept calling him until he stopped breathing. Now I can still hear my own voice at that time. Whenever I hear it, I feel that this is the gravest wrong I have done to my father" (2:289; see also Lee 1987, 8).

More than two decades after his death, the father still haunts the son, tormenting him with a heavy burden of guilt for his participation in a "cannibalistic patricide." This psychodrama could be read as just another symbolic reenactment of the author's hatred and self-hatred. The fact that the adult Lu Xun was still completing his mourning when he wrote this piece reveals that "his father's illness and death must have propelled a psychological crisis in the young Lu Xun by bringing to a head all the 'dark' forces that had figured in his childhood world" (Lee 1987, 9). In describing Lu Xun's relationship with his father, Lee further notes: "As the eldest son, Lu Xun was already . . . put in a position of responsibility: he was expected to redeem his grandfather and father and restore the family name. . . . Within a traditional Chinese 'extended family,' this psychological burden does not necessarily lend itself to Oedipal conflicts. Rather, it seems to have contributed to Lu Xun's early maturity" (7).

What does it mean for a father-son relationship to be without Oedipal conflicts? It could lead us to speculation about a Freudian post-Oedipal identification. But Lu Xun's identification with the father takes another turn. He is not just the son who succeeds the father by honoring and accepting his death; he wants to redeem (the loss of) the father at the same time. In Lee's reading, the redeemer, a term he borrowed from Erik Erikson's study of Gandhi, is to restore the lost family honor and prestige, typical of the eldest son's role in traditional Chinese society. Given the circumstances of the father's illness and death and the son's tormented memory, to redeem the father is a twofold act intended to symbolically avenge a wrong perpetuated against the father (traditional medicine that ultimately kills him) and thereby psychologically release the son from his own guilt of complicity.

I have argued that Lu Xun has inherited the discourse of cannibalism as a legacy of colonial modernity. But the theme of revenge pervasive in his writings seems to suggest also his unwitting inheritance of so-called revenge cannibalism. Eating for revenge signifies hatred in devouring the enemy. It is a ritualistic act that avenges the eaters through consumption. The dead body is not only invested with meaning, but also *re*-invested in its consumption by ascribing to it such a "sacred" value that it can only find its cemetery in its enemy's stomach. The dead body of "revenge cannibalism" serves as the site where society can reproduce its social relations and revitalize its moral energy through a different kind of "Communion." This recycling of human flesh indicates the mutability of hatred and the circularity of revenge.

This feature of revenge cannibalism provides another venue in which to explain Lu Xun's obsession with the specter and the spectacle, his father's revenge, and his fear of being devoured. When this specter, the dead father, returns, it returns necessarily in a spectrum/spectacle that stages the dramatic ritual of revenge and redemption. What is recycled in these spectacles is not human flesh incarnate but human flesh as symbolically consumed in "cannibalistic feasts" (Confucian morality, traditional medicine, the iron house, and the execution). What is changed in the ritualistic performance is Lu Xun's own transformation from an actor to an observer, transformed because human eating as a form of revenge can no longer be condoned. What remains unchanged, however, is its theme and symbolic structure.

Lu Xun's outcry in the iron house thus pours forth like a remote echo of his desperate call at his father's death. He is neither the successful mourner, who remembers the dead by remembering that the father is dead, nor the failed mourner, who commits suicide or suffers a breakdown. Lu Xun belongs to the third type Freud describes: the obsessional neurotic who "fetishizes" death-as-loss.[16] What Lu Xun cannot "forget" is not only that his father died by being "swallowed" but that the author is guilty of unwitting complicity in the crime of aggravating the father's pain. Because of his complicity, he must fulfill the duty of avenging his father for the boy's sinful act and yet cleanse his conscience of guilt. Dramatically embedding the scene of the father's death in a discourse of remorse and guilt, the narrator attempts to distance himself from both the "devoured" father and his own guilt, which is attached to the body.

This is another reason why death, disease, and the fear of being devoured are leitmotivs in Lu Xun's works: the mourner is a "neurotic."

Lu Xun's allegorical embodiment of the diseased and the deceased manifests, among many other things, his own "dis-ease." Returning to the two questions I raised at the beginning, my point is not simply to repsychologize Lu Xun. A probe into his "heart of darkness" not only can deepen our understanding of his subjective formation but also can unveil fundamental power relations not completely comprehensible apart from the constitution of intersubjectivity. This has everything to do with what Jameson emphatically calls "the role of the third-world intellectual," one that must be fully situated at the juncture of China's turbulent experience with modernity and colonialism. Above all, Lu Xun was one of the few modern Chinese writers whom my generation of mainland students grew up reading, and we read him with varying degrees of political fervor if not religious reverence. Then, overcharged with political polemics and combative rhetoric, our reading was molded in such a fashion that we were ill equipped and hardly emboldened enough to raise questions about the "father" and his "dark heart," not to mention the "mere trope" of "eating" and its materiality–despite, ironically, the mandatory education in historical materialism. What is disturbing to me in my rereading of Lu Xun is not really the dark side of his mind, the trauma of which arouses much sympathy and pain. I am most disturbed by the persistent hatred and self-hatred, disgust and disdain, unleashed through his allegorical representation of cannibalism, disease, and other evil forms, toward one of the most impoverished of all peoples, who not only did not eat human beings but did not have much to eat.

3. Shen Congwen's "Modest Proposal"

In 1930, Shen Congwen witnessed a public execution. This was just a few months before his best friend, Hu Yeping, a young leftist writer, was secretly executed by the Kuomintang (KMT) regime. The incident prompted him to write a reminiscence.

> In the Fall, I went to Wuhan University to teach prose-writing. . . . Whenever I went out of the campus, I would see soldiers, street barbers, and sometimes public executions. This drab and foolish world perplexed me, but nevertheless refreshed my memory of some of the colors and noises I had lost touch with in the past ten years. Once again like a jobless vagrant, I drifted to street corners, or found myself packed in a filthy mass of spectators, watching the street scene unfolding before my eyes. A bloody human head falling under the executioner's sword, and the dirty heads still sitting on the necks of many—this is a street scene I once saw, an extremely painful picture engraved in my memory.
>
> Under those circumstances, I entertained nothing but my own melancholy (*wode youyu jiushi wode yule*). There is no way to shake myself apart from the miserable scenes of the past, and my life is forever cast in their ghastly shadows. (1984, 88–89).[1]

If this spectacle of decapitation is déjà vu, Shen Congwen's viewing and response was markedly different from Lu Xun's. This perspective may help us understand how Shen Congwen, after Lu Xun, came to terms with social misery in writing. Although it would be too simplistic to read the two writers along bifurcating political and ideological lines, as they have been treated in PRC historiography,[2] Shen's self-conscious but low profile among the "filthy mass of spectators" certainly complicates, and perhaps reverses, the subject position Lu Xun established in viewing and framing modern China. As David Wang has noted, "these two writers' stories of decapitation form a dialogue, pointing to . . . the major argument as to the ethical and aesthetic limitations of a realist writing" (1992, 210).

In the broad sense that modern China often presents itself to Chinese intellectuals as an allegorical spectacle of the deformed body around which social reform and cultural revolution are inscribed to restore the head, Shen Congwen's position in this particular scene is also emblematic of his place in that history. Thanks to his military experience during the chaotic time of the late 1910s and early 1920s in his war-torn homeland, Hunan, Shen may have witnessed more decapitations and other forms of killing and mutilation of ordinary people by warlord troops than any other Chinese writer in the modern era. In his early years in western Hunan, he witnessed how local people were killed for being bandits and rebels, or randomly without any charge, sometimes hundreds or thousands of people in a single day. Under those circumstances, however, he did not echo Lu Xun's "call to arms." A former soldier, he knew the destructive power of arms only too well. In a time of unequivocal political polemics, his refusal to identify with the modern, panoramic vision of history and his uncertainty about the capacity of literary writing to approximate material reality and promote social reform were often seen as a politically ambiguous posture. His public stance often leaves the impression that he was an "apathetic bystander" who "enjoyed" watching brutal spectacles until the 1949 victory of real armed struggle swept him to the political dump site of oblivion and silence.

Although his "apolitical" stance and personal disposition kept him from offering himself as a martyr, Shen Congwen continued to write with a tormented conscience. To the extent that Lu Xun squeezes his "milk" to feed the "children," his writing describes an externalizing process of putting the mouth into words. Shen Congwen's writing, in contrast, is characterized by an internalizing process of putting words into the mouth, analogous to ingestion and digestion. To him, the world is the "large book": only the most rugged stomach is able to absorb and possess the substance and spirit of its texture. Even the least palatable experiences can and must be chewed to gain insight into the ugly truth of the world or ruminated to season a "perverse" cultivation of wisdom. In the above execution scene, the decapitated head and the heads of the executioners and spectators are assimilated into the interior space of melancholy, which in turn feeds on the lonely subject for its "self-entertainment." The term *yule* (entertainment) echoes the mask of *shangjian* (enjoyment), which Lu Xun puts on the faces of the crowd. Instead of the killing, however, what Shen Congwen "entertains" is the melancholic effect of his self-enclosed digestion of the visual misery. In this sense, Shen Congwen is a "big eater," if not an outright "cannibal," and his writing is an oralized form of the "large book" in its bits and pieces.

This mode of internalization indicates that, as David Wang points out, "Shen Congwen never makes irony a mode overpowering other modes" of representation. Ironic as his use of the term *entertain* may seem, its exterior register of cruelty is dissolved in the erosive yet enabling mood of melancholy. From the "entertainment" of melancholy or the digestion of its biting pain has arisen what Wang calls a "critical lyricism." Understood as a "mixed expression of lyricism and irony," critical lyricism reflects a "different moral pose" that "stems from the long Chinese tradition that stresses the ethical dimension of rhetoric" (1992, 209). Putting words into the mouth rather than the other way around, Shen regrounds the external body on his own so that the raw materials of absurdity and atrocity can be equally processed through the "big eater" and then expressed in a lyrical fashion without losing their critical thrust. The deformed body is re-formed à la the textual embodiment of his own body. Instead of connecting it to the diseased nation in the symbolic of the "father," Shen Congwen attempts to piece the deformed body back together through the imaginary, on the site of the symbiosis with the "mother" at the "oral stage."

The interior space of melancholy thus is mobilized into a temporal scheme of what David Wang calls "imaginary nostalgia." In Shen's writings, Wang elaborates: "[T]ime is reorganized or 'anachronized' " so that the writer can "reconstruct the past in terms of the present" and "see in the present a residue of the past." Corresponding to this dialectic of time is the "idea of displacement" in space, one that "implies the condition in which [Shen] is situated, the method he employes in search of a lost time and place, and the result he obtains in words." For the very idea of nostalgia presupposes the present state of alienation, only the displaced yearns to find a place to settle in, and home symbolizes a safe haven only for those already in exile or fearful of becoming homeless. Thus "nostalgia is equatable to the insatiable desire for more narrative and more memory"; the more one desires to find the home, the more one has to activate his imagination (1992, 251–53). As Shen's melancholic internalization of social misery is refashioned through imaginary nostalgia, his insistence on staying within the realm of signification sets off Lu Xun's leap out of language into faith. Equally important is the fact that his incorporation of the "large book" is not characterized by a "denial of loss," which "is the form of melancholy" in European romanticism (see Kilgour 1990, 170). What is lost is irretrievable in reality and in metaphysics, the oral stage is evoked only to fulfill the present hunger of the dislocated self, and the dismembered can only be re-membered in words. This aesthetic aspect of his critical lyricism is compatible, and in fact cognate, with its ethical dimension. The existential irony, the curse of the present void, thus is poeticized in a rare juxtaposition of the grotesque with the lyrical, the uncanny with the familiar, violence with serenity, death with eternity, and existential lack with imaginary fulfillment.

Shen Congwen's different approach to orality and visuality can also be traced to his childhood and his family's socioeconomic conditions. Raised in a well-to-do household, Shen did not have to face the snobbish cold world Lu Xun experienced. His remembrance of childhood is enriched with oral pleasure as much as Lu Xun's is fraught with the fear of being devoured. A recurrent image repository in Shen Congwen's writings includes the mother, the hearth, the clan, and the warmth of eating at home or in the wonderland of western Hunan. Often skipping school, he encountered outside the Confucian classics a world as fantastic and exotic as the one Lu Xun found in ancient myth, folktales, and vernacular fiction. Unlike Lu Xun's world of books, however, Shen's is the "large book," sizzling with local colors and flavors, which come into sharp contrast with Lu Xun's more ambiguous distaste of his own hometown.

Behind his motivation to write about his oral pleasure is the real hunger he had to endure as a poor country youth, often jobless, in the Beijing of the 1920s. In "Postscript to *Alice's Adventures in China*," he recalls that "poor and hungry, I had to ask for food at least fifty times" (1:204). Even half a century later, Shen still remembered a meal to which his mentor Yu Dafu treated him during their first meeting, an occasion Yu initiated in response to a desperate call for assistance and guidance from the then completely unknown Shen Congwen. After Yu learned that Shen did not have anything to eat, as Shen related to Yu's niece in the 1970s, "he took out five dollars, took me out for a meal, and left me all the change. How much five dollars was worth at that time!" (see Wang Jizhi 1992, 30). In contrast to his view of Yu Dafu, Shen had mixed feelings about Lu Xun. In "Remembering Hu Yepin," noting the meager income he then earned as a young unknown writer, Shen stated explicitly that "had Lu Xun resigned from his post in the Ministry of Education and his college professorship, relying just upon his royalties, he would have ended up just as desperate and laughable [as I]" (9:54). Writing in 1931, three years after Shen had become a college professor himself, he was quite vindictive about his early desperation and humiliation. If Lu Xun never wrote seriously about hunger because it was not his personal problem, Shen's experience of real hunger in Beijing sharpened his memories of home and his distaste for the city.

But the country-city dichotomy did not lead him to the single-minded, antimodern nativism that mystifies the "spirit of the folk." Lodged in this symbolic demarcation is a concrete personal and cultural ambivalence that refuses to totalize modern Chinese experience simply as a locality of culture between tradition and modernity or between the East and the West. Shen was humble and perhaps confused enough to know the limitations of fictional writing in saving China. Writing is only a venue for reconstructing experience in words; words, if necessary for political purposes, can at the most be used only for protest. An important aspect of Shen's writing is a dialectic of nostalgia and political protest. In the PRC's official version of history, Shen's nonpartisan stance and his entanglement with Lu Xun, Ding Ling, Guo Moruo, and other leftist intellectuals have given him the bad name of a "reactionary." That had more to do with factionalism, misunderstanding, and his largely "liberal" political views than with his literary work. Conversely, it is the artistic value of his works and his distance from partisan politics that have earned him high status in the canon of Western literary studies of China and, partly because of his popularity abroad, his revival in the post-Mao era.[3] For different reasons, his message of political protest has not received sufficient attention. His protest against social injustice is best represented in *Alice's Adventures in China* (Ailisi Zhongguo-youji, 1928), a fantasy novel that belongs to neither the genre of native soil nor that of urban life. Through ingenuous parody of fantasy, satire, and the grotesque, he made a "modest proposal." It not only turned his own imaginary nostalgia into a powerful social protest, but it rewrote the very structure of visuality and orality that had been initiated in Lu Xun's cannibalistic thesis.

Alimentary images and motifs in Shen Congwen's work are not as condensed in a few allegorical spectacles as they are in Lu Xun's. They often season the main narrative like little side dainties served at big banquets, barely noticed unless they are missing. While alimentary images may seem to be mere ornamental devices for detailing local customs and exotic life, their persistent use charts a consistent undercurrent upon which his taste for the larger historical drama can be measured. On the one hand, Shen's alimentation is not located in the center of political scenes but belongs to the "minor" margins such as memory of carnal pleasure and pain, everyday anecdotes in the kitchen and at the dining table, and the coexistence of the idyllic and the grotesque on the periphery of the national space. The minor site of orality reveals itself as a battleground for multiple libidinal and political forces; eating, sexuality, and speech are interlaced in the phantasmagoria of the body, poetically frozen in words yet historically figured in a larger pattern of conflicts.

To explore these margins, the rest of this chapter is divided into three sections largely following the chronological order of Shen's early fictional writings. The first section examines his alimentation of the country and the city, with detailed analysis of the stories "Lubian" (Hearthside, 1926), "Xue" (Snow, 1927), "Lansheng tong Lanshengtaitai" (Lansheng and his wife, 1926), and "Songzijun" (Gentleman Songzi, 1926). The second section discusses the novel *Alice's Adventures in China*, focusing on the rabbit's story of growing up in hunger and the "modest proposal" the narrator makes to the hungry China. The last section explores his poetic rewriting of the least poetic topics of Lu Xun (cannibalism, disease, madness, death, and perversion of eating and sexuality) in the stories "Ye" (Night March, 1930), "Chuzi" (The cook, 1931), "Sange nanren he yige nüren" (Three men and a woman, 1930), "Yisheng" (Doctor, 1931), and "Shangui" (The mountain ghost, 1927).

Assimilating the Country and the City through the Palate

For a self-proclaimed "country fellow" living and writing in urban centers, one's "native soil," the source of agri/culture, symbolizes the place and time when life began, where the experience of food punctuates the eater's emotional and intellectual development. In this part of the world, food is an authentic signifier for real life experience, warm in the child's sense of familial bonding, simple and unpretentious in meaning, yet richly sensuous in flavor. In contrast to the idyllic rural past, the diet of urban life is out of balance and contaminated by poor taste. The dichotomous mapping is inscribed, among other things, in the figurative distinction between a hungry nostalgia for imagination and an excessive appetite for fabrication. Nostalgic as he is, however, Shen is not romantic about any real return to "home." Precisely because one can never regress to the "oral stage," the desire of return has to be preserved in imagination and desseminated in writing. Food and word are ineluctably blended to afford him a shelter in the storm of social turbulence and moral collapse. Conversely, alimentary images and tropes in his city stories are themselves symptomatic fabrications of the very urban palate that deprives life of its authentic flavors in the first place.

In his *Autobiography* (1931), Shen Congwen recalls: "I was as sturdy as a piglet before I reached four years of age. When my mother was teaching me to read characters, my maternal grandma would give me candies to eat" (9:107). Reading and eating ritualize the boy's entry into culture. As words and food are the materials that nurture a strong sense of familial bonding, they always draw the adult Shen back to the days of a bygone era. In "Wangshi" (Things of the past, 1926), that the uncle matter-of-factly picks unpeppered beef for the boy elicits an authorial comment, "How nice my Fourth Uncle is!" (1:6). "Yeyu" (Night fishing, 1926) contains a more homey picture: a grand-aunt persuades him to eat more at the table and after the meal holds him in her bosom to massage his belly for digestion (1:15–16). Nowhere is Shen's nostalgia more explicit than in the story "Labazhou" (Holiday fruit congee, 1925), which begins with this rhetorical question: "From babies who've just learned how to call out Papa, to big kids who can go outside to call for a rickshaw, to old children with a growth of white hair beneath their lip, who doesn't get a delicious taste of sticky sweetness in his mouth at the very mention of holiday fruit congee?" (1:23; cf. Kinkley 1987, 115). What food evokes in the mind of the narrator, making him "regress" to an "old child," are the colors of the congee blended with various lucky ingredients, the hiss of bubbles and boilings in the pot, and the sweet smell that permeates the festive air. At the center of the familial scene is the loving mother orchestrating the domestic ritual of feasting.

"Hearthside," as homesick as the title sounds, is a story spiced with even more lavish colors and flavors. But it is also a piece that reveals the imaginary nature of nostalgic desire and the impossibility of fulfilling that desire in existential reality. In a space of seven printed pages, a fine menu of two dozen local foods is presented to the reader, ranging from gourmet delicacies such as swallow nest porridge, lotus seed gruel, and pigeon's eggs to common items like peppered noodles and glutinous rice cakes. One passage details candies:

> [The candy peddler's] big wooden tray was partitioned into sections, each with its own kind of treat. Some had different flavors even though they were of the same color and shape. Others tasted the same but looked different. Mint candies, wrapped triangularly in red or green paper, were cool but sweet to the taste. Sliced ginger candy was slightly hot. There were all sorts of fruit candies, round or triangular, five or ten coppers for a big piece and one or two for a small one. Lotus root candies looked like the real thing, with pock-marked pod and segmented root stalk. There were hollow hot pepper candies, red as a real chili. You could blow into one and make a noise like a cow horn if you bit off the two ends, including the root stalk. Eggplant candies were much smaller than real eggplants, but they were just the same in shape and color. If you poured tea into one and then sucked it out, you'd have some sweet tea, too. Then there were treats molded into the shapes of the gods. The smallest was the size of your thumb, but you'd need more than a catty of sugar to make the whip-wielding God of Wealth with his big belly. That Hubei candy peddler would put him right in the center, with the little gods and other candies arrayed around him in ranks. (2:71; cf. Kinkley 1987, 116–17)

This passage might well be used as a candy guide for children. At the same time, it also localizes the writer's memory of the past and locates that memory in the present moment of writing. If the exquisite depiction of the candy tray condenses the locality of culture into a miniature, this local space is woven into a hungry nostalgia embedded in the narrative time. The story's structure is deceptively simple at first glance.

The first sentence, which also forms the entire first paragraph, depicts a minimal tableau: "Four people [sat] around the hearth to warm [their] hands." The domestic serenity is reinforced in the next sentence, equally controlled: "Mother, and I, and Ninth Sister, and Sixth Brother, just those four of us." Time, then, is introduced: it is set at eight o'clock in the evening, when the three children are waiting for their late evening snacks to be served before bedtime. For that particular evening, duck porridge will be offered. The food, however, is yet to come when the story ends abruptly with this sentence: "Before the duck porridge reaches our mouths, we all feel empty." Only at the end of the story does it occur to the reader that within the narrative time the mother and the three children have never left the hearth, nor have they touched any food. They are just sitting at the hearthside, talking and waiting for the arrival of the evening snack.

The feasting is only imagined. All the delicious foods, including the candy tray, are inlaid in the narrative of *waiting for food* by a series of apperceptive associations, projections, and recollections. First, it is the shouting of a peddler who sells fried meat and vegetable rolls outside that reminds the children of their snack time. This touches off the narrator's account of their favorite snacks and the little tricks they play with one another and with the mother in making their orders. Following this rehearsal of the family routine, the smell of the duck porridge being prepared in the kitchen brings the narrator back to the narrative present. Then the sound of bamboo clappers suggests that a noodle vendor is passing the house, a sound is soon replaced with the chiming of a small brass gong, the candy peddler's instrument. "All those sounds were difficult for us to take," the narrator comments as he imagines these delicious foods. "Attached to each sound was a food that would make our mouths water. . . . We felt empty in stomach when they came, and we felt empty in heart when they were gone" (2:70). Carefully inlaid in the diegesis of waiting for food is the mimesis of imagined extravagance and gratification. What makes the children's imaginary feasting so real, at least in the first reading, is the absent presence of foods as food signs.

Situated in the time of the author's actual writing of the story, the inlay of the lavish imagery within the narrative of waiting for food reflects the author's own existential condition and his act of putting words into the mouth. Just as the children's hunger is activated by an array of sounds, smells, shapes, and flavors in words, hunger motivates more desire for remembrance and imagination. Figured in the textuality of eating is the lack, material and otherwise, that he acutely felt as a poor country youth in Beijing. The temporal structure of "Hearthside" corresponds with the author's existential moment of writing, and the food signs in the text sensuously materialize his present desire as much as they signify the desired objects. Because of the absence of food in the textual world of the story and in the real world in which he wrote the story, the more hungry he felt, the more writing he needed to do to fulfill that hunger; the more desire for writing he felt to fulfill his hunger, the more he needed to tap into the memory of the past by activating food imagery. Interwoven in the signifying structure of "Hearthside" thus is the paradoxical truth of hunger and extravagance, remembrance and existence, nostalgia and wish fulfillment, desire and deferment.

Shen Congwen's desire to appease his nostalgic hunger through writing is made even more explicit in "Zaisishu" (At school, 1927). Presumably a retired soldier's memoir about his early education, the text is about anything but his formal schooling, recounting instead how the boy repeatedly skipped class and drifted into the world of bounty. One of the narrator's favorite places to visit was the village fair, where quail fighting, cockfighting, martial arts shows, food stalls, and craft shops lined the bustling street. Following a seductive sketch of local goodies, the narrator remarks that he will "write a piece of five thousand characters only to introduce a special pickled lettuce," adding that such a long piece would still be considered "too simple" by the villagers (1:173). In more than two decades of writing, the author has certainly honored his promise.

Shen Congwen was so homesick at times that he had to take vicarious trips back to the country to eat his fill. The story "Snow" depicts such a journey. Congwen, the I-narrator and a soldier, has been invited to join Shuyuan (the given name of one of the author's close friends) in visiting the latter's mother in a remote village. The story depicts a brief moment in the early morning. A heavy overnight snow has made it impossible for the two friends to go out hunting as they had planned, so Shuyuan told Congwen not to hurry to get up. Confined indoors, they would chat and eat, and chat about eating. Shuyuan first roasted chestnuts in the stove. When they finished up the chestnuts, he went to the kitchen to "steal" cured meat and glutinous rice cakes against the mother's will. She was afraid that food taken before the breakfast would dull their appetites for the special treat of fried quail she planned to prepare for them. While the son was away getting more food, his mother arrived. She noticed all the pieces of chestnut skin on the floor, adding that she also caught the son in the kitchen. Congwen felt guilty for not having followed the hostess's request, but the mother, so as not to embarrass her guest, talked more about fine cooking. Upon Shuyuan's return, she only teased the son. After she left to prepare the special breakfast, Shuyuan grinned at Congwen and sneaked out of his pocket half a dozen slices of dried date paste. The story ends with Congwen still in bed, gobbling everything.

Conjured around the adult children's indulgence and the pampering mother is an idyllic picture of peasant hospitality and the extravagant simplicity of country life. Meanwhile, the topic of eating also functions as the topos, the "place," where the two conflicting outer spaces of the city and the country are condensed in the inner space of orality. For the narrator, as for the author, his retreat to the country gives him an opportunity to explain the different "tastes of the city and the country." Before the trip, he was afraid of getting physically sick in the village. "After I came here, I have mouthed in the entire beauty of the countryside" (1:138). Through these metaphors, the outside world is assimilated, as sensually as the food is, through the palate. In addition, the portrayal of rural beauty also rewrites the medical code introduced in the narrator's fear of disease prior to the trip. When Shuyuan invited Congwen to eat roasted chestnuts, the latter told the former that he had to rinse his mouth. His insistence on this hygienic practice—a scientific practice that stands for the superiority of urban modernity—met with Shuyuan's teasing mockery: "What a city person you are!" Congwen immediately recognized that Shuyuan teased him in the same way the city person would ridicule Shuyuan as a "country bumpkin." Enjoying their roasted chestnuts, the two went on comparing the city and the country. "Tell you this," Shuyuan said to Congwen, "we country folks have lots of fun. We would be roasting sausages right now if my mother had not told us she would fry quail for our breakfast." "In no way will I make fun of country people anymore," Congwen responded (1:137). The otherwise unclean practice of eating before teeth brushing turns out to be more "healthy."

As homey as the story is, it would be just another on a theme too cosy for the melancholic subject to entertain. Shen Congwen was aware that there would be no real return to the native soil. Just as displacement generates nostalgia, nostalgia leads to more desire for home, and thus more writing. If Shen's imaginary nostalgia is implicitly encoded in "Hearthside," "Snow" makes it more conspicuous. Here the dialectic of displacement and nostalgia finds expression in the vicarious travel of the self in both the enunciated subject and the subjective mode of enunciation. The subtitle of the story is revealing: "In the Countryside of Shuyuan's Homeland, a Story about You, Shuyuan, and His Mother." The "You" in the subtitle turns out to be the first-person narrator Congwen, the author's own name. Such a split inserted between the enunciation of the autobiographical narrator and his double in the enunciated "You" creates a spatial and temporal distance for the author's self-reflection. What happens between the narrator in the text proper and the "You" as an extratextual sign is a dialogical monologue that safeguards the illusion of self-identity *and* a monological dialogue that stands for the split self. This *dédoublement* figures the divided subject in the imaginary, in the image and discourse of the mother. The narrator is fully aware of his divided existence but nevertheless insists on maintaining his illusory imagination. Above all, fulfillment of hunger is a temporal movement, nostalgically to the "oral stage" and futuristically to the open-ended "next meal" at the same time. Cannibalism, on the other hand, signifies the ultimate state of negativity in the symbolic, whose solution lies in the leap into faith. Self-reduplication seeking different solutions—this may help us explain why Lu Xun had to abandon fictional writing to fight as a self-proclaimed soldier (though still with his pen), whereas Shen Congwen, a former soldier, continued to write fiction with increasing aesthetic refinement in an environment of mounting politicization of culture.

Shen's nostalgia could not ease his real hunger when his words failed to exchange food. Nor could the imagined home shelter a poor country fellow against the cold of reality. That is one of the reasons that in his eyes the city is sick, among many other things, in the way people eat. Food in his urban stories does not sizzle with the sensations of authentic life and genuine human desire. Instead, alimentary images and tropes become signs of decadence of which its superficial palate is just a symptom.

The story "Lansheng and His Wife" features a husband's obsession with his wife's hairstyle, yet this seemingly unrelated topic is carefully presented around food images. Lansheng is a middle-aged petty functionary in the Ministry of Finance, and his wife, who looks much younger than he, is a housewife. When the story begins, we learn that the husband has recently developed a habit. Instead of taking the bus home during his lunch break, he is spending about half an hour walking. There are two reasons for this: he does not want to get home too soon to do the kitchen chores, and he can leisurely eye the young women students, their hair dressed in a new fashion, from a nearby secondary school. The route he takes from his work to his house on "Steamed Roll Alley" passes "Pastry Lane," "Tenderloin Mansion," and "Turnip Alley." The couple usually has a nice division of labor in preparing food. The wife shops and cooks while the husband washes up and takes care of other logistic work. If the women is in a bad mood, as she is at times, the man will take over the cooking. When both are not on good terms, a neighborhood eatery sees two more patrons.

On a September day when Lansheng had received his salary, he happily ordered a bowl of boiled meatballs from the neighborhood restaurant, knowing also that on that particular day he would be spared his task of cleaning up the kitchen. The extra dish "changed the normal triangle of three dishes on the table into a quadrangle, and the wife's face brightened a bit more than the day before, too" (2:35). Spiced with a special treat, their table talk shifted from the routine topic of their daily menu to the new fashion in women's hairstyles. The husband then suggested to the wife that she might look even better if she followed the trendy fashion. The topical switch at the table, however, disrupted their voracious gulping of the meatballs, for she was vexed at his implied comparison of her with younger women. "When she turned her chopsticks away from a meatball to the dried vegetable braised in soy sauce, her irritation was also obvious on her face"—it looked like the dark-colored dried vegetable as well (2:36). The man later had to find other ways to persuade her to accept the new style. And once she did he resumed taking the bus. We learn from "Morning," a story written three months later about the same couple, that Lansheng had taken over the entire duty of cooking, a price he had to pay for updating his wife's appearance.

The image of the "superfluous man" is clearly borrowed from Ivan Turgenev, Shen Congwen's favorite Russian author. The emerging petty bourgeoisie is distasteful to him. In their life, not only is food depleted of its rich flavors but food signs have also changed to trivial signposts. From the alley and mansion names, to the arrangement in the kitchen, to the portraits of the wife's changing facial expression at the table, food signs are attenuated in the discourse of superficial and trendy tastes, advanced under the then fashionable banner of "new culture." Once hunger is absent from the petty bourgeoisie, it is replaced with greed in the form of excessive appetite.

Excessive appetite, along with pathetic sexual fantasy and seductive deception through textual fabrication, is the subject of "Gentleman Songzi." If the author mocks the shallow yet harmless Lansheng and his wife with some comic humor, that mild mockery is turned into a more pungent ridicule when it comes to the portrayal of a group the author finds more repulsive: the modern literati. An almost penniless country youth, Shen seemed as resentful of the commercial success of popular writers as of some figures in the serious literary establishment. But the hierarchical distinction between the different grades of writing was already a false one to Shen Congwen in that writers of any quality feed on the market principle of extracting economic and cultural privilege by selling themselves. Furthermore, the author was aware of his own quandary: as ambitious and serious as he was, his writing nevertheless was governed by the market principle. Through a narrative interlacing of both "brows" around eating and sex, "Gentleman Songzi" blurs the borderline between serious and popular literature and inadvertently inscribes in it the author's own predicament.

The I-narrator in "Gentleman Songzi" is a literatus who at least has read Gogol and learned Western painting. He is affluent enough to be able to afford a cook and a male servant. On hot and humid summer afternoons, he would relax on a camp bed in the shade of a giant pagoda tree, reading leisurely to ease himself into a long sound repose. Occasionally he may wake up at three to the noises of a cow and a calf, a hen and a cock, or mating crickets. "But that rarely happens, only when a light lunch awakens [him] with an empty stomach." He is rarely disturbed because his cook "seldom makes bad food." In his normal schedule with his normal intake of lunch, he would sleep well up to a quarter past four, when his friend Songzi would drop in and shake him awake. At times, Songzi may remember he is a gentleman and refrain from interrupting his host's "beautiful dreams of kissing beautiful women." When Songzi behaves himself, the narrator may sleep even longer until he opens his blurry eyes to catch Songzi dozing off in a chair before him (2:41).

Gentleman Songzi is a man of letters smart enough to tap into the cultural market of popular taste. He comes to converse with the narrator on a broad range of topics, from current affairs, philosophy, education, and nationalism to sex and romance. During their daily interlocution, Songzi needs a good deal of food to maintain the smooth functioning of his mouth. On the day he comes over to discuss a new popular romance he has just finished reading, he consumes up to ten big apples—his appetite would have allowed him to take more had the servant not saved ten apples for the narrator. Well provided for, Songzi in return provides the narrator with books he finds particularly interesting. Just in the past few days he has recommended *Two Volumes of Love Letters* and *A History of Sex*. According to the narrator's refined taste, these cheap books, though their prices are not cheap, are "poorly written," only suitable to "the average young men and women who are as fascinated with sex as they are hungry for food." Some of the things in the books afford them a crude "hand-on" after they have "exhausted their pure fantasy," guiding the married man to experiment on his partner or the unwed man to masturbate. The narrator "felt cheated by Songzi" to have been exposed to that sort of writing (2:42–43).

It needs to be noted that sex is not taboo in Shen Congwen's works. On the contrary, he celebrates what he believes to be the primitive energy and vitality embodied in the more spontaneous sex and love of the country folks, represented in stories such as "Baizi," "The Border Town," and "Long River." Meanwhile, from what we can gather from his works and other sources, Shen Congwen in his early years in Beijing was a shy young man, inexperienced sexually. His low socioeconomic status, lack of formal education, and country manner and accent—these may have kept him from erotic encounters. Although it is oversimplistic to treat his imaginary nostalgia merely as a fetish in his imaginative compensation, there is a clear trace of "personal lack" in his portrayal of "social excess." And this dialogic intersection is located right in the split voice of the narrator.

In "Gentleman Songzi," the narrator speaks in two voices. One is clear, authoritative, and judgmental, as when he describes the external world and his encounters with other characters. It is in his superior and sometimes sarcastic voice that Gentleman Songzi comes alive, almost like a clown when he is wolfing down the ten big apples. But when the narrative turns inward to the narrator himself, another voice emerges. It is ambivalent and uncertain, making fun of himself as he would otherwise scorn the stupid Songzi. Yet this narrative voice is not self-conscious on the part of the narrator and only belongs to the invisible author. After Songzi brings him the sex books, for instance, his biological clock fails him for the afternoon repose. As distasteful as he finds these books to be, "I just can't fall asleep, even though I had a lunch today as good as ever. . . . Probably it's because my body contains too much energy. . . . That porridge made with that half of the chicken left from yesterday, so tasty. Perhaps today's lunch was too heavy, more than what I had yesterday" (2:41–42). The narrator, as it turns out, has as lustful an appetite for food and sex as Gentleman Songzi does. To make it even worse, he is perplexed by his failure to sleep and is not aware of its cause: he is being seduced by Songzi's cheap sex books even though he feels cheated by them. By hiding his sexual impulse behind a misplaced self-diagnosis of the symptom, the text paradoxically reveals the truth that, as a popular ancient saying goes, "sufficient shelter and food awakens sexual desire" [*wenbao sheng yinyu*].

Gentleman Songzi not only seduces and cheats the narrator into his "self-awakening"—his inability to sleep. Seduction and deception serve as the central narrative principle of the text. The popular romance Songzi is writing, he claims, is based on the real love story of one Mr. Zhou, a college student of literature and a mutual friend of the two. Zhou is said to have confided to Songzi his recent tragic experience with a young married woman. The woman seduced him out of pure sexual lust, but Zhou took it as a serious romantic affair. After he came to realize her seduction and deception, the brokenhearted Zhou was driven to the edge of a nervous breakdown. Songzi then developed this story into a young man's fictional diary, supposedly having incorporated Zhou's real diary. Seeking advice and comment, Songzi brings his manuscript to the narrator. Its sentimentalism further sets off the voluptuous details of sexual fantasy. Songzi's dramatic telling of the story even keeps the narrator, as the listener, awake almost to midnight, when he finally departs, leaving his host the manuscript and the peels of ten big apples thrown all over the place. Days after the narrator has finished reading it, he meets the story's persona dramatis and inquires about his diary. It turns out that Zhou, a skinny man who has been trying to build up his weight and only records his daily progress in the diary, never had such a romantic experience. "Songzi has fabricated the entire story," it finally occurs to the narrator. And he is the one who has been seduced and deceived by this fabricated romance. In the end, we learn that Gentleman Songzi has fabricated Zhou's tragic romance because "recently he himself has been entangled in a love affair."

The circular and self-reflexive structure of signification, the double embedding of seduction and deception, and the theme of fabricated desire and the artificial mode of its fabrication—all these reveal a "double orality" of eating and speech at work. The model of double orality developed from the mythological tale of Yi Yin assumes the material primacy of food signs in alimentary discourse. This oral primacy generates the form and mode of articulation as much as cooking/eating thematizes the tale's content. Its signifying process is one of metaphorical transformation that nevertheless insists on its rhetorical approximation of materiality. But double orality works in opposite themes when it is applied to the semantic difference of the country and the city. In the country, Shen Congwen insists on the primordial materiality of food and encodes it in the imaginary of the motherly. Illusory as the imagined object may be, the authentic experience cannot simply be fabricated because imagination signifies the natural function of human desire. In "Gentleman Songzi," on the other hand, eating and speech are pathologically inscribed in the deceptive effect of textually manufactured desire and taste. In the cities, not only has food experience lost touch with the native soil and the healthy desire of imagination but food signs are appropriated into the signifying system of seduction and deception symptomatic of the cultural machinery that manufactures cheap lust.

Songzi's voracity, for example, is consistently figured in his speech just as it characterizes his excessive appetite. The story describes each of the ten apples as *bubai* (filler) in Songzi's telling of his story. As a journalistic term, *filler* denotes how these ten apples fill the blank space of his insatiable stomach and punctuate his telling of sexual fantasies. At the same time, the term suggests that his story is only good enough to fill in the tiny blank space on the pages of popular magazines. As if that was not sarcastic enough, Songzi himself suggests to the narrator that his piece will be "published in the magazine *Huapian zazhi* (Spoken fragments) (2:53). When Songzi mocks the skinny Zhou, calling him "Fatty," "his own face becomes as happy as *yuanxiao* (sweet round dumplings of glutinous rice flour used to celebrate the Lantern Festival)." Songzi even tells Zhou the plain lie, right in front of the narrator, that the narrator "is the one who covets your diary, repeatedly egging me on with his apples." The narrator and Zhou are embarrassed by Songzi's shameless lie, and they are only "spared his silly fabrication when the servant brings in walnuts and peanuts," which again "fill in" Songzi's boasting of "how he makes his face round" (2:58). For the shameless eater and fabricator, the food that fills his mouth can only be translated into the words that seduce and deceive. For the seduced and deceived narrator, he is at once the provisioner of the big eater and the consumer of his big lie. It is ironic that the narrator, with his fine taste in words and food, has to be awakened to his lust only to find out that he is already ensnared in the recycling of distasteful fantasy and fabrication.

Shen Congwen's "Modest Proposal"

Hungry nostalgia for imagination and excessive appetite for fabrication are two important tropes in Shen Congwen's early fiction. By assimilating the rural and urban spaces, he inscribes cultural conflicts around differing tastes. As noted above, his persistent emphasis on the form of representation has in the past resulted in Shen's dismissal from the communist canon and celebration overseas. Both sides have ignored his novel *Alice's Adventures in China* (henceforth *Adventures*), which contains the single most overtly political message he ever delivered. But I choose this text not to correct the "apolitical" image of the author—a problematic image that in my opinion was largely an effect of the hot and cold wars—but because the novel offers a rare window into the author's unrefined opinions and marks a turning point in the development of alimentary discourse in modern China. With his ascent into relative fame and security, Shen's discourse of hunger, prevalent in his early texts and this novel, gradually disappeared in his more acclaimed works of the 1930s.

From a formal point of view, the novel's narrative structure is quite episodic, yet it lacks the kind of lyrical flavor of his more refined native-soil stories. The author acknowledges that the novel is a "failed work" because it "turns a friendly and amiable rabbit into a Chinese gentleman" and imposes "fashionable political slogans" on Lewis Carroll's fable (1:202–3). Yet precisely because of his failure to strictly imitate the borrowed genre and theme, the novel stands out as an anomaly in modern Chinese literature as well as Shen's own corpus. In this sense, Shen Congwen, not Lu Xun, should be deemed the predecessor of Yan'an literature.

Interesting enough, Shen Congwen also approaches the problem of writing through a linguistic-cum-medical trope, but he completely deviates from the Lu Xun model. As he explains in the postscript to *Adventures*, he "casually picked the topic" with the intention of rewriting the fable for his little sister. But his "translation" was not really meant to amuse. He simply wanted to make the tale plain and easy to read "so that she could tell it to [their] mother to ease her pains of illness." As the son's words were to be assimilated through the daughter's mouth in order to "feed" the ailing mother, his act of writing must be taken as a symbolic gesture of familial piety directed at the physical body of the mother. This feature coheres with the author's position in the "minor." Above all, Shen's ethnic and regional background, his persistent love of home and homeland, and his marginal(ized) place in modern cultural politics must be taken at face value.

Shen Congwen's own judgment on the "failed work" is indicative of the artistic standard he sets for himself and as such reveals the very paradox of how literary writing appropriates the idea of the real and approximates its materiality. In the midst of writing the novel, he was shocked to find himself "blending social misery with pure humor and innocence," producing a "shallow and crude satire" rather than what he originally had in mind. Yet he could not change it because, as he put it, "I had so much in my heart that I couldn't help venting it." Moreover, he asks, what else would Alice and the rabbit see in China except the picture he has depicted? Both the social reality and the author's reaction to it justify the generic misuse. Since the novel resulted from such spontaneous self-writing, he simply could not have its explicit political and moral edges "rounded and softened" (1:202–3).

From writing to alleviate the mother's illness to writing to expose social disease, Shen also prescribes his "medicine." The cure he offers, though borrowed from Jonathan Swift, is indeed a "modest proposal." It is "modest" in the sense that he did not follow Lu Xun's example in envisioning the totality of modern China. The novel might well stage from the two travelers' "innocent" viewpoint an allegorical spectacle for the modern nation. The reason for Shen's refusal to play into the symbolic of the "father" lies in his self-positioning at the margin of the allegorical spectacle and is tied to his literalization of the word in relation to the flesh of the "mother." The fact that the novel spontaneously mixes Swiftian satire with Alice's dreamland captures Shen's subject position at the margin of the master narrative. The irony of history is such that the "reactionary" Shen Congwen approaches the problem of eating from a standpoint much more materialistic than the "revolutionary" Lu Xun's.

The novel consists of two books, each with ten chapters. It was written for the magazine *Xinyue* (Crescent) in serial form. The first four chapters are set prior to the journey and can be read as the novel's prologue. Chapters 5 and 6 depict the first two days Alice and the rabbit spend in China, in which the author launches his political protest. The rest of book 1 and all of book 2 shift from pungent political satire to mild comic fantasy and romance. In a novel written in the heyday of the White Terror for a magazine that advocated "art for arts' sake," the author's shift to a more politically safe genre and topic after the publication of the first six chapters reflects the larger environment of cultural production and his response to it, an issue to which I will return later.

In the first four chapters, two distinct sets of alimentary images and themes are juxtaposed against the two main characters' preparation for the journey. One set belongs to a Mr. Harper, an English gentleman who has traveled extensively in the Orient and has just returned from China. The text parodies the guidebook discourse of *chinoiserie* in Mr. Harper's cultural initiation of Alice and her rabbit companion. He first invites them to drink tea in the manner of the Chinese gentry. The rabbit can hardly appreciate that cultural ritual, and his funny behavior further reinforces the motif of exotica. Their pretravel acculturation culminates in an exquisite dinner of Chinese cuisine prepared by Mr. Harper's own Chinese-trained chef. The dinner scene plays on the most familiarly alien images—from the rabbit's awkward handling of chopsticks to his olfactory reaction to *choudoufu* (fermented beancurd with a strong odor). After the dinner, Alice and the rabbit "felt as if they had already been to China once" (1:212). For the author and his intended reader, the flavor of a foreign fairy tale is doubly seasoned in the text's comic manipulation of orientalist clichés and stereotypes. The authorial control of textual signification is obvious in his intertextual "free play" with the signifiers of an extremely self-conscious form, the fantasy novel, and in his burlesque inlays of orientalist fantasy within that fantastic genre and discourse.

The construction of a fantastic land anticipates its head-on crash into harsh reality. In fact, the introductory chapters already overdetermine the inevitable collision by inserting a parabolic bildungsroman depicting the rabbit's growth. The rabbit's social initiation and coming of age are presented as a process of negotiating for food to obtain knowledge, a survival story that has little to do with Lewis Carroll's original text. When the rabbit was about four or five years old, it occurred to him for the first time that "his body only belonged to himself because he had to find food to appease his hunger" (1:216). His first social encounter was with two dogs fighting over a loaf of bread. As their battle intensified, the rabbit realized that the importance of the bread was as an emblem of honor more than nourishment. His recognition of the new meaning of food led him to take advantage of the situation. He asked for the bread, and the dogs gave it to him under the condition that he serve as the witness to their duel. "No longer hungry after he ate the bread, the rabbit leisurely watched their battle for glory under the beautiful moonlight." The way he secured food the first day, comments the narrator, "amounts to a page in the history of mythology" (1:217–18).

On the second day, the rabbit learned another lesson. He begged food from a human, the son of a Parliament member at that. Unlike the glory-hungry dogs, the rich kid demanded humility and flattery from the beggar. For the rabbit, the exchange of words for food was not a bad deal at all. However, this truth about the exchange value of words was challenged on the third day, when the rabbit was unfortunate enough to run into a poor jobless man and attempted the same words-for-food tactic. The poor man taught him the hard lesson that creatures of their kind had to work for food or, when they could not sell their labor, rob or steal. Theft is an act that signifies self-shame and thus is a sign of human evolution. Robbery, on the other hand, is a less-civilized deed to which only creatures of lower intelligence would resort. Thus, the rabbit planned to steal food on the fourth day from a rich rabbit girl. It turned out that the girl was literally fed up with all the delicious food she had, and the hungry pauper simply helped rid her of a piece of sausage she didn't want in the first place. After many more days and more tragi-comic turns and twists, the rabbit finally landed in the hands of an affluent bachelor and became his servant. When the rabbit turned nineteen years of age, the master died and left him a large fortune. Now in his mid-forties, the gentleman rabbit is about to accompany Miss Alice to China.

Devoting the entire second chapter to the rabbit's story of growing up in hunger, the author obviously makes the tale more familiar to his intended audience. In the process of cultural translation, the innocent rabbit is transformed into a mythological figure of materialism. It is materialistic in that the meaning of food is not a given. Rather, food is a central locus on which meaning is produced and contested and social relations are constituted and organized. Meanwhile, such a materialist genesis of history is embedded in a narrative so mythological that the pathos of the hungry rabbit becomes allegorical of the mythos of humankind. What emerges from the tension of economic pathos and transhistorical mythos is that hunger must be taken as a universal problem but nevertheless be understood in a specific social context.

It is interesting to note that in re-creating the rabbit, Shen Congwen also renames him John Nuoxi. His surname, translated by Kinkley as "Beloved of the Nuo Gods" (1987, 93), is homophonous of the Nuo play of the Miao people, known for its ritual-dramatic performance, shamanistic chants, mythical themes, and grotesque masks. Intended or not, the act of hybridizing a foreign given name with a folk religious surname generates a defamiliarizing effect in line with the fairy tale's use of animalist imagery. The hybridized name corresponds well to the novel's overall thematic and generic reconfiguration of intercultural ingredients. Cultural encounter is not seen here as a totalizing process of territorializing international space—the West versus China in the modern context. Instead, that already totalized space can be reterritorialized by blending the minor images of fairy tale from the West with folk culture from the Chinese periphery. John Nuoxi's story, his formation via hungry experience, the transnational character signified by his name—all these prefigure his inevitable encounter with his Chinese counterpart and provide the pre-text for reading Shen's modest proposal.

In the novel, the proposal is made by a "hungry but upright ordinary person" in a newspaper article entitled "A Modest Proposal to the Impoverished Chinese for a Convenient Solution of Their Predicament." It is presented to John Nouxi by a man who "looks like a skinny dog, a walking skeleton wrapped in rags" (1:260). Instead of begging food from the two travelers, he asks John Nuoxi to kill him, one of the three choices proposed in the article. This logic is beyond the grasp even of the well-seasoned rabbit. He has to read the article through the maze of all the images of massive impoverishment. The naked poverty of the majority sets off the lavish waste of the few; the grisly condition of the poor is exploited to generate excessive profits for international capital; the collapse of social order serves as the excuse for extravagant military and law enforcement expenditures aimed only at protecting the haves; and moral decay and cultural decline prompt the pathetic call for preserving the old or introducing the new, all in the name of the nation and to the neglect of the common people's real needs. Since Chinese and dogs are not allowed to enter public parks in the international concessions, there is no point in the generous foreign powers advocating the conservation of Chinese cultural relics; their philanthropy may keep some from immediate death, but even the shabby survival of the poor population would strain the limited resources and contaminate the national landscape.

While venting his outrage, the author makes three proposals in the name of patriotism: let foreign powers take over the burden and allow the poor Chinese to serve as their slaves, so that the vast manpower of China can be utilized to develop the economy; let them starve themselves to death to spare philanthropic agencies and government officials the trouble of paying lip-service; or, if these solutions require too much coordination, each individual should take action and get killed. As for the children, Swift's Irish model provided a perfect example. Since China has so many children that their flesh may depress the market demand for salted and spiced meat, some of the young bodies should be kept alive to maintain a sufficient reserve of concubines, maids, and prostitutes for wealthy Chinese and to maintain a large pool of cheap labor for international investment. If Shen Congwen is known for his distance from politics, his modest proposal serves as a rare proof of his unreserved opinion. His protest stems from an enraged heart overwhelmed by the scope of the social atrocities and ideological absurdities of the time.

This outburst of social protest, however, is carefully juxtaposed with a more self-consciously performative mode of narration so that it cannot be easily appropriated into any particular vision of totality. The diverse views of the spectacle of modern China deserve more attention. The traveler's China is not only a tourist scene but also a theater. As "Mr. Nuoxi's sole purpose for this journey is to watch exciting scenes," on the first morning he left the hotel to sightsee without notifying Alice. When Alice learned that there were dramas to watch in the theater, "she did not believe that the Chinese were capable of acting on the stage; then she realized that everything unfolded before her eyes just like an interesting dramatic show, even the way the Chinese walked" (1:246–48). Exotic tourist scenes continue to unfold at the end of the novel, but the travelers' cultural encounters with the natives are presented in such a comical and parodic fashion that any interpretative attempt at some allegorical totality outside or beyond the tale's thematic and generic boundaries is bound to prove no less burlesque. Specularity, once pushed to its theatrical extreme, turns out to be nothing but the effect of linguistic performativity.

Because the overall performative nature of the novel prevents the narrative from conjuring up a total picture, the modest proposal is able to unleash a serious counterpoint to Lu Xun's national allegory. When Shen Congwen is presenting his solutions to hunger, the spectacle of decapitation resurfaces. Explaining why he wants to make the proposal, the author of the newspaper article writes:

> Some men are so hungry that in their desperation they put on a dreadful face to rob others. They may have their stomach filled for the time being; but once caught they surely will have their heads chopped off for good. When I see their deformed bodies, tears well up in my eyes, all the while the four-thousand-some bloody and filthy human heads lost under similar circumstances I have seen in the past come back to my mind. Those human heads, hanged on ropes or placed in wooden cages, are displayed at points of bustling traffic, *so as to let* (*haorang*) those who still have the head on the neck raise theirs to *appreciate* (*xinshang*) the scene. The pallid countenance of the dead would gradually turn sallow, crimson streaks of blood getting darker. Displayed are the might of the law and the fate of the weak. You can find such easy solutions anywhere in China, assisted by foreign powers at times. That—and the belly of the dead body ripped open, the liver and the gallbladder removed—I have seen more than four thousand times. Seeing this with my own eyes, I can't help shedding tears. *The truth is you'd better close your eyes.* . . . If you have been exposed to this kind of stuff for too long, probably you will feel that, as they say, "It's better alive than dead." (1:265–66; emphasis added)

Before we analyze this spectacle, let us recall two features of the slide described by Lu Xun: the body is actually in good shape ("they are all sturdy fellows") and the head symbolizes the diseased national spirit despite the body, which is thereby deemed dispensable ("the people of a weak and backward country, however strong and healthy they might be, could only serve to be made examples of or as witness of such futile spectacles; and it is not necessarily deplorable no matter how many of them die of illness"). Compared to Lu Xun's reading of the slide, the first thing one notes in the above scene is the chain of events. Since it is the hunger of desperation that leads to decapitation, the head is chopped off the body *because of* the abject material condition, not *in spite* of it. Repositioned this way, the head is reconnected to the existential lack of the material body, "the fate of the weak," and serves as a metonym for the violent excess of power, "the might of the law." Once the fundamental power relation is anchored in materiality, the *episteme*, the mode of knowledge production ingrained in the public display is itself on display as well. The discursive practice of the penal system exists prior to, and thus imposes its regime upon, the spectators; it demands the "appreciation" of its own atrocious exhibition. Unlike the mask of "enjoyment in apathy" Lu Xun puts on the crowd, the audience's "appreciation" is the effect ("so as to let") of the brute machinery that displays its power and cuts the body in half. From Lu Xun to Shen Congwen, there is a clear shift of the representational focus away from psychology and morality toward discourse and power relations.

As part of the modest proposal, this scene anticipates the author's outcry just a couple of paragraphs later: "The rich possess everything; the hungry contribute everything to humanity. The sacrifice of the hungry Chinese made China's historical past glorious. The entire culture of China has survived on the back of the poor people" (1:267). One does not have to invoke the familiar terminology of Chinese Communism to see how much Shen Congwen has in common with the peasant revolutionaries. Given the context of this outcry in the ebb of the revolution and the high tide of the KMT's anti-Communist witch-hunt, one would wonder why Shen Congwen did not turn to Marxism. The clue, however, is provided in the very scene.

The autobiographical, and indeed "confessional," nature of the fictional newspaper article is obvious. The counting of beheadings is traceable to the author's early experience, and the recounting of the gruesome details is reinscribed in many of his fictional and autobiographical texts. The most revealing part is his "confession." While tears keep welling up, the eyes should be closed to shut off the gazing, not so much of the beheaded as of the displayed. Is it a defiant gesture of refusing to be absorbed into the overwhelming spectacle of intimidation or is it a timid act of protecting the disturbed and frightened self from violence? Or would too much sight numb the heart or drive it to the edge of madness?

There is no clear answer to these questions—questions that perhaps should not be raised in terms of psychological (or any) dichotomy in the first place. Equally vague is a sigh of agonized helplessness, released in the midst of his most vocal protest, that his own life would have to drag on for no other reason than to keep it free of death.

Like the Shen Congwen in the scene of decapitation that opens this chapter, the narrator turns his eyes inward for a moment in melancholy. Turning inward means putting the visual world into the mouth, swallowing the tears to lubricate the rumination of horror. But the ruminated stuff is put back into words, suspended in the tableau vividly detailing the most gruesome: the colorful image of the colorless face of the dead, the belly ripped open with the liver and the gallbladder removed. The latter image recalls the postmortem removal of Xu Xiling's heart and liver. But, unlike Lu Xun, Shen Congwen gives us no moralizing, no divine call, as though hunger or some mythical-medicinal recycling of flesh could justify the "detailing," that is, "cutting into pieces," of the body. Instead of the author's psychic secret, the questions we must ask are these. Why did he persistently depict the most macabre scenes in his trademark poetic language? What do these beautiful images of the ugly mean? Where does that poetics of the ugly leave him in the cultural history of modern China? These are the same questions that often leave his reader in a limbo of profound bewilderment, very much like what is captured in the image of the ripped belly: a "mouth" wide open, the inside emptied out, a chasm poised like a huge question mark that begs for answers.

Shen Congwen's "Flowers of Evil"

I do not propose a comparative study of Shen Congwen and Baudelaire—one involving Lu Xun, especially his *Wild Grass*, would be more appropriate, as I have suggested. Above all, Shen Congwen's "flowers of evil" not only blossom in the cities but yield the most colorful fruits in the homeland. Furthermore, nostalgic as he seems at times, Shen Congwen has hardly entertained the idea of transcendental negativity, as Walter Benjamin has detected in Baudelaire as well as in Nietzsche.[4] The idea of the all-powerful Almighty, not to mention His death, never existed for Shen Congwen. As far as nihilism is concerned, the kind of eternal return found in the work of some fin de siècle European intellectuals does not pose to Shen Congwen a teleological problem nor require of him some metaphysical solution. "Eternal return" is already a given in the artistic legacy he inherited from ancient China, all the more so in western Hunan's mesmerizing forms. My borrowing from Baudelaire is only meant to foreground a *rhetorical* presence, via Benjamin, of what I would call a "phantasmagoria" of bodily dismemberment and remembrance as a dialogical counterpoint to Lu Xun's allegorical embodiment.

Like the French "lyrical poet in the era of high capitalism," Shen Congwen presents the phantasmagoria of turbulent China through a poetic lens of allegorical negativity. But he does not tie the broken pieces of the world to the transcendental absence of truth, as Baudelaire does, nor does he restore them by turning the present curse into a futuristic blessing as in the case of Lu Xun. Instead, he insists on the very surface meaning of atrocity and absurdity, seeing in the present void the ancient figure of emptiness whereby wisdom is to be gained and humanity freed from existing dogmas. Inscribed around the decomposed body is a "com-posing" language that recomposes the shattered pieces, not into a unifying totality but into what David Wang calls "discordant harmony" (1992, 217). His "flowers of evil," then, are less an end result of irony than a point of departure for a poetic approximation of all life forces in their fragmentation.

Shen Congwen, to be sure, can be as angry and melancholic as Baudelaire, but his moral rage and intellectual solitude are not located in the "spleen." As blood bursts from the beheaded, it circulates tears of indignation and pain in the heart. When the injured heart tries to recuperate to gain melancholic insight, it is nurtured by the emboldening fluid of the gallbladder—the source of courage in the Chinese system of symbolic anatomy. If boldness means having the "guts" (or gallbladder) to confront the world again, insight reopens the eyes to an epiphanic glimpse of truth. When Shen assimilates this recomposing process to alimentary discourse, writing becomes verbal cooking, storytelling signals feeding, and the writer/storyteller assumes the role of the mythical chef. In a time of severe material scarcity, the body and its sanity cannot survive without a rugged stomach and a rustic gallbladder.

The only detailed account of real cannibalism in Shen's work is found in the short story "Night March." This rare example reveals Shen's ambivalent and eccentric view on this subject. The story is based on the author's own military experience. Through the voice of the I-narrator he recalls his daily routine:

> Unless I had something very important to do, I always went out to see for myself how people [his fellow soldiers] actually cut out the hearts and livers of human beings [after their executions by the troops]. This performance I saw altogether eleven times. Once I saw a man inject fine powdered silver into a human gallbladder. I was told that thus impregnated that human organ became even more efficacious than bear's gallbladder in curing strange ailments such as heartache only some [sentimental] women and rich people can afford to suffer. But what I wanted to know most was how the heart looked in the frying pan. I had been told that it would quiver and jump about fearfully. I found that this was not true. *Those stupid creatures! If their hearts had been living, pulsating things, they would not have allowed others to cut off their heads without a struggle.* Since they did not resist being killed and never tried to cut off other people's heads, it was no wonder that their hearts did not jump in the frying pan. . . .
>
> One day the gatekeeper told me how he once ate a piece of a woman's tongue. He was serious and not just telling a tale. He said a friend of his had quarreled with his mistress, who later had an affair with a tinsmith and plotted with the latter to murder his friend. But the tinsmith refused and leaked her intention. After the gatekeeper's friend learned about this, he went to the woman's house, pulled out her tongue and cut it off. The gatekeeper happened to visit his friend at the time and was invited to partake of his solitary feast. It was not until later that he found out what he had eaten. He vomited for half a month but still felt sick.
>
> *To eat a piece of human flesh is not so weird, though the city people always associate it with the savages.* That's because they are sentimental and ignorant of the conditions of China. In fact, *these incidents of cannibalism are only different in the manner humans are eaten. Even now I have frequent opportunities to see how certain groups of people are devoured by others.* It is for this reason that I am able to talk, without undue show of emotion, about the strange and savage things I have seen. (1982, 260–61; emphasis added)[5]

In some aspect, Shen Congwen seems to share Lu Xun's view. He too blames the victims' lack of resistance and moves from the details of flesh eating to the metaphoric feast where ordinary people are devoured in political violence. But what he offers here is a country fellow's perspective, opposite to that of the more "civilized" city people. Precisely because people are devoured in all forms of oppression, cannibalism differs only in manner but not in kind. Moreover, he is reluctant to make undifferentiated judgment of the devoured and is consistent with the thesis of his modest proposal that in a situation of unequal power relations "certain groups of people are devoured by others," thus avoiding the sweeping culturalist diagnosis of collective self-eating. Even the victims' lack of "guts" is located in the organ of passion, the heart, which is not attributed to the source of the nation's rational spirit, the head. Defying the "civilized" mode of interpretation, Shen Congwen persistently shows the unfolding drama of social collapse "without undue show of emotion." From this seemingly detached viewpoint (detached from what he considers the sentimentalism and ignorance of the city people), he explores the possibilities of rekindling the decency and passion of the country folk.

The short story "The Cook" contains enough raw material for Shen to dish out an autophagic tale like Lu Xun's "Medicine." The gallbladder, for example, migrates into this story as medicine to ease heartache, a clue to the big question mark posed around the ripped belly. But the author blends this and other macabre anecdotes into a poetic narrative that revolves around a number of images and leitmotivs prevalent in his writings such as uninhibited primitive sexuality, the persistent pursuit of romance in its most earthy but truthful way, prostitution, and suicide—all to be eventually recast in the theme of basic human decency and honesty. What is most remarkable is its framed storytelling. Instead of cooking a meal for the host and his guest as originally arranged, the cook tells the framed story to "feed" them. Rather than consuming the dinner to which he was invited, the guest, the I-narrator of the framing narrative, ends up having a mouthful of words and hosting his host and hostess by taking them out for a late supper. Through multiple role switching and narrative doubling, Shen has composed a delicious verbal dainty out of incredible ingredients.

The story consists of three sections, with the first and the third set in the present and narrated by the guest and the second told by a third-person narrator about the cook and his lover. The protagonist, a young bachelor named Daoqing, has just left the military and is working as a cook for a college professor, a scientist as strict with his students as he is particular about his family chef. In the past six months alone, he has fired three cooks all because he suspected them of stealing the family's food and cooking utensils. Daoqing is hired as a compromise, not because of his professional savvy but for his unpretentious looks and manner. On the first day of his employment, the host invites his friend, a colleague, to test the new cook's skill, adding that the retired soldier might be able to make braised dog meat, apparently the guest's (and surely the author's) favorite dish. The cook's failure to prepare the dinner ruins the occasion, and after he finally shows up it turns out that he failed to perform his duty because of a young prostitute named Er Yuan or "Doubly Sturdy."

The second section could well stand alone as a perfectly self-contained tale. Located in a brothel, the squalid milieu sets off the decorum of the modern gentry. The style is also markedly different from the framing narrative, seasoning an otherwise tragic romance with calculated crudeness and vulgarity. Er Yuan is characterized as "a creature made of rough materials," "able to thrive on whatever nutrients are available to her." While possessing "an innocent heart that will never fade no matter how dirty a business she has to deal with every night," she is "as strong as a mare and energetic as a boar, carefree as the routine of life passes and shamelessly lustful when indulging in sex" (4:243). Reconfigured with opposite genders (i.e., the mare and the boar), this image cancels out the conventional mores that equate selling one's flesh to losing one's soul. The celebration of vital life force even subverts the political posture in the post–Lu Xun literature of social realism, which tends to dramatize the misery of the prostitute as a means of underscoring the theme of class oppression. Shen seems to suggest that the prostitute is not just a sexual object by trade but a courageous creature grown out of harsh economic necessity who stands for the unabated libido of survival in times of historical catastrophe. But he cautiously refrains from spinning her too far into a fetishized ideal symbol of folk vitality. To avoid the closure by objectification and narcissism characteristic of melodrama, Shen crafts a particular rhetoric of "heart" that "circulates" the blood of bodily sensuality and, through rhetorical circularity, collapses the sanctified mode of hierarchic embodiment.

Daoqing, the narrator of the framed story, has been courting Er Yuan for quite a while but is frustrated by his inability to win her heart. On his way to the market that afternoon, he dropped in to continue his pursuit. While Daoqing is waiting for Er Yuan's return, the madam, a woman in her seventies, asks the former soldier why he never brings her the human gallbladders she has repetitively requested to alleviate the pains of her heart disease. Although a bear's gallbladder is more effective, the human organ is a "cheaper" substitute she can afford. Since only the military has access to freshly executed bodies, and only the executioners have the guts to dig out that sort of stuff, she has to depend on his provision. But the young man does not believe in the alleged medicinal function of human gallbladders and has no intention of using his connections to procure any. Furthermore, his own heartache needs treatment, too, as he jokingly tells the madam "the only good cure that I know is Er Yuan" (4:246). The dilemma he faces is an economic tradeoff. In order to access Er Yuan's body and win her heart, he must buy the madam's permission by providing her with human gallbladders. Since he is unwilling to trade on that economic level, the only deal he proposes is, as he tells the old woman, "you want gallbladder, Er Yuan wants heart, so here you are: Let Er Yuan kill me. You can take my gallbladder, she may have my heart" (4:245).

The question remains whether Er Yuan wants to take his heart. It turns out that Er Yuan chooses to stay in prostitution because she is afraid that her departure would mean the end of the old woman. The old woman worked her entire young life as a prostitute herself and is left with nothing but a broken heart and a "shriveled body—withered almost to the point of vanishing from sight." An early portrait of her as a "dying bitch, tucked in a huge wooden chair, eyes closed and motionless" (4:244–45) suddenly emerges in a new light. The metaphoric contrast between the "dying bitch" and the "strong mare" can no longer hold the familiar moral and political dichotomies inscribed between the malicious, oppressive madam and the innocent, exploited prostitute, as such a metaphoric polarity is displaced into a metonymic chain that joins the two otherwise opposed hearts. In place of the conventional moral contrast is the circularity of the heart, a compassionate heart revealed in the most poignant moment, when Er Yuan sees her own bleak future in the image of the madam's shriveled body and yet is unwilling to abandon her.

Shen Congwen, however, insists on the surface rhetoric of the heart by refusing to endorse any particular brand of humanitarian love and compassion. As a matter of fact, Er Yuan's intention to stay in her dirty business for the sake of the old woman is not pronounced in the narrative, and the reader can only infer it from the casual remarks she makes. Nor is her compassionate heart figured as the noble prostitute or loyal concubine in the traditional shrine of women's heroic self-sacrifice for men.

She is simply not educated enough to behave that way, and the cook is by no means a sentimental prince or scholar. And their romance falls short of tragic closure at the very moment death looms large.

The framed story ends with Er Yuan singing "Oh, the Miserable Whore a Poppy Flower" (*Tan yanhua*). She has just learned that another woman has swallowed opium to kill herself, making that four suicides committed in the same alley of brothels in the past week. *Yanhua* (poppy flowers), a poetic euphemism for "female prostitutes," can also mean "fireworks," which explode in darkness with a flashing display of colorful light. As the woman swallows the crystallized substance of the poisonous but beautiful flowers, she "swallows" herself to complete a fleeting life cycle from orality to orality, turning her own body into a floral display of the evil world. Yet at the point the metanarrative of history would appropriate death into its overarching shadow, Shen closes his eyes to put the "flesh" into the mouth, this time by re-membering the devoured body in the poignant melody Er Yuan sings. The tears that well up in her eyes flash like the same tears the author found himself shedding and swallowing.

In poetic fashion, the framed story ends without even hinting the outcome of the romance other than associating it with the implied fate of all *yanhua*. What we do learn, in the last short section, is that the cook stays with his lover until she stops weeping. When the guest takes the host and hostess to a nearby restaurant, he suggests to his embarrassed colleague: "You should keep him [the cook] because he did not lie. As for me, I just want to say that I was completely satisfied with this cook" (4:255). He is as satisfied as if he did have his stomach filled with fine food. Given that the I-narrator is a college professor and the cook a retired soldier, the author seems to suggest that he is pleased with his own verbal cooking, one that insists on truth and authenticity but nonetheless foregrounds its construction through the double-tongued narrative. Considering also the example of "Gentleman Songzi," the narrative double of eating and speech cuts both ways. If fabrication feeds on an excessive appetite for seduction and deception, honest storytelling can assimilate material lack to a heart of abundant love and compassion.

The truth is that love and compassion cannot be articulated in excess of the material condition of the body at a time when the very articulation of love and compassion for the downtrodden is already inscribed in the excessive discourse of the head. What Shen Congwen achieves in the story is a phantasmagorical reconfiguration of the bits and pieces of the body without assuming a preestablished model of totality. Reconfigured with the multifaceted "heart"—diseased and broken yet loving and compassionate—are otherwise grossly incompatible figures: "recyclable" human organs, conflicting animal images, disease and vitality, poisonous drugs and colorful flowers, self-eating and oral re-membering, the cook and the storyteller, and the listener and the narrator. One has to have a gallbladder to mouth such a feast, digest all these ingredients, and blend them in a text about the "cook."

When he could have written a chilling story of flesh eating, like Lu Xun's "Medicine," Shen Congwen turned his eyes inward to the heart. Where no real cannibalism was involved, he would curiously invent one. The story "Three Men and a Woman" details such horrors as decapitation, the exposure and harassment of human corpses, madness, suicide, and necrophilia—anything but the actual eating of flesh. Yet the rhetoric of cannibalism permeates the narrative and culminates in the suicide victim's coffin, the lid removed, the dead body gone—"an empty wooden box with its wide open mouth poised to eat humans" (6:47).[6] It must be noted that although alimentary motifs in Shen's works range from the most gastronomic to the most grisly forms he rarely recycles the term *chiren*, perhaps an overbaked cliché to him. When he does deploy that archetypal metaphor, the human order also goes mad. But the author denies us any path out of language into faith, as though he wanted to test the ultimate limit of how much we could stomach at the edge of total breakdown. By framing the story in a reflective, melancholic mood for "self-entertainment," he turns madness itself into a poetic food for sober thought.

David Wang has identified in the text a "lyrical project," which parallels "the tedium of army life and the sheer irrationality of war" with "the uncanny romance" and "links [these] two irrelevant worlds together, letting them form a new pattern in which war is defined by bizarre romance, and gothic horror is counterpointed to military boredom." We follow the soldiers in their intrusion "into a benign, pastoral world-in-text which finally refuses our further advances" (1992, 223). What motivates the outsiders' intrusion can be described as an oral-sexual lust to capture what is "inside." When the "inside" is emptied, as in the coffin, the outsiders become suspended at its wide-open mouth where the inside and the outside merge. Given all his nostalgia for the warmth of the homeland and the "oral stage," Shen shows in the story a sober understanding of how easily the seduction of the "motherly" can slip into the nightmare of destroying her for repossession.

On the day the troops move into the village, two well-bred, plump dogs catch the attention of the narrator and a crippled bugler and "spark [their] imaginations." "Wherever we go," the narrator explains, "the sight of a fat dog would usually call forth murderous impulses most difficult for us to suppress." The urge to kill and eat the dogs is quickly subdued when they hear the calling of a young woman, the dogs' owner. The initial encounter with the objects of their gastronomic and sexual fantasies leads to the central stage in the village bean curd shop, where the two soldiers compete with each other and with the young shop proprietor to gain the favor of the girl, who resides across the street. In his comment on their lust, the narrator's allusion to a popular saying serves as the central organizing trope of the story: "The ugly toad wishes to eat the *rou* (flesh/meat) of the swan" (6:32).

If bean curd implies the familiar metaphor for the spotlessly white, soft, and smooth body of the belle, the narrator takes one more step to firmly clinch the rhetorical configuration of eating and sex, describing the "swan" as a "handsome creature" who echoes her well-fed dogs (6:32). This "handsome creature" further brings into sharp relief other animal images, such as the sow and water buffalo, used to depict crude peasant women (6:35). The cross-reference between eating and sex consequently sets the desirer and the desired in circular and exchangeable positions. In order to approach the dogs, the two soldiers squeeze their thin pockets to feed them. Once they have to face the hopeless reality that the daughter of the chairman of the local chamber of commerce is definitely beyond their reach because of their lowly status, the two soldiers get drunk in despair, denigrating themselves as "pigs," "dogs," and "filthy, ugly toads."

The soldiers' fantasy about the "swan" semantically reciprocates as its opposite the infernal condition in which they are existentially enmeshed. In addition to their daily spectatorship at the bean curd shop, there is a weekly execution of "bandits" staged in the village square. The two soldiers challenge their rival, the bean curd maker, to see if he has the guts to watch the public beheading. "When we arrived at the blood-stained ground," the narrator says, "there were four bodies, all naked to the waist, just like four dead pigs sprawling in the dirt. A few little soldiers in their oversized uniforms, with utterly mischievous looks, were poking bamboo sticks at the holes of the severed throats of the dead. A pack of hungry dogs had gathered around, sitting on their haunches and fascinated with this strange scene" (6:36).

The nightmarish spectacle in the daytime corresponds to the abject plight of these professional killers. In their drunkenness, the narrator asks himself and his crippled buddy: "Who are we anyway? Four dollars a month and look what we get: wading in mud when we pull out; drills and roll-calls when we settle down; sleeping on straw pads at night to let bedbugs suck our blood. Our mouths're meant only for tough old horsemeat and sour greens, and our hands only for cold rifle barrels. . . . We're dogs and pigs, all lined up in formation" (6:37). From the swan to the ugly toad, from the well-bred dogs feeding the murderous impulse to the starving dogs lurking to devour the corpses, and from the bloody murderers to the blood-sucking bedbugs there emerges a phantasmagoric world with its own mouth wide open, ready to devour whatever is available to appease its insatiable appetite. This is such an autophagic world that it is no longer clear who is coveting whom. Even the least contaminated "swan" would "swallow" herself to death as she swallows gold to kill herself, an older method of suicide, especially for ancient female beauties, than the swallowing of opium. Yet giving no clear explanation for her tragic suicide the text blocks an otherwise sensational development of the drama and thereby opens up another lyrical scene at the craziest moment.

For her two secret admirers, the young woman's death is like the "breaking of a flower pot," tragic because they feel that their lives, too, have been "dashed to pieces." At the same time, they find themselves "feeling somehow released," since it is better for her to die a clean death than fall into dirty hands (6:42). The author, however, is not interested in adding just another portrait of female martyrdom to the millennial altar of divine chastity. If the previous effort is to cast the narrative in the overwhelming shadow of symbolic cannibalism, Shen Congwen seems to want to pursue a bleaker followup to Lu Xun's Madman, retaining him in the language of madness. After the burial of the young woman, the crippled bugler makes two nightly trips to her tomb. When he has just returned from the second visit, he tells the narrator that he saw a robbed grave. At the very crazy idea of what the bugler intended to do at her grave, the narrator "jumped up like a perfect madman," shouting: "What's on your mind? You—beast!" (6:46). Yet at the moment the story is spilling its madness into a Lu Xunian outcry the narrative takes another turn, as the bugler cooly offers an explanation. He visited her grave the first night in case she might be still alive and crying for help—an act perhaps more delirious than crazy. He went the second night to dig her up after he learned about the folk belief that a woman who killed herself by swallowing gold might come back to life in the arms of a man within seven days. Coincidentally or not, her tomb is also described as a *mantou*, or "steamed roll," as in Lu Xun's "Medicine," before it is robbed and turned into "a wide-open mouth poised to eat humans." Attempting to sort out who "ate" this *mantou* and what had become of her body, the narrator finally accepts the bugler's explanation. "If I hadn't expressed my trust in him," says the narrator, "he could easily have gone mad and strangled me right there." As the narrator puts it: "Either I was going mad, or he [the bugler] must be" (6:46–47).

If the text deliberately shifts the focus away from the woman's story of a plausible tragic romance so as to keep her suicide a mystery, it also suspends the two soldiers' story of gothic mystery in order to explore the depths of madness. When what eats and what is eaten become infinitively reversible, madness becomes contagious as well, figuring the crazy world in its sober state of self-eating. Such a reversibility generates an epistemological aporia as to what defines madness and threatens to shatter the moral foundation of what constitutes the human. While the narrator's outcry "You—beast!" does reveal a conscious, moral rage, the ambivalent discourse of madness nevertheless lures us to take a dazzling glimpse at what lies beyond. From this point on, any hermeneutic search for truth and reality is halted and legend and magic take over. The key to understanding the narrative probing into madness, then, must be located in what actually lies beyond the grave.

In the diegetic world of the story, neither the culprit nor the woman's body ever shows up after her death. In fact, the young bean curd maker never speaks but puts on a smiling face before his own mysterious disappearance. The author implies that the woman loved this young man, a hopeless situation because of their class differences. Her despair may have led her to commit suicide. For the quiet young man, however, their romance must continue after her death. What we have learned are only bits and pieces of rumors spread in the village. "A bit of the news said:

'Somebody found the girl's body in a cave. . . . She lay completely naked on a stone ledge. Wild blue chrysanthemums were scattered all over her body and on the ground.' " This, the narrator comments, reveals how "human ignorance embroidered these news items, turning the obscene into the fantastic" (6:48). His judgment of human ignorance notwithstanding, the point where the obscene is turned into the fantastic marks the borderline where moral consciousness ceases its advance and the "beyond" world-in-text takes over.

Here we must take a detour to examine how this bizarre anecdote of necrophilia is circulated in Shen's other stories. Two autobiographical accounts introduce the same bean curd maker and illustrate Shen's impression of him. As depicted in his *Autobiography* (1934), Shen Congwen talked with the young man and witnessed his execution. There we learn that the young woman in fact died of an illness. The bean curd vendor dug up her body and stayed with the corpse in a mountain cave for three days before he carried it back to the grave, where he was caught. Now facing imminent death, he looks alarmingly calm, even telling the author how he almost fell into the coffin. To Shen's question about why he should have done that crazy thing, he returns a quiet smile, "as if I [the author] were a little kid who had no idea about love," and then murmured to himself "beautiful, beautiful." When a fellow soldier in Shen's troop dubs him a "crazy man," the necrophiliac dismisses this with another quiet smile "as though he were saying 'who knows who is crazy.' " His smile, Shen admits, "has maintained a clear impression in my memory for more than ten years" (9:160–61). In contrast to the reserved voice in the *Autobiography*, a more nostalgic mood emerges in *Western Hunan* (1938). Taking the bean curd vendor's act as reflecting the "crazy and bizarre passions" of his magical homeland, the author feels sad that such passions have vanished in the past decades (9:389). Nostalgia thus intersects a "voodoo" country of poetic fantasy.

The image of the cave decorated with wildflowers resurfaces in a number of stories and is reinvested with unrestrained ecstasy. In "The Doctor," an erotic thriller and gothic romance, a crazy young man abducts a doctor to a mountain cave to save the life of a young woman dead for two days already. The abductor is so lunatic that, after the doctor has told him that the woman is dead, he insists: "I ask you to save her just because she is dead!" (4:191). The "beautiful peach blossoms" he has gathered for the woman resonate with her "peaceful and serene countenance that looks like someone in sound repose" (4:195). The mountain cave, far removed from the world and decorated with flowers, is a recurrent image in some of Shen's most fantastic stories. There the last "noble savages" of the Miao people passed the last Rite of Spring through communal chanting and commensal feasting before they were massacred by invading government troops in "Seven Barbarians and the Last Rite of Spring" (1929). There, a young Miao couple immortalize their carnal and spiritual union by choosing to kill themselves in "Meijin, Baozi, and the White Kid" (1929). Slightly changed to an ancient castle on a mountaintop in "Under Moonlight" (1932), a Miao prince and a beautiful girl, forbidden by local custom to marry, turn their first night of marriage into a passage to eternity when "they happily swallow poison pills, lie amid withered wildflowers on a stone ledge, and wait with smile for the arrival of death" (5:57). Since these three pieces are either based on the folklore of the Miao people or adapted from popular Buddhist legend, the enclosed space of the cave or the castle marks the point at which the outside world ends with its contingency of flesh and the inside begins its open and open-ended search for eternity.

The dreamland in the cave and its motif of fantastic romance recall the "mountain ghost" in the namesake story, written as early as 1927. Because the title is borrowed from the ancient Chu poet Qu Yuan, the story reveals the intended connection of madness to a mythical tradition of poetic ecstasy, thus crystallizing the intertextual meaning of all the cave scenes. A talented folksinger and storyteller, the mountain ghost is the recognized "king of children" in the village. A skillful farmhand, he nevertheless would walk ten miles to view the peach blossoms in another village. As a member of the ethnic Miao people (known as the Hmong overseas), like many of Shen's characters, he exists on the margin of the Middle Kingdom. In mythological times, the Miao people were chased into the mountains of southwestern China and never benefited much from the civilizing order. The protagonist became insane after he was wrongly accused of abetting bandits and threatened with beheading. The harsh reality is visualized in the mother's fear that he would be forced by some bully to eat dead rats after her death.

The madman's disappearance in the story is deliberately designed to contrast the cannibalistic reality with the idyllic dreamland. The herdsman who discovers him describes the scene in the cave:

When I heard a familiar voice, I gathered I must know this person. If two people were talking, how come I only heard one voice? He said: "Eat it, why don't you eat it. A little bit, look at the yams I have just roasted, just take a little bit please! Let me feed you, mouth-feed you." Then there was a brief pause before he started again, this time singing: "My sweetheart, you are spotlessly white; I am pitch dark. Splash my black ink on your white paper, and see how we match." He laughed a lot, too, enjoyed the hell out of himself! (2:138)

The madman's brother immediately goes to the cave after he hears the boy's story. In the empty cave, some withering wild Chinese roses and a water container taken from his house convince him of the truth. A few days later the mountain ghost shows up quietly, dispirited and thin. Without the desire to talk with his mother, he has no appetite for the chicken she prepared for the gods and brought back from the village shrine for him.

Leaving much to the reader's imagination, Shen nevertheless blends poetic refinement with the most primitive passions of the madman through the double-tongued mode of signification. In the cave, an enthusiastic lover cooks and feeds, sings and laughs; in the real world, the disheartened loner lacks the desire for food or words. Linking the cave in "Mountain Ghost" to other cave scenes, we are asked to take an epiphanic look at the author's own poetic ecstasy and madness, crystallized in the erotic zone of the mouth. As Shen remarks in "Seven Barbarians": "Their [the Miao's] mouths are meant to kiss and chant praising songs of love and nature, not to tell lies like the rest of China does" (8:323).

While "Mountain Ghost" presents the most detailed depiction of ecstatic insanity, it also leaves room for poetic imagination because the cave scene is "blocked" from our voyeurist gaze. But intertextually placed side by side with the other cave scenes and the author's autobiographical accounts the "empty" cave is not empty at all. It is decorated with wildflowers, and the madman has a companion. Who is the "phantom," a mute or perhaps even a corpse? A simple flip of the coin may turn our hermeneutic and moral nightmare around: probably there is no *body* else in the cave; probably it reflects the madman's fantasy, so that desire becomes an intransitive figure, purely linguistic and poetic.

If our detour can only sketch a misty silhouette of the missing body in "Three Men and a Woman," it suggests to me that the body is not "missing" but "displaced." Its intertextual travels from the autobiographical accounts to the fictional writer's imagination delineate a transgression of the boundary between reality and fantasy. Given that those pieces were written at different times, transgression through displacement seems to indicate not so much an intentional act on the part of the author as an effect of his imaginary nostalgia. As such, the displaced body circulates a profound semantic and hermeneutic uncertainty and locates the writer at the intersection of multiple historical sites. History and fiction, remembrance and imagination, are mixed up to such an extent that Shen Congwen is as condemned to staging his psychodrama in his fictional cave as Lu Xun is forced to stage it in his autobiographical spectacle. The difference is that Shen's position on the cultural margin allows what is suppressed in the realm of the symbolic to resurface through a metonymic mode of signification that reconfigures otherwise contradictory signs into lyrical transgressions.

The textual displacement of the body from the coffin to the cave also symbolically shifts the body from the place of biological death to the site of poetic eternity. It reveals how cultural imagination is transcribed into a utopian desire that suspends the contingency of time. "Turning the obscene into the fantastic" thus embroiders the narrative of "Three Men and a Woman" as well, in the sense that the body (as the signifier of the obscene) in the cave is not completely naked but *covered* with wildflowers (the fantastic). At the same time, the cave scene is not enunciated by the narrator but is "quoted" as a rumor, more like an unintended Brechtian *gestus*, which defamiliarizes our aesthetic perception from what governs our ethical conception of the obscene. If the "naked" body lays bare the naked truth of evil, a wreath made of wildflowers is perhaps the only fantastic thing left to decorate the grotesque. Conversely, the wreath may well serve as a garland set at the liminal site where physical death becomes the starting point for a new life in the imagined world. The paradox of a naked body covered with flowers thus captures the ruptured coming-into-one of reality and fantasy, a phantasmagoric tableau frozen in "discordant harmony."

Such an epistemological and ethical aporia threatens to destroy the rhetoric of civilized norms. From the native-soil writer's standpoint, however, the invading forces from outside are the real cannibals. Shen Congwen is unabashedly candid in teasing the intruders. In the eyes of the villagers in the story "Xiao Xiao" (1934), the educated youths from the cities "bite people, like the officials; they only eat simple folk; they munch even the bones and don't spit up the remains" (6:225).[7] For the "ugly toads" in "Three Men and a Woman," their insuppressible lust to "eat" the "swan" transforms an otherwise simple narrative of intransitive desire into a doubly ambiguous narrative of destruction and self-destruction. "Eating" here is shown with its double edge: the desire to incorporate the object can easily slip into the wildest impulse to annihilate it for possession. If the rule is eat or be eaten, no one can escape being swallowed sooner or later. If such is the naked truth of the human condition, only magic can spare us the nightmare of being devoured. Given the author's fascination with the real bean curd maker, Shen Congwen has turned the tables of cannibalism around to see what a crazy food maker would eat. And it turns out that he eats no one and speaks little. It is the "mountain ghost's" lack of appetite in the real world that makes him a romantic poet; it is the ugly toad's cannibalistic lust that nails him to the coffin.

Once the tables are turned, Shen Congwen literally spins a clinical necrophiliac into a romantic, "life-saving" hero. Or is it not our entrenched view of "clinical truth" and the conventional moral code that restrict us into believing that he is truly crazy, failing to see who is crazy and who really understands love? Does his "obscene" obsession not reflect a more "divine" view of what is sacred precisely because he refuses to believe that life ends at death? Although the author as a modern writer may not be prepared to cross the fine line between poetic ecstasy and clinical insanity, his ambivalence about the past makes it impossible for him to separate the obscene from the fantastic, nightmare from dream. Narrative thus becomes the tool with which he can exorcise the demons and relive the beauty at the same time. By the same token, if one pushes the "mountain ghost" just one step further to see how he would act if he were to find himself in the bean curd maker's cave, the borderline between a neurotic poet and a hysterical necrophiliac would collapse under the unbearable lightness of being "mad." It is frightening for readers living in the late twentieth century to even entertain such ideas of civilized taboos. But the return of the uncanny in such beautiful forms holds us in awe of the magic of imagination unleashed at a time of devastating historical catastrophes.

Shen knows that what is real can become unreal once you change the telling of it. At the end of "Three Men and a Woman," the I-narrator remains uncertain as to whether his audience is convinced of the truth of the story, which is perhaps too bizarre to be real. In his characteristic confessional mood, he finishes up the story in this way: "What do I think [of the horrible incident]? I have become somehow melancholic. . . . I always feel disturbed, as the past often comes back to haunt me. Some things keep gnawing at my heart, but you would think I made them up if I told you. None of you understand how one feels as life drags on under the weight of hundreds of stories like this one" (6:49). The completion of "Three Men and a Woman" is dated August 24, 1930, about the same time that Shen Congwen saw the public beheading described at the beginning of this chapter. Instead of answering the question he raised to himself, he once again looked into his own heart, a heart so lonely and troubled that even he could not describe it—except on the pages of these beautifully written stories, which feed to readers otherwise utterly inedible stuff.

In his preface to Book II of *Alice's Adventures in China*, Shen Congwen made an almost desperate plea that the deeply divided critics and readers not classify him under any political or ideological "-isms." He sets out to explain his philosophy of writing in terms of "self-expression regardless of [political and ideological] doctrines, [the idea of] the epochal, and other theoretical schemes." Neither a revolutionary writer nor a literary opportunist, as some characterized him, he writes that

> my humble self is no good at crying out the Way, as my ill-fated life is always mired in poverty and disease. Awkward yet pedantic when I talk, I simply vent my rage and grief as they arise. It would be a mistake to call me a "comrade" as if I were to use my pen only for combating the upper class; nor would it be necessary to keep a vigilant eye on me as though I were dangerous [to the rulers]. (1:344–45)

In trying to lower his political profile, he makes it clear that his "attack on imperialism and the Chinese gentry was not meant to gain applause from a certain [i.e., the working] class." Since he was ill equipped to do anything practical to help the poor, he says, his "sympathy and empathy with the sufferings of the downtrodden could only be expressed in words" (1:344–45).

Shen Congwen and Lu Xun started with similar views of a Chinese society that was undergoing social disintegration and moral collapse.

Both writers are "neurotic," both for their fixations on repetition and for their repetitions of what is fixed in their memories. The difference is that Shen has always attempted to stay within language, turning it into a faith and exploring various figures and paths to what is ultimately impossible in reality. His own body is sick, voice vacillating, vision divided, and conscience torn. Writing served to heal the self, so words have become food to sustain life. Politically uncommitted and morally not an advocate of self-sacrifice, no wonder he has outlived Lu Xun by five decades and survived in virtual silence all those years of social catastrophe and personal suffering. If Lu Xun's legacy is his moral and political commitment to historical change, history has proven him right because he was a major force in shaping it. As for Shen's minor legacy, only post-Mao literature, especially that of the native-soil writer Mo Yan, remotely echoes it. Between Shen Congwen and Mo Yan runs revolutionary hunger and hungry revolution.

II

Writing Hunger: From Mao to the Dao

This part of the book delineates the hunger narrative in Yan'an literature and the postrevolutionary rewriting of it. Hunger was something the early Lu Xun overlooked because his diagnosis of the social body was directed at the diseased "head" of the nation. It is not that the phenomenon of poverty escaped him; rather, it is his allegorical reading that transformed destitute reality into a symptomatic sign for something beyond the immediate material realm. His visual focus on the "upper body" is an apt illustration of the culturalist tendency of May Fourth literature. On the other hand, it was a more deliberate act on the part of Shen Congwen to treat hunger in a personal and poetic fashion. His "modest proposal" linked social misery to the depleted body and anticipated the rise of a socially committed literature in the 1930s. But Shen Congwen himself backed away as he became more skeptical about the marriage of literary writing and radical social change. The fundamental question about the empty stomach had to be addressed through a revolutionary critique and transformation of the political economy. Literary writing was thus given a mission of engaging and changing material reality in a realistic form thereby determined.

Although some realistic works approached class disparity around the problem of hunger prior to Yan'an literature,[1] the major force behind the rise of revolutionary literature was the need for a Marxist-inspired analysis of, and solution to, the core issue of alienation in an agrarian society: the producers of food deprived of what they produce. As Maoism eventually defeated the urban-centered Stalinist line in the Party, Yan'an literature, aimed at mobilizing the peasants, prevailed over the leftist social realism prominent in the cultural scene of Shanghai—helped of course by the shift of the battleground to the country after the Japanese invasion. It is no surprise that a realistic writer engaged in class analysis may completely ignore hunger. Mao Dun, a leading advocate and practitioner of social realism, exemplifies many leftist urban writers' blindness to a basic needs of the masses. If hunger is absent in his *Midnight* because it is about urban capitalism, the motif is also missing in his stories about rural poverty and the exploitation of the peasantry. The same is true of Ding Ling's representation of Communist land reform in *Sunshine over the San'gan River.* Above all, prolonged hunger is primarily a personal experience that shapes and reflects the individual writer's sensibility. Agrarian focus and realistic form do not by themselves lead to the writing of hunger. As a result, the revolutionary narrative of hunger is always invested with personal desire even when the particular genre—predominantly realistic fiction in this case—is politically oriented.

In light of the tragic ending of the Chinese revolution and the restrictions imposed by officially sanctioned realism upon two generations of Chinese writers, one would be hard put to treat revolutionary literature as anything more than a body of texts for ideological indoctrination if not as merely political propaganda. So I would like to raise a different question, which underscores my approach: how can we negotiate a theoretical space that will problematize the self-serving ideology of the party-state without at the same time erasing the historicity of the revolution and the writing of desire? In a roundabout way, I propose to rethink the aesthetic question. What is foregrounded in the selected readings is a dialectic interplay between the social reality of hunger and a revolutionary desire for its appeasement. This dialectic is exhibited in the tension between the political and aesthetic aspects of hunger. If material lack is the central question in the rebellion, the revolutionary movement is able to mobilize the "masses" because the so-called masses are made up of individuals stranded in poverty and eager to eat their fill. If the Communist-led rebellion can be described as a hungry revolution, the revolutionary masses are motivated by nothing but their revolutionary hunger, physical and symbolic at once. Even in the theoretical discourse of Maoism, the abstract thesis of class struggle is fleshed out with an older rhetoric of the body, which legitimates peasant revolt when the table is not equally shared. Because the interlaced double nature of hunger has undergone an ideological short-circuiting from a political *and* aesthetic complementarity to a political *versus* aesthetic bipolarity, it is my intention to reopen the personal, aesthetic dimension of the revolutionary narrative.

I use the term *aesthetic* very loosely to describe anything that is repressed by or deviates from systematic political domination. This is because politics in Chinese Communism is not simply concerned with power in the broader sense. The Communist Party and the state apparatus have attempted to mold almost every facet of social life with the definite meaning of class struggle. Food consumption in this process has become a political act with a prescriptive ideological meaning. Yet eating is rooted in the experience of the carnal body, and the open-ended desire for fulfillment defies complete closure. The aesthetic of eating not just signifies the feeling and sensation of food but works as a general theory on the civil, psychological, and physiological activities of the body.

While I am aware of the bad name aestheticism has in current critical thinking, there are two reasons for foregrounding the personal-aesthetic aspect of a basically politicized discourse. First, in Western leftist thinking, aestheticism is conceived as fetishizing the text by severing it from the (political) context. Thus, to politicize the text is a resistance to its ideological closure. But when the system speaks the very language of "revolution" and "liberation," the situation requires many Chinese writers to deploy an aesthetic strategy in order to undermine or circumvent ideological restrictions. My second concern has much to do with Western Marxism, whose celebration (in the 1960s and early 1970s) of Chinese Communism has been replaced with a resilient silence since the atrocities in the PRC began to come to light in the late 1970s. In distancing itself from socialism as it is practiced, academic Marxism has yet to fully and seriously address the "Chinese question" beyond simply attributing it to orientalist constructs such as the "Asiatic mode of production" or "oriental despotism."[2] Above all, Chinese Communism was from the very beginning a major part of the *international* movement of anti-imperialism and social revolution. Its tragic ending cannot be explained away as just a *local* problem. Moreover, even the illiterate Chinese peasant eats food with invested human desire, not just out of mere instinctive need. The aesthetic attributes of the hunger narrative are where the eating subject enters into the socioeconomic realm and struggles to maintain a certain personal autonomy at the same time.

In his "Theses on Cultural Marxism" (1983), John Brenkman, among the earliest neo-Marxist writers addressing the problems of state socialism from within the heritage of Marxism itself, rightly locates the tragic absence of "ethical" concerns within Marxism itself. He calls attention to "a Marxist political economy which falls behind Marx's critique of political economy, and has furnished justifications for the abolition of human liberties in 'really existing socialism.'" Brenkman proposes to "revamp the social, psychoanalytic, and aesthetic elements of theory" so that cultural Marxism can face the missing "ethical," which he conceptualizes, via Freud, Lacan, and feminism, in the metaphor of "desire" (22). In light of Brenkman's thesis, the aesthetic of hunger has an ethical underpinning as well.

In chapter 4, a small sample of Yan'an literature is juxtaposed against a historical retrospection by two veteran revolutionary writers. I do not include works of "local color" such as those by Zhao Shuli and Ma Feng, two representative writers of the "school of potatoes" (*shanyaodanpai*) who have enjoyed vast popularity among northern peasants. Their folksy overture is less characteristic of the politicized discourse of hunger and merits a separate study. Nor do I cover the more canonical works by Zhou Libo and Ding Ling because their writings are either insignificant to the topic or simply do not treat eating in any meaningful way. I leave out all works published in the Mao era of the PRC since these are by and large replicas of the established Maoist model, with only minor thematic and stylistic variations. Instead, the section on revolutionary literature is followed by readings of two texts written by veteran revolutionary writers in the post-Mao period: Wang Ruowang's *Hunger Trilogy* (1980) and Lu Wenfu's "The Gourmet" (1983). Both texts attempt to reevaluate the revolution from a historical perspective. Their treatments of hunger are remarkably similar to early moments of Yan'an literature while their rethinking is located in the tragic end of the revolution.

Chapter 5 focuses on two novellas: Zhang Xianliang's "Mimosa" (1984) and Ah Cheng's "The Chess King" (1984). Although published only shortly after *Hunger Trilogy* and "The Gourmet," the authors address the problem of hunger from the viewpoints of those who did not participate in the Communist revolution. The term *postrevolutionary* is used to characterize the subject matter and the writers' positions, the former an issue concerning historical periodization and the latter a matter of narrative consciousness. Both writers have managed to bypass the revolutionary narrative by problematizing their own reading and writing. Food and words are once again entangled on the level of representation when their thematic incorporation of classical Marxism (in Zhang) or the Dao (in Ah Cheng) opens other possibilities for interpreting the meaning of hunger. This detour of revolutionary history outlines a contour of postrevolutionary cultural reconstruction in the 1980s. Paradoxically, the texts on material lack have provided some symbolic food for the ongoing rebuilding of the national body. Hunger thus comes to its own "consciousness" in the *writing* of desire.

4. Hungry Revolution and Revolutionary Hunger

Yan'an Literature: *Hungry Revolution*

The Chinese Communist revolution was inspired by Marxism while it also sinicized that nineteenth-century European theory. What actually happened in their mutually transformative encounter? Arif Dirlik has noted that the "predicament of Marxist revolutionary consciousness" involves "the difficulties in reconciling the universalistic premises of Marxism with the particular circumstances and needs of the Chinese Revolution" (1983, 183). Between theory and practice, then, is the crucial issue of assimilating the abstract and the "universal" to the concrete and the particular. This mode of theoretical adaptation can be read as a story about the Chinese eating of Marxism, embodied in Mao's own alimentary metaphors. In "On New Democracy" (1940), Mao argues:

> To nourish her own culture, China needs to assimilate a good deal of progressive foreign culture as resources of her cultural food (*wenhua shiliang*). . . . However, we should not gulp any of this material down uncritically, but must treat it as we do our food—first chewing it, then submitting it to the working of the stomach and intestines with juices and secretions, and separating it into nutriment to be absorbed and waste matter to be discarded—before it can nourish us. (2:700; cf. 2:380)[1]

Mao's theoretical alimentation provides a discursive model for epistemological and political incorporation of things foreign and abstract. In practice, one of the conditions for assimilating Marxism was that the Chinese masses—mostly illiterate peasants—not only could not understand the sophisticated *Das Kapital* but did not have much to eat. The task for Mao and his fellow Communist intellectuals was to feed Marxist nourishment to the hungry masses in a language easy for them to digest so that they could rise up to fill their own stomachs through revolution. In contrast to the speculative mode of the German philosophical tradition in Marx, Mao's early theoretical work was written in a style that a peasant with basic literacy could understand. In Mao's "Analysis of Class in Chinese Society" (1926), social disparity is often defined in terms of unequal food distribution. He describes the "petty bourgeoisie" as having "surplus money or grain." They "invariably desire to climb up into the middle bourgeoisie." Mao ridicules the snobbish petty bourgeoisie like this: "[T]heir mouths water copiously when they see the respect in which those small moneybags are held." As for the "semiproletariat," their hardship is measured by how long their earnings can keep them from hunger (1:5–7; 1:15–16).

The class analysis thus narrated, the struggle of the have-nots inevitably began with their attempts to "eat the rich." In his "Report on an Investigation of the Peasant Movement in Hunan" (1927), Mao presents "fourteen great achievements" of the movement. One of these is "hitting the landlords politically." The peasants did that in their "major demonstrations" in which they "eat at the offender's [the landlord's] house, slaughtering his pigs and consuming his grain as a matter of course." This kind of major demonstration, reported Mao with great enthusiasm, is represented by an event in his home county. There "a crowd of fifteen thousand peasants went to the houses of six of the evil gentry and demonstrated; the whole affair lasted four days during which more than 130 pigs were killed and eaten" (1:26; 1:37). Eating the rich is, then, an action that "hits them politically." Another achievement is "overthrowing the clan authority of the ancestral temples and clan elders, the religious authority of town village gods, and the masculine authority of husbands." These authorities are overthrown where the "old rule barring women and poor people from banquets in the ancestral temples has also been broken." Mao reports an event in which a group of peasant women "gathered in force and swarmed into their ancestral temple, firmly planted their backsides in the seats and joined in the eating and drinking, while the venerable clan bigwigs had willy-nilly to let them do as they pleased" (1:33; 1:44–45). The politics of eating and the populist mood of Mao's "report" aptly transplant the new concept of "class struggle" into Chinese soil, assimilating it into the millennial narrative of peasant rebellion best represented in the *Water Margin*, which fascinated Mao from his childhood to his last years. Written before the 1927 Nationalist-Communist split, Mao's work already anticipated the inevitable course the Communist revolution was to chart.

In the formative years of Yan'an literature, Mao called upon writers and artists to create a new literature and art to serve the people. A vast number of works produced in this period revolve around hunger and its revolutionary fulfillment, a corpus of *jingshen shiliang* (spiritual food) to nurture the hungry peasants and soldiers. The term *spiritual food*, which echoes Mao's *cultural food*, appeared in Communist publications at least as early as 1940.[2] The French-educated poet and painter Ai Qing advocates that, because "the working class is the creator of culture," "one of the goals for revolution is to re-appropriate culture from the privileged class and return it to its owner." This must be carried out by "integrating poetry into the ordinary people's life as the bank and the kitchen are to their life," and by "opening the palace of knowledge as if to open the granary."[3]

The analogy between knowledge and nutrition is nothing new in the Confucian tradition, which treasures the book. But the revolutionary theme of blending words with food is opposite to the ideal of harmony. Contained in the old bottle is now a new wine of revolutionary teleology from the old human-eating society to an egalitarian socialist feast. In poetry, Li Ji's "Wang Gui and Li Xiangxiang" (1946), the most celebrated long narrative poem, describes the fate of two young lovers in a narrative trilogy (from hunger via revolution to liberation) that fulfills their hunger for food and love. The telos of liberation owes its tantalizing appeal to the concrete structure of a Communist communion of sort. The following poem is quite typical of such a tale. At a local pub, the narrator relates his hungry journey: "Hunger, because of hunger, / I traveled hither and thither; / In the end, I came to the Soviet [Yan'an], / Where I don't worry about my next meal anymore." The audience then urges him to drink more: "Have one more cup, / for we are now Soviet brothers."[4]

In theater, the popular folk opera *Baimaonü* (White-haired girl, 1945) dramatizes the politics of eating as the core of the Communist rebellion. On New Year's Eve, the time for Chinese families to get together and make *jiaozi* (meat- and vegetable-stuffed dumplings), the poor peasant Yang Bailao stayed away from home to avoid paying a debt owed to the usurious landlord Huang Shiren, a loan he contracted to pay for his wife's burial. He returned home late in the evening only to find himself in the impossible position of repaying his debt by giving up his only daughter, Xi'er, as a slave housemaid to the Huangs since he could not come up with enough cash. Heartbroken, he killed himself by drinking a pot of bittern he had bought to make tofu as a meat substitute for the New Year's celebration. Shortly before this, Da Chun, Xi'er's lover, had brought her with a bag of flour to make *jiaozi*. When he returned later, the father was dead and the daughter had been abducted to the landlord's house. Urged by an underground Communist, Da Chun and some other young villagers left home to join the Communist troops. Later Xi'er managed to flee the Huangs' after she was repeatedly bullied and humiliated by Huang and his mother. She spent several years in the wilderness, becoming a white-haired "wild woman." At the end of the play, Da Chun, now an officer in the Communist army, ran into the white-haired Xi'er and brought her back to their now liberated home village. The play draws to its happy ending when the newly liberated Xi'er regains human dignity and becomes a revolutionary soldier.

It is significant that in this popular melodrama Yang Bailao drinks bittern to kill himself rather than utilizing more popular suicidal methods in Chinese society such as drowning or hanging. Considering that what he drinks is something to be used for making a special food for the New Year, an occasion symbolic of rebirth, such suicidal ingestion most intensely dramatizes social struggles around orality. Yet this suicide episode was to be altered some twenty years later in the ballet version, wherein Yang, instead of killing himself, fights the bully Huang and is beaten to death. In killing *himself*, the image of the poor peasant fails to represent the class consciousness of the oppressed and falls short of enhancing their revolutionary spirit. Such a change erases a powerful act directly ingrained in oral experience. In any event, the play's popularity is inseparable from its powerful appeal to its intended audience—peasants and peasants turned soldiers—and their basic needs and concerns.[5]

In fiction, Wang Ruowang's short story "Lüzhanzhang" (Director Lü, 1946) describes the hungry revolution in a schematic way.[6] Since I will examine Wang's *Hunger Trilogy* in some detail later, it is important to note that his later work can be traced to his early awareness of the importance of food. Even in his *Autobiography* (1991b), published four years after he was expelled from the Communist Party for his liberal influence upon the 1986 student movement, Wang repeatedly recalls the terrible hunger and starvation that he witnessed and experienced in the old China.

"Lüzhanzhang" is named after its protagonist. Lü was the director of a grain purveyance center in the Eighth Army's logistical branch. He was responsible for the timely and orderly supply of food to the frontline troops. One day his staff caught a thirteen-year-old youth stealing some seven pounds of grain and handed the boy to Lü. The poor lad, instead of being beaten as he expected, saw a smiling face asking him why he stole. After listening to the boy telling him the obvious reason, Lü let him off with the grain and told him not to steal again since the food was meant to feed the army, which was fighting for the poor. This, however, created a conflict of sort: his administrative duty was to safeguard the food supply for the troops rather than distribute it among the poor. But as an officer in the liberating force he also felt the moral and political obligation to help them, especially when he saw every day at the gate of the purveyance center poorly nourished peasants turning in their tax grain to help support the troops. Underlining his political consciousness was his personal story. Lü helped the boy because his own child had earlier died of hunger and because his wife had begged for food in the streets to feed his sick mother after he left home to join the army. He came to know this only after he returned to his newly liberated hometown and saw the soldiers there handing out emergency food and mobilizing the peasants for land reform.

Lü thus decided to solve the apparent conflict of interest between his moral obligation and his administrative responsibility by enlarging the range of the latter to meet the former. He first requested that emergency grain be distributed among the most needy and, in doing so, used it to mobilize local peasants. Because this region had just been freed from Japanese occupation, the peasants still had some doubts about his motivation. At the first meeting where Lü announced his plan for the emergency food distribution, an old peasant named Li Yihe expressed his distrust: "Food from the authorities won't agree with the stomachs of the poor. You feed chickens to get eggs." But their suspicion was soon alleviated by the mother of the boy Lü had helped. Only three days after the first meeting, Li Yihe became an organizer for the food distribution and educated other villagers, saying: "Remember what the Communist Party has given us while holding your bowls in hand. At my advanced age, I have never seen such a benevolent government and army." Lü further turned the occasion into an arena for political agitation, telling the villagers that the long-term goal of revolution is that "everyone can eat one's fill and has a plot of land of one's own." His words were "like a sunbeam penetrating into a dark room, shining upon the minds of the audience" (393–95).

In this way, the food that feeds the hungry becomes a powerful symbol to awaken and enhance the class consciousness of the peasants. Once assured of the sincerity of the new authority, the peasants were organized under Lü's leadership and set out to confiscate property from local bullies and collaborators of the old regime. But the path of land reform was not straight, and they met strong resistance at a village where peasants were still intimidated by the lingering shadow of the past. Again Lü used food as a political symbol. He grabbed from an old peasant a "dark pancake" made up of grass seeds and mashed yam vine, urging his audience to stand up and fight the landlords so that they would never again have to eat that kind of food. At the end of the story, because of his achievements outside his administrative duties, Lü was transferred from the army to the local civilian government and given charge of a whole district. To celebrate their newly established government and welcome Lü to his new office, local folks staged two plays. One play's title is: "Who Feeds Whom?"

"Who feeds whom?" is the central problem the Communist revolution has to address, and Wang's story offers a cogent footnote to this question. Along the sociological chain from production to distribution to consumption, Marx locates the class struggle in the realm of production, particularly in the relations of production. But to translate his abstract, theoretical category and concept (what are "relations of production" in the Chinese context anyway?) into concrete and tangible terms, Chinese Communists must mobilize the peasantry by playing on the most obvious disparity in consumption. This is where Wang's story begins: with the boy's stealing of food. When the lack of food for certain groups is contrasted with other groups' surplus, the problem of consumption in turn brings distribution to the focal point. Although Lü's job is supplying food to the troops, his role, as he actually plays it, is a metaphor for the ultimate goal of the whole revolution: (re)distribution of wealth. Lü's overstepping of his narrowly defined administrative function is not only justified but is eventually honored as a model by the higher authority and leads to his promotion. This enlarges his role as a distributor and metaphorizes his function in the overall social scope. Once social conflicts are laid bare in terms of distribution, revolution becomes a viable means for redistribution and results in a wide array of struggles to change the relations of production. It is another issue whether or not the revolution has solved these problems and succeeded in producing a socialist feast. It is important to note at this point that consumption is where the personal and the political are ineluctably intertwined in shaping the narrative of the hungry revolution.

"Who feeds whom?" is also a pivotal question the revolutionary culture must address. Lü's use of food for political agitation exactly corresponds to the way Mao defines the political function of literature and art. The notion of revolutionary culture means two things in Mao's works written in this period: (1) culture for revolution and (2) revolution of culture. The former defines the political mission of revolutionary culture in propagating Communist ideas; the latter addresses the modes of artistic representation by which revolutionary culture achieves its goals. If Lü as a character transforms food into a powerful political symbol that directly appeals to the peasants, this is achieved by the author's effort to reach out to the peasants through a theme and language familiar to their own experience.

This is precisely what the earlier Lu Xun was unable to do and the later, revolutionary Lu Xun repeatedly called for: a national and mass literature and art. In this process, writers and artists can no longer stand as critical outsiders, as the earlier Lu Xun did, but must participate in the revolution and "feed" the masses with positive "spiritual food" by way of absorbing and assimilating raw materials and artistic forms from the masses. This relationship of mutual "feeding" or nurturing between the material producer and the cultural producer is one reason that the literature and art of the Yan'an period have had such a political impact on the population. Mao himself has repeatedly emphasized that the two most powerful weapons for the Communist victory are *qiangganzi* (the barrel of a gun, standing for armed struggles) and *biganzi* (the shaft of a pen, which signifies cultural and ideological struggles). In brief, the Communist revolution is a hungry revolution, and revolutionary literature and art have both reflected and nurtured the peasants' revolutionary hunger.

Chairman Mao: God or Food?

In "Director Lü," when the old peasant Li Yihe reminds others that it is the Communist Party that has liberated them from hunger, his gratitude reflects a general cultural attitude. The story contains an anecdote most illuminating in this regard. After the liberation of a village, "Director Lü is said to be a living god" and is believed to have kept in his granary "some magic weapons that can expose the true evil nature of the bullies and Japanese collaborators." This leads many peasants to further stretch their imaginations: "If a [mere] director is so nice to us folks, how benevolent the Chairman must be!" (401).

Even though Mao was yet to become a full-fledged living god, his deification began as early as the Yan'an period, and Wang's story was not a rare case. He Jingzhi, one of the coauthors of *The White-Haired Girl*, wrote a poem entitled "Taiyang zai xintou" (The sun shines in our hearts, 1941),[7] equating Mao with the sun. The image of Mao as the sun was probably first created in the folksong "The East Is Red," which was to reach its apogee during the Cultural Revolution. What makes He's poem remarkable here is that he casts Mao directly from the image repository of the ancestral god Yandi.

The poem describes a peasant named Zhang San retiring from farming in the early evening. While on his way home with his ox he watches the sun setting and "another sun swells up in his heart." He reflects on his liberation and the bumper harvest awaiting him, asking himself why he is so fortunate. Not the gods, nor Heaven, but Mao has made all this real: "Chairman Mao is even warmer than the sun / He shines still longer. / Zhang San tears down the clay Buddha; / Into fire he throws the Kitchen God!" The poem ends with a set of images typical of this genre of liberation literature: the ox moos, Zhang sings a folksong, stars smile in the sky, and he sees a bright and straight path ahead.

The poem's theme and form are new in that it presumably describes a peasant from his point of view and in his own voice. It belongs neither to the ancient poetic tradition nor to the new poetry of the May Fourth period, characterized with its often contrived Westernized syntax and imagery. Yet precisely because it is new in this "uncultured" way the poem conjures up an "uncontaminated" picture that is anything but new. It depicts an idyllic scene as old as the ideal of the Chinese peasant. The images of the farmer, the ox, the crop in the field, and the sun all belong to the "primitive" image repository unified around the mythological god Yandi/Shen Nong. Within this unchanged symbolic world of China's agri/culture is the substitution of a new cultural icon for the old, namely, Chairman Mao for the Buddha and the kitchen god. The substitution of a new human authority for the old supernatural ones certainly points to the issue of the human agency crucial to positive social change. But the semantic substitution goes hand in hand with the syntactic reinscription of the timeless myth.

I have previously described the image of this dual-faced ancestral god and its embodiment in the term *mu* (to "ox"-herd/government) and argued that *mu* is a key concept for understanding ancient China's political culture. So central is the concept that, throughout the history of China's dynastic changes, the terms and the underlying structure of ideological legitimation for these changes have virtually never changed. Just as the sun always rises and sinks in its eternal recurrence, one emperor may be toppled after another but the Son of Heaven is immortal. If hunger leads to peasant revolt, the fulfillment of hunger must be reassured by creating another "kitchen god" in the image of the Noble Farmer, the projected ideal of the peasant himself.

It is true that the achievements of Yan'an literature are unprecedented in revolutionizing literature itself and in reaching out to ordinary people. However, Wang's story and He's poem reveal a tendency that compromises the formation of a genuinely revolutionary consciousness. This tendency was to culminate in the narrative closure of revolution, revolution as an open-ended process that is rooted in the irreducible desire of hunger. In this way, the revolutionary narrative embeds in itself a dialectic interplay between its utopian open-endedness and its authorial/authoritarian closure. By forcing open this narrative tension, hunger and desire cannot simply be reduced to mythological-teleological reification. Rooted in this hunger is the implication that Mao, if a god, must serve himself up as "food."

Ye Hong's "Xinkendi" (Reclaimed wasteland, 1939)[8] depicts a peasant's insatiable hunger for meat. Ma Qiuchang, who had just joined the revolution in order to eat his fill, was excited to hear his team leader promising that they would eat meat twice a week. His class consciousness yet to be awakened, Ma did not quite trust his leader's promise of a bright future and was unable to cheer himself up for the hard work involved in reclaiming wasteland. One day his leader told him that even

Chairman Mao ate millet during this period of austerity, meaning that Mao did not enjoy any privileges.[9] Although he was touched momentarily by Mao's egalitarian food consumption, Ma relapsed quickly into his gloomy mood and refused to accept the leader's empty promise of a future described like that of the legendary Soviet Union. Even with the gradual awakening of his class consciousness and his new responsibility of leading the team, Ma still disliked his better-educated teammates talking the big talk: "He wondered aloud why these educated city youth gave up their comfortable life and came here to suffer the hell of it! Damn their big talk. Let's talk about the farm. What if we could all eat our fill! Even after chasing the Japs out of China, you still have to fill your stomach first. He became excited: 'Let's get to work!' Awakening, [he realized] it was just a dream" (80). At the end of the story, his former team leader returned from the front lines with truly exciting news: the troops had robbed the Japanese of so much canned meat that they were sending some of it back. For the first time, he was convinced of a bright tomorrow: "We will have meat to eat! He thinks about tomorrow. What a happy day that will be!" (80).

Ye Hong's story was published three years before Mao's "Talk at the Yan'an Forum on Literature and Art." In this story, hunger is basically a problem of material lack, and its fulfillment is yet to be negotiated beyond that level. Even though Mao is invoked—and the protagonist "has heard he is a great hero" and "the savior of the common folks" (70)—he falls short of materializing the promise to satisfy the protagonist's more immediate voracity. Because Mao also eats millet, the savior fails to offer himself as a "meat" savory enough for the ravenous protagonist. Hunger, figured in a daydream, is paradoxically kept open-ended. In this way "hunger" can only signify its source of desire (i.e., hunger proper) as opposed to the image of Mao as the "transcendental signified" in He Jingzhi's poem and Wang Ruowang's story.

If Ye Hong's story defies narrative closure by inscribing revolution in a discourse of immediate need and insatiable desire, Qin Zhaoyang's "Anmen Maozhuxi youbanfa" (Our Chairman Mao has his ways, 1946)[10] literally turns Mao into the object of a verbal feast. "A folktale about Chairman Mao," as it is subtitled, the story is told within a story, a feast of words about a feast of meat. The primary narrator, presumably the author himself, relates to the reader a folktale. During a rainy season, a group of revolutionary youth gathered in the peasant's house and asked him to tell a story simply—this is of paramount importance—"to kill the time." Purely for pleasure, the tale nonetheless has a serious theme and subject: China's national unity and Chairman Mao's wisdom.

The old man's story is simple. A conference was held in Yan'an in 1937, with participants from all walks of life and all political persuasions. Some foreigners were also invited. After a month's discussion, the United Front was formed to fight the Japanese aggression. To celebrate its success, Mao suggested that all participants—three to four hundred—gather around a single table to enjoy a big feast so that they could show the world China's national unity. "But how can you get such a huge table for your feast?" asked some foreigners. Instead of answering their question, Mao led all his guests out onto the open ground, where braised pork in huge containers was ready to be served. Still unable to grasp Mao's point, his foreign guests tried to locate the table, only to find that by one table Mao meant the whole of China, claiming that this "table," with its inexhaustible supply of food, could provide feasts for all the Chinese people. In practice, however, the voracious crowd found it impossible to get the meat into their mouths other than by fighting one another, which was precisely the problem the conference was held to solve. If these leaders could not even dine in an orderly manner, how could they lead the nation to fight the Japanese? Bordering on the absurd, the tale again shows Mao's wisdom. He had his soldiers come up with bunches of five-foot-long chopsticks, urging his guests to help each other by passing the meat around to feed his or her neighbor so that everyone would have an equal share. When a youth in the audience asked how long a meal like that would take and how one could use such long chopsticks, the storyteller finally showed the truth of his own wisdom: "this is just a joke."

What makes the tale a palatable joke is its double-embedded narrative structure. Mao's feast as the "inner story" is interrupted at several points by practical questions his foreign guests have raised, questions that step by step push his grandiose idea to the verge of the impossible. In the same way, the old man's telling of that story is also interrupted at several points by questions raised by a youngster. The logic of the youngster's questions is the same as the foreigners', and each of his questions forces the storyteller to produce a solution, only to be further cornered to reveal the true meaning of the story. That is, as a joke told in order to kill the time it has no fixed meaning or reference outside the act of storytelling itself. The meaning of the story is only an effect of storytelling as signifying: *Chairman Mao*, *national unity*, and *China* are just signifiers, as are *feast*, *braised pork*, and *chopsticks*. Each signifier does not make sense apart from the others, and together all produce the text, the "pleasure of the text" as Roland Barthes might call it. What governs the text, exactly as shown by the peasant's "fabrication," is the principle of double orality.

Unlike Barthes's "pleasure of the text," this tale produces "oral pleasure" rather than the pleasure of "sexuality" or "bliss." This is determined by the subject matter—feast of meat—and the oral mode of communication. The tradition behind it is as old as the mythological chef/prime minister Yi Yin and the ancient genre of the well-cooked/wrought word. More specifically, the tale evokes the folk oral tradition derived from a variety of Buddhist dialogues such as the *koan* and its later variations, in which the meaning of words is "ruminated" only to be attenuated through the process of playing with the signifiers. This is not to suggest that the peasant storyteller shows disrespect to his "hero." Rather, if Mao is the savior, he must be made to fulfill his ultimate function of "feeding," of serving himself up as "food." Just as the fabricated feast projects a utopian desire, this desire projects a truly revolutionary hunger in the broadest sense of the phrase. It is a revolutionary hunger so utopian that it can only be fulfilled in words, words about feast, about Mao, and about braised pork.[11]

In contrast to the drab, heroic asceticism that dominates the assembled products of revolutionary literature in the PRC, Qin's folktale displays the humorous aspect of the peasants and their healthy "hedonism." By fabricating a thematically revolutionary story for fun and dramatizing this creative process, the text plays around a lofty ideal without being subsumed under a "higher" ideological metanarrative. Historically speaking, the tension between irreducible desire and the tendency of narrative closure was solved by the latter's repression of the former. But how was this irreducible utopian desire subsumed into the dominant mode of representation? Who, by assuming the position of authority, has dictated a single meaning of revolution and revolutionary literature?

Narrative Authority and Authoritarian Narrative

Liu Qing's short story "Tudide erzi" (Son of the earth, 1945)[12] describes in a nutshell the actual process of narrative closure. Like many works of this period, the story tells about hunger in the old society and the fulfillment of hunger in the new. In the old society, the peasant Li Laosan was deprived of his land and forced at times to pick discarded rotten cabbage leaves for food. Extreme poverty eventually drove him to cheat and steal, and once he was almost beaten to death after he was caught stealing crops in the field of a nearby village. An outcast, he was persuaded by the new government to take a new path in life and earn a living for himself. The old social system, a local government leader told him, must be held responsible for the crimes he had committed. As long as he works hard and leads an honest life, he can become a new citizen. The leader also advised him to take up masonry, which his father had taught him, and referred him to a government-run construction project. After several years of hard work, Li has saved enough money, bought a small farm of his own, and become a son of the earth once again.

The story of Li Laosan is another example of the liberation theme narrated as "the old society turned humans into ghosts." "The new society turned ghosts into humans" (*jiushehui shiren biancheng gui; xinshehui shigui biancheng ren*), a formulated couplet first used to interpret *The White-Haired Girl* and later to describe almost all works produced on this model. But Liu Qing's authorial narrative, as opposed to Li's personal story, incorporates the latter as a mere footnote for constructing a narrative authority corresponding to a dictated reference of meaning. As a matter of fact, the story is told in the first person from the point of view of a government official rather than that of the "son of the earth," and the latter's past only appears in the second section as a historical backdrop. This first-person authorial narrative supersedes Li's past story and circumscribes the space in which its meaning is defined.

The first section begins with a scene on New Year's Eve. A low-ranking functionary in a regional government, the narrator named Liu (a homophone of the author's surname, whose job in the government is similar to the author's at that time) received a guest, Li Laosan, and along with him a New Year's gift, a small basket of *momo* (steamed rolls in the local dialect). Receiving an unexpected guest with a New Year's gift at this time, Liu became suspicious of Li's motive. He asked why Li wanted to give the government this gift. Knowing Li's past, Liu even asked Li if he intended to bribe government officials in order to evade the grain tax. This drove Li to self-defense and forced him to tell the truth. He explained that he only wanted to thank the new government for his good fortune: he had just bought a small farm. Seeing Li's sincerity, Liu accepted his gift.

In the second section, the narrator, while chewing Li's *momo*, recounted his past. Through this flashback, the narrative uses the gift as a witness to historical change and defines the relationship between the giver and the receiver as that between a debtor and his creditor. The peasant is "simply" repaying a moral debt to his liberator. "Simply" is what makes the gift acceptable because the giver does not harbor ulterior motives that might undermine the legal and economic contract between the tax collector and the taxpayer. Thus, the food simultaneously signifies a number of things and its structure of signification reveals several layers of social relations between the Communist government and the peasantry. For the "son of the earth," the gift expresses his genuine gratitude for the new society. The fact that he can afford such a "luxurious" gift is itself a telling example of his new good fortune. It is something he never could have offered in the past, and yet it is more than what his legal obligation requires him to give. At this level, the food defines the relationship between the individual citizen and his government in excess of a "mere" economic and legal contract. This excess or "surplus value" is emotional and affective, which is not difficult to understand in the context of a peasant's liberation. Food, above all, has an absolute value in the culture and constitutes the key issue in the revolution; it thus must serve as the centerpiece.

For the narrator, the meaning of the gift is rather ambiguous, and his function is to clarify and define its meaning either through his own authorial voice or by forcing, as he does in the text, his peasant character to speak for himself. What makes the gift ambiguous, however, is precisely its "surplus value." This surplus value is suspicious in that the gift might be intended as a bribe, which would undermine their contractual relationship. Trying to define the gift's meaning as purely emotional, the narrator ironically reveals their real social relation. The government, however new, must collect taxes; the peasant, even liberated, must pay taxes. For thousands of years, Chinese peasants have taken it for granted that they must pay taxes to the state, and the revolution certainly has not changed that basic social contract.

The issue is not whether the Communist government, or any government for that matter, should levy taxes; the question is whether the peasant must pay two kinds of "taxes"—one in grain and the other in steamed rolls—to the state in return for the liberty to produce food to feed himself. The second "tax," the gift, is what at once subsumes the real social relations and moralizes such relations into a narrative hierarchy. If the peasant's gift echoes an ageless cultural unconscious, the official's acceptance of that gift as a necessary moral "surplus value" reinforces the hierarchical structure of the society.

This power relationship is fully acted out on the level of meaning production, established in the authorial intervention into a spectacle of pleasure. In section 3, the narrator and the commissioner go to Li's home village to watch a show the day after the New Year. The reader is told that the village *yangge* troupe has created two plays based on real stories. One of the plays is entitled *Li Laosan's Liberation*, the dramatis persona of which is the same "son of the earth." On their way to the village, the two government officials met Li and his two sons walking to their farm. Recognizing Li's devotion to his newly purchased farm, the narrator nonetheless asked him to watch the show about his own story. Li dismissed it as "pure fabrication," ashamed perhaps of his own past. The narrator's remark reveals his or the author's view as regards the function of literature and art: "The play is created to educate the audience (*bianxi quan shiren*). What does it matter [whether it is fabricated or not]?" Li left anyway, apparently with mixed feelings. But the narrator would eventually intervene in the show:

> *Li Laosan Fanshen* was the last show. It was extremely appealing to the villagers because it was created and performed by their own folks according to a true story of a local character. Regrettably, however, the show was flawed, and this must be pointed out. That fellow Ying Wanger who played the role of Li Laosan was well-known for his funny tricks. His performance was peppered with trivial pranks that induced one wave of laughter after another from the audience. This somehow diminished the tragic effect of the original story. For this reason, I, being the secretary of the local government, must point this out to the troupe's art director and after the show say a few words to the villagers. . . .
>
> "Folks," shouted I in a high-pitched voice, "don't laugh when you watch the show! My tears were running when I was listening to Li Laosan bringing up his past. You folks didn't fare much better than he did in the old society." (461)

The narrator thus turned the spectacle of pleasure into an arena for political agitation, asking the villagers a series of questions about their past misery and present abundance. In the end, the dialogue culminated in the topic of eating. He asked them why they bought so many spices in the last month. A middle-aged peasant replied:

> "We used them for cooking, of course. . . . Now that we are doing fine, in the New Year we want to eat meat. Doesn't that need more spices?"
>
> The last question again induced a wave of laughter. But it was immediately overwhelmed by a round of shouting of [revolutionary] slogans. (462)

The slogans, as the narrator hoped, attribute the villagers' liberation to the Communist Party. These slogans were contrived by the authorial voice. The text in this way exemplifies class education based on the historical contrast between the old and the new society. This contrast is called in Communist terminology *yiku sitian*, "recalling [past] bitterness and thinking over [present] sweetness."

For an agriculture centered on grain production, meat is a luxury for the peasants. That is why meat is the focus of dreams in Ye Hong's story about a peasant's insatiable hunger and the topic of a verbal feast in the folktale. Unlike these two stories, Liu Qing's text succeeds in repressing the laughter induced by the mere mention of meat. Meat eating, laughing, and storytelling are thus the major tropes that organize a different politics of orality, a politics of oral pleasure centered around the interplay between the two functions of the mouth. Just as eating figures the pleasure of being at one with the world, the folk storytelling and the folk-comic "pranks" display the playfulness, the "noninstrumental" mode of communication, through which individual human beings join one another in the shared utopian desire for an egalitarian community. These are the few sparks that illuminate a mass revolution and its literature.[13]

It is illuminating to compare Liu's narrative strategy with that of the folktale about Mao's feast. Both frame a story within a first-person narrative. While the folk story "deconstructs" its inner story by embedding it in the telling of a joke, the narrator in Liu's text intrudes into the folk show, dictates what is correct or incorrect, and imposes a fixed doctrine on the peasants and *their* revolution and liberation, only to establish the narrator's own authority in the end. It is important to note that the "hero," the "son of the earth," is not present in the scene. His story, his existence, is merely a "nonpresence" (i.e., his "past" and his diegetic "absence") against which the narrator constructs the narrative authority of the Party's omnipresence. By submerging Li's life story into a higher structure of meaning and by further repressing the folk representation of that same story for indoctrination, the narrative consciousness at work is nothing other than authoritarian. This authoritarian model epitomizes the closure of revolutionary discourse in modern China. Many aggravated problems in the later development of literature and art in the PRC, such as official control and ideological indoctrination, can be traced to the Yan'an years.

It is easy to blame—as it was in the 1980s—the peasants themselves. Like Li Laosan and the characters in "Director Lü" and "The Sun Shines in Our Hearts," the peasantry need a savior, a benevolent leader, to accomplish their liberation. But this kind of argument misses a critical point: the Communist leadership is supposed to be the agency for transforming the people's consciousness according to Marxist principles. One of the Marxist principles is, as the *Internationale* chants, that there has never been a savior and the slaves must break the shackles themselves. But this simple truth would have to wait more than thirty years before it could be once again voiced in literature, despite the fact that the *Internationale* is one of the most frequently heard songs in the PRC.

In sum, hunger is a predominant theme of the Communist revolution, a "master" (or "slave") trope on which revolutionary discourse is modeled. Central to this theme and trope is the hungry desire for food, meat, laughter, and social justice. It is not surprising that, once this revolutionary process is closed and revolution itself is gradually turned into a rhetoric for ideological legitimation, revolutionary literature must be reopened afresh from its roots in hunger.

The Bittersweet Rewriting of Revolution: Wang Ruowang's *Hunger Trilogy* and Lu Wenfu's "The Gourmet"

Written by two veteran revolutionary writers, the *Hunger Trilogy* and "The Gourmet" overrode the wave of "scar literature" in the early post–Cultural Revolution period by extending their rethinking into the pre-1949 Communist revolution. Wang's text captures three moments of hunger and juxtaposes them in such a way that a poignant question arises: what has gone wrong with *our* revolution? The revolutionary enthusiasm and resolve depicted in the first two parts of the trilogy is contrasted with the devastating experience of being deliberately starved in a

Communist prison during the Cultural Revolution. Presenting all these as heroic and tragic, the text sings a mixed song of eulogy and elegy for the revolution.

Covering the period from the eve of the Communist victory in 1949 to the early 1980s, "The Gourmet" reveals a profound ambiguity between hunger and extravagance, lack and excess, and the entanglement of politics with aesthetics. Posing itself as a social history, the text problematizes its own politics of eating through an aesthetic of resistance.

"Eating a Meal to Recall Bitterness"

This expression, *chiyikufan* in Chinese, is taken from the opening sentence of Wang Ruowang's autobiographical novel. The phrase describes, in the author's words, a "religiouslike ceremony" during the Cultural Revolution. By swallowing steamed rolls made of chaff, carrot leaves, or yam vines the eater is supposed to recall the bitterness of the old society. It was believed that such a "masochistic" act would enhance and purify the eater's proletarian consciousness. In the political vocabulary of the time, *chiyikufan* meant a specific oral enactment of *chiku* (eating bitterness or enduring suffering), an organizing trope for revolutionary sacrifice. One of the central themes of revolutionary literature since the Yan'an period has been "heroic and noble sacrifice," represented in a variety of ways of "eating bitterness." The coarse food is invested with sacred meaning, signifying the eater's faith in a quasi-religious ideology. This quasi-religious pre-text is one of the discursive practices Wang's novel sets out to undermine.

"Eating bitterness" only makes up one stage in the teleological narrative. In the phrase *chiyiku fan*, the meal is meant for *yiku*, or "recalling [past] bitterness," with the emphasis on the implied "past." But *yiku* aims at mobilizing the next conscious activity, called *sitian*, "thinking over [present] sweetness," with the same emphasis on the implied "present." *Yiku sitian* describes, in aesthetic-psychological terms, a temporal structure that organizes the political discourse of modern Chinese history by splitting it between the bitterness of the old society and the sweetness of the new. The idiom functions at the same time as the most economical trope: it thematizes history by means of flavors and incorporates temporality through the palate. This gustatory-historical structure is another pre-text that Wang's novel engages.

Dwelling on these religious-historical pre-texts, Wang makes it clear from the outset that his story tells about eating bitterness in its most horrifying form. "My past suffering was not from eating coarse food, but from the inability to scrounge up even anything coarse to eat." It is about, as he puts it, "the extraordinary hunger . . . that makes you wish for death." Meanwhile, he also lays bare his intent: he is not telling the story "to strengthen any sort of proletarian consciousness, but to express a hope." "Twice is bad enough," Wang confesses with bitterness, "three times is too much; I only hope not to have to face starvation a fourth time" (116; 3).[14]

The irony of modern Chinese history could not be more painfully played out than in the evocation of "hope" made sixty years after Lu Xun cried out his hope that the old feast of cannibalism could be overturned. To make it even worse, Wang's hope is reduced to a mere animal need for food. Yet by juxtaposing the first two segments of the trilogy prior to the 1949 Communist victory with the third one in a linear narrative the novel collapses that historical landmark between the old and the new society and stands the rhetoric of *yiku sitian* on its head.

When the narrator transgresses the clear-cut bitter/sweet dichotomy that organized the revolutionary teleology, his feeling toward his whole life as a veteran revolutionary is none other than bittersweet. It is sweet because he still cherishes the memory of heroism and noble sacrifice from the first half of his life. It is bitter not so much because he made that sacrifice and swallowed lots of bitterness as because his sacrifice for a sweet new society has yielded another bitter fruit. This ambivalence toward revolution displays the dilemma faced by many revolutionary writers, who feel betrayed by the Party yet unable to disown their past. Since his revolutionary struggle ineluctably constitutes who he is, the author must paradoxically turn the whole structure of *yiku sitian* upside-down. That is, the reader is asked to read his text as recalling past sweetness (his participation in the revolution) and thinking over present bitterness (the tragic failure of that revolution).

The first two parts of the trilogy describe the narrator's experiences in a KMT prison and during the guerrilla war against the Japanese. Starvation is couched in a narrative of heroic sacrifice. Lurid details of animal instincts are presented matter-of-factly and sometimes with incredible humor, so that heroism is embodied in the narrator's omnivorousness for survival. For the sixteen-year-old Wang, then a political prisoner, hunger was the necessary test and redeeming path to becoming a full-fledged Communist. This personalized embodiment of Communist history is narrativized in the near-ritualistic practice of swallowing anything that passes for meat. In the KMT prison, the rice is "partially eaten away by maggots," with "lots of cooked maggots" in it. These maggots, a senior Communist suggests, "should be treated like a kind of meat" because they provide "a source of protein" (117; 5–6). It is a tale of survival that deliberately crosses the fine line of what is edible and what is not. When hardship requires a more stoic heroism, the trial of the palate stands in for the revolutionary spirit. When the narrator and his group are stranded in no-man's-land during a Japanese military campaign, they eat grasshoppers "as if they were a deep-fried shrimp" and swallow green worms "like raw eggs." To deceive one of their comrades who would rather die than eat worms, the group convinces him that they are "dried beef" (137–38; 50–53). On both occasions, the Communists consume all kinds of raw "meat" with a sole purpose: to survive so that they can build a new socialist society. Although worms and other insects are swallowed uncooked, they are "cooked" in a revolutionary spirit with the sweet flavor of comradeship. So it comes as no surprise to find that the less edible the food is, the more heroic the narrative becomes. Between the lines, there seems to be a narrator of tall tales somehow removed from his own excruciating experience, a hero showing off his omnivorous guts.

The effect of such heroic omnivorousness anticipates the narrative reversal of the hero, imprisoned later by a system that he had helped create. In the Communist prison, the narrator's identity reversal from a veteran revolutionary to an old "counterrevolutionary" is most poignantly displayed in the reversal of his relationship with insects. This time, his own body is served up for bedbugs, which "suck blood from every part of [his] body." To make things even worse, the Communist prison authority has rejected a request that it issue some powder to exterminate the bugs. The "revolutionary" logic is: "Mercy toward bedbugs is cruelty toward political prisoners!" If the eating of worms is the utmost measure of the instinct for survival, cruelty is stretched to its most gruesome extreme when bugs are allowed the extravaganza of the political prisoner's body, already tortured by deliberate starvation (148; 77).

Comparing the Communist prison with the prison of the past, the narrator remarks: "There we were starving as we are now, but the hunger had lasted only two or three days and everyone's morale had remained high throughout. Today, there's no end in sight; the hunger's an evil prank, and we suffer for nothing. Compared to our present situation, the hunger back in the woods became, ironically, a happy memory" (162; 107). With no end in sight and morale low in the Communist prison, raw "meat" can only ease his hunger, containing no heroic flavor.

While raw meat signifies the eater's primitive instinct and the utmost test of human endurance, cooked meat aestheticizes appetite and desire. If consumption of maggots, worms, and the like gauges one's physical endurance, braised pork signifies the desire that pork itself cannot completely fulfill. In the KMT prison, braised pork is served the day the new warden takes office. The event is described as "a miracle." With only one piece for each, the narrator recalls: "I tore my piece in half and held each in my mouth for about fifteen minutes, unwilling to chew it. I thought this was just my own childishness, but I observed that my cellmates, too, were holding the meat in their mouths, pursing their lips, their cheeks bulging" (119; 10). The prolonged sensation cannot satisfy the empty stomach, but it does sharpen the ravenous desire for more. The more one desires, the more the writing of the desire.

In the KMT prison, the Communists demand a better diet by staging hunger strikes. They insist on three conditions, including the addition of a piece of braised pork once a week. On the fifth day of the strike, each prisoner is offered a piece. The narrator had been told by his older cellmates not to take the pork before the authorities met their other demands. Resentful and disappointed, the teen-aged Wang has to suppress his "joy and appetite, which had just been stirred up." The suppressed voracity is then displaced upon a mental "screen" on which "there was a beautiful, glistening, sweet-smelling piece of pork." The author describes his projection as follows:

> This mirage was even more enticing than the real thing, and more harmful. It was as if my whole body had turned into a steaming piece of meat. When I pressed my fingers together they felt greasy and oily; when I opened my eyes, even the water stains on the ceiling resembled pieces of gleaming pork; my ears were full of the sound of pots being dragged along the floor announcing "time to eat." (123–24; 17–18)

While his hunger is a physiological experience under an extreme circumstance, the physical depletion is compensated by a mental feast. As a favorite food and a cultural institution, the braised pork once again serves as a powerful sign of the struggle between the political body and the physical body. Sacrifice, then, is embodied in the blurry boundary between the flesh and the pork, a rhetorical feature of *rou* that will resurface in works by Mo Yan, Li Ang, and Amy Tan. The feast of braised pork was, of course, only a hallucination. It was made real in the end, however, when the KMT authorities yielded to the prisoners' four demands: to improve the quality of the food, supply better-quality rice, add one piece of meat each week, and allow the prisoners' relatives to bring in legal publications. This victory, the author remarks more than forty years later, "was the first time in my life that I reveled in the joyous taste of victory, the sweet flavor of revolutionary struggle" (125; 21). The author's self-portrait of his omnivorousness is captured even in his rhetorical posture. Alimentary writing is above all composed of words of food.

That is why the meaning of the revolution must be chewed over and over again when the author finds himself tasting the bitterness of his historical achievement. During the Cultural Revolution, Wang is imprisoned in the same cell in which he had been interrogated by the KMT police four decades before. The authorities' policy is governed by the slogan: "Mercy toward the enemy is cruelty to your comrades." The brutal treatment is measured once again by the food ration, now reduced even below the level of the KMT prison. Even worse, the time-honored weapon of the hunger strike fails to work this time. The KMT warden at least was afraid that the death of a political prisoner would ruin his career if it were leaked to the outside world. In the Communist prison, should the "counterrevolutionaries" refuse to eat, they deserve their own deaths and will help conserve food for others.

History returns as the same ghost but in a different name, and the author dishes out one bitter dose after another, all in the haunting imagery of the familiar past. The weekly ritual of masticating a piece of braised pork recurs in the Communist prison. But this time pork figures in a completely negative way. Because braised pork was initially served on Thursdays, on Wednesdays "everyone was eagerly looking forward to Thursday's piece of meat," "praying to himself, hoping that his piece of meat would be a little bigger, a little fattier." Yet one Thursday the authorities change the menu, substituting preserved eggs. This substitution is not only an exchange of food items: it inverts the relationship between the eater and the eaten. One inmate, a "bourgeois musician," finds inside his egg a black smelly liquid and asks a guard to exchange it.

The guard not only refuses to do so but calls him a "bad egg." Chasing him into the cell, the guard "pulled him out and smashed the egg over his head, swearing furiously, 'You counterrevolutionary! Rotten egg! You're just the kind of bastard who should be eating rotten eggs. If you want to eat well, why the hell don't you eat at home? Why come here to be so picky? How can you reform your ideology like this?' " (154; 90–91).

The pun *huaidan* (rotten or bad eggs) is of course a popular device. But its two "referents" are blended in such an entanglement here that food symbolism not only signifies, but shapes, entails, and justifies direct action that completely collapses the distinction between discourse and practice. Such cruelty activated through the violence of language can only make sense in the context of the Cultural Revolution that "slaughters culture" (*gewenhaiming*). Parallel to such a brutal politics of eating is the no less brutal suppression of reading, reading as consumption. While three of the four demands of the hunger strikers in the KMT prison were about food, the other one was about reading books. In the narrator's experience, as he puts it, "reading—beneficial in itself—is the best method for curing hunger." Before the narrator joined the revolution, he had only an elementary level of schooling. He considers the KMT prison his "university," in which he read several hundred books and even learned Japanese. But in the Communist prison all he is allowed to read are Mao's works. Learning a foreign language is out of the question, even though one of his cellmates is an American-educated medical doctor. This is because learning English involves the risk of being accused of "propagating Western culture," thus adding to their "crimes" (149; 79). Just as food must be reduced to a minimum, books must be banned. If food culture and written culture are two of the most significant legacies of ancient Chinese civilization, the Cultural Revolution is no doubt best represented in the text as cultural destruction.

Instead of "eating a meal to recall bitterness," Wang shoves down the reader's throat one dose of bitterness after another, only to force us to face the total lack of food, of human decency, of social civility. Yet all these lacks are wrought under the excessive craze for "revolution," "liberation," and "socialism." Because of this ideological and rhetorical excess, there is a double burden on the narrator. The narrator still believes in good faith that his participation in the revolution ties his personal past to the past of the present regime and thus makes it untenable for him to protest outside the established revolutionary rhetoric. He cannot stage a hunger strike because that posture would simply confirm his opposition to the Cultural Revolution and his failed ideological reform. Nor can he condone suicide because killing oneself would simply be another piece of evidence that one has lost faith in the new China. As an old cellmate reminds him: "We should uphold and protect the Party's prestige wherever we are"—even when they are in the Party's prison for "crimes" they have committed while protecting the Party's prestige (161; 104).

What is left for him to ruminate on is nothing but the past. In a rare emotional outburst, the narrator shouts:

> Motherland, plagued by great disasters, seventeen years after the revolutionary victory, how could you have the heart to put your loyal sons and daughters through a bloody bath of untold danger once again?
>
> I had already been through two devastating bouts with hunger. How could it be that this great land, for which I struggled with sweat and blood, could so savagely torture its beloved son? Is this regime worthy of being called a dictatorship of the proletariat? Is this kind of Communist Party worthy of being called an organization of the proletarian vanguard? (148; 77–78)

The narrator's outburst may sound pathetic to today's reader, especially when it is contrasted with the overall cool-headed "cruelty" with which he depicts the lurid details of starvation. It may be impossible for Wang's generation to wean themselves completely from the nostalgia of a glorious past. However, *Hunger Trilogy* also sings a song of elegy and eulogy mixed with a futuristic "hope." Hunger, like a recurring specter haunting the bloody path of history, may once again season our bitter memory about one of the most tragic atrocities in the modern world.

Between Gastronomical Pleasure and Political Pathology

Commenting on a joke from the Czech writer Milan Kundera's *Book of Laughter and Forgetting*, Terry Eagleton has detected a "pathological overreading" in Communist society. If we disregard the problematic teleology implied in his neologism of "post-capitalist" and substitute the PRC for Eastern Europe in the following passage, Eagleton's remark provides a cogent entry point to Lu Wenfu's "The Gourmet":

> In the post-capitalist bureaucracies, even vomiting is made to assume some kind of instant symbolic meaning. Nothing in Eastern Europe can happen by accident. The logical extreme of this attitude is paranoia, a condition in which reality becomes so pervasively, oppressively meaningful that its slightest fragments operate as minatory signs in some utterly coherent text. Once the political state extends its empire over the whole of civil society, social reality becomes so densely systematized and rigorously coded that one is always being caught out in a kind of pathological "overreading," a compulsive semiosis which eradicates all contingency. (1987, 25)

"The Gourmet" offers a compelling example of how a politically compulsive semiosis traverses the oral space of eating and how eating's political overreading has turned oral pleasure into aesthetic resistance. Lu's novella further complicates the total politicization of food in the PRC by tracing it to the "origin" of food's political systematization in the pre-1949 China. The pathological overreading in post-1949 China thus is historicized as an end effect of a justifiable cure for the existing social disease. Reflecting a social history of food consumption, the text describes a rare picture of socialism as it has existed for a Marxist reading that must address a whole set of ethical issues concerning desire, pleasure, and consumption.

Lu's novella delineates three stages from the eve of the Communist victory (sections 1–2) via the first thirty years of the PRC (sections 3–8) to the post–Cultural Revolution era (sections 9–12). The first part is organized around a binary opposite between excess and lack. The second part describes the reversal of the old social structure governed by the principle of a pathological asceticism. The third part brings into play these two pre-texts and leaves their historical conflicts and ironic outcome open to histrionic ambiguity.

The bipolar structure juxtaposing a politics and an aesthetics of eating is embodied in the two major characters: the first-person narrator, named Gao Xiaoting, and the gourmet Zhu Ziye. Gao and Zhu represent two distinct attitudes toward consumption, and their narrative entanglement underscores the conflicts of two opposing hermeneutic codes of food. Speaking in and for two worlds of cultural (un)consciousness, their textual dialogism captures in a nutshell the historical mapping, unmapping, and remapping of the carnal body. As the narrator summarizes it at the beginning, Zhu "haunted me like a specter for forty years. I despised, I loathed, and I opposed him, but in the end I turned out to have no special capacities, while the gourmet succeeded precisely because of his obsession" (4; 97).[15]

By "have no special capacities" the narrator means that his career is a joke. His has been a career, it turns out, of taking over a famous restaurant and turning it into a disaster. Ironically, he took the post of restaurant manager simply because, as he confesses, "I hated eating" in the first place. On the other hand, it is Zhu's obsession with fine food that gives him the title "gourmet." Through the two characters' narrative entanglement, a third voice will come to the fore to identify neither. While it oscillates between the two to weave their interplay into a social history, the third voice also ironizes itself when it has to face the ambiguous picture it has created. In this way, the author has created a shadow of himself in the narrator just as the gourmet has haunted the narrator like a specter. The path of this third consciousness marks the author's travel from faith to irony. His faith, no matter how lofty it is, must ride on the hungry tide of ever-changing history.

The gourmet occupies a position that is neither politically harmful nor reliable to the Communists. In fact, his story shows the footsteps of pathological overreading when eating enters into a strictly political realm of interpretation. Before the liberation, Zhu inherited some real estate and spent his life collecting rent. He had no interest in business, was carefree about his clothing, and never got married. An owner of real estate, his own shabby residence only meant for him a bed on which he could fall asleep. Otherwise, his life was totally devoted to gastronomical pleasure. From dawn to dusk, Zhu's daily routine was marked with an itinerary between breakfast noodle shops, teahouses, restaurants, taverns, and the bathhouse, where he indulged in after-lunch digestion.

In the earthly paradise of Suzhou, the so-called Venice of the East, known (in the West first through Marco Polo) for its exquisite food, gardens, arts, and culture, eating is treated as a cultural ritual and fine art. "Unlike Oblomov," the prototype of the lazy Russian landlord widely known in China, Zhu was rather "diligent" even though his obsession with food was coupled with a more general code of laziness in the pejorative sense of *haochi lanzuo* (gluttonous and lazy). "As with other art forms," the narrator comments on Zhu's oral pleasure, "the art of eating depends on how well one is in command of time and place." A gourmet, in other words, is an active eater like an actor in a show. For Suzhou, cuisine has its "complete structure" and stages the gourmet's commensal dining as a "drama." Its inexhaustible variety not only provides rich sources of gustatory gratification but generates insatiable oral pleasure of another kind: table talk. In their table conversations, the diners "ruminate" over dainties they have just savored and discuss future menus to sharpen their palates. Eating and talking, and talking about eating, anchor life solidly in oral extravagance.

The sensual experience must be prolonged through digestion until the pleasure of food is thoroughly absorbed by the body. Digestion requires "concentrated rumination with no external distractions." Soaked in warm water and sunk in "the void of the external world and the emptiness of the mind," Zhu "feels the gentle movements of the stomach and the indescribable ease and pleasure of the whole body" (7). Playing on an old holistic understanding and practice of relaxation and using Chan Buddhist terms, the narrative inscribes the gourmet's digestion in a discourse of idealistic "hedonism." The pleasure of fine food thus embodies an ageless text of pleasure whose meaning is figured in the eater's refined taste for, and leisurely attitude toward, mundane life.

This age-old aesthetic of eating, however, is superimposed by the narrator's political reading and dissolved in a discourse of class struggle. The narrator, a high school student at that time, is remotely related to Zhu. After his father's death, poverty forces him and his mother to seek refuge in Zhu's residence. In return, he must run errands after school for Zhu's daily routine. "Every evening," the narrator recalls:

> I would wait at the tavern door with a bamboo basket [to take orders from Zhu and his company for items the tavern does not serve and pick them up from other places]. When the neon signs went on, Zhu and his friends, clean and fragrant, with ruddy cheeks and in good spirits, would arrive in a line of gleaming rickshaws, bells ringing and horns bleating, weaving their way through the pedestrians like a festive dragon. . . . [T]hey were greeted . . . by two rows of ragged, filthy beggars with their bony trembling hands outstretched. Zhu was prepared, and with a wave of his hand a small bill would fly toward the beggars' leader. "Off with you," he'd say.
>
> The beggars dispersed with a cheer, and I, a beggar of a different kind, would walk up to Zhu with my hungry stomach, basket in hand. This beggar was different because he knew something about the world and history,

about liberty and equality, and had read about [Sun Yat-sen's] Three Principles, and because he disapproved of gluttony and believed in human dignity. (8; 104)

The class contrast is reinforced by a series of scenes the narrator encounters on his errands between various restaurants and food stalls and culminates in the reinscription of the Tang poet Du Fu's famous couplet: "Behind the scarlet gates meat and wine rot, / On the road men lie frozen dead."

More than thirty years later, the narrator still looks back on the old society from this perspective: "I didn't start becoming a believer in Communism by reading *Das Kapital* or the *Communist Manifesto.* I was probably spurred on to it by Zhu and his like, who made me realize that all extravagantly elaborated 'isms' were futile and only Communism could solve our problems. Zhu could hardly have assumed such important airs if his property had been confiscated" (9; 107). This moment corresponds exactly to the narrative of the hungry revolution.

Food thus politicized, eating becomes a symbolic act in itself. On the sociological level, the gourmet's extravagant consumption no doubt has some political-economic implications related to the unequal distribution of food. This is exactly what the Communist revolution had intended to change. However, Zhu's consumption is also an aesthetic act with no intended political implication. The problem with the narrator's political overreading is that he shifts a political *and* aesthetic act into a political *versus* aesthetic binary, erasing bodily pleasure by means of a revolutionary asceticism. This political short-circuiting of the aesthetic, if it could be justified in the revolution, anticipates its own reversal in the post-revolutionary era.

The political pathology began to penetrate the fabric of the everyday when political power changed hands and food started to be encoded in a new set of rules. After the Communist victory, the narrator returned to his hometown and was assigned as a representative of the new government to running a famous restaurant. He came back to realize his revolutionary ideal to "overthrow the human-eating old society" with a specific goal: "the life-style of parasites like Zhu Ziye had to come to an end." His "parasitic" history notwithstanding, Zhu fully embraced the Communist government. Not only did none of the policies of the new government affect Zhu adversely, but his property was left untouched because he had been a simple rent collector, a member of the "national bourgeoisie" under protection before the 1956 socialist reforms. "Apart from being a glutton he hadn't really done anything" to the detriment of the revolution and the new society. With a most ironic twist, as Zhu puts it, "the Communist Party is good because it has got rid of all these robbers, thieves, ruffians, vagabonds, gambling and opium dens"—all the social evils that used to hinder his freedom to pursue gratification in one way or another. Even the restaurants were less crowded because many of the rich people either fled the mainland or were imprisoned. Now he could indulge in extravagant eating in a much more peaceful and stable environment (11; 110–11).

At worst a harmless parasite, Zhu's total devotion to food with no interest whatsoever in politics and business nonetheless is subject to the compulsive semiosis of the new regime. The irony of revolution for the narrator could not be greater than the fact that "revolution meant liberation" even for such a parasite, whose lifestyle had prompted the narrator to join the revolution in the first place. So he tried everything within his power and the law to deprive Zhu of his remaining privilege. When the socialist reforms were introduced in the mid-1950s, he provoked his staff into heated discussions about how to transform the restaurant from a place that mainly served the wealthy into one the workers and peasants could afford. In this socialist transformation, every detail of the restaurant became a political symbol and underwent a systematic overhaul. The neon lights at the door and the colored lights in the windows were taken down since they were "nauseating remnants" of the old society's "lavish display" and "represented the decadence and overindulgence that were the source of wickedness." The interior was remodeled by tearing down all the partitions of the private rooms: "Only bloodsuckers wanted to eat in hiding," and the workers and peasants with their clean money should not be afraid of eating in public. Service had to change, too, as waiters and waitresses now should behave like equal members of the society and get rid of the old manner of servility including "oversmiling" (17).

Substantial reform requires reevaluating the meaning of the menu. As a result, the restaurant only served foods the ordinary workers and peasants could afford—and could cook at home. When it reopened after such reforms, the eatery was crowded with working-class members. Many of the new patrons had never dined at a restaurant because of the high cost; some had entered it only by the kitchen door to supply raw materials.

Welcoming slaves to their former master's dining place, the narrator was deeply touched by his accomplishment. In retrospect, he still firmly believes that "[he] wholeheartedly engaged in a great cause that appeared insignificant in magnitude" (17).

The restaurant manager would appear to be a well-qualified practitioner of "cultural criticism." His endeavor is "insignificant in magnitude" because, above all, it only deals with eating, a private and personal matter. On the other hand, his action is part and parcel of a "great cause." Every facet of the restaurant must be scrutinized through a political overcoding in accordance with an overriding symbolic system. Under the name of socialist transformation, political power encroaches upon the realm of the aesthetic (neon and colored lights), the private (room partitions), the civil (service manner), and the physiological (menu). This is only an "insignificant" instance of how the state-sanctioned ideology collapses the boundary between the public and the private, the political and the aesthetic, and the symbolic and the bodily by "remodeling" the space in which the body interacts with the world.

However, the outcome of the dismantling of a civil space is anything but an egalitarian socialist feast. Once the working-class' curiosity about watching a political drama has faded away, they come back to the restaurant to satisfy their appetites rather than strengthen their revolutionary consciousness. Yet the absence of "servility" means rudeness, and the absence of "extravagance" dishes out only a menu of poor quality and little variety. And "ninety percent of the complaints were made by social members who do not belong to the bourgeoisie" (21). The simple truth, as one of the narrator's comrades lectures, lies in "a strange physiological phenomenon: the palate of the bourgeoisie and the proletariat is not in the least different." "Suzhou cuisine is famous," his comrade stresses, because "it's something created by laboring people over a long period of time. If you destroy it, history will hold you responsible" (22–23; 135–36). By appealing to the universal of human eating and to the cultural tradition of the earthly paradise, the story takes a dramatic shift and anticipates the final triumph of the gourmet.

Just as the narrator stands for the political pathology of food, the gourmet represents its aesthetic resistance. After the socialist reforms, Zhu is not only driven away from the poor food served in the restaurant—and most of the others run by the state—but he goes "underground" to find a new source of fine food. To the gourmet's amazement, there exists another school of Suzhou cuisine of which he has never heard, let alone tasted. It developed, with reference to *The Dream of the Red Chamber*, from a long tradition in which the high-ranking official-scholar in "feudal" China secluded himself in his high-walled mansion and entertained at homemade banquets. This school of cuisine is "a crystallization of material culture and a cultivation of taste." "It expresses the rich substance of Suzhou cuisine in a natural form, refining it in such an artistic fashion that artificiality dissolves in the appearance of simplicity" (19). With the narrative shift, the style also changes to a more colorful portrayal of food to contrast the drab description of the socialist restaurant.

The representative of this "underground" school of cuisine is named Kong Bixia, the celebrated concubine of a former KMT politician who fled the mainland and abandoned their child shortly before the Communist victory. A highly cultured courtesan from the old society, she could not make ends meet in the new. With nowhere to spend his money, Zhu found his way into Kong's house. And complementary to each other's needs, each found the other indispensable. But Kong's kitchen would not make an "underground restaurant" when her supreme cooking became known to members of the proletariat. The head chef from the narrator's restaurant, now deprived of the opportunity to utilize his skills, was invited to Kong's house, only to find a chef superior even to himself. But his visit was reported to the narrator, who investigated the incident with the conclusion that Zhu "had gotten away from socialist reforms." The symbolic significance of this incident, the author comments in hindsight, is that "the Cultural Revolution may have destroyed many other cultural legacies, but the heritage of fine food has been sustained and survived like an ever-flowing river" (20).

If Kong's art of cooking belonged exclusively to the private home of the ruling class in the past, the private art form has paradoxically become a private, artistic form in resisting the ubiquitous political pathology. Art, which might well serve one group in a particular historical context, should not be the ruling class's monopoly. A former ruler's privileges may well be used to serve as a means of opposition. Just as the plot of the story thematizes the dichotomy between political domination and aesthetic deviation, the narrative entanglement of the narrator and the gourmet offers a metaphoric structure that governs a postrevolutionary rereading of history. *Dixia*, meaning "underground," is a densely coded political term in the Communist vocabulary. It is associated with the Communists' dangerous but heroic *underground resistance* before the victory and with *surreptitious crimes* against socialism thereafter. Coupling it with *restaurant*, which represents a "private" space, *underground* becomes a revealing metaphor for the repressed desire. The persistent symptom of political repression is not simply a psychoanalytic pathology; it is displaced from a historical fact. To foreground what is repressed "underground," the text simultaneously opens up the repressed desire and the forgotten history. By manipulating the multiple semantic meanings of *underground*, the narrative turns the rhetoric of liberation on its head.

Parallel to this subversion of the official rhetoric from within its own semantic space is the reintroducing of actual hunger immediately following the narrator's awakening to common sense. The mass famines in the 1960s bankrupted the ideological legitimation of the Communist regime and found the narrator and the gourmet unlikely comrades. Hunger neutralized their antagonism when the two had to share a cart of pumpkins to survive. As capitalists and disgraced cadre members of the Cultural Revolution, both were victims of the madness of the massive persecutions. Starved during his nine years of exile during the Cultural Revolution, the narrator "has sufficiently thought about the problem of eating." Now at the age of fifty, he reflects, "it occurs to me that I have accomplished nothing" (31).

While the narrator painfully admits that he has turned out to be good at nothing, the gourmet in the end rides on the tide of the post-Mao economic reforms to the fame of a specialist in fine food. Their entanglement once again pushes the narrator to resort to the memory of the bygone ideology. Unable to reconcile his glorious past with the fact that history seems to have traveled back to where it started, he projects the old compulsive semiosis onto his one-year-old grandson. At a family banquet, the child is praised as clever because he "prefers chocolate to hard candy." "My head was spinning," the text reads, describing the narrator's response to his grandson's innocent voracity:

> When he grew up he would be another gourmet. I had spent my whole life unsuccessfully trying to change Zhu; surely I could change this little creature. I grabbed the chocolate and forced a fruit candy into his mouth.
>
> He started to wail.

Everybody present was stunned, thinking to themselves that I at this advanced age had gone crazy. (45)

With such an abrupt ending, the reader seems to hear a remote echo, through six decades of modern Chinese literature, of the Madman's plea to "save the children." The shocking effect not only is felt by the audience in the text but is also directed at the reader. Not until the end is the reader fully convinced that there is an ironic distance between the author and his first-person narrator. If Lu Xun traveled from irony to faith, Lu Wenfu started with faith and ended up in irony. His ironic voice separates itself simultaneously from the gluttonous gourmet and the paranoiac narrator and comments on a drama not of their own making. This textual space of ambiguity allows the reader to face a complex picture of the body that ingests food, digests meaning, assimilates nutrition, and eliminates waste, the body that also talks, shouts, and wails. This oral space defies ideological totalization.

In concluding this chapter, we must consider the ideological constraint embedded in the revolutionary literature of hunger as well. The tragic closure of an emancipatory aesthetics in Mao's China cannot be attributed exclusively to the rise of the authoritarian state and its repressive policies in controlling the process of cultural production. The form of realism, with its insistence on representational truth and narrative authority, has provided the discursive model for the ideological legitimation of the party-state. One of the consequences is the four-decade reproduction of hunger as a historical master trope for social reality. It is not that such a social reality should be ignored; the problem lies in the prescriptive method of interpreting the meaning of hunger within the established discursive field of Maoism itself. This narrow range of interpretation closes the door on other possibilities of artistic imagination. Wang Ruowang perhaps best exemplifies this tired form of realistic representation. Set apart by more than three decades, "Director Lü" and the *Hunger Trilogy* share the authorial insistence on the referential truth of writing. The power of realism is such that in attacking the party-state *Hunger Trilogy* ends up reinscribing the very rhetoric and narrative model of the revolution. In "The Gourmet," similarly, the third voice of a more distanced author stands at the very edge of breaking away from realism, especially when the ancient art of oral pleasure is evoked as a counterpoint to Communist asceticism. But the overriding narrative of linear history prevents the third voice from being fully developed, leaving it stuck between the empirical reality of an authentic revolution and the author's ironic commentary on his own dilemma. It is against this double constraint of official ideology and its realistic mode of narrative containment that a postrevolutionary rewriting of hunger was to arise in the mid-1980s.

5. Postrevolutionary Leftovers

Zhang Xianliang and Ah Cheng

Compared with the revolutionary narrative of hunger as a whole, the most striking feature in Zhang Xianliang's "Mimosa" and Ah Cheng's "The Chess King" is the foregrounded relationship of food with words. Above all, the meaning of hunger is always mediated in its writing. Once the constructive power of the word is recognized, writing hunger can no longer be contained in a strictly realistic form. The paradox can be seen in reference to per capita grain consumption in China, which increased from two hundred kilograms in 1977 to more than three hundred in 1984, thanks to the post-Mao agricultural reform. Writing hunger in a time of relative abundance must therefore be grasped as part of the collective effort to reconstruct historical memory. To the extent that literary writing and eating represent two primarily personal activities of the mind and the body, postrevolutionary narratives of hunger should be defined as a rewriting of the revolutionary legacy, that is, a retrospective digestion of the "leftovers." This chapter pays equal attention to food and words.

The first section focuses on Zhang Xianliang's revision of the two central icons of the revolution: Marx and the people. In the second section, the hunger motif of "The Chess King" is situated in the context of the root-searching nativism and the cultural fever of the mid-1980s. Both texts incorporate food and words in response to the search for symbolic nutrition of the time. The two intertwined aspects of consumption are localized around the cultural body as one that ruminates whatever is inherited from the "ancestors" beyond the immediate legacy of Maoism. Both authors bypass Maoism by activating older sources of writing, namely, classical Marxism in "Mimosa" and the ancient Dao in "The Chess King." Put together, their blending of multiple historical leftovers produces something new: the Dao of Marx for survival.

Feed Me, Marx! Feed Me, the People!

Like many of Zhang Xianliang's fictional works, "Mimosa" generated heated debates in critical circles. Those who defended the Party's dogma accused the author of exposing the dark side of the PRC, especially the lurid scenes of the famine in the early 1960s.[1] Critics who opposed the Party's old policies were also angered by his wicked exposé, which they believe tarnished the image of suffering intellectuals and their moral integrity.[2] These differing and opposing views were indicative of the dynamically changing horizons of interpretation in an era of cultural vertigo. Just as the haunting memory of poverty had to be rechanneled into a national drive for economic modernization, various cultural forces were competing to fill the symbolic void wrought by the collapse of the official ideology. The hunger for material wealth has nourished the desire for new sources of symbolic capital and artistic imagination.

The contradictions manifested in the debates are attributable in part to the explosion of signs in the novella itself. Lack of food in reality is juxtaposed with extravagant allusions to more than two dozen foreign and ancient Chinese writers, artists, and thinkers. Peasant slang and four-character proverbs, folksongs and poetic expressions, political jargon and philosophical dicta, and even lengthy quotations from *Das Kapital*—all these are cramped into the text which dishes out one mouthful of images after another in a language that is silver-tongued to some, yet refreshing to others after decades of cultural anemia. Indeed, rhetorical extravagance is a trademark of the author's showy style as much as a symptomatic reaction to the prolonged malnutrition of the cultural body. The symbolic fulfillment of hunger is now achieved by displacing material lack into semiotic excess, which in turn generates generic transgression of realistic conventions. This dialectic of lack and excess is epitomized in the narrative disparity between the two sides of the first-person narrator/protagonist. Zhang Yonglin is at once the protagonist who lives his material existence much like a desperate animal and the self-reflective narrator who feeds on his own bodily depletion for an extravaganza of words. As a result, social contradiction is best displayed in his struggle for sanity against the madness of the history in which he is caught.

It is this conflicting voice that has caused enormous confusion to the reading public. The author is certainly guilty of subjecting the haunting madness of intense hunger to a facile moralistic explication. Conversely, Zhang Yonglin's self-reduplication into the diegetic and the reflective worlds stands metaphorically for the excruciating experience of a post-revolutionary society attempting to make sense of its catastrophic past. Thus, we need to read the protagonist Zhang Yonglin in spite of the narrator Zhang Yonglin—or the former rightist intellectual Zhang Xianliang in spite of the now famous author Zhang Xianliang—even though they make up the same textual and historical entity.[3] Historical contradiction, in short, is embodied in the protagonist's *dédoublement* as much as the text offers a formal solution to his split.

Eating Marx

In the prologue to the story, the author stakes out the central theme by quoting from volume 2 (1918) of *Ordeal* by the Russian-Soviet writer Aleksey Tolstoy: "Thrice wrung out in water, thrice bathed in blood, thrice boiled in caustic." Following the quote, he describes himself as someone who "indiscriminately absorbed feudal and bourgeois culture," who "after a long 'ordeal' finally becomes a Marxist." His fictional book is thus entitled *The Revelation of the Materialist* (Weiwulunzhe de qishilu), with "Mimosa" being the first in a series of nine novellas and novels he plans to write. The Chinese rendition of *Ordeal* is *Kunan de licheng*, meaning literally "Historical process of bitter suffering." Of the original title of the author's unfinished book, *qishilu* is the term for "apocalypse" in Chinese translations of the Bible and Coppola's film *Apocalypse Now*. This quasi-religious rhetoric is crucial to the materialist's identification with Marx and the people.

The materialistic-cum-religious posture, however, is not self-contradictory in light of the deification of Marx in Mao's China. Nor is the juxtaposition of hunger with "divine revelation" intended for an iconoclasm of Marx himself. Rather, Zhang's critique is launched within the fluid boundary of Chinese Marxism as part of the dynamic process of renegotiating the Marxist legacy. The quasi-religious encoding of suffering manifests precisely the internalized symptom of an asceto-Marxism that falls behind Marx's critique of political economy. A historical subtext here is the young Marx's *Economic and Philosophic Manuscripts of 1844* and the critique of "socialist alienation" that was initiated in Eastern Europe and embraced in China by some leading "liberal" Party intellectuals in the early 1980s.[4] What the theorists advanced on the ideological front was echoed in Zhang's literary indictment of social misery in Chinese state socialism. This critique of socialist alienation will come forth in a powerful fashion later in Zhang Yonglin's fantastic bibliophagy of Marx. But before we move to that remarkable episode the lofty rhetoric of the prologue must be further dissected.

Intertextually, the novella's prologue reminds us of Lu Xun's "Diary," though the sense of irony is played out not around linguistic and formal clashes that embody the confrontation of tradition and modernity, as in Lu Xun's story. Rather than valorizing the head at the expense of the body, "Mimosa" highlights the split between the head and the stomach so as to show the very ironic consequences of a revolution that promised a socialist feast. Intratextually, however, between the prologue and the story proper, the ironic distance derives less from an authorial design than from a textual embodiment of a historical "truth by default." The ambivalence of the authorial voice is postponed until its quasi-religious mood breaks down when it becomes impossible to reconcile itself with material reality. Indeed, historical contradictions can no longer be contained in terms of the character's split consciousness alone. If by authorial design Zhang Yonglin is torn between his moral conscience and the human animal in his body, the conflict between mind and flesh cannot be solved within the "inner," psychological world. The mind-body clashes generate a phantasmagoric feast of words that is at once "readerly" and "writerly," realistic and hallucinatory. In other words, the intratextual contradiction between the prologue and the story proper reveals an abyss between the protagonist's animal instinct and the narrator's desperate attempt to transcend flesh via Marx, when, so to speak, Zhang Yonglin wants to have his cake and eat it too. In the end, the failure of the quasi-religious mood in the prologue to contain suffering returns us to the abject condition of material existence. Here, a hermeneutic probing into the aesthetic realm is necessary for reopening the critical space of materiality.

If the split personality of Zhang Yonglin is figured in his simultaneous embodiment of material lack and semiotic excess, this existential condition would make him a Kafkaesque hunger artist. However, hunger is not chosen by him for the cultivation of wisdom, nor does art for art's sake help him discard the body that cries for food. His is the ordeal of a bourgeois intellectual so starved that starvation turns him into a materialist by default. His consciousness is caught in an aporia whereby the lofty posture of idealism does not cohere with his primordial experience. The madness of history can only be contained as a signifier of emptiness: the lack of food miraculously becomes a sort of Eucharist for his communion with Marx, the opposite of the normal mode of religious participation. Like the Madman's story, there are two modes of the allegorical at work. The deconstructive mode of the Benjaminian allegory stands the ruins of history on the empty stomach, whereas the constructive mode of the Hegelian allegory sutures the teleological narrative of the ordeal from moral downfall through repentance to the final redemption. The negative allegory then allows us to enter the world of the materialist in spite of the quasi-religious revelation advanced by the author in the prologue.

What the allegory of the materialist reveals, first of all, is that the protagonist's downfall is not a moral problem. When the story begins, Zhang Yonglin, at the age of twenty-five, has already spent four years in a Chinese gulag because of an alleged anti-Party poem. A young romanticist, he has almost lost his life in coming to understand the seeming truism that "if you fill your stomach you don't feel hungry." This is a folk saying that sounds redundant, but he "found [it] more difficult to grasp than Aristotle's *Poetics*" (257–58; 83).[5] His nightmare is not death in hunger but the decay of the soul when a poet bred in the spirit of *Poetics* has fallen to the squalid state of animals. In the labor camp, even the rats died out because "they had nothing to eat but [were] in danger of being eaten [by humans]" (210; 41). Released, Zhang Yonglin stood 1.78 meters (5'10") tall but weighed only forty-four kilograms (ninety-seven lbs). Riding in a cart and watching the driver whipping the horses that were "in no better shape than [he]," Zhang Yonglin saw his own fate in that of the horses. "I could understand the driver's callousness," he remarks. "Hungry? So what? While there's life in you, keep going. Hunger, far more terrifying than his whip, had long since driven all compassion from our minds" (182; 14). When the poet was entrapped in the battle for mere existence, he utilized his mighty mind to compensate his feeble limbs. He made a trick container, taking advantage of an optical illusion to fool the cooks of the labor camp into giving him 100 centimeters more gruel at each meal. Freed from prison and working on a resettlement farm, he crafted an arithmetical trick to cheat an illiterate peasant and took away more than a pound of free carrots. These were, recalls the narrator, places "where my education came in handy" (190; 22).

However, being educated is also a burden on his conscience when the moral self of the poet interferes with the instinct of the human animal. "In the daytime," Zhang Yonglin reflects:

> my instinct of self-preservation drove me to ingratiate myself and resort to all kinds of tricks [to obtain food]. At night I was horrified by the contemptible behaviors, revolted by my conduct during the day. I shuddered and cursed myself.
>
> I was fully aware of just how low I'd sunk.
>
> I don't believe that decadence is entirely due to objective circumstances. If that were the case and will-power counted for nothing, then men would sink to the level of beasts. True religious believers can lay down their lives for God. Materialist poets take high ideals as their god. Since I was not dead, what was I living for? Just for the sake of living? If so, how utterly futile. (205; 37)

Again, the analogy between "true religious believers" and "materialist poets" should not confuse us. In the protagonist's world, this comparison is just another example of how two contradictory conscious worlds are interlocked in the narrator's attempt to make sense of the reality and his "natural" response to it. The inner conflict exhibits his equivocation between the abject reality and the sense of guilt, with the former inscribed in the discourse of the latter. This confusion, because it results from internalizing external contradiction, manifests a pathological reaction to the brutal world. By internalizing objective circumstances as moral decadence, the narrator obviously has to read history in such a way that he can reconcile his meaningless life with his tortured self. And the source that would save him from the futile life is *Das Kapital*.

The classic Marxist text is the only book that the protagonist reads during the course of the story (all other books are referred to in his memory of the past). When a philosophy teacher hands it to him as a farewell gift, he advises Zhang Yonglin that "maybe you can find out from it why we're where we are today," stressing that the collective "we" means more than just this particular group of Rightists and that "our fates are closely bound up with that of our country" (186–87; 18). Subsequently, the text resorts to Marx as a critical weapon to indict the Communist regime on its own terms of legitimation. In this sense, *Das Kapital* stands for the source of truth and meaning much the same way that it functions in Communist history. To highlight the religious nature of the official version of Marxism, the author lets a Muslim peasant refer to it as Zhang Yonglin's version of the Koran (324; 153). By the same token, the narrator describes his Marxist enlightenment with the Buddhist term *dunwu* (satori), which "gives birth to a new life" inside him (317; 145). "This book," he comments, "was now my sole link with the rational world of the intellect, the only way I could rise above buns, carrots and gruel, and could become different from a starving beast" (207; 38). By distinguishing the masterpiece of historical materialism from primordial material subsistence, "Marx" becomes the "transcendental signified" that redeems his moral downfall. This transcendental tendency subsumes the social-historical critique intended by the philosophy professor.

However, hunger resurfaces in a more powerful form once the consumption of Marx's book supersedes the quasi-religious posture. After all: "Hunger can become a palpable weight pounding against your stomach. Can scream to each nerve in your body: I want food!" (208; 38). The weight of hunger is so formidable that the sacred book of Marx in the end has to serve itself up as food. On a snowy day, Zhang Yonglin reads Marx like this:

> I could really believe Chaplin's portrayal of that famished prospector on a snowy mountain who mistook a man for a turkey. That wasn't a stroke of imaginative genius. Chaplin must have heard about it from somebody who'd known what it was to starve. When I read [in *Das Kapital*], "Commodities come into the world in the shape of use values, articles, or goods, such as iron, linen, wheat, etc.," I savored the word "wheat" instead of concentrating on the meaning. I had a mental picture of bread, steamed buns, flapjacks, even cream cakes which made my mouth water. Then came the equation [describing the exchange of commodities].
>
> A "coat," "tea," "coffee," "wheat," what a feast! Imagine wearing a spotless white coat [instead of huddling in a torn quilt], with some Keemun tea or Brazilian coffee in front of you [rather than an empty tin], cutting up a cream cake [not a carrot]—that would be a feast fit for the gods! My imagination enabled me to blend all the banquets I'd ever attended, seen

or heard about. But all those delicacies distracted me from "The Fetishism of Commodities and the Secret Thereof." And on that cold silent winter day there wafted over that appetizing smell of the food I'd been imagining. I started to have stomach spasms. (231–32; 60–61)

It is the social reality of hunger that shifts the focal point of reading from the quasi-religious allegory to its own deconstruction. For one thing, Marx could not possibly have imagined that his thesis on commodity fetishism would become the very object of consumption, the secret of which is revealed in his disciple's imagination as nothing grandiose. This episode perhaps ought to be taken as one of the few truly "creative" readings of Marxism in Communist history. Hidden in this passage of semiotic overcoding is the poverty of life wrought by the distorted implementation of that social theory. An exhausted theology of emancipation from the shackles of necessity to the promised kingdom of freedom eventually has to serve as a necessity for survival.

In deconstructive terms, the extravagant imagination of the book goes hand in hand with the disruption of signification and the depletion of accepted meaning. The signifiers of commodities are completely taken out of the text and regrouped in a series of plays on words. This seems to be a strategy characteristic of postmodernism. Yet all the time there is a persistent return of material referents to obstruct our free play with the signifiers. If "wheat," "coffee," "tea," and "bread" shortcut their signifying chain and merge with their referents to create a hallucination, the projection is motivated by nothing less than real hunger, which in turn engenders bodily dysfunction such as stomach spasms. In a most ironical way, the grand narrative of utopia is seen in a physical dystopia. In this reversed order of food and words, the daydream of food that spawns the pathological meaning-production of words fades into the horrifying nightmare of reality. At the same time, the daydream is also reinvested with the libidinal impulse of eating in a truly materialistic digestion of the book. The boundary between food and words, between consumption and reading, is completely erased in distorted playfulness not for the mere sake of play. Verbal playfulness generates nothing but intense pains of the body.

Obviously, a deconstructive reading must be modified here to take account of the material underpinning of language use. Meanwhile, we need to note that alimentary writing has a long poetic tradition, which stimulates other carnal responses than stomach spasms. The pleasure of the text compensates for the pains of the body. The Chinese materialist poet may surprise aesthetic Marxists when he literally consumes Marx's words as gastronomic images. Later, Zhang Yonglin's mental ingestion of *Das Kapital* becomes increasingly aestheticized when it assimilates Marx through the gastronomic palate for a verbal feast that eases his artistic hunger. He is uncertain whether he can "assimilate the nutrition made up of abstract concepts." So he decides to chew the concrete images: "Marx used such vivid, graphic images to illustrate economics that, though I didn't fully grasp his meaning, I was gripped by his fluent literary style." Abstract concepts not fully accessible to the poet, he savors the "vivid images" and "the evocativeness of poetry" (296–97; 121–23). This strange consumption of words of things eventually connects commodity production with aesthetic intoxication. As he puts it:

> The ability to express rational ideas in terms of graphic images from real life is a rare gift for any thinker or artist. And Marx was an unsurpassable master at this. I was starting to read *Das Kapital* seriously as a fine work of literature, in which I admired each sentence. Literature can work miracles in people's minds. Can smash their preconceived ideas and reshape them.
>
> Both art and abstract ideas have the power to intoxicate human beings. Together they are doubly potent. Though still unable to grasp to the full the subtlety of this wine, it was going to my head. (298; 123–24)

Once again, one wonders how Marx would respond to the poetic ecstasy generated by *Das Kapital*. The metaphoric equation of art and poetry to wine is one of the oldest topoi in the Chinese and European traditions, of course. Yet only by transgressing the rigid generic and thematic boundaries can the abstract theory of political economics intoxicate the reader—a feeling of intoxication "doubly potent" at that. Here Zhang's bibliophagy produces a different kind of hunger artist when words are sipped to ease the pains of the flesh rather than tapped for the transcendence of the soul. It is in the aesthetic blending with materiality that gastronomic intoxication enables the narrator to come to terms with the situated truth of Marxism. As aesthetic consumption deconstructs the dualism of the body and the mind, words become the material bearer for reconstructing historical memory. In the end, the word is the wine that sustains life by soothing the pains of madness.

The aesthetic depoliticization of Marx corresponds to the general cultural environment of the 1980s. From a purely political point of view, reading Marx in a seemingly glorifying narrative is an ingenious way to head off official censorship. But the subversive intent is aimed at opening a new ground of interpretation that infuses pleasure into asceto-Marxism, injects desire into political economics, and inscribes a playful human face around the sober weapon of critique. The corresponding formal strategy is a generic transgression of the rigid boundary between the political and the poetic modes and the consequent breakdown of the symbolic hierarchy embedded therein. Poeticized for verbal consumption, Marxist theoretical discourse now takes a new emancipatory form perhaps never intended by Marx himself.

Zhang's approach to Marx may well be called materialistic aestheticism. The logic of the nondualism of food and words lays bare the interconnectedness of production and consumption, writing and reading, and construction and interpretation. The backward leap to Marx is based on a forward move out of established modes of reading, a creative reading that is simultaneously "readerly" and "writerly," realistic and deconstructive. It is "readerly" and "realistic" in that the reading is figured in consumption, caused by the lack of food/book in the reality. But the reading is also "writerly" and deconstructive because through metonymical displacement the fixed meaning of the book is diluted and reinvested with subversive desire. This strategic displacement through "reading as consumption" produces a different "writerly text" and foregrounds the material nature of language use.

To problematize these poststructuralist concepts is meant here to highlight the complex picture of cultural politics in a postrevolutionary society. If the theoretical shift from classical Marxist critiques of production to Stalinist critiques of consumption has turned historical materialism into asceto-Marxism, this restrictive practice must be re-turned. In an era of international travel, Zhang Xianliang's wicked yet brilliant pastiche of asceto-Marxism delineates a brief contour of a "second-world" theory that has traveled to a "third-world" country and is debunked through a playful consciousness similar to that of the postmodernism of the "first world." These labels of global cartography are not strictly applicable to the Chinese situation because the postrevolutionary culture of China assembles bits of all yet resembles none of the three worlds as they are classified in our current theorization of geopolitical and ethnocultural configurations. Conversely, while we are tempted to celebrate formal hybridity in cultural formations, the thematic substance of the "materialist revelation" must be taken seriously as an earthy yet schizophrenic outcry: Feed me, Marx!

Problematic of the People

The project of rewriting Marx cannot be completed without critically addressing another major cultural icon of the Communist revolution: the Chinese peasantry. For the poet, the feast of Marx's words is accompanied by the seeking of real food from the true provisioner. The narrator's relationship with the peasant characters illustrates less a matter of reimagination than a real problem of the continuous social disparity between the modern literati and the masses. Some critics have pointed out that the author idealizes the peasants in order to dramatize the protagonist's moral downfall and his final transcendence of his petty self. What is most problematic is Zhang Yonglin's relationship with the peasant woman Ma Yinghua, for whom "Mimosa" is named. The story of an educated young man who is saved by an underclass woman, only to part with her in the end, has simply reproduced an old-fashioned melodrama of sentimentalism.[6] Thus, we need to disentangle the issue of gender from that of class so that we may reappropriate her alterity to foreground an alternative social history.

The image of Ma Yinghua resembles what Rey Chow (1991, chap. 4) calls the "loving woman." As Chow has pointed out in her reading of some early-twentieth-century Chinese texts, the image of the "loving woman," often assuming the position of the mother, is paradigmatically structured as "affection versus sensuality" or "reverence versus eroticism." The "idealization of a woman depends on a conception of her as clean and untouched by sexuality." This "dissociation of affection and sensuality" deprives the woman of her "psychic life" and demobilizes her as a fetish (149–50). In "Mimosa," the male construction of the loving woman hinges on the narrator's recurring doubts and repeated dismissal of his doubts about Mimosa's sexual "cleanness," his contrived account of her voluntary suppression of erotic desire, and his later rejection of her body to valorize her moral purity. In the end, she is immobilized into a redeeming figure whose only function is to nurture Zhang Yonglin's body and save his soul.

Approached from this angle of male projection, the author's revision of "the people" to deconstruct the key category of class is undercut by his reinscription of an even older "mother-son" complex. For the loving woman is not only deprived of her sexuality but is also a replica of the feeding mother, long established before the political dissociation of women from their womanhood. There is a consistent retrieval of the "oral stage" that sets up their narrative encounter in the "baby's" imagination of the "mother." The first time the hungry Zhang Yonglin went to Ma Yinghua's home by himself, he "was spurred by a natural impulse to raise the lid of the pan and lift the curtain to see what there was to eat." He acted as if he were a starving child gazing at the food his mother has prepared for him (214; 45). When he was invited to her house the next time, he dreamed of "a wife and a big beef and cabbage stew," a line from a Russian poem. Yet there was no wife nor Russian menu but a big steamed roll offered to him by the hostess. Insisting that he should not be ashamed of taking food from a single woman, she treated him just like her own child. When she was feeding her own boy, she promised more food to Zhang in a speech act directed at her child. "Ershe," she asks her boy, "tell Uncle: Don't worry. So long as I have food there'll be some for you. Go on, say" (237–42; 67–70). Thereafter, Zhang Yonglin would visit her home whenever he was hungry. Hunger not only turns Zhang into a schizophrenic eater of Marx's words but it also returns him to the oral phase of the baby.

Their symbolic relationship is consciously recognized by the narrator himself. In fact, he enjoys it very much. After a few weeks of dining at her home, he finds his body literally growing up. "Each time I stoked up with real grain there," Zhang Yonglin remarks, "I felt myself growing stronger. It wasn't my imagination either. . . . I could feel my cheeks filling out, feel my good muscle tone. For the first time in my life I was full of energy. . . . Many novels describe the sound of plants growing at night or shoots breaking through the soil; but I had the unique experience, as I lay in my ragged quilt at night, of hearing my own cells divide" (264; 90). By the same token, when Ma Yinghua is stroking his cheek, he feels as if it is "a gentle breeze" and "could hear strains of Brahms' 'Lullaby' " (281; 106). When he was angry with Mimosa over the suspicious source of her dumplings, she "teased him like a child with her smile" (318; 146). Her teasing, however, also prompts him to conclude that "she seemed incapable of taking anything seriously" (ibid.). Along with the narrator's physical growth goes his recovery of self-consciousness, the recognition that he is not her child. But their separation takes a form rather similar to the family drama when the "father" intervenes. Not a physical presence, the "fatherly" is an older figure of social disparity. As Zhang Yonglin reflects: "Nothing could bridge the cultural gap between us. . . . Much as it upsets me, I felt that we were incompatible" (317; 145). The cultural gap is once again structured on the age-old opposite of the cultural elite versus the working people. "While I read Marx," the narrator reflects, "he wanted to transform my outlook, bringing it in line with that of the working people. On the other hand, my past experience made me conscious of a gap between them and myself. I was superior to them mentally, on a higher intellectual plane" (312; 140). In the end, literacy marks their class difference, and the age-old social gap reinscribes the imagination of the "motherly" in a hierarchy of class.

All the repeated references to the "motherly" and its association with food is indicative of the age-old male fantasy of the loving mother. To make it even more problematic, the object is not a biological mother, nor even an elderly substitute from the narrator's clan. Just as the quasi-religious mode of the narrative attempts to reduce the socioeconomic nightmare to a moralist self-redemption, the intellectual's self-awakening is no more than his painful recognition that it is ultimately impossible for him to be at one with the social other. Consequently, the "mother" and the "child" have to be separated when class and gender differences are brought to the fore. A question then arises: what value does the story contain in rewriting the revolutionary image of the people?

A similar distinction has to be made between the subjective use of the woman for the intellectual's redemption and the social condition in which Ma Yinghua and other peasant characters manage to survive. Much as the split between the head and the body creates two allegories of Marx, Ma Yinghua has two faces, so to speak. If the writerly transgression of Marx defies moralistic closure, the otherness of the woman can be reappropriated from the male idealization of the "motherly." By shifting to her own point of view, we will encounter a peasant woman who manages to control her life. As the repressed narrative unconscious surfaces in Zhang Yonglin's hungry ingestion of Marx's words, sensuality reasserts itself in the libidinal realm of eating. What makes her a powerful figure of survival, ironically, is precisely her marginal position in the symbolic parameters of the people.

Ma Yinghua is uncharacteristic of the people in a number of ways. Illiterate, she displays no class consciousness of the idealized revolutionary heroine. A descendent of a central-Asian ethnic minority, she has an "illegitimate" child and is thus "uncivilized." Located at the bottom of a hierarchical society, she "unashamedly" takes advantage of her social status. If a poor peasant woman is fated to the domestic space, she will turn out the fittest in the struggle for food. Although the authorial narrative uses her as a textual trope for the narrator's transcendence of flesh, the radical difference embodied in this uneducated poor minority woman provides a powerful subversion of the people.

A schematic review of the Communist idealization of the peasantry is necessary before we proceed further. From Lu Xun to the Yan'an years, there was a process of historical change in the name of the people. The negative diagnosis Lu Xun initiated was transformed into a positive consciousness-raising strategy. The narrative subjectivity of a lonely searcher and the telos of a vague hope for a similarly vague future in Lu Xun were reformulated in the revolutionary narrative of Yan'an literature, with the new "socialist feast" as its telos and the collective revolutionary consciousness as its subjectivity. In his 1942 "Yan'an Talk," Mao particularly called upon intellectuals to remold their thought in order to bridge the gap between cultural and material producers. However, this process evolved into idealizing the people to the exclusion of the intellectual. The exclusion of the intellectual was to create a potential social tension that would come to the fore in the class struggle in the realm of ideology after the founding of the PRC. Meanwhile, the idealization of the masses produced an idealistic type that culminated in the "model dramas" of the Cultural Revolution—an idealistic type that no individual member of the masses could live up to and a totalizing type that has denied his or her real needs and reasonable desires. In retrospect, the totalizing concept of the people is inseparable from the centralization of power in the hands of the party-state, paradoxically because the political power is exercised in the name of "the dictatorship of the people's democracy."

Once the masses are deemed in theory to be the masters of society, they must respond to the party-state's repeated call for their "noble sacrifice." Indeed, the industrialization of the first thirty years of the People's Republic was based on a disproportionately high accumulation of capital on the back of the peasantry. This Stalinist sacrifice of rural interest was further aggravated by the prolonged Maoist political campaigns, which disrupted the basic rules of socialist construction. Toward the end of the Cultural Revolution, the rhetoric of class struggle became so preposterous that the propagandist organs blared everyday the slogan "[Chinese land] would rather grow socialist weeds than capitalist seedlings," a graphic metaphor for what was left in the bowls of the masses. Contrary to the myth that gives all credit to reform-minded leaders such as Deng Xiaoping, the post-Mao economic reform actually started as a bottom-up peasant revolt.[7]

The heroic idealization of the people went hand in hand with the impoverishment of the rural people who were the backbone of the revolution. Further complicating this historical irony is the fact that intellectuals such as Zhang Xianliang found themselves in a similar situation. Not only did they have to go through the "ordeal of bitter suffering" but this ordeal was the necessary condition for their thought reform.

When intellectuals were forced to perform hard labor among the peasants, however, their experiences had some positive effects. They found themselves in a position to understand the peasantry better than their predecessors did. The age-old social gap between the elite and the peasant was in this way leveled by "egalitarian poverty" rather than around the table of the envisioned socialist feast. Zhang Xianliang himself seems to see in his experience of hard labor a good opportunity that put his literary writing into a different perspective. The narrator reflects toward the end of the story: "It struck me that in the Chinese and European literatures that have nurtured me, there had been no characters like these peasants: humble, crude manual laborers with their own moral code, yet intelligent and capable of the finest feelings." In his view, " 'the People' don't exist in the abstract, they are like Mimosa, Team Leader Xie, and Hai Xixi, though they may fall far short of the grandeur of the [revolutionary] literary characters." As a result, Zhang stresses, "fate had given me the chance to discover these rough diamonds, and I must remember each and every one of them" (336; 166–67). It is their ambiguity, like rough diamonds, that demystifies the aura of the people.

The peasants's moral code is vividly manifested in their actions and attitudes toward food. Theoretically, as the producers of food, they have the "natural" right to feed themselves with the food they produce. Yet, in a state socialism where peasants' basic livelihood is sacrificed for industrialization in the name of public ownership, personal survival becomes ineluctably political. For Hai Xixi, the Muslim cart driver, his livelihood depends on a piece of wasteland he has reclaimed on which to grow soybeans. This political "encroachment" on the public land has the tacit approval of Team Leader Xie, an official who represents resistance within the Party because he is a farmer himself. But their actions are governed not by their different moral code but by the fundamental ethic of stoic survival.

The narrator's often excessive moralistic reading of the peasants is in sharp contrast to the latter's transgression of that hypocritical moral concern. Mimosa can make the best of food shortages by taking advantage of the lack of "morality." She turns her status as a young, attractive, single woman into a powerful resource to "seduce" men into providing her with whatever food they can steal from the public farm—without ever letting these men take advantage of her. To her, this is not cheating. "Who is fooling whom?" she asks the narrator, who questions her behavior. "Just think, they didn't pay for the grain they brought to me. If I didn't take it, they would hog it themselves anyway" (341; 171–72). In the massive famine, "she had a store of flour, rice, glutinous millet, maize, sorghum, soybeans, peas [and] whatever grew on the steppe" (258; 84). She appears immoral only to those who moralize her according to a rigid self-righteous code of conduct.

Interestingly, the clash of different moral codes even has much to do with global politics. Opening her home like an "American restaurant," she respatializes an "immoral" space into a home of bounty. "As time went by," recalls the narrator:

> I learned what other farm-hands meant by "American Restaurant." It was just a figure of speech based on their understanding of the world. It wasn't a restaurant in the usual sense, but anyone could drop in for a chat; so it was more like a teahouse. And the men who frequented it showed their appreciation by keeping her supplied with extra grain. The intriguing thing was the use of the adjective "American." To the farm-hands America was an outlandish, promiscuous, immoral country, but so rich that no one worried about food and clothing. They weren't insulting Mimosa, just poking fun at her. (259–60; 85–86)

During the Cold War, when the United States was the top enemy of China, Chinese peasants in one of its remote corners could remap that space in an "immoral" woman's home that provided the warmth of food and chat. This double spatialization transgresses the ideological and political mapping of the world and is based on the peasants' incorporation of the world through orality: eating and chatting. It is in this simple but ambiguous space that social relations are reestablished outside state-sanctioned parameters. And this newly opened space is symbolic of the oral space that was originally ingrained in the mother-child relationship but was now transformed into a dynamic and mutual responsive process. By making her home an unofficial center of village life, she not only decenters the political landscape of the everyday but stands as an active, loving woman. Because she controls food and the microspace of eating, cooking, feeding, and nurturing, she adeptly manages to control the lives of herself and many others in the face of the uncontrollable torrent of historical catastrophe.

To return to the two sides of Ma Yinghua, the narrative's ultimate inability to contain her within any established type of characterization paradoxically leaves her image open-ended. As the poet and critic Shao Yanxiang points out: "Instead of idealizing her character and connecting her image with our old civilized and barbarous traditions, I can only say that her image evades our established modes of cognition. . . . She comes to life, not from the author's intention, design, contrivance, and construction, but out of the true life-experience and from the bottom of the author's heart" (1984, 24). Perhaps it might be better to ignore the author's openly stated intention and instead treat the contradictory and controversial text as an allegorical (in the Benjaminian sense) embodiment of a postrevolutionary moment. What is laid down by the changing tide of history is nothing less than a sediment of cultural pathology that exhibits the deep-seated ambivalence of the time.

The narrative ambivalence toward the peasant woman is particularly indicative of the intellectual's anxiety to relate to his social other. It is unfortunate that he had to come to understand the harsh conditions of the peasants through forced labor. Nevertheless, his ordeal of bitter suffering yields some sweet fruit. It certainly has not erased their social distance, but intellectuals like Zhang Xianliang have adopted a more humble attitude toward those who feed. In the tradition of alimentary writing discussed up to this point, Zhang Xianliang is more self-conscious about the relationship of food and words. This captures the real economic exchange whereby the writer trades literary work for food. In his rereading of Marx, he blends food and words for a verbal feast so that Marxism can be recycled for a new round of critique. With the people, he is anxious to repay his debt to those who fed him. In the end, however, ink can only be shed on paper to commemorate the paradox of material poverty and semiotic plenitude.

Surviving (in) "The Chess King"

Like Zhang Xianliang's "Mimosa," Ah Cheng's novella "The Chess King" has attracted enormous critical attention. Ah Cheng's low-key treatment of eating, chess playing, and storytelling fed the emerging cultural nostalgia for a lost way of life by single-handedly touching off the "searching for roots" movement in the mid-1980s. The lingering image of the ancient Dao has even found its way onto the Internet. On July 11, 1994, the electronic mail Chinese magazine *Huaxia Wenzhai* (China digest) devoted an entire issue to reprinting the novella under the editorial title "Selected Literary Masterpiece." For a piece of fiction supposedly too new to deserve the title "masterpiece" yet too old to sustain attention for novelty in an age of mass reproduction of culture, what has made it so appealing to the national (un)consciousness, so unerasable from the historical-cum-electronic "memory"?

It might be helpful to trace the novella's greatness to an earlier moment in its dissemination. In 1986, Li Oufan (Leo Ou-fan Lee), Li Tuo, Gao Xingjian, and Ah Cheng published the proceedings of a "roundtable" discussion entitled "Literature: Overseas and China" (Li Oufan et al. 1991). Though not solely devoted to Ah Cheng's work, their discussion started with Lee's opening remark with regard to how belated the transmission of contemporary Chinese literature was to readers abroad. He cited "The Chess King" as an example, noting that its enormous popularity in overseas Chinese reading communities came *after* its reprinting in the influential Hong Kong journal *The Nineties*. The editor of *The Nineties*, however, decided to reprint the novella *after* he was introduced to it through a short commentary Michael Duke wrote and published in the same journal (the novella was reprinted in the next issue; see Li Yi et al. 1992, 46). Though Duke did not exactly say how he came to know it, he indicated that the mainland literary critic Feng Mu had told him about the author during Feng's visit to Canada when Ah Cheng had just attracted a great deal of domestic acclaim (See Du Maike 1985, 82). The novella's early triangular journey between China, North America, and Hong Kong, and its more recent resurfacing on the Internet, involve all three major modes of cultural transmission, from the most "primitive" oral communication through printing to the information superhighway. During these ten years, moreover, we witnessed the way three "local times" were unraveling and emerging at once: the unraveling of state socialism in the PRC and its "peaceful transformation" into what could only be called "state capitalism with Chinese characteristics," the unraveling of colonialism in Hong Kong and its increasingly strategic role in the emerging "Greater China," and the shifting tides of opinion in North America toward the Pacific Rim.

I propose to read the text's trans-Pacific circulation as a witness to the trace of the (in)famous "always already" at work while at the same time taking the e-mail reprint as testimony to the other half of the slogan: "never ever." In this section, I first delineate a moment of the "always already" in the text's early reception, an important instance that has contributed to the rebirth of cultural nationalism in post-Mao China. Later I will attempt to push open the "never ever" by uncovering the textual alterity that has been crossed out and thus must be returned to constitute that which *survives.* Inspired by the chess master in Ah Cheng's masterpiece, I adopt a reading tactic modeled on chess playing. Reading the process, not the outcome, of each game is very much like reading the trace, the trail, and the movement of language. Each piece is like a signifier, whose signified is determined by its position on the board in relation to other signifiers. Conversely, each move may also change the meaning of the whole text, differentiating between the pieces on the battlefield so as to defer the final closure. There are as many chess texts as there are players. The same player may never perform the same game in the way it was played before. To the extent that displacement figures each and every move on the board and survival signifies the process of constant negotiation, displacement is the existential condition of survival as much as its strategy. This dynamic, ever-changing, open-ended game offers a model for reading Ah Cheng's novella and the various interpretative moves in the critical literature.

While chess playing provides the model for a deconstructive reading, chess is nevertheless a cultural institution implicated in the construction of the nation. In traversing "territories" and crossing "borders," chess in the modern world has been appropriated by nationalism to embody the teleological movement toward the final identification with the transcendental signified: the defeat of the opponent in the name of the king.

In post-Mao China, especially where Chinese players are likely to win international titles (such as in *go* or women's international chess), chess matches have played into the writing of the nation and are often broadcast via television to foster patriotic sentiments. This double nature of chess being both an open-ended process of signification and a reified embodiment of teleology is a microscopic effect of the ambivalence of nation-narration.

As Homi Bhabha has pointed out, the construction of the modern (European) nation hinges on a discursive address to the "people." This appellation defines the "people" at once as "the historical 'object' of a nationalist pedagogy" and "the 'subject' of a process of signification." The discourse of nationalism thus is figured in "a split between the continuist, accumulative temporality of the pedagogical, and the repetitious, recursive strategy of the performative." Such a "conceptual ambivalence" between the pedagogical object and the performative subject of modern society "becomes the site of *writing the nation*" (1990, 297; original emphasis). If chess playing and nation-narration share a similar ambivalence, it is the former that consciously valorizes its playfulness and performativity and seeks to repeat the pleasure in the game's irreducible uncertainty and infinitive variety. The primary process of chess playing thus not only lays bare its double nature, imposed by the ideology of nationalism, but it can be used to examine the traces of ideological containment and concealment. As such, chess playing and nation-narration signify the bipolar tension between the performative and the pedagogical. Such a tension is already inscribed in the title, inserted yet hidden between "Chess [and] King." It is these two figures that provide a metonymical configuration of the ambivalence of nation-narration.

Post-Mao Nostalgia for "Roots"

In the narrow sense of the term *survival*, Ah Cheng's story has much in common with the so-called scar literature that preceded it. The latter is a narrative precedent that represents personal experiences under political persecution, economic impoverishment, and emotional trauma in Maoist China. In the early years of the post-Mao era, two groups of survivors—the "rightist" writers and dislocated city youths—were the major voices repudiating the Maoist legacy. In contrast to scar literature, which exposes the sufferings of the survivor as a political victim,

Ah Cheng's story extols the triumphant spirit of the survivor as a cultural hero. With little reference to historical catastrophes, "The Chess King" portrays the individual's survival as a positive experience: what is capable of surviving the catastrophic must be anything but excessive sentimentalism and narcissism. This thematic change shifts the focus of postrevolutionary literature from humanistic self-pity and outrage to nativist rewriting of the political and the ethical. What the text brings to the fore is the problem of how to bypass the haunting images of the immediate past and reconnect with ancient "roots."

Wang Meng, a former "rightist" writer who served as the minister of culture and resigned after the 1989 crackdown, was among the few early commentators who sensed the problematic of writing Ah Cheng posed. Soon after the novella's publication, Wang wrote that "for a long time I haven't seen this kind of language, this kind of style, and this kind of narrative." He then cited a few examples, ones that have become classic quotations of Ah Cheng's work. "Not only is the language special," Wang continues, "but the substance is also unique." He sums up its uniqueness as the textual valorization of the protagonist's integrity, the reversal of the narcissistic pathos of scar literature, and the Chinese Way of chess, which powerfully evokes abstract ideals beyond the game. Against the creative writer Wang Meng and his fascination with the novella's language and theme, however, the cultural apparatchik Wang Meng in the end downplays the historical significance of "The Chess King," considering it a mere "strange tale" tinged with the escapism of ancient China. This "strange tale," according to him, is incompatible with the "mainstream of literary development" that "represents real struggles in the spirit of the age" (1984, 43–45).

Wang Meng's split voice captures in a nutshell the two conflicting forces in determining the meaning of the text and negotiating its position in the larger political context. For one thing, his final negative encoding of the text in mainstream ideology sets the standard away from which, in hindsight, the literary development was actually moving. His critique of the text's "escapist" tendencies points to the detour of a literary movement in search of "roots" rather than "the spirit of the age." His official view aside, the creative writer Wang Meng's reading is indicative of the way the overwhelming majority of critics approach the text. Located at an ideological intersection, the recurrence of a particular style of fictional writing must be understood first and foremost by accounting for its historical absence: "For a long time I haven't seen this kind of language . . ."

Once established as a cultural signifier for a historical *absence*, the text is called upon to re-*present* the lost past through its stylistic affinity. It is called upon to reconnect the linguistic and aesthetic particulars of a preexisting but disrupted world with their reemergence and then to transform this particular form of sensibility into a general manifestation of modern China's historical trajectory. Wang Dewei, for example, has noted that the celebratory response of readers from overseas Chinese communities reflects a "homesick reading" (1991, 139). Readers in Taiwan and Hong Kong have explicitly linked the historical absence to the loss of native culture at the hands of Chinese Communism. Since it is the Communist revolution that dislocated many expatriates from their homeland, the return of a pre-Communist native tradition cannot but elicit their memories of the past. And even though critics in the PRC have to navigate the political minefield with much caution they are no less "homesick" than their overseas counterparts. Their celebration of the native's return was coupled with the pleasant estrangement the text generated in their initial encounter with it—estrangement from their habit of reading shaped by the then still dominant official discourse. But most critics took their feeling of defamiliarization as a point of departure for something to be refamiliarized. Unlike the forward-looking Wang Meng, they looked backward to recenter this strange tale around the native tradition. As a result, a story that "tells" about human survival also "shows," by virtue of the fact that it signals a historical return, the much applauded survival of Chinese tradition.

Theodore Huters has suggested that what C. T. Hsia calls modern Chinese literature's "obsession with China" may be reinterpreted as "less a marker of nationalistic sentimentality and more a deep-seated perplexity about . . . the past" (1993, 270). His observation may well apply to the nostalgic response to Ah Cheng's novella, which clearly is internally oriented and backward looking. But how has this temporal move played into the space of the modern nation, a territorial and a symbolic space that can only be constructed by its borders or external differences? It ought to be noted that in the text the only explicit use of the term *China* or *Chinese* is in the phrase "the Chinese Way of chess." It is used only once toward the end of the story, where the protagonist's opponent, an old man depicted in the image of a hermit, finds in the protagonist the true Dao of chess and exclaims: "The Chinese Way of chess has not declined at all" (Zhonghua qidao bijing butui). This phrase has been repetitively identified as the transcendental signifier and has generated a grand allegorical transformation culminating, for instance, in Michael Duke's pronouncement: "The Chinese Way Has Never Declined At All" (Zhonghua zhidao bijing butui, the title of his article published in *The Nineties*). His substitution of *zhi* for *qi* in the phrase brackets the qualifying phrase "of chess" and lays bare the otherwise less visible trace of what Kam Louie criticizes as "abstracting tradition" (1987, 1).[8] Duke writes: "Wang Yisheng's 'Way of Chess' is presented as embracing the Three Teachings of Chinese philosophy—Taoism, Buddhism, and Confucianism (*tao, chan, ru*)—as well as the fundamental concepts of Chinese cosmology—vital essence and principle (*qi, li*)—and thus to be a comprehensive symbol of the priceless spiritual heritage of traditional China" (1987, 57).

Obviously, Duke is more concerned about the survival of traditional cultural values than the construction of the nation-state. But there is a clear working of what Derrida calls the "irreducible excess of the syntactic over the semantic" (1981, 221; also see Bhabha 1990, 4) in the repeated use of the configuration of "tradition" with "nation" in spite of the intended stress on the former. This is even clearer in the case of many Chinese critics, in whose work the temporal component is hardly distinguishable from, and often is interchangeable with, the spatial component. What contains the temporal and the spatial and makes them exchangeable is the umbrella category of culture and its correlating linguistic and aesthetic manifestations. An article on Ah Cheng's "aesthetic search" by Su and Zhong (1985a) employs all these terms: "China's national culture" (zhongguo minzu wenhua), "strengthening national cultural consciousness" (qianghua minzu wenhua yishi), "China's national traits" (zhongguo wenhua tese), "Chinese cultural spirit" (zhongguo wenhua jingshen), "traditional Chinese culture" (zhongguo chuantong wenhua), "China's national character" (zhongguo minzu qizhi), and "China's traditional artistic ideal of humanity" (zhongguo chuantong yishu renge). The authors contend that Ah Cheng's work contains China's entire traditional culture. According to them, reconstructing China's cultural identity by revitalizing its tradition is the precondition for its membership in the international community of arts and letters, just as China's political independence is required for its membership in the United Nations.

Because the imagination of a great tradition is based on a literary text, culture is equated with aesthetics, cultural consciousness with narrative consciousness, and traditional cultural traits with stylistics. "Aesthetic consciousness and style" in Ah Cheng's story is defined as "something immersed in China's traditional culture." The protagonist Wang Yisheng represents a synthesis of Daoist and Confucianist ideals. This ideal character leads a simple life in the peace and harmony of nature. The story's narrative structure is of course "not Aristotelian," not for dramatic effect, but unfolds at a leisurely pace. The story's ending is "typically Chinese," fading into tranquility and vanishing into an open blank space. All this is due to the language that expresses "national cultural consciousness." "As a matter of fact," these two critics argue, "China's pictographic characters [*sic*] are in aesthetics superior to the alphabets of the West," a linguistic superiority Ah Cheng puts to good use (Su and Zhong 1985a, 54–59). Elsewhere Su Ding (1986, 90–93) calls upon contemporary Chinese writers to identify with the lost traditions, supporting his argument by invoking the rebirth of ancient Greek culture in the Renaissance, the impact of Eastern cultures upon modern Western avant-garde arts, and the convergence of oriental mysticism with modern physics—an unspecified reference probably to Fritjof Capra's *The Tao of Physics*.[9]

A more insightful critic, Ji Hongzhen, juxtaposes Ah Cheng's attitude toward life with his aesthetic sensibility, which corresponds to the author's intent to "create an atmosphere of national culture in order to bring Chinese fiction into dialogue with world literature" (1986, 49–51).[10] It is important to note that not only has the absence of nativist writing generated the temporal move to the past but its present return must be relocated at the "border" of external differences. Such a cultural imagination "represent[s] the nation's modern territoriality, in the patriotic, atavistic temporality of Traditionalism" (Bhabha 1990, 300). At the same time, traditionalism is given the rather futuristic mission of redefining for China its contemporary cultural boundary and reentering the world. Ironically, this mission reproduces exactly the central theme of opening up to the world in the post-Mao era, despite the semantic change of the "spirit of the age." The "irreducible syntactic" of nation-narration thus circumscribes the "semantic of traditionalism" within its own metanarrative, turning a nativist story into a national treasure, where tradition merges into modernity, the performative into the pedagogical.

Wang Xiaoming (1988), one of the few mainland scholars who have criticized Ah Cheng and the searching for roots movement, points out that the notion of roots is very vague and the searchers are not really concerned with the enormous complexity of China's traditional culture and society. They simply try to imagine something "primitive" to work out their own frustration and confusion in a time of drastic social change. Wang Xiaoming clearly points his finger at the problem of what Bhabha calls "the ethnography of the 'contemporary.' " What cultural dynamics lies beneath the "contemporary," the subtext and context implicitly inscribed in the imagination of a mythical past?

A most striking feature of the critical literature surrounding Ah Cheng's fiction is that its vocabulary and mode of interpretation are directly transplanted from the discourse of the "cultural fever," the "second new cultural movement" in twentieth-century China (after the May Fourth), as it has been called. The sudden increase in intellectual attention to the problem of culture in the second half of 1984 coincided with the publication of "The Chess King" and the subsequent "craze of searching for roots" in literature. According to Chen Kuide, these two movements, one involving academics and the other fictional writers, were two of the three major forces that shaped the public discussion of Chinese culture from 1984 to 1989.[11] Chen points out that Li Zehou, a leading intellectual historian and philosopher, was one of the driving forces behind the "cultural fever." Underlying Li's complex and eclectic thought are his persistent efforts to redefine traditional culture, especially its "cultural-psychological structure" (wenhuaxinli jiegou), and his repetitive call for cultural reconstruction after the catastrophic years of Maoism. Li's culture-centered approach has destabilized the authority of the official discourse, complicating the latter's linear interpretation of history by injecting the nebulous and "cyclical" notion of culture. Li's influence upon the younger generation of scholars and critics was such that he was hailed as "the guardian and teacher of youth." While his thought is often crudely assimilated and at times misused, deliberately or otherwise, his vocabulary pervades the writings of the younger generation and molds the discursive practices of literary and cultural criticism.[12]

Also influential upon the "cultural fever" and the discussion of "roots" was the groundbreaking article "On '20th-Century Chinese Literature' " by Huang Ziping, Chen Pingyuan, and Qian Liqun (1985). A key notion that breaks new ground for rethinking twentieth-century literature is the "cultural rupture" of the May Fourth period. Even though this term was originally used to describe the May Fourth radical break from the old China, it has become a predominant trope in the discourse of searching for roots. Often, the use of *rupture* indicates such a nostalgia, as if a lost ancient tradition could be transplanted back into contemporary minds. More revealing is a series of articles in which this trio elaborates on its twentieth-century project (Chen Pingyuan et al. 1985–86). With the exception of the first and the sixth pieces, which deal with the initiation and the methodology of the project, the titles of the other four articles deploy exactly the kind of terminology that permeates interpretations of Ah Cheng's stories. These articles are entitled "Global Outlook" (Shijie yanguang), "National Consciousness" (Minzu yishi), "Cultural Perspective" (Wenhua jiaodu), and "Artistic Thinking" (Yishu siwei). As in the discussions of "The Chess King," their groundbreaking project is constructed upon the international-national dichotomy, centered on the formation of a national consciousness as its ultimate goal, with culture as the organizing concept and the aesthetic, stylistic, and linguistic components as the building material.

Since the category of culture covers a complex ensemble that encompasses everything from the belief and value systems governing social practice and behavior to the structural arrangements of everyday life, its semantic ambiguity signals an apparently depoliticizing function in post-Mao reconstruction. Both movements set out as culture-centered attempts to depoliticize Maoist ideology, which treated cultural and artistic practice as a mere propagandist instrument, and engage on its own terms contemporary sociopolitical issues. Even though these two movements later proliferated in many conflicting directions, the construction of a national allegory around "The Chess King" arose when the term *culture* became a catchword displacing the official term *ideology*. Wang Meng's commentary embodies that emerging moment of negotiation, and the split in his voice epitomizes the ongoing ideological conflict.

To recenter the public discourse around culture, both movements had to back it with enough political weight by configuring the term *culture* with powerful temporal and spatial appellations such as *tradition* and *nation*. Their configuration finds expression in the phrase "the traditional national culture" (chuantong minzu wenhua) or its two anagrams: "the nation's traditional culture" (minzu chuantong wenhua) and "the nation's cultural tradition" (minzu wenhua chuantong). In whatever order they appear (which may differ in the denotation), the three signifiers together circumscribe the discursive boundary within the unity of time, space and its inhabitants, and shared identity. This strategic configuration is indicative of historical contradiction and discursive constraint. Before the "cultural fever," there were several attempts at symbolic response to the catastrophic experiences of the immediate past: the appeal to humanism and modernism in "scar literature" and the "misty poetry," respectively; the rediscovery of the "young Marx with a human face"; and the subsequent debate on "alienation in a socialist society." These moves either died out or were repressed in the Anti–Spiritual Pollution Campaign of late 1983. Under this historical constraint, what is available for resistance, which must also be politically viable, is the alliance of "nation" with "tradition" under the umbrella category of "culture." The phrase "traditional national culture" is thus a "politically correct" (or safe) rearrangement of the limited symbolic resources available to the postrevolutionary period.

As the term *culture* is employed to replace *ideology*, *tradition* is evoked to counter *modern*. This modern ideology, though not stated explicitly due to the official repression of dissent, implies and implicates the signified version of Marxism. It is under the rubric of Marxism that the systematic destruction of culture and tradition was carried out in the Cultural Revolution. The displacement of "foreign ideology" by "native culture" is not simply a political move disguised in changing terminology. It has as its top priority the reconstruction of the society's belief and value systems on the cultural desert left by more than ten years of fanatic class struggles. From a global perspective, Marxism as it was practiced is, to postrevolutionary China, what the colonial legacy is to the "third world." Although in the "third world" Marxism still can serve as a viable resource for resistance, the Marxist legacy in China is exactly what postrevolutionary cultural nationalism attempted to demolish. Situated in this immediate context, the call for traditional national culture was a strategic move of displacement as well as a reconstructive move intended to fill an ideological void. It signaled the collapse of the grand narrative of "cultural revolution" in modern China, a narrative that is uniquely a "third-world" practice of a "second-world" theory that originated in the "first world" as its opposite.

To approach post-Mao China's cultural reconstruction in this way may pose a series of theoretical questions to Marxism and postcolonial studies. For the former, the issue at stake is not theoretical but historical in contemporary China, where the very term *Marxism* signifies less a theory than the dominant ideology and, under its banner, the entire apparatus of state power. The linkage of China to the "third world" has long been made by Jameson, but the specific linkage of postrevolutionary China to the postcolonial "third world" is completely of my own making, far beyond what neo-Marxism would ever acknowledge. To make such a linkage would seem rather suspicious: my mere mention of the "postcolonial" is vulnerable to the kind of critique Aijaz Ahmad (1992) has made against the postcolonial studies developed in the past two decades in the Western academy. This is so because I propose a reading of the Chinese cultural scene of the 1980s that could be (mis)interpreted as labeling Marxism as a form of cultural imperialism in modern China—a controversial topic that has a long history of its own in the field of Western sinology as well as across the Taiwan Strait. Moreover, Chinese Communism mobilized the society by advancing the banner of anti-imperialism, and its modes of operation and organization were arguably more nativist than internationalist, particularly in the case of Mao himself. In the post-Mao era, highly acclaimed Maoist "third worldism" was replaced with the "first-worldist" modernization agenda. All these problems indicate a profound theoretical quandary and perhaps set the very limit of theorization. But, precisely at the point where theory runs into the stone wall it helped create, theory collapses into discourse.

The discourse of postrevolutionary reconstruction must be treated as a "natural" response to the conjunctual crisis of the time. It is a natural, and perhaps even an instinctive response, not just to the immediate catastrophic consequences of "class struggles" but, more importantly, to the failure of history to transform this locality of culture in its own image. As much as it attempts to displace the official ideology on the discursive level, displacement also figures the historical path and existential condition of modern China, as it does of the entire "third world." It is a natural response also in the sense that what constitutes "nature" is nothing but the "native." In Ah Cheng's fiction, for instance, "nature" and the "native" converge in the Dao (of chess), the tree ("The King of Trees"), or the native language in its "natural" form–the dictionary ("The King of Children"). Portrayals of massive impoverishment and deprivation, the destruction of the natural environment, and the de-education of the young in these stories reveal the ruins of history and loom large in the cultural landscape of the 1980s. If we dismiss cultural reconstruction as nothing but the figment of a bad nationalistic imagination, we will miss the underlying logic of rewriting local history for collective survival.

At the same time, this "natural" response is also a symptomatic reaction. To rewrite local history is one thing; to replace one grand narrative with another is entirely different. In displacing the official version of totality, the national allegory has reinscribed the former's totalizing structure, substituting cultural mystification for ideological deification. In other words, if the postrevolutionary crisis offers an opportunity for rethinking the ruins of history, such totalizing categories and concepts as "traditional national culture" can succeed only in reconstructing the semantic; it hardly changes the syntactic of the preceding ideology. When a literary text is called upon to speak for such a new totality, it once again is turned into a footnote of a metatext. It is this recurrence and reinscription of the "always already" that must be further displaced.

The Games of Naming, Eating, and Chess

Since there is an overwhelming consensus in China and abroad that there is something essentially Chinese about "The Chess King," one must ask what it is in the text that has made such interpretations possible. Ah Cheng's comment on how the story should be read offers a convenient point of departure. He criticizes the realistic readings of his novella by pointing out the narrative mediation between two "worlds": one told from the unnamed first-person narrator's point of view and the other from the protagonist's. According to him, "Wang Yisheng represents the objective world" whereas "I" the "subjective world." Admitting that the author or the narrator does not have access to Wang's inner world except by relating his experience to the narrator's interpretation, Ah Cheng emphasizes that such a correlating process through cross-reference between the narrator and the protagonist, between the self and the other, is completed at the end of the story (see Shi Shuqing 1987). Elsewhere we have learned that the text was actually created out of a story Ah Cheng "fabricated" for an audience of his friends (see Li Yi et al. 1992). The author clearly advocates a phenomenological reading guided by the first-person narrative. The reader is asked to follow the narrator's storytelling and engage in a hermeneutic act from the author/narrator's standpoint. An alternate reading thus requires a dialogic approach to the interplay between the narrator and the protagonist. A dialogic reading aims at unveiling the ambivalence of the narrative, as figured in the split between the pedagogical voice of the author/narrator and the performativity of the chess player. This ambivalent split can be detected first of all in the textual tension of the protagonist's appellations.

The protagonist has three names: "Chess King" (*qiwang*), "Chess Fool" (*qidaizi*), and Wang Yisheng. As a given, a name is the first sign for a person's "identity" and the last piece of his or her "property." The sign system demands that each name signify metonymically for an entity only proper to that so-named body. A person may have or be called several different names, which may even contradict one another, but the different names of one person ultimately complement each other and, put together, symbolically round up the "pound of flesh." But what if a name—in fact the very title of the text—does not belong to the protagonist at all? Perhaps the question should be raised not in the figure of possession or *identity* but in terms of cancellation or *différance.*

Underwritten with the author's signature, "Chess King" first of all is the name the author gives Wang Yisheng, who does not even know it. The name is used only once, in the title, and never appears in the story itself. As such, "Chess King" is a supratextual sign for authenticity and authority. This "title," in other words, is that which the author gives his other, for the reader, on behalf of the "king's" tradition. As the title of the story, it circumscribes the text within a master narrative and predetermines the reading toward a glorious realm of signification. This master narrative operates on the ascent of the protagonist from a fool to a king. What governs the operation of this reversal is the principle of condensation and displacement. Coincidentally, the two characters (*qiwang*) of the story's title are respectively the first character of the other two names: *qiwang* is stolen from *qi daizi* and *wang yisheng.* In Chinese nomenclature—and in many other linguistic systems of naming for that matter—the given name marks the difference while the surname subsumes that difference under the paternal genealogy. By condensing the surnames of the Chess Fool and Wang Yisheng and then displacing the two to enthrone the Chess King, this title/name usurps the corpus, textual and physical, and subordinates it to its supratextual authority.

But the king's discourse cannot erase the traces of its usurpation, not even in the title. The king, above all, is only a chess king and between *chess* and *king* is the very split of the performative and the pedagogical.

Moreover, the Chess King does not recognize that he is enthroned: he is only called "Chess Fool," often shortened simply to "Fool," in his own diegetic world. This Fool figures otherness to the King, and his "foolish" existence is excluded from the realm of pedagogy and knowledge. The nickname Chess Fool, by virtue of being a nickname, is at once the semantic opposite of and the discursive supplement to the title/name. This nickname contains the other within a binary opposition between norm and idiosyncrasy and between the addresser, who is capable of knowledge, and the addressee, who is not. Yet the king-fool dichotomy is never fully stabilized until the end, where it is the narrator who elevates the fool to the status of king. In this process, the other is "recognized" by the narrator and is thereby incorporated into the narrator's subjective world. Corresponding to the title/name where reading begins, the end of the story turns the fool's experience into the narrator's rewriting of history. This is achieved, uncharacteristically given the text's generally undramatic mode of narration and the narrator's restraint, by staging the last scene as a highly dramatic spectacle on the objective side and by transforming the spectacle into the subjective reconstruction of monumental history. As Huters points out: "The openness of the earlier part of the story is suddenly closed off" in the narrator's "firm assertion of cultural judgement," a judgment that "reduces the epistemological force of the earlier part of the narrative, with its promise of a new pluralism" (1985, 414).

There is no question that the text plays around a *semantic* ambiguity in order to destabilize the king-fool or master-slave binary and collapse the social hierarchy embedded therein. But the *symbolic* solution of the opposites in the title and its corresponding closure ultimately *structures* the fool's experience in a narrative of ascent that only belongs to the discourse of the king. Situated in the bifurcating imperial-populist discourse of China's long past, the fool was always "entitled" to become the king but the narrative of ideological legitimation for his ascent never changed, and in fact only reproduced the same *histoire*. The issue I am attempting to problematize, then, is not the text's obvious semantic subversion but its narrative containment. The strategy of narrative containment, according to Jameson (1981), is a "politically symbolic act" that functions very much like the Freudian dream, though the repressed "political unconscious" is grounded in the historical rather than the libidinal realm. Thus, it is in the text's naming tropes—that is, condensation and displacement, the two Freudian formal mechanisms for organizing the unconscious into dreams—that one can locate what has been repressed into the political unconscious. And this political unconscious is manifested in the third name: the protagonist's real given name.

The given name Yisheng, as Wang Yisheng himself explains, means separately the numeral "one" and "living" (*shenghuo*). As the first numeral, "one" is the smallest number, closest to zero or nothing. In philosophical Daoism, the only explicit reference in the text to some Chinese essence, "one" is that which the Dao engenders and through which it multiplies the naming of the world ad infinitum. The Laozian order of things predicates "one" as the first name (because the Dao cannot be named), that is, the first metaphor that names. Looking it up as the first entry in any Chinese dictionary, we find that the semantic field of "one" is as fluid as its generative capacity is open-ended. This capacity lies not only in its being the "first" but also in its being a verb: the Daoist "equation mark." The smallest, yet all-encompassing, "one" occupies the core of the Daoist dialectic. The combination and convergence of ambiguity and simplicity in the numeral "one" makes it open to interpretation, depending only on its concrete use.

Coupled with *sheng*, Wang's given name could simply mean "a life," as plain as this English translation may sound. But located at the conjunction with the king's discourse, *yisheng* embodies the unconscious world of otherness. The context in which Wang Yisheng explains his name and the subtext of his explanation delineate the symbolic space in which his name signifies. The person to whom he explains his name is called Ni Bin, two characters that in Ni's own exegesis mean "man" and "civilian and military," respectively, and put together are symbolic of the entire civilizing structure viewed from the ancient emperor's throne. Though not in the least militant, Ni Bin is a cultured man from a privileged family. In their first meeting, he towers above Wang, who must strain his neck to see him. As a character foil as well as a signifying trope, Ni Bin, through his height and his name, defines the way the reader must see Wang Yisheng.

Parallel to this descriptive contrast is a political and metaphysical subtext. When the Chess Fool explains that *sheng* means "living," as opposed to "life" (*shengming*),[13] he is still refusing to read Jack London's "Love of Life" (Re'ai shengming) the way the narrator (and the culture) would want him to during their earlier conversation on the train. This subtext must be further highlighted against a larger ideological background. Portrayed as "the Gorky of American literature," Jack London is a major figure in the Communist canon of critical realism. His "Love of Life" was made known to many young readers in China through Lenin's extolling of the story on his deathbed. Sanctified by the founding father of the world Communist movement, London's life and death battle, set on the nineteenth-century American frontier, was erected as a monument to heroism. Wang Yisheng's choice of "living" over "life"—his inexorable insistence on reading London's story as meaning nothing but eating—signals a "perverse" resistance to encoding his name in the official symbolic system.

The three names, three signifiers of the "proper," are like three chess pieces signifying different positions. It is largely the king's narrative that is responsible for the grand allegorical transformation of the text into a "master-piece" on the board of contemporary cultural politics. But the king only exists as an extratextual title, in the text's title/name, who calls on other pieces to sacrifice themselves for him just as his counterpart does on the battlefield of chess. His authority, designated by the author, would immediately collapse if the other pieces were allowed to make their own moves and voice their own stories. What emerges from this deconstructive reading of the textual system of nomenclature must therefore be read as stories of "a living" and a "fool" whose objective experience unfolds around the two major motifs of the story: eating and chess playing.

Taken as a whole, the author is most honest and sympathetic with the fool's attitude toward food. Or, conversely, the king's narrative is unable to reduce the primordial need to eat to a pedagogical function. In the unpublished version of the story, Wang Yisheng is so "foolish" that instead of accepting his promotion to the provincial chess team he decides to stay with the prefectural team simply because the latter provides better food.[14] But the trace always leaves its trail, and it resurfaces vindictively in the author's official speech.

Ah Cheng's "A Few Words," a speech delivered at his first public appearance as a celebrity (and published in 1984), can be read as such a return. In a ceremony awarding a prestigious national prize to his first novella, he refuses to play into the self-serving spectacle; instead, he distances himself from the typical self-congratulatory ritual by foregrounding the impoverishment of postrevolutionary society. He describes his family's meager income, which could not satisfy the son's innocent voracity, famines in the countryside he has witnessed and heard of, public callousness toward beggars and the disabled, and the hardworking but poverty-stricken peasants. He says virtually nothing about his own writing. On a public occasion designed to evoke the three-thousand-year-old grandeur of the written word, the prize-winning writer emphatically talks about the "exchange value" of his writing in balancing his family's budget. In this sense, Ah Cheng's words must be read as food, food that keeps Wang from ascending to the throne. Hence, my reading follows the erased ending.

To the extent that the text has been read as a national allegory, it also allegorically (in the Benjaminian sense) reveals the ruins of the nation in the most brutal form of starvation and hunger. In so doing, the text rewrites the representational history of hunger. The claim that Ah Cheng's work bears on the entire traditional culture of China is relevant if—and only if—one reads the text against the grain of the dominant alimentary discourse dating back to the earliest myths and Confucian classics. This long tradition has shaped hunger as a "master trope" in a fundamentally "slave," that is, *critical*, discourse, despite its having been employed by historical figures ranging from the Confucian sage to Lu Xun, from Mao to post-Mao "humanists." Any attempt to confront hunger in this tradition would once again reproduce its rhetoric and thereby continue the age-old discursive practice. To rewrite hunger without being implicated into that entrenched politicized discourse thus requires a strategic redeployment of the trope in a way that is neither confrontational nor compliant, neither narrowly political nor purely aesthetic. What makes "The Chess King" postrevolutionary in the syntactic is its reconfiguration of Wang's experience of hunger with neither the official rhetoric nor its "humanistic" critique in the post-Mao era. Rather, hunger is reintroduced as a "nonpolitical" trope so that it can reconstitute its fundamental corporeality.

A youth growing up in the "new China," Wang is from the beginning deprived of the "luxury" of having his stomach filled. This is because his father is a sick worker and unable to feed the family. So hunger is a matter of fact for "a living." As a matter of fact, starvation must be taken matter-of-factly. Nothing could be more political than such an "apolitical" dilution of the heavily loaded theme. By not allowing the familiar politics of hunger to come to the fore, and thus denying it the status in the "master" narrative it has long enjoyed, the text paradoxically highlights eating as an absolute material experience. In other words, food is restored to what Huters calls "an absolute value" (1985, 397). It becomes regrounded in the body physique, always caught in, but never completely erasable by, the body politic.

Wang's approach to hunger, as noted previously, is displayed in his deviation from the allegorical meaning of London's "Love of Life." He insists that the story be read as manifesting desperation under extreme conditions of starvation. Refuting Wang, the narrator tries to persuade him that "it is not a story about eating at all; it is a story about life." Wang's stubbornness finally makes the narrator conclude that "you really deserve to be called the Chess Fool." To the narrator, Wang's foolishness lies in his lack of comprehension that food is for thought and digestion is an act of ruminating the abstract flavor of "life." Just as they differ in interpreting London's foreign story, they argue about a folktale. Wang insists on reading it in terms of eating, whereas the narrator takes it as a parable that encourages thrift (65–66; 93–94).[15]

At the same time, Wang also makes a clear distinction between "hunger" (*ji'e*) and "gustatory greed" (*chan*) and dismisses Le cousin Pons in Balzac's novel to the latter category. He distinguishes himself from the narrator and other youths because they do not understand hunger. Even if they may sometimes feel starved, their feeling expresses more gustatory greed than real hunger. As the notion of "life" signifies an abstraction in excess of material subsistence, greed manifests an excessive lust the hungry also scorn. To him, the lack of firsthand experience of persistent hunger generates gustatory greed, and greed, exhibited in excessive appetite, corresponds to the "surplus meaning" of food. Wang seems to insist that food's materiality resides neither outside nor inside the realm of meaning; it is rooted in the irreducibly nondualistic body physique. This forces the narrator to recognize the economy of a double lack: the lack of an abstract meaning of food in Wang's metaphysical world as a result of, and a response to, the lack of food in his material life.

If hunger is often conceived as an oral lack and perceived as a facial or frontal deficiency, the text respatializes our perception by dislocating this brutal lack on the other end of the ingestion-digestion-elimination system: the bottom. As a matter of fact, it would be more faithful to translate the original *pigu* into "butt," rather than "bottom" and "backside," as in the two English versions. One critic has noticed Ah Cheng's use of the term in serious literature and cited it as an example of calculated crudeness and vulgarity (Jiang Yuanlun 1986, 82). *Pigu* appears in two parting scenes from the narrator's point of view:

> The windows on the side of the carriage next to the platform were already crammed with the departing youth from many different schools leaning outside, joking or crying. The windows on the other side faced south, so that the winter sunlight slanting in through them was shining coolly on the many bottoms on the northern side of carriage. (56; 85)

> Wang Yisheng adjusted the strap of his satchel and hurried off along the highway, raising the dust with his feet, his clothes waving. His trousers flapped about as if he had no backside inside them. (88; 113)

Wang's difference is illustrated here in two kinds of lack. In the first scene, he lacks interest in having anyone see him off to the countryside (in fact he is keeping his sister from finding him). While other youngsters are "facing" the narrator with their butts, he finds Wang his only company. Wang's explanation for his staying aloof is quite simple: "I'm going where there's food to eat, so why all this crying and snivelling" (56; 86). Compared with "scar literature," which represents the traumatic experience of the city youths' forced relocation, Wang's apparent indifference displays his different perspective: he is leaving a place he would rather not face. And the reason he lacks interest in city life is brutally foregrounded, in the second scene, by his lack of a backside—a sign, in hindsight, of prolonged hunger and malnutrition during childhood and adolescence.

In contrast to the narrator's attempt to elevate Wang to the throne, the economy of lack has enmeshed the narrator in Wang's world of primordial subsistence. If early in the story the narrator must ruminate about food's abstract meaning, from the second section on he digests food for the body to absorb its "valuable" nutrition and eliminate its "meaningful" waste. In section 1, the narrator comments on Wang's ravenous gobbling with irony. Wang is described as a "reverent" (*qianchengde*) and "merciless" (*canwu rendao*) eater, the former a religious term used to describe the faithful's total devotion and the latter a political term describing total disrespect for human suffering. These two terms were frequently used in the post–Cultural Revolution era to ridicule the Red Guards' fanatic worship of Mao and to condemn their ruthless persecutions of class enemies. The irony figured in these two terms reveals the narrator's deep sympathy toward Wang. However, this irony also inserts a sympathetic distance between the observer, who pities, and the observed, who is put in the position of the pitiful. But this ironic distance gradually disappears in eating scenes that take place in the country, such as the "snake feast" in section 2 and the group gorging in section 3. With the disappearance of the narrative distance between the narrator and the protagonist, they eat food as "mere" food, an absolute value unto itself. The age-old political alimentation is thus eliminated by returning the figure of lack to the site of the corporeal, the body that must survive.

Most commentators on the novella, who are also proponents of digging up some pure Chinese roots in the text, find their evidence in the Chess King's "Dao of chess." Opponents charge that this invocation of Daoism is a sign of decadence and passivity. Meanwhile, a Daoist scholar deems it not pure enough for "Chess King" to claim the true Dao (Huang Fengzhu 1987). Ah Cheng is disingenuous but does point out that these critics and commentators "all speak their own words" (Shi Shuqing 1987, 51). He is disingenuous in that the king's discourse invites the glamorous celebration of Wang's triumph in revitalizing the lost Dao, but he is also right because the Dao of chess, like the true Dao of anything, cannot be named and identified. If the text has generated all these different words, this phenomenon simply testifies to the ultimate truth: the principle of the Dao that governs the movement of the trace originated in the irreducible void and points to open-ended infinitude.

Like Wang's experience with hunger, his Dao of chess is also figured in a fundamental lack and defies ideological reappropriation. In fact, the most valued chess set his mother gives him is *blank*. The mother used to be a prostitute and was impregnated and abandoned by Wang's natural father, whom the son has never met. The illiterate mother made the set out of used toothbrush handles and left it (still blank) to the son at her death. Blankness signifies nothingness and is symbolic of her whole life. Although many commentators have tried to inject some abstract meaning into the poor woman's blank legacy, from her point of view she had nothing mysteriously abstract to offer her son.

From the son's point of view, however, the blank chess set represents everything his mother left to him. On it is inscribed the mother's love that finally overcame her disapproval of the son's obsession with chess (because she could not expect the boy to make a living by playing it).

Written on the blank set is the paradoxical truth of lack and survival, nothingness and extravagance, reality and pleasure, and death and memory. But this paradox has never been fully played out in the son's consciousness. He talks about the Dao of chess in a multivoiced discourse that he does not really understand.[16] His chess is so "empty" and at the same time so filled with his affective memory that its meaning is ambiguous. Even at the end of the story, Wang's invocation, "Ma, today, I . . . Ma—", does not stabilize the meaning of the blank set. Thanks to this final uncertainty and ambiguity, the text leaves the meaning of the chess set blankly indeterminate.

What is most remarkable about the Dao of chess is its paradoxical principle of negativity and performativity, of displacement and survival. Corresponding to the mother's blank set, the son often plays the game in "blank," too—the so-called blind game as in his final victory. As the Chess Fool describes it: "I'm hooked on chess. Once I start playing I forget about everything else. As long as I am immersed in chess I'm happy. When I haven't got a board or pieces I can play it in my head. It's no skin off anyone's nose" (75; 102–3). To him, chess is a world onto itself, a performative experience neither within nor outside language. This is the site of marginality where language, including its material carriers (the board and the pieces), collapses into *écriture*, purely imaginary and performative. If this world is one of "pure signifiers," his "free play" no doubt is an "escapist" move with which he manages to elude complicity in the madness of history and yet survive its catastrophe. Only at this point can one positively embrace its "Chinese essence." This returns us to the beginning of this section: the trace of that "never ever," which traverses Ah Cheng's text, and Wang Yisheng's chess playing, which directs my reading. It is from this negativity, the very site of lack, that desire can be reintroduced as that which survives.

When asked if there is a hidden meaning behind the text, Ah Cheng once remarked that " 'The Chess King' is a koan" (see Li Oufan et al. 1991, 533). The rediscovery of Chan Buddhism, as well as philosophical Daoism and the *Yijing* (or *I Ching*) was a hot topic in the movements of "cultural fever" and "searching for roots." In the post-Mao cultural reconstruction, Chan and Daoism inevitably were incorporated into the ideology of nationalism, a process that reminds us of D. T. Suzuki's dissemination of Zen in the rise of Japanese nationalism.[17] But Ah Cheng emphasizes that Chan is a state of mind. Repeatedly talking about Chan is just a sham or, to borrow a familiar Chinese idiom Hu Shih once used in his famous debate with Suzuki, "Chan of the mouth-corners" (*koutouchan*, which simply means "one's habitual phrase"). For Ah Cheng, that state of mind called Chan is "spaceless and timeless." Relating it to "searching for roots," he points out that such a search must "open up our sense of time and space," "not return to an old time and space" (Li Oufan et al. 1991, 535). To avoid sliding once again into the Zen discourse of Suzuki, we must study the modes in which language works in anything labeled as Chan. For a heuristic purpose, let me formulate in the following the way "displacement for survival" traverses the text:

The game of naming	Wang is a king Wang is a fool Wang is both a king and a fool Wang is neither a king nor a fool
The game of eating	Food is for (abstract) thought Food is for (gustatory) greed Food is for both thought and greed Food is for neither thought nor greed
The game of playing	Chess is inscribed Chess is blank Chess is both inscribed and blank Chess is neither inscribed nor blank

Beyond yet still between this neither/nor, the ultimate negativity of Chan and deconstruction, is the text of pleasure, the pleasure of (reading the) text, the syntactic dissemination of a genuinely *post*-revolutionary un/consciousness that redefines a local history. If this is a "Chinese essence," it is one located in, not outside of, time.

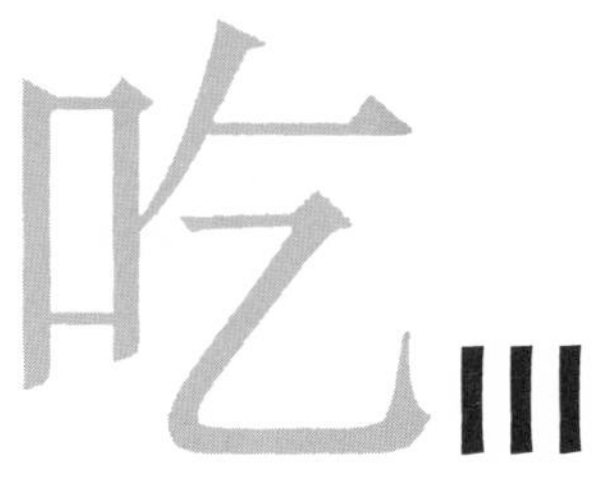

III

The Return (of) Cannibalism after Tiananmen, or Red Monument in a Latrine Pit

"The human-eating old society" is one of the most hackneyed political phrases in the vocabulary of Chinese Communism. As a topos, however, cannibalism is absent in revolutionary and the postrevolutionary literature. Above all, hunger is irreducibly a reality in modern China, fitting well in a literary tradition shaped by the principle of realism. Cannibalism, on the other hand, is always tinged with a touch of surrealism, and the kind of social allegory invested in this genre requires the laborious interpretation of a well-educated reader. So it comes as no surprise that cannibalism reappeared first in a highly experimental story: "Gudian aiqing" (Classical love, 1988) by the young writer Yu Hua, a leading figure in post-Mao avant-garde literature. It is one of the most poetic stories Yu has written—and probably the only text that contains a detailed portrayal of cannibalism in post-Mao Chinese literature published by nationally known writers before 1989. Not a realist piece, the story is not allegorical, either, in the sense that the Madman story is. Yu's playful exploitation of horrifying scenes of human butchery and consumption only serves to highlight his brilliant yet wicked pastiche of the classical convention of love stories. Yu's is a different agenda, and we would be disappointed if we tried to uncover any hidden political allegory in the text.[1]

That Yu's story bears no significant weight of social criticism of contemporary China is nonetheless very significant to our study. As a student of literary art, I am fascinated that the tired political metaphor can be treated with such a poetic touch in a well-wrought work of fiction entirely different from the modern discourse. As a student of cultural genealogy, I find that what is most significant about the text is what is missing from it: the dazzling madness in Lu Xun's textual and conscious world is completely absent in Yu's playful rendering of the "subject." As pointed out previously, the correlative between cannibalism and madness is a trademark of the Lu Xun model. His sociopolitical criticism and allegorical representation of history are informed with an excruciating sense of intellectual crisis and emotional trauma. This kind of national allegory can only recur in response to another intellectual crisis of similar scope, this time the June Fourth incident. The three texts to be discussed—Zheng Yi's book-length reportage *Hongse jinianbei* (Red monument, 1993) and Liu Zhenyun's novella "Wengu yijiusier" (Revisiting 1942, 1993), in chapter 6, and Mo Yan's novel *Jiuguo* (Liquorland, 1992; also published as *Mingdingguo* later in the PRC) in chapter 7—were all written and published after that major event. And all three texts are intertextually connected with the Madman's discourse. Their intertextual connection is what links the May Fourth and June Fourth incidents in our trilogy—a historical connection forcefully articulated in the mass protest movement. To return to Yu Hua, then, the absence of Lu Xun's ghost in his pre-1989 story points to the post-1989 tragic milieu in which the three works under question were produced.

The periodization of intellectual and literary history around major political events always runs the risk of simplification. It must be complicated and complemented by examining the ongoing socioeconomic dynamics accompanying those events. A brief summary of contemporary alimentary discourse is thus in order.

In the second half of the 1980s, the narrative of hunger disappeared from the literary scene. Coupled with the fading interest in writing hunger was the emergence of a postrevolutionary consumer society. After a decade of economic reform, a sufficient food supply became a reality for the vast majority of the population. The reform itself was articulated as metaphoric progress from the broken Maoist "iron rice bowl" and "big cooking pot" to the Dengist slogan "it is glorious to get rich." The definition of getting rich may differ between the new entrepreneur and the peasant, but the bottom line for society at large was that individuals now had to take care of their own stomachs rather than continue to take part in an illusive "socialist feast." Just as the standard narrative of economic development was constructed as a process from *wenbao jieduan* (the stage of basic but sufficient clothing, shelter, and food) to *xiaokang jieduan* (the stage of being well-to-do), the agenda in the average Chinese household was increasingly organized around the desire for more "luxurious" consumer goods, better housing, and improved transportation. Food must not be neglected, of course, as it still constitutes the largest expenditure for the ordinary family. Instead of adequate quantity, however, qualitative improvement of the diet, especially meat consumption for more protein intake, was emphasized, sometimes in connection with the call for strengthening the physical body of the Chinese "race."

While the economic reform generated unprecedented prosperity, drastic changes also intensified existing social contradictions and created new social ailments. Rampant corruption and abuses of power provoked popular resentment and gave rise to the mass protest movement of 1989. Increased upward mobility for some left others behind and heightened the sentiments of inequity and relative deprivation. In the absence of successful, systematic, political reform, the party-state mobilized a redefined, more nativist-bound ideology of nationalism to relegitimate its authority and diffuse popular resentment, while the population, especially in rural areas, revived traditional customs in order to cope with feelings of disorientation. Even the long-forgotten Mao was brought back for a brief moment. His image was recirculated in the popular imagination as part of a longing for a lost egalitarian system, only to be wholesaled in a lucrative market of nostalgic commodities ranging from talismans of the great savior to specialty eateries that serve his favorite dish of braised pork.[2] Except for the remnant Maoists, however, few would seriously consider returning to a society of "equality in scarcity." Capturing the mood of the time is the double-tongued popular saying: *duanqiwan chirou, fangxiawan maniang* ([People] hold up the bowl to eat meat but put down the bowl to curse the mother [that is, the authorities]). It is an ironic, yet apt, illustration of the historical change from the reign of Mao, when there was little meat to eat and a mild growl against the authorities might land one in jail, to the success in meat production and the relative political tolerance of Deng's China. In this rapidly changing social environment, the international fast food industry has also penetrated the world's "largest potential market," led by the meat-intensive packages of McDonald's and Kentucky Fried Chicken. *Chirou* (eat meat) has finally replaced the age-old pathos of *chibao* (fill the stomach).

"Eat meat," of course, is not the same as *chiren*, "eat human." Although the 1989 crackdown was in retrospect only a brief setback for China's economic modernization, its political impact was for quite a while immensely traumatic, especially for the intelligentsia and in the domain of high culture and literature. If we take the five-decade narrative of hunger as an interlude, on the two ends of it lie the May Fourth and June Fourth incidents. Unlike prolonged disasters such as the wars before 1949 and the famines in the wake of the Great Leap Forward and during the Cultural Revolution, May Fourth and June Fourth were abrupt political events of such faith-shattering magnitude that they stood out as the two most catastrophic moments of intellectual crisis in twentieth-century China. If traumatic shock can only be absorbed in madness, nowhere can madness be better contained, expressed, or disseminated than through the horror of being devoured. In contrast to the presence of material destitution and symbolic fulfillment in the preceding narrative of hunger, cannibalism is rather emblematic of moral and intellectual "lack." Since the political cliché of *chiren* has been so naturalized in the official discourse, one has either to come up with hard evidence, as Zheng Yi and Lu Zhenyan try to do, or present it in a surreal fashion, epitomized by Mo Yan's novel. The haunting recurrence of cannibalism thus puts into narrative form the political unconscious of the time, symptomatically revealed in the most visible linkage of the recent trauma to the "original scene" of Chinese modernity. The spirit of the age is once again framed in the struggle "to eat or be eaten."

The three writers in question share the same cultural legacy in their response to the madness of history. Through the same signposts as those found in the Madman's travels, their texts approach political violence and social breakdown in terms of the familiar cultural image of the infernal journey. But these works differ fundamentally in whether they take the modern mythology of cannibalism for granted (as Zheng Yi and Liu Zhenyun do) or question its underlying assumptions (as Mo Yan does). Such a difference is epistemological in nature and therefore generates axiological questions beyond these works' immediate political implications. *Red Monument* fully embraces the Madman's legacy and pushes it to an even more radical extent. Except for the author's own absolute authority over truth, nothing is left unchallenged, proving once again the resilience of the modern apotheosis. "Revisiting 1942" enters the discursive field of hunger and cannibalism from a refreshing narrative point of view but ends up taking recourse to the same exit as in the Madman's story. Both texts are written with an unquestioning claim to historical veracity. They approach the facts with a blind eye to the ways in which ideology generates contradictory meanings of lived reality and conceals its own contradictions at the same time.

By contrast, Mo Yan's rewriting of modern mythology shifts the alimentary narrative from the height of the visual-moralist trope of *chiren* to the bottom-up angle of an oral-materialist probing at the human ecology of *chirou*. In the same process, the rhetoric of madness is also dissolved in the drunken stupor of alcoholic spirits, thus turning the Madman into a schizophrenic, his outcry into the devil's laughter. The novel is at once a sweeping parody of the metanarrative since Lu Xun and phantasmagoric revelation of a nightmarish world yet to come. Such an ending of heroic apotheosis in twentieth-century Chinese literature paradoxically suggests that the cultural landscape of post-1989 China can no longer be crystallized through a historical totality in spite (or because?) of the excruciating impact of June Fourth. The irreducible multiplicity of flavors, tastes, positions, and viewpoints, even in the writing of cannibalism, should be recognized as a landmark of the 1990s.

6. Monument Revisited

Zheng Yi and Liu Zhenyun

The "Redness" of *Red Monument*

Red Monument has little "scientific" value, as the author claims, beyond its documentation of a few cases of flesh eating during the Cultural Revolution. It is the *writing*—the narrative strategy, rhetorical posture, and subject position—that is worthy of serious attention. I propose to read it simply as a *text*. In this section, I will first reconstruct the historical incident as represented in the text. Next I will analyze it intertextually against Lu Xun's "Diary of a Madman" and the discourse of cannibalism. In treating the book as a text, I do not mean to diminish the undisputable horrors it contains. Rather, only by examining the ways that these facts are re-presented can we grasp their historical significance.

About Guangxi Cannibalism

Cannibalism did take place in the heyday of the Cultural Revolution in the Guangxi Zhuang Autonomous Region. But before I move to that historical incident, I would like to clear up a conceptual muddle. My question is: were the violent acts systematic and organized, as the author claims they were? Many cases do reveal their organized nature, while a few others do not. Since it occurred only at the county and the commune levels in remote areas of Guangxi, I tend to view the incident as "locally organized." But I seriously doubt how "systematic" it could be, given the virtual collapse of the "system" during the factionalist civil war. In the context of the mass violence of that period, the locally organized action was nevertheless an "isolated case." Once I state my view as such, I want to honestly say that I am not prepared to argue whether it was "systematic" or "isolated." This is not just because of the lack of access to what actually happened. My reluctance has more to do with our current discourse on political violence in general and that on the People's Republic in particular.

Systematic and *isolated* are terms that act inevitably to generate a false dichotomy whereby one has to make an either/or choice, that is, either to attribute the violent "behavior" to the "isolated individual" or the "organized violence" to the "totalitarian state." Just as the former category neatly reduces a complex social phenomenon to the "personal," the latter conveniently packages the "political" (broadly understood) around the party-state simply because it is presumed to be "totalitarian." Is there anything that lies between that polarity or even outside it? Is the "total" not just a thin veneer full of holes, through which the former Soviet Union and its satellite states fell? More importantly, the question about the false dichotomy is related to the central issue of representation. In modern China, the mere *writing* of cannibalism is always a totalizing act as far as the writer takes the Lu Xunian moralistic-political stance and makes the claim of absolute truth relative to the totality of history. As a result, the representation of cannibalism is bound to be "systematic" in fictional form or otherwise.

Zheng Yi's investigation was centered on Wuxuan County, where the worst incident occurred. There fighting broke out in January of 1968 but not until after the founding of the county's Revolutionary Committee on April 15 did killing and cannibalism intensify, as the winning groups began to retaliate against their enemies. Zheng Yi summarizes the Wuxuan incident in three phases, namely, the "beginning phase," in which organs were secretly stolen from dead bodies; the "heightening phase," in which flesh eating became increasingly and openly acceptable; and the "phase of massive madness," which saw even bystanders who did not belong to any faction participate (90–91).[1] The violence was stopped in July after Premier Zhou Enlai received a shocking report and sent in troops of the People's Liberation Army to intervene (93).

In the late 1960s, Wuxuan had a population of 220,000 people, among whom 524 were killed during the six-month civil war. Of those killed, more than 100 were subjected to anthropophagy according to the author and Wang Zujian, his main informant, though the official investigation conducted in the early 1980s found only 76 such cases. Livers were the favorite target, followed by hearts, and there were 18 bodies stripped of all flesh. As for the anthropophagi, the official investigation puts their number at more than 400, but the author claims the true number to be between 10,000 and 20,000, though he admits that it would "remain a historical mystery never to be solved" (98). In some extreme cases, the victims were mutilated, their organs extracted even before their deaths, though again there is no way to know how many died in that brutal way. In the wake of the official investigation, only thirty-four offenders were convicted and sentenced to imprisonment from two to fourteen years. Many more were punished through administrative measures. Leniency toward the criminals was attributed in part to the general "forward-looking" environment of the 1980s and in part to a coverup by many local officials who were responsible for, or implicated in, the bloody event.

The act of cannibalism, in the author's view, resulted from the comprehensive waging of "class struggle" and "revolutionary revenge." While the victims fell into all demographic categories, most cases involved members of losing factions or other "bad elements" such as former landlords, out of favor Party officials, "rightists," and "counterrevolutionaries." Under the rubric of class, the violent acts defy clear-cut generational, familial, and gender classifications. A male teacher, after he learned that a young woman's heart could cure heart disease, instigated the killing of a teen-aged female student by calling her a "counterrevolutionary" and then took her heart in the dark of night (44). Conversely, a young woman who took the lead in a number of anthropophagic activities proved her firm "class stance" and later was promoted to vice chairperson of the county's Revolutionary Committee (74–75). As a group of youngsters consumed the flesh of one of their teachers (71), a group of teachers and school staff mixed a student's flesh (killed by another student) with pork (81). Even the corpse of a would-be father-in-law was cut apart by the young woman engaged to the victim's son (81).

In this chaotic situation, however, some activities were less orchestrated than the predictable narrative of "class struggle" would lead one to believe. For example, a group of men killed one of their enemies, cooked him up, and "forced two female co-workers to join them because these two women failed to take a firm stance [to support the group]" (68). In contrast to this case of implicating "enemy sympathizers" by coercive inclusion, four schoolteachers were excluded because they were "black elements," considered "not good enough to eat the flesh and only qualified to collect and bury the [victim's] bones" (82). Furthermore, flesh was consumed not simply out of "class hatred" or "revolutionary revenge." Livers and hearts were taken for other reasons: to "embolden the eater" (27, 28) or to cure the eater's ailments (23, 81; see also the case of the "beauty heart" cited above). On many occasions, individuals partook in the eating not because they were politically committed to any faction or hated the victim. These were bystanders who wanted a share for personal reasons. For instance, some old men took the brain of a dead victim while an old woman suffering from an eye ailment sought the eyeballs (91). Filial piety and parental duty motivated some young individuals, who took pieces of flesh home for their parents (74–75, 81), and some mothers brought their sick children to the site of the butchery for a piece of liver (23). Various culinary procedures adopted seem to suggest the presence of "gourmet cannibalism" as well. Therefore, while it is true that anthropophagy occurred as part of the violence unleashed in the chaotic situation, some individual acts were motivated by factors other than political violence. They do not cohere with any "system" of classification.

Three men stand out, all of them Party members who had joined in the Communist revolution before 1949. They represent, respectively, the perpetrator, the victim, and the hero. Xie Jinwen, the perpetrator, is featured in three photographs as well as in the text. One of the pictures shows the 1984 official resolution expelling him from the Party for his participation in cannibalism. When he was the chair of the Revolutionary Committee of a production brigade, seventy-two "class enemies" were massacred after a memorial service for a former member of the winning faction. Many of the bodies were later cannibalized. During a 1986 interview, Xie even recounted to the author the "glorious history of his eating human livers" (26). In 1948, Xie and his fellow guerrilla fighters killed a KMT informant and roasted and ate his liver for "self-emboldening." The author recalls: "On a whimsical impulse, I asked him: 'which tasted better, the one you roasted before or the one you boiled this time?' His answer was: 'the roasted one was delicious, the boiled one tasted bad.' " This source, Zheng Yi comments,

> suggests that cannibalism is a continuous phenomenon in the history . . . under the banner of class struggle and the proletarian dictatorship. All the events of cruelty that occurred under communist rule in the past decades

originated from the [Marxist-Maoist] thorough repudiation of the universal, general, moral standard and from the denial of the abstract [idea of] humanity and love" (27).

Huang Jiaping's story features the tragedy of the victim. A middle-school vice principal at the time he was killed, Huang was raised in a wealthy family and was well educated with progressive ideas. Sympathetic to the poor peasants, he joined the Communist revolution in 1947 and served as a deputy county commissioner after 1949. During the 1954 purge of former Guangxi underground members of the Party, Huang was found to be a "traitor." In a battle with KMT troops, he was forced as a guerrilla chief to surrender after he learned that the enemies were holding more than eighty villagers hostage and would kill them all if he refused to submit. Even though he did not implicate his comrades after his surrender and joined another guerrilla band upon release, he was expelled from the Party and removed from his official post. Twelve years later, on the eve of the Cultural Revolution, his judgment of "treason" was revoked, his party membership was reinstated, and he was appointed as a school vice principal. An occasion otherwise worth celebration turned out to be an even worse disaster. The former "traitor" was singled out by the school's Red Guards and went through the ordeal of beating and humiliation until he was killed on July 1, 1968, the forty-seventh anniversary of the founding of the CCP. The next day his body was exposed in the schoolyard as a "struggle session" was held. After the meeting, the group robbed the corpse, leaving only the head and bones. According to a female participant—the one who was engaged to Huang's son: "I believed it was the right thing to do to carve his body up since he was a traitor" (81). After the Cultural Revolution, Huang was politically rehabilitated for the second time—this time posthumously, of course. Three people were charged and two convicted, but only one was sentenced to ten years of imprisonment. Given that Huang's tragic life and death derived from his early act of self-sacrifice to protect innocent villagers, he was, in the author's judgment, "a martyr of humanistic ideals" (85).

The book devotes an entire chapter to Wang Zujian, the hero who reported the Wuxuan incident to the central government and pushed fiercely for the post-Mao investigation. Wang's story is presented as a historical saga. His grandfather, Wang Kezhong, was the famous Supreme Court judge who presided over the trial of the student activists of the May Fourth Movement and acquitted them all, declaring that "patriotism is no crime" (139). His father, Wang Shaohui, went to France to study civil engineering and later quit school to take part in the anti–Yuan Shikai rebellion. The father became a major figure in bridge engineering in modern China and was highly respected by leaders such as Zhou Enlai and Ye Jianying. His "French connection" later helped his son to pass an urgent message to Zhou Enlai. Wang Zujian himself was introduced to revolutionary ideas at a very young age, wrote for the Communist *New China Daily* during the War of Resistance against Japan, and was mentored at one point by the late foreign minister Qiao Guanhua. He was a student activist in Beijing and became an underground Party member in 1947. After the liberation, he volunteered to follow the military to Guangxi and chose to work as a county Party chief in order to gain firsthand experience among the peasants and collect materials for a historical novel on the Taiping Rebellion.

Governing a rural county led him to see the mounting contradictions between Communist ideals and state policies, as the government began to centralize grain purchases and distribution at the expense of peasants in 1954. Wang questioned that policy after he learned that nearly two thousand people had died of famine in his county in the first year the policy was introduced. During the 1957 Rectification Movement, Wang openly criticized the state monopoly over food production and distribution policies and their catastrophic consequences. Because of this, he was expelled from the Party, labeled a Rightist, and sentenced to hard labor. In 1960, his Rightist label was removed and he was reappointed as the director of the county's cultural center, though he had to wait until 1979 to have his Party membership reinstated. During the bloody months of 1968, Wang, already a "dead horse" who posed no threat to any group, stayed on the sidelines until the civil war deteriorated into the "phase of massive madness." His connections in Beijing made it possible for his report to reach Premier Zhou Enlai. Although the violence was stopped after the military intervention, Wang paid a high price. The county Revolutionary Committee soon found out that he had leaked the news, and once again he was subjected to "struggle sessions" of humiliations and beatings and sentenced to hard labor for the next five years.

In contrast to Xie Jinwen, Huang Jiaping and Wang Zujian are two "red monuments" of profound irony in a book that aims to erect a Red Monument of communist inhumanity.

Neither a participant in nor a victim of cannibalism, Wang Zujian is portrayed in the book as a heroic survivor morally obligated to seek and tell the truth. "Seeking truth from facts" is the central theme in the post-Mao repudiation of the Cultural Revolution, but the politics of "telling the truth" reveals a more complex network of historical forces at work. Wang Zujian's uphill battle did not cease after the military intervention. The struggle intensified in 1978. During a county-level meeting of Party delegates, a couple of alleged offenders were not only left unpunished but promoted to the powerful County Committee. Enraged, many delegates boycotted the meeting. Wang Zujian, then still awaiting his own redemption, wrote a long exposé and sent it to the Central Committee in Beijing, pleading for a thorough investigation and justice. The piece was published unaltered in the "internal edition" of the *People's Daily* (distributed only to high-ranking cadres). Soon Wang described the incident to a group of writers and journalists attending a provincial conference. Even with more and more horrors surfacing almost every day in post-Mao public discussions of the Cultural Revolution, few were prepared to believe Wang's story of actual cannibalism. Many were so flabbergasted that they thought it "a fabricated tale resembling a parable or a piece of mythology" (136).

The central government's investigation went on with little success until the removal in 1983 of the former Guangxi Party boss, Wei Guoqing, and his oligarchic clique. As the last province to rectify the wrongs of the past, Guangxi suffered more than a hundred thousand "unnatural" deaths during the Cultural Revolution, the largest in the country in proportion to the local population. Under pressure from the new Dengist reformers and the general public, local officials responsible for the horrors but still in power pretended to cooperate with the investigators while they tried desperately to withhold critical information. The most sensitive pieces of evidence they attempted to cover up were those related to cannibalism. As the fact became indisputable, the focus of the investigation shifted to the number of victims and perpetrators and eventually to the culprits and the terms of their punishment.

As with the local officials' efforts to mitigate the horrifying effect of the crimes, the post-Mao regime used cannibalism as a pretext for the suppression of "ultraleftist" elements in the Party. If we can only guess that cannibalism was what in the end stunned Zhou Enlai into recognition of the macabre extent of the violence, its shocking effect on his successors is much better documented in the author's presentation of the investigation. It will suffice to cite the most devastating example: "The investigative team from the Central Committee of the CCP reported that Wang Wenliu (female), vice chair of the Revolutionary Committee of Wuxuan County, was alleged to have mutilated and eaten male reproductive organs. [The leaders of] the Central Committee were so shaken that they made numerous phone calls in May and June to press for her expulsion from the Party" (52). She was found guilty, expelled from the Party, and removed from office, though no specific charge was leveled against her for her alleged obsession with male organs because of insufficient evidence. Nevertheless, the gravity of the offense was gauged, in the order of symbolic importance, not by the act of cannibalism alone, nor simply by a case involving a female, but ultimately by a woman's alleged mutilation of a penis. Increasingly, the seeking and telling of the truth was heightened by the people's reactions to the outrageous violations of civilized taboos and by the sensational treatment of such extreme cases as Wang Wenliu's. If the perpetrators had to be eliminated from the Party, the next logical step was to quarantine the body politic from epidemic madness.

The focal point of the investigation was not how barbaric cannibalism was. Precisely because *chiren* has been conceptualized as *the* most barbaric form of inhumanity and its effect of madness rooted in the cultural unconscious of modern China, the very knowledge of the horror must be contained. The immediate threat was that the telling of it would shatter the social order, which had yet to be fully stabilized, especially when the atrocity could be easily attached to the image of the Party at the redefining moment of reform and opening up to the rest of the world. According to a local official, Guangxi authorities once had a policy directive sent to subordinate organizations dictating that "all Party members who participated in human eating [will] be expelled." Copies of that directive were soon recalled, though the "spirit" of the order was deemed still valid. The provincial authorities recalled the written document for fear that the news might be leaked to the media of Hong Kong. Should that happen, the policy directive would speak for itself "as such clear evidence of rampant cannibalism that it should lead to a Party directive exclusively aimed at the offenders with disciplinary terms clearly laid out" (52–53).

In other words, though the historical search for facts was conducted to cleanse the collective body, the written record of the search had to be erased from public knowledge so as to safeguard the image of the Party.

In the end, Wang Zujian, the courageous truth seeker and truth teller, found himself unwilling to let the story travel abroad as well. In a personal correspondence in 1988, he told Zheng Yi why he did not want to discuss the Wuxuan incident any more. His self-censorship resulted from his conscientious identification with the highest interest of the Party and the nation. He was inspired by Chen Huangmei, the vice minister of Culture and a veteran playwright and film critic who had been persecuted during the Cultural Revolution. In a speech to a Guangxi audience, Chen Huangmei had cited cannibalism as the worst example of the Cultural Revolution. But when Chen told the audience that he had heard about someone planning to include the materials in a fictional work he made an earnest plea: "Please never ever write such a piece! Should it be known to the outside world, how devastating it would be to the reputation of China, the Party, and the Chinese people!" Citing Chen's plea, Wang Zujian in his letter asked Zheng Yi: "Did you take the recent trip to Wuxuan in order to collect materials for your writing? Now that twenty years have passed, is there still the need to write it in a literary work? I don't know what the Central Committee will think of this. As far as I am concerned, I have no plan to do so" (141–42).

These two veteran Communists' fears were not groundless. Their concern indicates their understanding of the power of writing and the ethical responsibility of the writer in a world where historical facts can never be presented completely free of ideological overreading, where the notion of truth can always be misused to generate untruth. At the same time, however, their self-imposed silence paradoxically reinforces the power of words and misplaces their genuine concern for the protection of the image of the Party in the name of the Chinese nation. No matter whether one speaks out or remains silent, historical generalization and ideological totalization cuts both ways. For the overloaded image of cannibalism is always already "ethnicized" in modern times as *the* signifier of barbarism. In the modern world, cannibalism has never been—and I fear will never be—treated as just another crime. Above all, the number of victims of cannibalism in Guangxi was a tiny fraction of the total number of "unnatural" deaths, and the physical cruelty inflicted on the victims was not necessarily more painful than other forms of brutality (or even "painless" if the body was robbed after the victim's death). But the hundred thousand victims of "unnatural" deaths served as a mere statistical figure tucked into the backdrop of a violent history, the sole purpose of which was to highlight the sensational drama of human eating in Zheng Yi's search and presentation of "truth." Obviously, Zheng Yi has only reproduced the sensational approach of the official investigation, even though he strove to expose its "hidden truth."

In the end, the Wuxuan incident became a focus for repairing the existing social order upon the ruins of its own making. Since the very idea and memory of cannibalism are constituted in a totalizing epistemic mode and moral code, implicating all parties in a state of "madness," its contagious effect had to be diluted for the mental health of the nation. A life and death battle, started by the survivor for the survival of all, was thus transformed into one for the sanity and sanitation of the body politic. It has to take another shattering instance of madness—this time the Beijing massacre of 1989—for "tell the truth" to explode into "tell the world," the most frequently shouted phrase in the wake of the mass protest movement. It took the fugitive Zheng Yi four years, after his first trip to Guangxi, to start writing *Red Monument* (the book was written between October of 1990 and July of 1991 while the author was on the run because of his involvement in that movement). Zheng Yi concludes the chapter on Wang Zujian as follows:

> Even such an upright and courageous intellectual as Wang Zujian could not break loose from the complex of Qu Yuan [the ancient Chu poet] that confuses patriotism with loyalty [to rulers]. What could be more tragic than such a self-imposed fate for Chinese intellectuals! They may put their lives on the line against social injustice but never face up to the highest authority. . . . Probably the bloodbath of June 1989 has awakened them; perhaps they are still torn between abstract philosophy [i.e., the Communist ideology] and brute reality. In any event, his mission has run its course. *In his generation of Communists, he is a true human being, a capitalized Human Being.* Each generation has its own mission to carry out. What he is incapable of accomplishing is left to us. (142; original emphasis)

We do not know exactly what caused the author to delay the writing of the book until after the Beijing massacre, in spite of his professed urgency to tell the truth. In the preface to *Red Monument*, however, Zheng Yi admits that he did not anticipate the tragic outcome of June Fourth and scolds himself for having stayed away from Beijing in the final days before the tanks rolled in. The time and the circumstance of his writing the preface is key to understanding the narrative as well as the thesis of the book. After a two-year flight from the police and spending the latter half of that period writing the book, Zheng Yi had completed the manuscript and was about to deliver it into safe hands in a few hours. "I realize that I have created a miracle," the author claims. The writing of the manuscript and telling the truth to the world are in his view such acts of rebellion that he invokes "Adam and Eve's stealing of the forbidden fruit," "Prometheus' stealing of fire," and "[the Chinese mythological figure] Gun's stealing of the heavenly clay to control the flood." The irony is that the mass protest movement of 1989, whose tragic outcome perhaps was the decisive factor that convinced Zheng Yi to write *Red Monument*, invoked none of the above.

Imagined Journey to Hell

Zheng Yi's inflated sense of self-importance has much to do with the demigod tradition of modern Chinese intellectuals. But what is at stake here is the impact of his apotheosis upon the writing of the book. It is predictable that he follows Lu Xun in his thematic treatment of cannibalism but less so that he would also allow himself to be immersed in the *subjective* mood of the Madman in the presumably *objective* narrative of "investigative journalism." In spite—or rather because—of their contextual and generic differences, the presence of the Madman's discourse in Zheng Yi's nonfictional work testifies to the resilience of a particular discursive practice that has nevertheless been reified as the universal path to historical truth. What links May Fourth and June Fourth is therefore not just the obvious recurrence of the topic of cannibalism per se, but the inscription of emotional trauma and historical catastrophe in the narrative enunciation of madness. How are personal and historical experiences intertwined in a book that claims to tell the truth to the world? What formal strategy is adopted to organize the narrative and construct the consciousness?

Setting out on his first trip to Guangxi, Zheng Yi jokingly dismissed his decision as "crazy." After all, as he puts it, the Guangxi of 1986 featured "peaceful and bustling southern China basking in bright sunshine." But this self-mockery turned out to be quite accurate: like Lu Xun's Madman, the I-narrator Zheng Yi was about to embark on a heroic journey of descent into a human inferno. "Although I was yet to collect the materials [of evidence]," he recollected later, "I felt that what had happened there was not an isolated incident. . . . Based on my knowledge of the Communist regime, I knew I was about to enter a forbidden zone, a dark forest of bloody crimes." The journey would require extraordinary courage and self-sacrifice on the part of the fact finder and truth teller, who, as the author describes his role, "bears the heavy Cross of the Guangxi incident" (4). Once such a "holy" duty is assigned to the I-narrator—which tends to reinforce the comparison of himself to Adam and Eve, Prometheus, and Gun in the preface—and once the narrative of his telos is shaped prior to the actual trip, the matter becomes a simple task of presenting the case in accordance with the *predetermined* subject position and its mode of enunciation.

As he was approaching his destination, Zheng Yi reconfirmed his anticipation: "I thought I really had entered a dark forest full of evils; I came to see a red monument brushed over with human blood" (20). Days spent listening to gruesome stories about human livers became a gut-wrenching experience. When a dish of fried pork liver was served, writes the author, "I tried very hard to suppress the urge to vomit after I picked two pieces from the dish, instantly turning my eyes away" (28). Like the fish eyes that caused the Madman to vomit, the evil blood was contagious. Exhausted and stressed, Zheng Yi became "suspicious that my previous hepatitis had recurred" (76). In this way, the blood-producing organ that embodies the symptom of the larger political disease is literally rejoined by the author's diseased liver. Fortunately, his fear proved only a false alarm after a medical checkup, but the feeling heightened the narrative primacy of the personal experience over the historical search. As a result, the farther he ventured into the "dark forest," the more blurry the line became between fiction and reality. Inevitably, Lu Xun's Madman and the I-narrator met in a scene of "eye contact":

> Several days had passed, and I was no longer a stranger in Wuxuan. . . . Whether I knew them or not, the number of my "acquaintances" was growing larger. Some of them looked at me with a sincere smile; some eyed me with cold, hostile glances. The most frightening were the pene-

trating gazes of those who harbored unfathomable motives. All this made me feel like the character depicted by Lu Xun in his ingenious story "Diary of a Madman." (89)

On quoting a passage about the Madman's "eye contact" with the villagers in Lu Xun's story, Zheng Yi admits: "Maybe my fear was ungrounded, maybe not. Lu Xun's Madman suffered from schizophrenia, I was normal; the Madman was a fictional character, the Wuxuan incident a bloody reality" (90). Thus, between the fictional story created in 1918 and the bloody reality of 1968, Zheng Yi had to figure out his own reality in 1986. In the end, he turned himself into a fugitive on the run, reminding us of the author's underground experience while writing the book. In his fear that the materials he had collected would disappear as he himself vanished from the world in some premeditated "accident," he hastily sneaked out of the "dark forest" on a bus, alert all the time to any suspicious-looking individuals and surroundings (108).

Lu Xun's fiction, the historical memory of the Wuxuan incident, the author's 1986 trip, and his post-1989 ordeal—four narrative strands are thus interwoven in the pages that depict his search for truth. What ties these different elements together is the discursive practice of the "imagined" journey. By "imagined" I do not imply notions such as "invention," "fabrication" or "falsity," a reductionist equation that Benedict Anderson warns us against in *Imagined Communities* (1983, 15). In technical terms, since Zheng Yi is not an eyewitness to the historical occurrence, he has to first visualize, then verbalize, what his informants have told him. While the referent may be the fact, the fact is made to signify in the way it is told (by the informants) and retold (by the author). When the author narrates the historical event from a predetermined journey, cultural imagination takes hold as a necessarily mediated textual strategy that assigns form and meaning to writing and reading. The anecdotes cited from the writer's account of his personal feelings clearly indicate that the telling of the fact is inseparable from larger patterns of cultural imagination and historical memory. It is the imagined journey that allows the narrator, as well as the reader, to travel between different times and places.

As a fiction writer, Zheng Yi is meticulous about the plausible details of the historical event while all the time transcribing the reconstructed details into the larger network of signification. He believes that all the existing human imaginations of the underworld would pale in comparison with what he has "seen" in Wuxuan. There, as the text describes it:

> A fever of cannibalism swept the land like a plague and culminated in —I don't mean to be hyperbolic—"feasts of flesh." The feasting took place after public struggle sessions that involved indiscriminate beating and killing, and the butchering of victims still alive. Hearts, livers, gallbladders, kidneys, chest muscles, tenderloins, limbs, hands and feet, ribs, etc., were boiled in water or oil, roasted, fried, braised, or cooked with other methods. Everywhere—even on school campuses, in the county hospital, in dining halls of government agencies all the way up to the county administration—the feasting went on and on as cooking smoke kept curling upward. The shouting of drinkers' finger-guessing games was mixed with the loud bragging of one's achievement [in the violence] and the noisy demand for appropriate rewards. (92)

The "detailing"—"the cutting into pieces"—is mobilized to "flesh out" the whole. Immediately following the above scene, the author asks:

> Has the human race ever encountered such a hell of madness and horror in any religious classics? The most horrifying picture of Hell in the West is perhaps the Inferno described by Dante. But this great poet's wildest flights of imagination *do not go beyond (ye buguo shi)* images [such as wasp biting, decapitation, extraction of the tongue, mutilation, drowning in blood and filth, and other Chinese renderings of the forms of punishment in the Inferno]. In the East [*sic*], the Hell called Fengdu on the Yangtze River was the deepest abyss one could imagine. As brutal as the mount of cutting blades, the vast wok of boiling oil, the piercing of the heart by ten thousands of arrows, torture, mutilation, extraction of the tongue, beheading, grinding under millstones. . . , the worst, the condemnation to the karma of animals for the next life—all these were *just so so (ruci eryi)*. . . . The proletarian dictatorship is *ten times and even a hundred times* more cruel and inhumane than anything the human race has imagined. (92; emphasis added)

Once the trip is constructed to symbolize the descent into the inferno by following the familiar path of the Madman, the imagined journey is bound to end with the Lu Xunian type of allegorical totality. The conclusion is predictably a new and expanded version of the Madman's:

We have sunken step by step into Hell like a horde of beasts! My fellow Chinese, let's think, let's ask ourselves: Did it [cannibalism] only happen in Guangxi, carried out only by those ten thousand some individuals? No, Guangxi is not just a province, it stands for China! Not just those individuals are human eaters, our entire nation is composed of cannibals! We not only eat others, but we eat ourselves. By self-eating I don't just mean the killing among ourselves, between the elders and the youngsters, brothers and sisters. I mean the self-eating of our soul—our human nature, essential for our survival and for the building, with the whole human race, of the ideal kingdom of humanity. (107)

One wonders, in a small way, how "realistic" the scene of "feasting" is, given the small number of cannibalized victims in proportion to the overall population and the time span of the "feasting" over three months. What is most shocking, however is not really the "feasting" itself but the detailed imagination of the "festivity" as a compelling fact. If Lu Xun's Madman can draw a sweeping conclusion on the millennial Book of Confucian Virtues and Morality without giving a "detailed reading," it is because the text is a short story and thus only has to fulfill the demand for allegorical truth and formal coherence. In *Red Monument*, the imagined journey must meet a higher standard in order to lead the reader from details to totality. This requires a double strategy to reconstruct a local scene and then to frame it in a presumably universal reference—that is, to the medieval European and ancient Chinese versions of the underworld. The local detail has to be as horrifying and uncanny as one can depict while the horizon of interpretation must be all-encompassing and familiar in the given realm of cultural imagination, so that the reader can easily make sense of the local according to the signifying frame of the universal. Although the meaning production is governed by a set of expectations different from that of Lu Xun's story, Zheng Yi's text must fulfill its "literary" or formal demand in order for the content to be accepted as standing for some higher truth.

Yet at the very point that the text proceeds with its metaphorical transformation of descriptive detail into allegorical totality, the significance of the local scene suddenly surpasses that of the "archetypal" underworld, turning the latter into something *ye buguo shi* and *ruci eryi*. These two phrases on the "margin" of the text are not marginal for the textual production of meaning. For one thing, they signify nothing but the entrenched belief that cannibalism must be treated as the worst of all human vices and evils. But this is not the issue as long as one takes it to be an *opinion* that the author (or anyone for that matter) is educated to believe. Rather, the opinion reveals a deep-seated historical contradiction and hence a symptom of modern China's cultural pathology. On the narrative level, these phrases are signs of "syntactic excess." As such, they reveal the "free travel" of the cultural imagination across generic and spatio-temporal boundaries in spite of the pronounced positivism of the investigation. The moment the author jumps to an "outcry" in the name of the human race, he also becomes the judge of the very "universal" imagination on which his interpretation of the particular is grounded. On the ideological level, these signs of "syntactic excess" are the same as those of "semantic lack" in the sense that any concrete historical experience can no longer be presented apart from the abstract edifice of transhistorical human nature.

Ironically, if "syntactic excess" characterizes the rhetorical primacy in ideological (re)production while "semantic lack" signals the absence of material substance in that rhetorical posture, they are two of the most resilient fixtures in the official ideology. By "official ideology" I do not simply mean, in the narrow sense, the rhetoric of "revolution" and "class struggle" repeatedly manufactured by the state apparatus. I refer it, more importantly, to the powerful effects of ideological appellation upon the population—including here its most ferocious critic, Zheng Yi. Informed readers of the discourse of the Cultural Revolution will immediately recognize the familiar logic behind phrases such as *ye buguo shi* and *ruci eryi*: A (say, the oppressor in the old society) was bad enough, but compared to B (say, the counterrevolutionary under attack), A *ye buguo shi ruci eryi* (A was only so so, hence B is even worse). This "marginal" connection between the author's rhetorical strategy and the discourse of the Cultural Revolution foregrounds the problem of reinscription. And the most salient sign of ideological replication is the author's repeated, unquestioning invocation of the term *the people* throughout the book.

Taken as a whole, *Red Monument* is not a book of investigative journalism at all. All the "red monuments" are crudely brushed up in the first half of the book, only to pave the way to a second half that seeks "theoretical and scientific explanation" with regard to the violent history of the People's Republic. But the author's "theoretical and scientific" endeavor is nothing but an all-out polemical charge at Mao and what he considers the two ideological foundations of it: Marxism and Confucianism. As Zheng Yi launches his attack at the three historical figures, he reproduces exactly the same rhetorical figure of "the people." Especially in reevaluating the Cultural Revolution, he separates the "high-level power struggles" from what he calls "the people's revolution" (181), even replicating at one point the Maoist invention "within the people" (*renmin neibu*) to describe the civil war of the Cultural Revolution (186). In the argument for "the people's revolution," he recycles the very language of violence and hatred of the Red Guard Movement, which, in fact, fired up the mass fever of revenge and killings. On a purely theoretical level, any serious "theoretical and scientific" explanation of history cannot simply ignore the fact that Mao was the most eloquent rhetorician of "the people" in twentieth-century China. Above all, the prayer "Long live Chairman Mao" and Mao's response "Long live the People" epitomize the most dramatic moment of a long historical process in which the deification of the "great savior" goes hand-in-hand with the reification of "the people." The author's uncritical use of the latter against the former not only paradoxically reaffirms that ideological appellation; it leaves the door open for another round of "people's revolution," lacking only a new "great leader" (a role Zheng Yi seemed to intend to assume).

Unlikely as the alliance between Marx and Confucius is, the logic behind this wild "theoretical" reconfiguration is rooted in the radical antitraditionalism that has existed since May Fourth. What has changed is that Maoism—and Marxism, its ideological ancestor—has become just another "tradition," added to the dustbin of history along with the longtime "dead horse" of Confucianism. The linkage of Maoism to what is called Confucianism does not even cohere with the author's own appeal to idealized humanism. Despite many conceptual problems with the notion of "Confucian humanism," there is no question that the "class struggle" has divorced the idea of being "human" from "Confucian virtue and morality" and replaced the abstract "human love" with the no less abstract "class hatred." By the same token, the political category of "the people" is just a gross extension and attenuation of the classical Marxist concept of "the proletariat" for strategic reasons (because the Chinese proletariat was too small a force to single-handedly carry out the Communist revolution). The category of a social class defined in the political economy of nineteenth-century Western Europe is superseded by an empty but all-powerful figure for establishing a new system of class(ification). Situated especially in a postrevolutionary society of state socialism, the content of "the people" lacks a socioeconomic basis; its boundary has been drawn and redrawn according to changing ideological needs and political whims, and its application to the everyday life has proven disastrous. In short, the ideological concept of "the people" feeds on a grandiose rhetoric of invented social formation with catastrophic consequences.

Zheng Yi's "uprooting" of Maoism by tying it to Confucianism and Marxism also reinscribes a more recent version of radical antitraditionalism, namely, the "cultural fever" that preceded June Fourth. In the previous chapter, I described the "protraditionalist" branch of the cultural movement represented by the discussions around "The Chess King." While Zheng Yi was one of the earliest advocates of the "literature of searching for roots," his approach was at odds with Ah Cheng's, as is reflected in such fictional work as his 1985 novel *Old Well* (Laojing) but more visibly in his participation in the 1988 television miniseries *Death Song of the River* (Heshang). The central feature of radical antitraditionalism in the second half of the 1980s was its totalizing gesture of attributing contemporary China's problems to the cultural roots of the ancient "Yellow River civilization." The "death song" is chanted by those enchanted with the [Western] "Blue Ocean civilization" in the post-Mao cultural imagination of the global landscape. The comparative reading in *Death Song* is filtered through the lenses of nineteenth-century European social evolutionism, civilization theory, and the Hegelian teleology of history as well as images derived from contemporary fantasies of the "West." The end product is just an updated version of May Fourth antitraditionalism, which views China's "historical stagnation" in the past centuries as resulting from "oriental despotism" and its Confucian ideology. Time and again Confucianism has served as the archetypal scapegoat upon which intellectuals vent their frustration with present social conditions. While the two branches of the "cultural fever" differed in their thematic treatment of tradition, they shared the same cultural syntax in inscribing the contemporary around the reinvented past. Once freed from official censorship, Zheng Yi simply lets the previously muted attack at the current system come to the fore and squarely (mis)places the tragedy of the People's Republic on the "roots" of Confucianism.

Imagined Journey to Paradise

As the infernal journey often embeds in itself the transcendental path to a paradise, Zheng Yi's imagination also travels in a heavenly direction. Having read about his first trip to the "underworld," however, we should not be surprised that he also has constructed an idyllic wonderland out of utterly poetic fantasy while unabashedly proclaiming its "scientific truth." In the text, this ascent to paradise develops through the narrative of his second Guangxi trip.

Zheng Yi admits that he faces "a serious theoretical challenge" (187) if he is to convince the reader to accept the connection of the local incident with the totality of history. Because cannibalism is said to have occurred only in Guangxi, it would be very easy for a Han Chinese writer to attribute it to the customs of the ethnic Zhuangs. To avoid what he dismisses as "Han chauvinism," he returned to Guangxi in 1988 to search for "the mysterious answers hidden in Zhuang culture and history and conduct a comprehensive study of Zhuang nationality from the angle of cultural anthropology" (188). His "fieldwork," then, is a pivotal link between the reconstructed incident of cannibalism and the sweeping conclusion regarding Mao, Confucius, and Marx. In a similar vein, the writing of the second trip constitutes an "ethnographical" detour in the text's transition from "investigative journalism" to political polemic. The question is not whether a fiction writer is qualified to play the role of the professional cultural anthropologist but how he goes about his "fieldwork" and what knowledge his work produces about the "indigenous" culture.

The quest for the mysterious answers consists of two parts. The first describes his excursion into some remote villages and includes largely impressionistic samples of local hospitality, festivities, ritual-religious practices, folklore, and courting and wedding customs. Of course, he found nothing that would suggest any connection of the violent acts with the Zhuangs' sociocultural practices and belief and value systems. This leads him, in the second part, to look into Zhuang legendary tales and then juxtapose them with some historical and fictional accounts of Han cannibalism. His reading of the local customs and historical records without exception follows the larger pattern of the predetermined narrative, though the specifics are different from what he searched for in the 1986 trip.

Let's read of his textual search first. A Zhuang legend indicates that human flesh provided a source of food in prehistoric times of extreme scarcity, and older people were said to be more vulnerable to anthropophagy after their deaths. This practice was stopped by a young man named Teyi. Instead of giving up his mother's body to the villagers, Teyi killed an ox and handed out the meat. After the gods' failed intervention, the practice of killing and eating an ox replaced anthropophagy. Today, the ritual of ox killing is still observed in the region, usually held as the opening of social celebrations and feasting. To the author, the tale "describes a historic progress of morality, and Teyi is a cultural hero in human civilization deserving of our commemoration" (212).

What is sanctified may not always be followed. After the First Emperor of Qin established his empire, Han invasion and influence accelerated. The imperial order from the north gradually transformed the local "clan commune society" into a "society of patriarchal slavery," which lasted until the time of the Northern Song dynasty. During this millennial interval, "much of the old ways from the primitive age" remained; "some vestiges have even survived up to the present day" (220). The book provides no account of anthropophagy in the region from the point of view of the Zhuang people (due to the absence of a written language perhaps), nor does it demonstrate the connection between sociohistorical changes and the practice of cannibalism. All examples of flesh eating in both the Han and Zhuang regions are cited from Chinese-language sources. In the end, the author summarizes his findings in four points:

1. The Zhuangs are a people too innocent to understand the evil.

2. Zhuang cannibalism as documented in historical records occurred in prehistoric times just as it occurred in other cultures.

3. Yesterday's custom should not be subjected to today's moral standards. The flesh eating of the past can only be judged according to the moral standard of nature as a necessary means of survival. As the Zhuangs entered civilization much later [than the Hans], they are not so far removed from the past. As a result, previous customs can resurface if they are agitated by evil forces.

4. For nearly three thousand years, the Hans have been adversely influencing the Zhuangs through their own criminal acts of flesh eating. (238)

Based on this summary, Zheng Yi explains the roots of the most recent tragedy in Guangxi: "Cannibalism has a different moral content in different historical phases. In primitive ages, it was only a means of survival, not an expression of hatred [as in the Han culture]." The different forms and contents of cannibalism between the Zhuangs and the Hans lie in the distinction between innocence and vice. "Once the [Han's] vicious content is injected into the [Zhuang's] innocent form, vice will disguise itself in the innocent form to sweep the society into uncontrollable madness." The reason why cannibalism did not take place in Han regions is that "the Hans are too far removed from primitive ages, and it is just too naked a form of barbarism for them to undertake." For the Zhuangs, however, "cannibalism existed in their memories up to the fairly recent past and has been deposited in their collective unconscious. . . . When it was stirred up by the 'hurricane of class struggle,' the consequences were catastrophic." The conclusion is: "The origin of barbarism is in the north, in Han culture, even though it [cannibalism] only occurred in the Zhuang region." Therefore, Mao and the Party were the "chief criminals" (239–40).

Zheng Yi's "anthropological discovery" contains a few useful points. His treatment of past anthropophagy is by and large historical and materialistic. The attempt to understand the Zhuang people and their history is an earnest moment in a book written elsewhere with an explicit ideological bias and political polemics. This "border crossing" is a gesture aimed not only at transcending the ethnic divide but reaching the terrain of grassroots cultural-religious practice. However, despite his attack on Mao and Marx, the narrative account of historical "stages" reduplicates the discourse of history books published in the PRC. This is consistent with his borrowing from the Marxist-Maoist vocabulary throughout the book (which is not ironic, though, given his upbringing and his romantic view of "the people's revolution"). The main flaw of his "anthropological" search is that this work of "cultural anthropology" provides no empirical evidence or informant accounts to support the alleged but crucial connection between the violent acts of 1968 and some esoteric sediment from the mythical past in the "collective unconscious" of the Zhuangs. The author fails to explain why the "collective unconscious" escaped the memory of the overwhelming majority of the Zhuang people. Moreover, the evolutionist narrative also fails to explain why the violence broke out not in the less "civilized" villages but almost exclusively in the relatively modern and urban surroundings of county or commune seats. Among the fifty-six officially designated minority nationalities in China, the Zhuangs are arguably one of the most "sinified" ethnic groups, which the author himself repeatedly points out. In light of all these factors, how could there continuously exist a "pure ethnic form"? How could it be that the indigenous culture of the Zhuangs has survived in isolation where in fact the Han influence has continued for more than two thousand years, not to mention the more recent penetration of what is supposed to be "totalitarianism"?

The very moment he tries to dig out some pure ethnic cultural relics Zheng Yi turns a blind eye to the most salient signs of cultural hybridity. It is illuminating to "watch" the cultural space in which a presumably "primitive" sorcery performance was carried out. In a room in a mountain village, "the icons of Heaven, Earth, Emperor, Father, and Teacher stood there, worshipped just as in every house" in the village. Across from these Han cultural icons, "spread all over the side walls, were movie posters, mostly foreign ones, which featured glamorous and fashionable stars and exotic metropolitan landscapes" (194). Much as the civilizing order of the ancient Middle Kingdom shaped remote village life in the past, the "postmodern" collage has also reached this corner of the world. The image of the metropolis is as exotic to the villagers as their "indigenous" culture is to the visiting "cultural anthropologist."

Although the second trip is told as an ascent to Heaven, diametrically opposed to the first one in theme, it is still anchored in the narrative of an outsider's travelogue. Neatly organized within the framework of civilizational narrative, the traveler's imagination of Zhuang religion and culture is inscribed in the space of idyllic Eden. After his observation of the ritual performance in the room decorated with foreign movie posters, the author's cultural fantasy takes off:

> In Zhuang culture, the ghost world is the human world, and a common world capable of mutual understanding at that. It is a world of beauty and charm: the ghosts are no different from humans, all simple and loving beings; males farm and females spin, joyfully wed for peaceful life. There is no Last Judgment, no karma and cycle of punishment, no Hell. There are only pastoral serenity, glittering sunlight, bustling streets, undisturbed villages, and naked men and women rejoining Nature, working in the fields. . . . In sum, the primitive religion of the Zhuang people depicts an otherworldly realm as beautiful as Eden. It gives death positive meaning and thus accords life the most positive affirmation. (198)

One does not have to be very imaginative to see the mismatch, in a "primitive" land, between "bustling streets" and the tranquility of "naked men and women rejoining Nature." The picturesque idyll is no less detailed than the infernal "feasting," showing once again the constant shift between poetic imagination and "scientific" search, between the fiction writer and the "cultural anthropologist." It operates on the kind of nostalgic longing for the lost homeland represented by Shen Congwen—whose rediscovery in post-Mao China was one of the roots of "literature of searching for roots." Zheng Yi, of course, is no disciple of Shen Congwen's. For him, barbarism and lyricism can never coexist in the form of "discordant harmony." One has to be either "critical" or "lyrical," governed by the moral principle of vice versus innocence, not the poetic principle of critical lyricism. Moreover, the uncontaminated Eden is not just a signifier for the dream forever lost; it must serve as the "transcendental signified" of what the author himself stands for. Eden, above all, is the land of God.

Zheng Yi's subjective position is none other than that of apotheosis in both of his historical trips to Guangxi. There is no fundamental difference between his "journalistic" investigation of evil and his "anthropological" search for lost innocence. Here is how the author describes his arrival in this wonderland. As he was warmly received by a group of local writers, he wondered why "they lent me their hands of hospitality." These little-known writers, the author points out, have been subjected to repeated intellectual robbery by well-known men of letters from outside. Those literary thieves have mined the hard intellectual labor of the local writers and turned the materials they collected into cheap products of exoticism. For quite some time, these Zhuang writers of lesser fame had refused to meet and accommodate visiting Han writers. Zheng Yi was the first one welcomed. The reason for their exceptional hospitality, the author speculates, "lies in our shared repulsion for cannibalism and our love for Zhuang people and culture. . . . Like the hundred thousand souls of unjust death, they knew what I was up to" (192). The inflated self-perception is just a subjective effect of the ubiquitous presence of the moral sage.

To the extent that the "scientific search" is narrated in the form of a fantastic journey, the meaning of that search is always written before the trip begins. The angle of his entry into the land of "mysterious answers," it turns out, is simply that of the Han elite. Even before he sets out for the "field work," Zheng Yi has made up his mind as to what kind of Zhuang culture he would discover:

> Just as I had found in my earlier research of historical [Han Chinese] sources, the most visible characteristic of Guangxi culture is shamanism. . . . If the Yellow River culture can be simplified by calling it the Confucian culture, and the Yangtse River culture (or the Chu culture) can be simplified by calling it the Daoist culture, the Red River culture (or the Hundred Yue culture) on the upper reaches of the Pearl River should be simplified by calling it a culture of shamanism and sorcery. After we arrived in Nanning [the capital city of Guangxi], we asked a few literary friends to tell us more about shamanism; we were totally absorbed [in their storytelling] and absolutely entranced [with the stories]. Shamanism is not just the primitive religion of the Zhuang people, nor does it simply characterize their worldview and their entire spiritual world; shamanism is their way of life. To understand a minority people, one must understand their religion. Thus, we embarked on another long journey (191).

This fascination with "indigenous" culture notwithstanding, his approach reflects the entrenched mode of the Han high-cultural imagination of the exotic Other, particularly in those minority groups living in southern and southwestern China. The essentialist move is not a strategic ploy meant to invert sinocentric dominance, however. It extends the sweeping stroke of "cultural fever" by remapping the national space into three neatly outlined cultural clusters. Of course, monolithic Confucianism (and its complementary bedfellow Daoism to a lesser extent) must be subverted to allow "primitive religion" to emerge as Chinese civilization's southern, and hence least soiled, outpost. But this move does not change the center-periphery axis of cultural cartography. The imagined journey to Eden follows the same old route of the displaced and disenfranchised literatus-poet of ancient times.

In conclusion, *Red Monument* is a monumental version of the grand journey of the Madman and his descendant. The *writing* of the book is saturated with the Madman's (un)consciousness of a "persecution complex" and "absolute superiority." The book can and must be read as a fictional text, despite the author's claim to historical accuracy and scientific truth. From May Fourth radical antitraditionalism to post-Mao radical antitraditionalism/anti-Communism, the historical irony operates in a hauntingly schizophrenic mode. Concrete practice of "Confucian virtues and morality" is crudely repudiated, only to see a bloody recurrence of the worst traditions. The value system is increasingly vacuumed as social critique becomes moralized in the name of human values for melodramatic effect. The more urgent the problems of the present time are, the more ugly the ghost of the past is made to appear so as to serve as an easy target of facile blame. Historical memory is so totalized under the banner of "continuous revolution" that revolutionary violence takes on a life of its own to shatter the basic civic order into bits and pieces. The rhetoric of ideological radicalism attains such heights of inspiring mystification that any attempt to dislodge meaningful social change from that rhetoric would appear to be too complacent, conservative, and even reactionary. Socioeconomic impoverishment of the population goes hand in hand with the heroic saga of "the people." All the while intellectuals are humbled to "produce milk" to feed the masses or are forced into hard labor as "cow-ghosts and snake-demons," they return triumphantly in the end like the savior to embody the highest social conscience and historical wisdom. If these are the legacy of the Madman, his sons and grandsons have greatly expanded the schizophrenic scope of his diary.

Revisiting the Madness of History

Zheng Yi is not the only writer who has attempted to reconstruct a historical incident of cannibalism through a fictional narrative of an imagined journey. Liu Zhenyun's "Revisiting 1942" follows a similar path, combining "journalistic" investigation, "ethnographic" interviews, and political commentary. The difference between these two post-Tiananmen texts is that Liu's was published as a novella, a novella with certain avant-garde features at that. The novella sets out on a "postmodernist" journey, then betrays itself to favor a documentary presentation of historical facts, only to betray once again that documentary narrative by jumping into the classical trap of allegorical totality. If the formal logic of *Red Monument* operates on a triple leap from "investigative journalism" to fictionalized "anthropological" research to political allegorization, "Revisiting 1942" reverses the order of the first two steps but ends up in the same allegorical totality.

What I find most interesting about the novella, however, is not the author's double breach of his own textual logic and narrative coherence but what his double betrayal reveals in terms of the relationship between literary practice and ideological reproduction. His formal experiment in the first leg of the journey does put the reader in a more self-conscious position vis-à-vis his storytelling. And his search for historical truth through existing documents and "ethnographical interviews" in the second section could broaden our horizons regarding the use of fictional writing in rewriting history. Yet the apparently self-conscious twist of generic boundaries and stylistic rules at the beginning does not persist as the narrative moves on to focus on historical facts, especially when these facts are absorbed almost like a textual footnote into the author's allegorization of truth. It shows once again a clear-cut pattern whereby *writing*, no matter how experimental in terms of generic border crossing, is always overridden by ideological principles if the underlying *episteme* of the discursive field remains unchanged. The triumph of ideological reinscription over artistic experiment not only points to the author's own limitations. It suggests that nothing is more resilient and unamendable than the modern mythology of cannibalism precisely because that mythology can assume various generic forms and stylistic masks over a long period of time.

History as Documentary Truth

Let me first address the second mode of writing in the novella—the "rediscovery" of a massive famine that occurred in Henan Province during World War II. This search makes up roughly half of the textual space and, in generic terms, stands in between the other two modes of the text: the "postmodernist" travel and the classical "national allegory." Liu's search is based on a few historical sources, of which Theodore White's memoir *In Search of History* (1978) is the most important. But the relationship of the primary text with the quoted sources is intended for documentary citation rather than intertextual play. White's account of the 1942–43 famine provides the basic "raw materials" from which the novella draws extensively. Indeed, most of the detailed descriptions of the disaster and the political maneuvers in the power centers are quoted from White's book, directly in some cases and indirectly in others, where White's narrative is mixed up with Liu's polemical attack and imaginative reconstruction. Those who have not read White's memoir cannot tell it from the text's extensive use of "indirect speech." This copious appropriation of White inevitably turns the American journalist into "the central figure" (*zhujiao*), as the author admits halfway through (51).[2] The term *zhujiao* means, literally, "major role(s)"; in literary criticism, it is usually translated as "hero(ine)" or "protagonist." But in this particular text of fiction the term is not used in the literary sense; White does not come forth as a literary character in the novella. A closer look at his textual function will later reveal a symptomatic working out of a lasting cultural pathology. From a literary point of view (if we still read the text as a piece of fiction), such a betrayal of the aesthetic principle results in the loss of a great opportunity to rewrite history. I will return to this narrative tension and its allegorical solution later.

What is called "1942," then, is a book (White's) published in 1978, and the "revisiting" is nothing but a journey through that book.[3] The authorial voice in the novella repeatedly emphasizes that White is "the *zhujiao* in this essay" (*wenzhang*, as opposed to *xiaoshuo*, or "fiction"), that the writer (Liu himself) is "not writing fiction," and that the reason for his extensive use of White's memoir is to "ensure historical truth" (51, 68). There is no *intended* intertextual parody and revision between the two texts; nor can we sense any reflective distance between Liu and White. Thus, we may simply revisit the famine as it is presented by White.

The famine devastated the KMT-controlled area of Henan to the south of the Yellow River (the northern part of the province was divided between the Japanese and the Communists). The province had a population of thirty million. Five million died or were dying in White's estimation when he arrived on the scene in early 1943. A severe drought, followed by a plague of locusts, destroyed the bulk of the crop of 1942. The bad news did not reach the KMT capital until very late and was dismissed by Jiang Jieshi (Chiang K'ai-shek) because he distrusted the local officials and suspected that they were attempting to deceive the central government so as to obtain tax relief and aid. As a result, taxation continued to be levied at the already high wartime level, taking away whatever harvest had been left for the peasants. Writing more than three decades later, White admitted that "[o]f all marks on my thinking, the Henan famine remains most indelible" (1978, 144). As he describes one grisly scene after another as an eye witness, White writes:

> [T]*he worst was what I heard, which was cannibalism.* I never saw any man kill another person for meat, and never tasted human flesh. But it seemed ir-

refutably true that people were eating people meat. The usual defense was that the people meat was taken from the dead. Case after case which we tried to report presented this defense. In one village a mother was discovered boiling her two-year-old to eat its meat. In another case a father was charged with strangling his two boys to eat them; his defense was that they were already dead. A serious case in one village: the army had insisted that the peasants take in destitute children and an eight-year-old boy had been imposed on a peasant family. Then he disappeared. And on investigation, his bones were discovered by the peasant's shack, in a big crock. The question was only whether the boy had been eaten after he died or had been killed to be eaten later. In two hours in the village, we could not determine the justice of the matter; anyone might have been lying; so we rode on. (1978, 148–49; emphasis added)

During the famine, some "good officials and officers" and Western missionaries made piecemeal efforts to help. But the sheer scope of the catastrophe called for national and international intervention. So White sent out a dispatch that somehow bypassed the system of government censorship. After the story broke in *Time*, it infuriated Madame Jiang (Chiang), who was visiting the United States. She asked Henry R. Luce, the publisher, to fire White (which Luce refused to do). As the controversy surrounding White grew, progressives led by Sung Qingling, the widow of Dr. Sun Yat-sen, took advantage of this window of opportunity and arranged for White to meet with Jiang Jieshi. When it finally occurred to White in the meeting that Jiang "did not know what was going on," he recalled, "I tried to break through by telling him about the cannibalism." Jiang objected that "cannibalism in China was impossible." In the end, White produced photographs, taken by Harrison Forman of the London *Times*, that showed "dogs eating people on the roads." As happened with Lu Xun, the visual image electrified Jiang. "The Generalissimo's knee began to jiggle slightly, in a nervous tic," White notes. In his defense, Jiang told White that "he had *told* the army to share its grain with the people" (1978, 155; original emphasis). Yet it was also a self-defeating indication that he *did* know at least something about the famine. Jiang's unwitting "confession" escaped White, and Jiang remained a good person (though a bad leader) in his mind.

When government aid arrived belatedly, the funds were either misused or attached with conditions to the disadvantage of the needy. For instance, the government banks "would discount their own currency; for a one-hundred dollar bill, they would give back only eighty-three dollars in small bills" (White 1978, 152). Since the bureaucratic system had already collapsed, it could not handle the chaos for which it was responsible, at least in a major part. The massive suffering and chaos led White to conclude that the famine had created "an animal theater" (153). In hindsight, he attributes the famine to three causes: the war and the violent damage to the ecosystem after Jiang ordered troops to destroy the dikes on the Yellow River to stop the invading Japanese; the drought, which may have had much to do with the ecological changes; and the lack of well-organized relief and assistance. In his view, "death might have been avoided had government acted." In reality, it was "anarchy that masqueraded as government," and therefore the "death was man-made" (150). Directing his indignation at the Nationalists, White lashed out against them:

> Had I been a Henan peasant I would have acted as they did when, a year later, they went over to the Japanese and helped the Japanese defeat their own Chinese troops. And I would have, as they did in 1948, gone over to the conquering Communists. I know how cruel Chinese Communists can be; but no cruelty was greater than the Henan famine, and if the Communist idea promised government of any kind, then the ideas of mercy and liberty with which I had grown up were irrelevant. (153)

In Search of History was published more than three decades after White's first book, the best-seller *Thunder Out of China* (with Annalee Jacob, 1946), which got him into trouble in the McCarthy era. Clearly he has lost his faith in the Chinese Communists, yet still he is defending himself against his alleged role in "losing China to the Reds." This of course is not the point in discussing his memoir here. Rather, Liu's novella would be worthless (at least to me) if he had only copied White's accounts. The significance of the novella does not lie in its documenting some historical facts—we may well read White's book or other sources for that purpose. What is valuable about the novella is its symptomatic manifestation of how difficult it is to transgress, if not transcend, the modern discursive practice that allegorizes historical totality around cannibalism. Liu's novella is capable of doing that, but it fails even to live up to its own promise, made on the opening pages.

The Pathology of Self-Eating

"Revisiting 1942" promises something different at the outset, which goes as follows:

> In 1942, a mass famine took place in Henan. An admirable friend of mine launched me backward to that time over a dish of soybean sprouts and two pig's feet. My farewell meal would probably have passed for delicious food in 1942; or it perhaps wasn't such a big deal. In February 1943, Theodore White of *Time* magazine, along with Harrison Forman of the London *Times*, went to Henan to investigate the famine. In a place where a mother cooked her baby for food, the officials of my native province treated the two foreign friends to a banquet. They were offered lotus-seed porridge, peppered chicken, beef stew mixed with chestnut, bean curd, fish, fried egg rolls, *mantou*, rice, two kinds of soup, plus three pancakes with sugar scattered all over. Even today we petty folks have the chance to come across such a banquet only when we read of it in the menus of fancy restaurants or in books. According to White, that banquet was one of the best he had ever had. I must say it would be one of the best I have ever seen. But White also noted that he was too conscientious to eat. I believe that wasn't a problem to those officials. The bottom line is this: folks back home then had trouble finding food, but that was their problem. Whatever happens in this ancient land of ours, officials at and above the county level never have to deal with this kind of problem, not just lack of food, but also lack of sex. (28)

It must be noted that the reference to contemporary China in this passage (and another reference to the 1960 famine at one point) are clear signals as to what the author wants to imply and whom he wants to implicate. Although Liu cannot openly attack the current regime as Zheng Yi does, he seems to have made a deliberate decision not to allude to White's positive comment on the historical role of Chinese Communism cited above. The author's attempt to transcend the established major history and blur the political-partisan divide between the Nationalists and the Communists is neatly packaged in a sarcastic narrative of revisiting a "minor" history. This intent becomes even more obvious when the I-narrator has reached the year of 1942—"through a boring tunnel that stank of aged piss," and found that his friend exaggerated the importance of his trip. The deaths of three million people is simply "a trivial matter" if one weighs it against the major international events of the time. Above all, the world then "revolved around the White House, No. 10 Downing Street, the Kremlin, Hitler's underground headquarters, Tokyo, and the official palace of Jiang Jieshi." What is remembered as history is not the famine but "Madame Jiang's visit to the United States, Gandhi's fasting, the Stalingrad campaign, and Churchill's cold." The satirical tone is doubled when we are told that even the narrator's grandmother, a survivor now at the age of ninety-two but still very sharp, fails to recall for quite a while what happened to her in the famine: there were so many famines in her life that it takes some time for her to figure out which one the grandson is asking about! Ninety-two is the number of years the twentieth century had traveled when Liu was writing the novella. As the grandmother stands in for our century, modern Chinese history becomes something to be "filtered out and forgotten," as the narrator points out. Only he, "a descendent of the trashed hungry," wants to take a trip off the political axis of the world. Thus, like a pig on the run, he "swallowed the two pig's feet together with the nails"—his admirable friend forgot to remove the nails in preparing the farewell meal. Oblivion is thus the rule of history. He is forgetful in only a minor way, though, because he is determined to crack open the forgotten abyss (30–31).

The opening section of the text shows some features of the avant-garde literature of the time. The narrative blends a double-voiced discourse that wickedly crisscrosses between times, places, subject positions, and rhetorical postures—all cleverly woven around alimentary images. His "interviews" with the survivors are well written with humorous self-mockery but still maintain a sense of sympathy and sincerity. The novella even includes an "appendix," which consists of two irrelevant personal announcements of divorce from local newspapers published during the war—an indication that the author is sensitive enough to approach the written text of major history from its margins. The narrative voice is serious and cynical at the same time: he cannot but be serious toward the weighty task of revisiting a catastrophic history, yet he does not take himself too seriously in carrying out that great endeavor. As a fiction writer, Liu seems to know that he must avoid the apotheosis of the Madman. Yet at the same time he cannot let the narrator turn into a complete cynic. To keep himself from crossing the fine line between irony and cynicism, without resorting to the familiar madness, the author assigns a split role to his surrogate narrator. When the narrator makes comments on his own role as a fiction writer, he is "cool" and cynical enough not to lapse into madness; when he approaches the historical event, he is a serious investigator.

This use of double-voiced narrative would logically lead to a highlighting of the textuality of the search for truth by incorporating White into its fictional space. I make this comment not because I find White's accounts inaccurate—on the contrary, I find them as controlled as any journalist could have made them given the sheer scope of the misery—nor because I want to fault Liu for his later departure from his experimental style. If his use of White to "ensure historical truth" does not cohere with the aesthetic principle of the opening narrative, it must be considered to be a question of cultural pathology as much as an aesthetic discordance, revealing once again the trace of the Madman's "leap of faith" in deviating from his narrative logic. This pathological revelation is quietly built up—perhaps the author was not even aware of it—until it culminates in telling the truth, not of history, but of textuality.

The textual truth becomes crystallized step by step as the double-voiced narrative of the fictional narrator is gradually subsumed under the voice of authority. The shift from fictional mode to historical account reaches its peak as the narrator cites the most lurid details from White's memoir (and a few other sources). With the vanishing of the experimental playfulness of the fictional narrator, the author suddenly finds himself "not writing fiction." Even the "interviews" with survivors, which are told with a mixed touch of irony and sympathy, quietly become more like footnotes submerged in the overarching narrative of major political history as it is looked upon from the top. The departure from the original intent to tell the minor history is voiced precariously by the narrator. As the narrator comments on one of his informants who is deaf and virtually mute: "It's no easy job to retrieve historical facts from the living" (48). Since those who are alive can no longer "speak" or do not quite remember it (like the grandmother), the written document of the major history has to usurp their voices.

What is most illuminating—yet not surprising—is that the narrative reaches another "breakthrough" exactly the same way White "tried to break through" at his historical meeting with Jiang. In summarizing White's account of the chaotic flight of the refugees to the "human-meat market" of dogs eating people, Liu writes:

> (5) Cannibalism. The wolf nature resurfaced in humans. When nothing else was left for food, people would become wolves to eat other people. White said that he had never seen any humans eat the meat of other humans before, but his Henan trip opened his eyes. . . . He saw [*sic*] a mother boil her two-year-old and eat it; a father strangle his two children and eat their meat to save his own life; and an eight-year-old, who had lost his parents in the flight and was imposed upon a peasant family by the troops . . . was discovered by the peasant's shack in a big crock—only his bones were found with no flesh left on them. There were parents who exchanged their children for food and husbands who exchanged their wives. *Writing up to this point, I feel* that those people should have taken to robbery, murder, or organized themselves like Ku Klux Klan or terrorist groups: to eat their own family members and children was such a waste of their daring. . . . *A nation has no hope whose members only know how to eat each other.* (55; emphasis added)

The significance of this passage is not the author's slip in misquoting White. For whether White "heard about" the cannibalism or "saw" it does not change his conclusion that "it seemed irrefutably true that people were eating people meat." Nor does Liu's addition of the exchanged children and wives make much difference here: it could have happened in the desperate situation to a few crazy individuals (among the thirty million). The three examples White wrote about in his memoir do provide a gauge of the severity of the calamity, as do references to flesh eating in ancient Chinese records. But these little errors made by Liu are significant when they add up to the critical point: Liu's additional departure from his textual logic finally frustrates his search for minor history. This time he moves away from White's narrative, which he has so far exploited to ensure historical truth. The American journalist at least maintains enough sanity in contextualizing human catastrophe in a most devastating war and "natural" disaster. Yet all of a sudden the author jumps in, literally inserting his authorial comment on what White did *not* say. If the first shift marks the point of departure from experimental fiction to documentary history, this second jump is another and more serious "betrayal" of the author himself. The "minor" personages—the victims of the famine—turn out to be even worse than the villains, now turned into an empty signifier for the same "national allegory" practiced by Lu Xun. This allegorical mode once again shows the consistent and persistent trail that defines and traverses the discursive field of cannibalism in modern times. The logic of Lu Xun in reading the "apathetic" crowd at the beginning of the century is echoed by an end of the century "outcry" with a more excruciating sense of madness; it is even more schizophrenic because the Madman at least never thought of murder, the Klan, and terrorist groups as viable means to "save the children" or the nation. Ironically, as much as the author condemns self-eating, his betrayal of himself "shows" the very pathology of a cultural (un)consciousness shaped by nothing but the historical logic of autophagic self-destruction since the time of Lu Xun.

The outburst of indignation is always disruptive of "normalcy," whether it occurs in the context of Jiang's meeting with White or in the context of the intellectual crisis of the 1990s. But it is also disruptive in this case of the writer's own agenda. Instead of "retrieving" a forgotten history from a bottom-up perspective as the story sets out to do, Liu's "revisiting" ends up with the same "leap of faith"—a leap now made twice over. To return to the significance of the novella, outlined earlier, Liu's double betrayal of his own narrative logic is not simply an aesthetic matter. It demonstrates that the theme of cannibalism is capable of bending all forms of writing to its totalizing mold. As long as one follows the same ideological and epistemological pathway to history, a "breakthrough" through generic and stylistic amendment paradoxically makes that hard-rock mold of thinking even more difficult to break and in fact only reinforces the symbolic power of the theme.

A fictionalized reportage and a fiction-cum-documentary history, *Red Monument* and "Revisiting 1942" provide the most pathetic testimony to the unsurpassable threshold of repulsion and fright built into our anthropocentric narrative of civilization. It takes a real leap of faith to dissolve the madness; such a leap can be found in Mo Yan's *Liquorland*.

7. From Cannibalism to Carnivorism

Mo Yan's *Liquorland*

Born into a peasant family and raised on the vast northern plain of China, Mo Yan is appropriately called a native-soil writer. The topic of eating and drinking is ubiquitous in almost all his fictional works. In fact, most of his published books contain agrarian and alimentary images even in their titles. The list includes his first collection of stories *Toumingde hongluobo* (Translucent turnip), named after a 1985 novella; his myth-making novel *Honggaoliang jiazu* (The red sorghum family, 1987); his most politically engaged novel *Tiantang suantai zhige* (The garlic ballads, 1988); and his more recent novels *Fennude suantai* (The garlic of wrath, 1993) and *Shicao jiazu* (The herbivorous clan, 1993). In light of all these, *Jiuguo* (Liquorland, 1992) could be read as "the carnivorous clan."

The novel paints a grotesque portrait of the fictional city of Liquorland. In the height of the post-Mao economic reform, the city has developed a strategy to promote gourmet tourism around brand-name products of fine liquor and food. Central to that development is the "invention" of a special banquet delicacy that uses the tender flesh of children. Demand has created a supply of meat babies "manufactured" solely for the market. After the provincial authorities learn about this hideous crime, a senior detective is sent to Liquorland. Through a series of role reversals, the heroic investigator not only fails to catch the criminals but himself suffers a breakdown, ending up drowned in a latrine pit. In the end, the I-narrator Mo Yan travels to Liquorland in order to work out a better ending for the detective than such a pitiful death. But instead of assuring the reader of any authentic truth, Mo Yan himself collapses into a drunken stupor during the official welcome banquet, leaving pages of schizophrenic rumbling and mumbling for us to sort out.

The novel is structured on a triple narrative embeddedness and displacement, and each of the three strands provides a distinct but partial entry into the textual world. Of the ten chapters, all but the last consist of three structural units. The first has a basic plot, is told by Mo Yan, and revolves around the investigator. Punctuating this narrative of seeking the truth are nine short stories about "gourmets." These stories are "written" by a local writer named Li Yidou, whose given name signifies his enormous capacity for drinking. A Ph.D. candidate who specializes in liquor mixology at the Liquorland University of Brewage, Li is more interested in brewing verbal than alcoholic "drink." His writing is highly experimental in style, packaging the ancient Chinese strange tale, late Qing social exposé, political satire, and wry folk humor with high modernism, literature of the absurd, and Latin American magic realism. In Li's fictional world, celestial fantasy and infernal misery form the two sides of the same coin; the magic of the spirits simultaneously inspires poetic imagination and destroys social fabric; exquisite culinary culture is combined with the brutal torture and butchery of animals; and the refined taste of gourmandism generates execrable filth. In parallel with Mo Yan's and Li Yidou's narratives are the letters of personal correspondence between them, which serve as the third structural component. Their exchange of ideas and information provides the reader with a guide to their respective fictional writings as well as their personal interactions. But this neatly constructed format is only a textual illusion, which is deliberately made so by the author's self-textualization. Mo Yan is "composed," on three interrelated levels, of the real author of the novel, the fictional narrator-in-text, and a character in his own epistolary writing. As Mo Yan travels to Liquorland but fails to find answers to the mystery of his own making, even that illusionary authority is erased.

Thematically, the novel juxtaposes baby eating with gourmandism, alcoholic drinking with madness. This thematic doubling can be traced to traditional Chinese alimentary motifs such as *jiuchi roulin* ([drink] pond of liquor and [eat] forest of meat) and *zuochi shankong* (sit idly and eat up all one's fortune). Moral decadence, social degeneration, and dynastic collapse all unfold around extravagant feasting and overindulgence. Situated in post-1989 China, *Liquorland* captures the social gluttony and historical madness of the emerging "meat market," a distorted mixture of the worst elements of the corrupt political system and the capitalist "free market." While this social allegory may sound familiar, the modern discourse of *chiren* (eat human) is also dissolved in an older rhetoric of *chirou* (eat meat). Placed side by side with the works of Lu Xun, Zheng Yi, and Liu Zhenyun, Mo Yan's novel signals a paradigmatic shift from cannibalism to what I would call carnivorism—a shift from morality and teleology to material practice and mythology. As moral decadence is regrounded on oral excess, poetic madness is attenuated in the magic of liquor. When linear history is replaced with the cycles of the flesh, the body is removed from the unifying point of authorial consciousness to embody the fragmented bits and pieces of a self-destructive world. Against this line of major history, Mo Yan also has moved beyond the minor legacy of Shen Congwen, appropriating the latter's textual remembrance of dismemberment yet tearing apart the faith in words at the same time. Unlike Shen's insistence on integrity of form, Mo Yan's self-effacement exhibits a "postmodernist" aesthetic. He even makes his own "postmodernist" strategy a target of ridicule, conveying an utter distrust of cultural fetishization and formal retrenchment. Lest it be misunderstood that Mo Yan is just another writer obsessed with the "free play" of language, the critical thrust is never missing in the text. The absence of pronounced moralism paradoxically makes the naked truth even more compelling and "apocalyptic." When the reader is awakened to the nightmare with no savior in sight, nightmare itself becomes the reality to be reckoned with.

So far, this study has largely treated eating and cannibalism as separate issues. *Liquorland*, however, links the two themes together to underscore their underlying interconnectedness, thus begging us to rethink their murky relationship in terms of bipolar complementarity rather than dualistic contradiction. Lurking in the background of this thematic double is the author's experience of growing up in severe hunger. In "Wangbuliao chi" (Can't forget about eating), Mo Yan recalls the horrible effects of the famine of the early 1960s. In the first few months, his family managed to survive by eating such inedible "foods" as grasshoppers and cottonseeds. When the winter came, even the skin of trees was peeled off for food. Many villagers died of starvation, and a few died from eating too much too quickly when relief food finally arrived. "That was the best time for [wild] dogs," Mo Yan recalls. "The dogs were so used to eating dead people that they became crazy, attacking living people for meat, too" (1997, 95).[1] It is only natural that Mo Yan should limit his exegesis of the character *chi* to the meaning of "mouth begging food" (which is cited in the introduction). In that desperate situation, one might expect some incident of "hunger cannibalism," as was often assumed in popular belief. Yet there is no reference to cannibalism in Mo Yan's nonfictional writing. While hunger is a ubiquitous phenomenon in his fictional world, it is embedded in an all-encompassing narrative of the "food web," the logic of which is incomprehensible apart from the maddening experience of a child forced to swallow such an inedible hodgepodge and witness dogs attacking people for food.

Mo Yan (1995) is emphatic about the way his peasant upbringing shaped his perspective and sensibility. Unlike the other hunger artists in post-Mao China, who are all urbanites, he deliberately mixes every aspect of "eating" to challenge our finicky palate, departing completely from all the previous models of representing hunger *and* cannibalism. In the sense that *Liquorland* provides an unprecedented assortment of all alimentary themes, it must be read as an allegory of our small human world in the larger food web.

In the rest of this chapter, I will first examine the strategic literalization of *chiren* as an act of *chirou*, and modify the conceptual framework of carnivorism as an alternative to cannibalism. Underlying this conception of carnivorism is a nonanthropocentric view that encompasses elements from both cannibalism and meat consumption yet belongs to neither. This liminality or betweenness is highly ambiguous, operates through a decentered discourse of the body, and is encoded in the rhetoric of *rou* (flesh/meat—I will use the original term throughout except when I emphasize its doubleness in English). This conceptual revision leads me in the second part to trace the decomposition of the body to an equally decentered figure of critical consciousness. Just as cannibalism is rewritten as carnivorism, the subject position of divine madness embodied in the Madman is literalized, and indeed "liquidated," in liquid spirits. The discussion finally points to the symbiosis of the "carnal," the "carnivore," and the "carnival." By way of Bakhtin's theory of the carnival, I will conclude this chapter with an account of Mo Yan's carnivalesque self-embodiment from his earlier nostalgic nativism to the shattered myth of the people.

Carnivorism and the Rhetoric of *Rou*

The most chilling scenes in *Liquorland* are described in two stories written by Li Yidou, entitled respectively "Rouhai" (Meat children) and "Pengrenke" (A lecture on culinary art). In the College of Culinary Art, the Department of Meat-Children Procurement opens its doors on a regular basis. The babies are rated first according to their gender. The market price for boys is higher than that for girls for reasons not given—probably an ironic indication that girls must be kept "cheap" under any circumstance or perhaps that females must be left for the sake of reproduction. Payment also varies according to the degree of tenderness, fatness, and cleanness of the children. Parents, the producers, must raise them accordingly. Once the baby passes the inspection, it is well nursed with nice food and given plenty time for rest and play. The victims are numbed with high-quality liquor before they are butchered; they also are kept completely drunk during the execution. Past experiments suggest that those who are not alarmed by the terror of slaughter nor feel the physical pain produce the best meat. Further, such "alcoholic euthanasia" is a more effective measure to reduce the baby's milky odor than postmortem treatment of the body with cooking wine. The method of ending the young life also requires precision: the artery in the sole of the foot is opened to let out the blood while the alcohol-numbed child is seated in a special chair so that the entire body remains intact in appearance. This is because the body must be prepared and served in its original wholeness as if it were still alive; visible cuts, bruises, and holes will violate that high aesthetic standard.

Central to the production and consumption of meat children is the social contract for "dehumanization." The signing of the sales contract comes only after a routine question-confirmation procedure. In sequence, the inspector asks the seller four questions: (1) "This child was born and has been raised for the exclusive use of the Department of Procurement, is this correct?" (2) "It is therefore considered not to be a human being, is this correct?" (3) "Therefore, what you sell us is a special commodity, not a child, is this correct?" and (4) "It is hereby agreed that this commercial transaction is carried out in good faith, is fair to both parties, and must be deemed final, is this correct?" (88).[2] The same logic is found in a culinary class. "To be a chef," emphasizes the instructor, "one must stay cool and dispassionate. The babies we kill and cook are not real human beings. They are just little humanlike animals, a special product selected strictly under the contract of mutual agreement to meet the economic development and market needs of our prospering city" (268).

What puzzles the reader at the beginning is not so much the cruelty of this lurid "commodity exchange" as the absence of any hint of compassion and outrage in the enunciating voice. The entire story "Meat Children" is narrated matter-of-factly. As it unfolds in a peasant home in the early morning, the reader has no clue to what will become of a lovely boy except that he clearly occupies the center of narrative attention. While the mother is carefully cleaning his body, the father is anxious to hit the road as if any delay would destroy some golden opportunity (he failed to sell the boy last time simply because it was too late when he arrived at the inspection site). The couple's brief conversation revolves around whether or not their son will sell for a good price. The husband tries to convince the wife: "Our Little Treasure will certainly be rated Grade A. No one has invested as much as we have—you have eaten a hundred pounds of soybean cake, ten carps, and four hundred pounds of turnips" (74). The mother, however, complains that all the food she has consumed has only transformed her body into a milk-producing machine, corresponding exactly to the man's enumeration of her feed. Slowly, the reader comes to the knowledge that the father is jealous of another couple in the same village. That couple has made a good fortune partly because the wife is more productive in childbearing and partly because a relative of theirs is an inspector—so their babies are treated more favorably in passing the inspection and getting a higher grade. In this unfair market, Little Treasure's parents can only hope that their baby will generate enough profit to be worthy of their hard labor and investment. If one substitutes a piglet for the baby boy, the narrative of "Meat Children" would be legible as a story about a peasant family's routine business. Even the mother's expression of attachment and protection is distorted. When the father is about to slap the boy to silence his crying, she intervenes, saying: "Don't hit him too hard. A bruise will lower his grade" (76). Only the surreptitious atmosphere surrounding the father's trip adds a bit of Kafkaesque absurdity and horror, as he constantly eyes other children to reassure himself that his boy will indeed make the highest grade.

The cold-blooded tone in the narrative of production, however, contrasts sharply with the warm tone in the narrative of consumption. The instructor's "dehumanizing" of the meat baby is only the pre-text for the enterprise of gourmet eating. The culinary class begins with the following remarks by the instructor:

Dear students, have you ever thought of this: eating is no longer just to fill the stomach. Along with the rapid development of our Four Modernizations and the continuous increase in the people's living standard, eating has become an activity for artistic connoisseurship. Cooking thus is a sophisticated art form that requires more than technical know-how. The culinary artist should be more precise and adept than the surgeon, more sensitive to colors than the painter, has a sharper nose than a hound, and possesses a swifter tongue than a snake. . . .

Meanwhile, the gourmet's expectation is getting higher and higher. His taste is refined and nuanced, like the playboy who constantly changes his partner or the emperor who always covets another's territories. In short, it is not easy to satisfy the fine taste of today's gourmets. Thus, we must work hard and be creative to fulfill their needs. This is essential to the prosperity of our city and to your future success. (266)

The climax of the lecture, as noted earlier, is the in-class demonstration of the "alcoholic euthanasia" of a baby and his "peaceful" death.

The absence of a sympathetic, authorial voice reflects the author's calculated cruelty. By incorporating an otherwise blatantly cannibalistic topic into the language of commodity exchange and gourmandism, Mo Yan allows the narrative to shift from the question of "human value" to the "invisible hand" that determines the body's "exchange value." Interwoven into this discourse of classical Marxist political economy are two subtexts: the lingering vocabulary of Marxism-Maoism and the Dengist lexica of the "socialist market economy." Mo Yan, however, does not simply show their contradiction (and complicity, as both are appropriated in the ideological legitimation of power relations). He makes another decisive move to inscribe the "exchange value" around the consumption of flesh so that the abstract value of labor in the Marxist formulation is given a concrete form, literalized as a piece of meat to be consumed. By taking such a "disinterested" posture, the author bypasses the tired master trope of *chiren* to zero in on the social condition of *chirou*, thereby shifting the moral question of cannibalism to a critical scrutiny of the material and cultural practice of carnivorism. In twentieth-century China, Mo Yan's calculated cruelty echoes Shen Congwen's "modest proposal" more than Lu Xun's "outcry." Political satire notwithstanding, the theme of *chirou* is derived from a different rhetorical strategy than Shen's —or Swift's—"modest proposal." Since *chirou* is deliberately configured with gastronomic taste, I would like to revisit the notion of "gourmet cannibalism" as a point of departure for our discussion of carnivorism.

Literally, *gourmet cannibalism* can be defined as the culinary refinement of human flesh for gastronomic gratification. There are several problems with this definition. First, it is largely based on a few unverifiable cases from ancient Chinese literature, such as the Yi Ya legend, the "black deeds inns" in *Water Margin*, and the coveting of the sacred flesh of Tripitaka in *The Journey to the West*. Second, it is conceptually reductionist because the social-political context always inscribes extra-alimentary meanings around eating. Furthermore, the term is "invented" in the process of cultural translation, as there is no existing equivalent in the Chinese language. Understood in the English form, *gourmet cannibalism* is an oxymoron in rhetoric and a contradiction in social practice. Underlying its paradoxical structure is the dichotomy of the "high culture" of gourmandism versus the "low nature" of cannibalism. This logic is similar to the way Lu Xun's Madman reads barbarism out of the Confucian book.

Problematic as it is, the notion of "gourmet cannibalism" nevertheless allows me to foreground two issues against more familiar modes of alimentation. For one thing, the treatment of the flesh as a source of "fine food" does imply an intrinsic gastronomic intent on the part of the eater, even though it is acted out in conjunction with social practice. Since it is motivated neither by the material lack of food, as in "hunger cannibalism," nor by moral-political excess, as in "revenge cannibalism," epicurean consumption of the flesh has nothing to do with physical survival under desperate conditions or the symbolic enactment of social hatred. Such a "neither/nor" logic is further complicated by another question. Contrary to the humanistic tenet (Confucian or modern) that prohibits the eating of the flesh *because* it is deemed sacred, the flesh is believed to be no less "sacred" and *therefore* a more valuable food. This is what happens to the sacred body of the Tang monk Tripitaka in *The Journey to the West*. In the few cases of liver and heart consumption in Guangxi cannibalism, the organs also embody a different kind of "sacred" value (though not necessarily articulated as such). Whether portrayed in a quasi-religious epic novel or practiced by a handful of anthropophagi, the "sacramental" nature of the flesh, when used as an inducement to consumption, plays havoc with our anthropocentric understanding of the body. It is also a far cry from the underlying assumption of communion in that the act of eating is not performed for the spiritual transcendence of the carnal body.

Let me summarize the logic of "gourmet cannibalism" in a less rigorous form: I want to eat your flesh not because I am dying of hunger, nor because I hate you, nor because I want to partake of you to become at one with your spirit; I do so simply because I desire your flesh for the sake of the longevity, health, or sensual satisfaction of my flesh. The act of "gourmet cannibalism," then, has to be located in the site of the body of the human animal, where the flesh is equated to meat—a special kind of meat of course. Now that flesh is the most abundant source of meat (due to the sheer size of the human population) and only morally off limits to its own kind, the equation of the flesh with meat not only transgresses that moral code but brings to the fore the carnivorous nature of the human animal. Thus, "gourmet cannibalism" can be conceptualized as a human form of carnivorism, contradictory in rhetoric but not in the material practice of meat consumption. It cancels out the rhetorical tension of "high gourmandism" and "low cannibalism" by putting each under the other's erasure.

In contrast to the familiar moralism that subsumes the cannibal in the category of the subhuman, human carnivorism subjects the eaten to "the law of the jungle" (hence the "commodification" of the meat children). The latter operates on a negative dialectic of normality and pathology crucial to the "dehumanizing" of the body. On the level of food practice, meat consumption is conceived as normal (except for the true vegetarian) and cuts across all carnivorous species, with humans standing as the most versatile carnivores at the top of the food chain. Of all species, I dare say, humans are the most creative and brutal omnivores. Yet our consumption of animal meat is never deemed pathological as long as we stay on the triumphant apogee in that biopower structure of evolution. It only becomes a pathological practice when someone eats the flesh. There is nothing abnormal once the flesh is detached from its sacred dwelling. Perhaps it is only too natural that those who eat others' meat should contribute their own to sustain the order of meat production and consumption. Above all, is it not true that, even in our enlightened understanding of being human, it is the carnal shell of the sacred Self—the "pound of flesh," as Lacan calls it—that has been systematically dismissed and repressed, if not totally discarded? If our flesh were indeed so dispensable, it would be natural to consign it to the order of prey.

I recognize the degree of absurdity in the above argument. One can simply ask me where we would leave the ethical question of "being human" once we were to do away with the moral precept of not eating our own kind. I want to make it clear, on a provocative note, though, that I am not prepared to advocate the consumption of the flesh to solve the problem of food shortages on our increasingly overpopulated planet, not to mention developing a gastronomic taste for it. I hope that such a cannibalistic solution will not be necessary. Or, to make it less repulsive but no less cruel, I hope that the problem will not be solved through "natural" means such as famine, epidemic diseases, wars, or "random violence." I simply argue that, by cutting to the rock-hard truth that humans also are carnivores, Mo Yan's novel plays havoc with more than the familiar conception of cannibalism. It also forces us to rethink the anthropocentric basis on which our food habits and related social practices hinge. The above argument sounds absurd because the human practice of *chirou* lays bare an absurd truth that links us to other flesh-eating mammals, a link that anthropocentrism tries to conceal and erase.

On the most visible level, *Liquorland* exposes the normalization of the flesh so that it can launch a sweeping critique of the "meat market" in post-1989 China. Human carnivorism provides a critical tool that is far less loaded than the worn-out tropes of cannibalism and hunger, thus opening new possibilities for critical subversion. Having pointed out this important aspect of the novel, I also hold that the text's strategic reconfiguration of history with carnivorism generates other implications beyond its immediate social context. If the theoretical assumption of cannibalism is always anchored on the Lu Xunian thesis in modern China, Mo Yan's investigation makes a "downward" move instead to show the deep-seated predatory nature of the human condition. Through an "apocalyptic" revelation of the naked reality of carnivorism, the totality of Lu Xun's anthropocentric *episteme* and evolutionist ethic falls apart as well. The discourse that shapes the course of Mo Yan's investigation is embodied in a culture-specific rhetoric of *rou*.

In the traditional Chinese sign system, there are two descriptive terms for anthropophagy: *shiren* and *renxiangshi*. In the long course of historiographical writing, they have become hackneyed metaphors for social calamity and natural disasters. The ancient word that bears a strong moral overtone is *roushi* (carnivorous in the "predatory" sense of the word). While *roushi* often refers to abusive, parasitic officials (sometimes called *roushizhe*), it is also a descriptive term in the same way that *carnivora* defines flesh-eating mammals. The first meaning of the word *roushi* applies to the social aspect of *Liquorland*, and the second could be deployed to link such a social critique to the carnivorous propensity of the human animal. This double reference is in part a morphological function of the term *rou*. As I have noted in the introduction, *rou* occupies a vast field of signification, from human flesh to all different kinds of animal and fruit meat, only modified by the animal or the plant's name as a descriptive attribute. As with the relationship of the Chinese term *chi* to the English term *eating*, *rou* covers a larger semantic field than *flesh* and *meat* and thus is rhetorically more powerful in generating ambiguity. It is understandable that a daring food culture should employ a single noun to bear the "substance" of all the carnivores, humans included. In this sense, *rou* posits the eater and the eaten in an exchangeable and reciprocal relationship, leaving the human body less differentiated than it is on the polarity between *flesh* and *meat* and, by extension, between human eating and meat consumption.

Of course, tensions have always existed between *rou* and spirit and between carnality and spirituality. In the vocabulary of Chinese Buddhism, for instance, the carnal body is called *roushen*, a transient chunk of *rou* to be discarded before the soul enters Heaven (as is said of the carnal shells of the pilgrims in *The Journey to the West*). Those who do not have the faith then possess only *rouyan* (eyes of *rou*), subjecting themselves to the perpetual cycle of "reincarnation" in the lower strata of beings. So the true Buddhist must stay vegetarian. In modern China, *routi* (body corporeal) is defined as opposite to *jingshen* (mind/spirit). Yet, because the body must be recognized for its human value in Enlightenment humanism or for its material value in historical materialism, *shenti* has replaced *routi* as the common term proper to the "physical body." It is interesting to note that *shenti* became the neutral(ized) term for the physical body through a linguistic-cum-cosmetic surgery that removed *rou* from *roushen* and *routi* and then pieced together what was left in them. Still, the "fleshless body" has managed to maintain a certain *benti*, or "ontology," on its own terms because the traditional character *ti* is made up of "bones," "liquor," and "grain." In the course of transforming the old, this primitive ancient body thus has to be radically modernized and "humanized" in the simplified character *ti*, which indeed simplifies the complex structure of bones and tissues into a word composition of *ren* (human) and *ben* (root, origin, or essence). No wonder (philosophical) "humanism" is often translated as *renben zhuyi*.

"Decarnalization," the removal of *rou* from the animal body of the human creature, has much to do with the conception of the sexual body. Like the English word *carnal*, *rou* has long been associated with the sexual body and often contains derogatory connotations.[3] A classic of ancient Chinese pornographic literature, for instance, is entitled *Rouputuan* (Carnal prayer mat). A graphic—indeed, ideographic—character for "penile penetration" is written by coupling *ru* (enter or penetrate) on the top with *rou* at the bottom.[4] In addition to *roushen* and *routi*, other compounds include *rouyu* (carnal desire) and *rougan* (voluptuous)—the latter a gendered term referring usually to the well-rounded female body. Interestingly enough, *rouyu* and *rougan* also have undergone a surgery similar to that of *roushen* and *routi*, civilized by the addition of less graphic character *xing* (sex, sexual, sexuality) into *xingyu* and *xinggan* in modern Chinese. Despite all these attempts to erase and conceal the flesh, *rou* remains to be circulated in the linguistic tissue of the everyday simply because it signifies a favorite source of food at the same time. It keeps crisscrossing between the two discursive sites of eating and sex and within eating between flesh and meat. As far as it remains natural for the human carnivore to eat *rou*, the term may always bring up other semantic associations to generate a broad range of metaphorical substitutions and metonymical displacements. The multiple signification of *flesh/meat* makes it impossible to completely delink one meaning of *rou* from another. This rhetorical ambiguity does not exist in a more differentiating system like the English language, at least not to the same extent as *rou* does in the vast field of bodily practice and cultural embodiment.

The Madman's fish eating and vomiting in Lu Xun's story, not to mention the too numerous lapses of unintended "border crossing" between flesh and meat in Zheng Yi's own discourse, inadvertently reveals the entrapping secret of *rou*. But the cross-signification of *flesh/meat* is best retained in folk expressions. "The ugly toad wishes to eat the *rou* of the swan" illustrates that (see the discussion of Shen Congwen's story "Three Men and a Woman"). A more crude saying reads: *chirou yidun, buru jinrou yicun*, approximating to something like "Not even a whole meal of *rou* can compare to an inch [of the penis] in the *rou*." In Zhang Xianliang's "Mimosa," the peasant woman Ma Yinghua laughs at her well-educated lover when the latter addresses her as *qin'aide*, a loaded translation of "darling" circulated only among "bourgeois" urbanites. Instead, she calls him *gougou* (doggy) and asks him to address her as *rourou*, a reduplication of *flesh/meat* indicative of a more carnal intimacy. A metaphor of local color mainly associated with the sexual aspect of the flesh, her self-naming as *rourou* nevertheless reinforces her image as the provisioner of food to the starved "doggy"—the male protagonist. Only the Madman and his descendants would take these folk expressions as reflecting cannibalism. Conversely, the various rhetorical tropes of *rou* reflect quite a unique cultural anatomy of the carnal body.

In sum, the human body is only a small chunk of *rou* intimately connected to the vast world of flesh/meat, bones, and tissues. Since such a body is as carnivorous as that of other flesh-eating animals, it is subject to the same rule of reversibility and reciprocity. Based on this linguistic economy of *rou*, cultural embodiment must be understood in terms of its discursive multiplicity, dispersal, and circularity, always open to the dynamic process of historical reconfiguration. If my brief account of *rou* returns us to the ethical question raised earlier, I hope that I have made my point seem less absurd. The expanded and qualified notion of carnivorism is concerned with larger ethical questions about the human experience, not just a technical concept in, say, zoology or the study of mammals. It is a major ethos of human history, even though I happen to approach it from a culture-specific angle. Meanwhile, I believe that the ethical is relative to the historical, just as our food habits are relative to material conditions. What I find so useful in the notion of carnivorism is not an ethical principle we must condone but a radically different point of view on the historically constructed bodies of *rou*. This almost lost *episteme* and its rhetorical elements are what enables Mo Yan to insert a fresh critical edge into the representational convention of cannibalism without reproducing its tired moralist overtone. If the canon of modern Chinese literature begins with the first text on cannibalism, *chiren* has resurfaced in another moment of intellectual crisis, restored to the older form of *chirou*.

Madness and Its Liquidation

As I have argued previously, the representation of cannibalism from Lu Xun to Zheng Yi is intertwined with an excruciating sense of madness. Together, madness and cannibalism constitute a self-other relationship that is moralized through a contrast of the sacred agent of apotheosis with the devouring world of barbarism. Madness defines, simultaneously, the social crisis in which that moral self is enmeshed and the mode of its symbolic transcendence. The passage to salvation follows the rhetorical pattern of visual reenactment of oral anxiety. It reveals a systematic practice of metaphoric transformation whereby the muddle of the material world surrounding the oral zone is symbolically resolved in the glorious order of vision. Madness thus spearheads the path to enlightenment. At the root of these subjective and figurative positions lies the outside traveler, historical or imaginary, a figure traceable to the "original scene" in Columbus's Great Voyage and his accidental composition of the term *cannibal*. Although the modern Chinese traveler is always caught in the agonizing isolation on the "border," he returns triumphantly in the end as the representative of the spirit of the age. In short, madness, visual gaze, and travel are the trademark of the modern discourse on cannibalism.

Now that Mo Yan's *Liquorland* has marked a paradigmatic shift from *chiren* to *chirou*, from cannibalism to carnivorism, such a strategy of literalization also alters the existing rhetoric of madness. Much as he moves downward to reground the eating of flesh on the consumption of meat, Mo Yan collapses the narrative of the outside traveler at the bottom of the abyss. Instead of visually transforming madness into a signifier for moral triumph, Mo Yan's hero mistakenly visualizes a latrine pit as a feast of flesh and is drowned in it. This reverses the established route from orality to visuality and literally turns the archetypal moral sage into a schizophrenic shit eater. What dissolves the spirit of the age is liquid spirits. Not only is the hero's nervous breakdown inseparable from his drunkenness, but the I-narrator Mo Yan has to travel into the inferno to "liquidate" his own authority in liquor.

The story of the outside traveler begins much like a detective story. Ding Gou, a middle-aged senior detective and Communist Party member, is sent by the provincial authorities to investigate the alleged case of baby eating in Liquorland and its subordinate Mount Lou Coal Mine. The reader enters his textual world through almost all the familiar signposts in the modern "travelogue" on cannibalism. No sooner is he embarked on the mission than the trip is cast in a dark shadow. As seasoned as Ding is, the thought of baby eating drives him crazy. Like the Madman and Zheng Yi's I-narrator, his visual experience is fraught with hallucinations of human eating whenever he sees little boys in the street (16) or in a traditional New Year picture (12), which in turn calls up the image of his young son. As he is taken to meet the local cadres, the phantom milieu looms large, "as if he had entered an old-growth forest," with the strange-shaped fruits hanging on a tree "like naked baby boys" (22). When the Party secretary and the general manager of the mine are walking Ding to the banquet room behind the "forest," he feels as if he is being taken to a court of law with himself reversed to the position of the accused. But he is determined to dig out the truth, "even if he has to descend to the inferno and walk into a tomb" (47).

Indeed, "the high-rise building in Liquorland leads to Hell, just as the skyscrapers in New York City point to Heaven" (104). This spatial compression sets a sarcastic tone from which the narrative unfolds further into a realm of excruciating neurosis. Once Ding Gou is sucked into it, there will be no exit. His fate is already encoded in the textual system of nomenclature. The character *ding* is written in the shape of a hook, and the character *gou* means "hook." A superb "double hook" with a glorious past, known for catching the most fishy of criminals, Ding Gou himself is to be "hooked" time and again in his journey. For one thing, the main suspect, named Jin Gangzhuan or "diamond drill," will prove not only too slippery to capture but hard enough to destroy even the "hook." Jin used to work in the mine and was promoted to his present post as the vice director of the Propaganda Department under the Party Committee of Liquorland. This turn of fortune resulted from his unbeaten record of outdrinking anyone at any banquet. This is a special gift because he can always serve as a surrogate drinker on behalf of his superiors and never lose dignity by getting drunk. In a time of extravagant squandering of public funds on banquets to promote "public relations," a bureaucratic function charged in the past with ideological brainwashing naturally has metamorphosized into an instrument to keep his boss "sober minded." According to Mo Yan's "postscript," this frivolous case of corruption is based on a newspaper article, written by a real guzzling cadre to confess his sin and condemn the infectious social disease, which inspired Mo Yan to write the novel (423–24).

Ding Gou's investigation of "official cannibalism," a job crazy enough already, thus faces an even more dazzling challenge. The tradition behind the spirits is just too powerful to resist. Distilled in the intoxicating liquid are the solid matter of manhood and masculine guts, public vanity, and intrinsic "spiritual" vigor. *Jiu*, the pronunciation of the numeral "nine" as well as that of "liquor," signifies the largest digit, the highest domain of Heaven, the art of social bonding, and the energizer for ritual-religious worshipping and feasting. In ancient Chinese poetics, the spirits brew the Lu Xunian *kuang*—"madness" understood as a state of poetic ecstasy. Meanwhile, alcoholic drinking also comes first in the sequence of the four fatal forces that destroy the human order, expressed as *jiu* (liquor), *se* (sex), *cai* (wealth), and *qi* (anger). Much as *rou* forges the rhetorical linkage among the material bodies of the world, *jiu* connects a myriad of mental and "spiritual" experiences in a cosmic scope. Once caught in such a maze, one either soars to Heaven or sinks to Hell. But Mo Yan chooses both the sublime and the obscene for his hero, only to cancel one out with the other.

This simultaneous movement toward the otherwise bipolar opposite is figured in the hero's ascent and descent at the same time. When Ding Gou is already drunk at the banquet, his chief rival Jin Gangzhuan shows up and adds more magic to Ding's bewilderment. The last trace of Ding's vigilance is soon dissolved in Jin's graceful manner of connoisseurship. As Jin moves to sip the last of the thirty glasses he bets against the investigator, the latter is entranced. He sees in Jin's gesture "a beautiful curving line like the motion of the bow on a violin," which then touches off a stream of poetic images: from "golden leaves drifting in an autumn breeze" and "a tiny white flower in front of a tombstone" to "a mountain brook quietly spilling into a deep pond of lush green." The moment the detective collapses into the exalted persona of a romantic poet, he begins to admire the alleged baby-eating connoisseur (60).

In conventional hermeneutics, a change of perception induced by alcohol would indicate deception, especially in a detective story structured in a narrative movement from the false surface to the hidden truth. Ding Gou's intoxication, however, marks his schizophrenic ascent into a realm of verisimilitude that is neither true nor false. When the last dish is being served to climax the banquet, an anticlimax is set right in front of the detective. "Sitting cross-legged in the middle of a large gilt plate is a little boy with a charming smile, a pleasant scent emanating from his oily, golden body" (91). Once the evidence so easily presents itself, Ding draws out his pistol to arrest the baby eaters. In a delirious moment, a divine calling compels him to trigger an aimless shot. It is a fatal blow that simultaneously knocks off the boy's head and explodes Ding's sense of sanity. The lovely boy turns out to be a culinary miracle: a honeydew melon sits on the neck; two grapes fill the eye sockets; a roasted piglet stands as the torso; and lotus roots and sausages fill out the arms and the legs. Pressured by the hosts to make amends for his silly rudeness, the detective even cuts two slices of lotus root from the boy's arm. His action, as his rival jokes, "is [evidence of his] complicity in our feast" (99–100).

Painted in this macabre farce is a caricature of the sublime. With the pistol pointed at his head, Jin pleads:

> Comrade Ding Gou, don't be so stubborn. We all have pledged in front of the Party banner to devote our lives to the well-being of the people. Don't think yourself the only man of virtue in the world. In the list of our guests who have tasted this special food, there are our national leaders and people from all over the world, including famous artists and a variety of public dignitaries. (94)

By the same token, Ding's schizophrenic experience is described in a burlesque amalgam of his official duty, fatherly love, disgust toward the archetypal "gourmet cannibal" of Yi Ya, and the Lu Xunian outcry. As the bullet is released from the pistol, we hear the detective shouting:

> Let injustice and inhumanity tremble in the pang of the gunshot; let all that is virtuous, beautiful, and fragrant join hands and smile. Long live justice, truth, the people, and the People's Republic! Long live my great son! Long live boys! Long live girls! Long live the mothers! Long live myself, too. *Wansui, wansui, wanwansui* [the last part of the prayer used in the imperial court as well as during the Cultural Revolution to pray for the longevity of the emperors and Mao]. (96)

Following such a celestial caricature, the detective "collapses like an aged, worn-out wall," "lying on the ground like a corpse just dragged out of a large vat full of liquor" (97).

When the intoxicated detective fails to conjure up a reality in terms of truth versus falsity, the frailty of human cognition is laid bare. As the exquisite dish of the boy escapes Ding's dualistic conception, cannibalism itself is turned into an effect of nothing but the "surface." The mesmerizing "liquidation" of a solid world furnishes the existential condition for the detective's cognitive vacillation and role reversal. Inevitably, Ding Gou's infernal journey passes the second threshold of the four evil forces, as he becomes besotted with a voluptuous woman, a femme fatale who turns out to be Jin's wife. The "double hook" himself is framed in a scandalous photograph that Jin takes of them having sex in his own bedroom. Following this reversal from a law enforcement officer to a "hooligan," Ding Gou embarks on an existence on the run as a beggar and a fugitive. One of the most devastating episodes is his encounter with a retired former Red Army soldier. A veteran revolutionary who still has to work by attending to a cemetery of revolutionary martyrs, the old man is a lone figure among the dead and a metaphoric figure for what is left of the heroic past of the revolution. The old soldier picks up the detective-turned beggar, who was lost on the street and being treated by the local police as a "crazy man" (278). On learning about Ding's mission and pitiful situation, the veteran revolutionary scolds him: "[O]ur generation planted the seeds of heroic tigers and wolves but harvested a bunch of pathetic bugs like you" (295). As if that were not tragic enough, the old soldier himself ends up with his ears, nose, lips, and hands munched away by a swarm of rats. When Ding Gou returns to find the grisly scene, he fires the old man's shotgun at the rats. The rats are gone and so is the old soldier. What is left is the site of an apparent murder.

At the end of his ordeal, the nightmare comes true. While the crazy detective is listlessly wandering about, a gaily painted riverboat in the ancient style drifts along in front of him. On the boat, a feast of flesh is reaching its climax. Many familiar figures flash among the diners, including himself. They are about to eat a plump, smiling, baby boy. In his final act of duty,

> the detective jumped toward the boat but fell into a huge, open-air latrine pit. Fermented in the cesspool was the thin soupy mix of vomited liquor and meat and defecated meat and liquor. Floating on the surface were inflated condoms and all imaginable articles of filth. Here was flies' heaven and maggots' paradise, a fertile ground for all sorts of viruses, germs, and

bacteria. He felt this place was his best destiny. As the warm, gruellike stuff was edging up to his mouth, the detective burst into laughter. In a few seconds, ideals, justice, dignity, honor, love and all that was deemed sacred had sunk to the bottom of the pit along with the woeful senior detective. (382)

I must admit that reading such a passage is not a pleasant experience, and translating it is even worse. To nowhere, not even the ancient Chinese imaginary world of the grotesque, can we trace this particular form of death, although the filthy hotchpotch was the first thing the author remembers of his childhood. In "My Homeland and Childhood," Mo Yan recalls that on a hot summer day he fell into a latrine pit and swallowed the dirty liquid to his fill until he was rescued (1995, 105). Just as the intense hunger Mo Yan suffered in childhood has metamorphosed into a fictional feast of "meat children," his memory of a childhood mishap has wound up in a wicked hyperbole. But it is consistent with his view that "literature is a cause of 'blowing the bull' (*chui'niu*) rather than 'petting the horse' (*paima*)," that is, an exercise of artistic imagination rather than fawning flattery (104).

Placed side by side with Lu Xun's "Diary," the hero's last jump may well be read as a "satanic" mimicry of the Madman's final leap to "save the children." It is a heroic journey that lands in the abyss, a vision of truth and justice that only regresses to the most pathetic form of "eating," and a divine calling that bursts out in the horrifying laughter of the devil. The images of the ancient boat and the feast of flesh reinscribe the Madman's reading of the Confucian book, only to be inverted into an illusionary trap for the hero's demise. Once the Madman's journey ends up in the detective's resting place, reality must be relocated nowhere but at the bottom of the carnal cycle. It is not the ingestion of meat and liquor, but the vomited and defecated stuff that shores up the "bottom line" of the absurdity of the human condition. If the investigator follows the Madman's footsteps to enter the discourse of cannibalism, his moralism is dissolved into the inescapable pit of carnivorism.

Once the Madman's vision is drowned in the filth, his outcry is distorted into a devilish laughter. Ding Gou's final outburst is truly a Baudelairian laughter of madness, without, of course, ascribing the negativity of lived reality to the absence of transcendental truth. The ironic mood of *dédoublement* is fully narrativized to the extreme of language where madness figures fate rather than fosters the leap of faith. Political satire, social exposé, historical allegory, and the literature of the absurd are all packaged in a postrevolutionary text to mark the end of history. To Mo Yan, however, the end of history is not some historic moment to be celebrated, either. Destruction does not necessarily lead to rebirth. If the "last laugh" echoes a devil's apocalyptic revelation of a historical nightmare, Mo Yan himself must descend to the underworld as well to end this grand infernal journey.

The I-narrator Mo Yan describes the ordeal he has to go through in finishing up the detective's story like this:

> The writing of the novel has reached the most difficult part. That surreptitious senior detective always eludes me. I am simply at a loss as to whether I should let him die right away or go crazy. Even if his demise is what I want, I can't decide whether he should just kill himself or drink himself to death. In the last chapter, he was drunk again. To ease the pain of writing, I got drunk, too. I didn't soar to paradise like those [ancient] immortals. Instead, I sank into the inferno and suffered the hell of it. The scene on that [other] side is the worst. (299)[5]

According to Mo Yan, Ding Gou was originally modeled on Detective Hunter, one of the most popular Hollywood heroes introduced to the Chinese audience at the time of the novel's writing. However, the reference to "Detective Hunter" is underscored by a sarcastic play on the trendy infatuation with imported mass entertainment, as is the heavenly inscription of the skyscrapers in New York City cited previously. After reading Li Yidou's strange tales one after another, Mo Yan finds the glorious image of his hero fading step by step into an utterly hopeless drunkard. "I could no longer write the story," Mo Yan admits. "So I came to Liquorland to seek some inspiration in order to work out a better ending than the way he is drowned in the latrine pit" (388). Once he arrives at Liquorland, he is sucked into the same world of schizophrenia and intoxication. His "travelogue" ends with his own collapse during an official banquet. The novel's ending consists of a four-page delirious interior monologue and is written in the unpunctuated, Joycean style of the stream of consciousness.

In twentieth-century Chinese literature, the authorial body is often implicated in the process of alimentary embodiment. This is where the author's consciousness is revealed in writing or his subject position is constituted through writing. Now Mo Yan presents himself as a fellow traveler of the detective—and a "follower" at that. Just as the conventional authority the writer enjoys is dismantled, the central figure of subjectivity that hinges on the romantic notion of *kuang*, or "poetic ecstasy," is dissolved in the blasphemous mumbling of the drunkard. Posing himself as another outside traveler, Mo Yan inevitably subjects his own body to the shift from cannibalism (which is the outsider's discourse) to the principle of carnivorism. For the first time in modern Chinese literature, a fiction writer explicitly narrativizes the lack of his textual authority by subsuming himself under the rules of the world-in-text. Along with the infernal death of the Madman emerges the postrevolutionary writer as just another textual signifier, besotted, bewildered, and bifurcated.

Postrevolutionary Carnival

Among major writers of twentieth-century China, Mo Yan is the one always prepared to offer his own *rou* as the organizing trope for his work. In dedicating *Red Sorghum*, for instance, he writes: "With this book I respectfully invoke the heroic, aggrieved souls wandering in the boundless bright-red sorghum fields of my hometown. As your unfilial son, I am prepared to carve out my heart, marinate it in soy sauce, have it minced and placed in three bowls, and lay it out as an offering in a field of sorghum. Partake of it in good health!" (trans. Goldblatt [Mo Yan 1993c]). The symbolic act of serving up his heart would look like a continuation of the tradition since Lu Xun. But, contrary to the Lu Xunian cow that eats grass to produce futuristic milk for the young, the son now is prepared to feed his heart to the rising cultural nostalgia that *Red Sorghum*—especially through its film version directed by Zhang Yimou—has helped to nourish. He offers his heart to revitalize the rugged spirit of the folk and reconstruct the forgotten myth of the native soil, recalling instead the kind of "backward look" we find in Shen Congwen. In this sense, the son's symbolic gesture reenacts the ritual of *geguliaoqin*, much like the daughter's soup making for the dying mother in Amy Tan's novel, so that he could redeem the old China slaughtered under Lu Xun's call to arms. While the form of metaphorizing the physical body for cultural embodiment remains largely unchanged, the substance of Mo Yan's "heart" suggests a historical reversal from radical antitraditionalism to cultural reinvention of ancestral myth.

More significantly, however, the heart carved out is marinated in soy sauce and minced before the pieces are placed on the imaginary altar of ancestral spirits; it is sacrificed for the health of those who partake of it. Were it not narrated from the son's point of view, the culinary detailing of the heart would resonate with the images of "gourmet cannibalism." Who would be the "gourmet," the wandering souls of the past or those of us who partake in the reading-as-eating? Probably both. Now that the son's sacrificial move is made without the slightest hint at "gourmet cannibalism," or any form of cannibalism for that matter, are we prepared to partake of it? Struggling between our educated horror of cannibalism and our no less culturally constituted obsession with a healthy diet, we are justified to take a closer look at the son's intent and the content of the bowls. We must ask: why does Mo Yan, on the page of authorial dedication, call himself "your unfilial son" at the very moment of performing the ritual of filial piety? What is unfilial about his act?

Red Sorghum, as it turns out, is narrated by the son of a *zazhong* (illegitimate child or bastard) about his heroic grandparents. Like a *zazhong*, the marvelous red sorghum wine is a magical product of *zajiao* (hybridization), as it is brewed out of the grandfather's urine. This "theme wine" has fomented the rebellious spirit of the folk in the novel and the film and excited the blood circulation of the national body. The film's theme song, "The Wine God," swept China and has since become a household melody. Instead of the son's heart, the reader/viewer has a mouthful of the urine-turned-elixir to celebrate the return of the grotesque and the uncanny. The brewing of such a mixed drink fleshes out the central theme of carnal transgression and carnivalesque blasphemy.[6] What is hidden beneath Mo Yan's nativist imagination of the Chinese folk is the very source of cultural parody: the authorial posture of offering some "dirty" stuff in the name of filial piety. Yet Mo Yan's ancestral commemoration is not an ironic gesture, either—as far as irony is posited as the negative figure for an authentic self experienced only in language. Rather, the self, including his "heart," is completely dispersed in the texture of myth and cultural unconsciousness. This is the reason why the reader is not positioned to see any implication of cannibalism in the author's heart offering—unless we impose a schizophrenic method of reading. It proves once again that what counts as cannibalism hinges on a specific narrative point of view. Neither moralistic nor ironic, the brewing of the hybrid liquid returns us to some "authentic" moment of primitivity. At this conjunction, Bakhtin's theory of the carnival may provide a linkage between the theme of carnivorism and the mode of carnivalesque writing.

Central to Bakhtin's notion of the carnival is "the material bodily principle" that is realized in the "images of food, drink, defecation, and sexual life." He defines the representational mode of the carnival as "grotesque realism." Aiming at "the lowering of all that is high, spiritual, ideal, abstract," grotesque realism is concerned with "the lower stratum of the body, the life of the belly and the reproductive organs." The degradation and debasement of the higher stratum of the body, however, operates on a dialectic of death and rebirth, destruction of the old in anticipation of the new. Through its festive laughter, the carnival unleashes a "temporary liberation from the prevailing truth and from the established order." What Bakhtin repeatedly emphasizes is the collective mode and mood of carnivalesque practice. "The material bodily principle," he writes, "is contained not in the biological individual, not in the bourgeois ego, but in the people, a people who are continually growing and renewed." "Carnival laughter is the laughter of all the people," he insists, "not an individual reaction to some 'isolated comic' event" (1984, 10–21). Writing during the rising terror of Stalinism yet critiquing the bourgeois notion of the individual subject at the same time, Bakhtin sees in the disruptive, cyclical, and communal activities of the carnival a possibility of redeeming the masses from their ideological appropriation.

In light of Bakhtin's theory, *Red Sorghum* is a text that attempts to reappropriate the notion of the people by changing its image from the "divine" to the "obscene." But Mo Yan lives in a time that the earlier Bakhtin perhaps never expected to see. In the post-Mao era, the concept of the people has become an empty signifier. This idealized vehicle thus is up for grabs because its content has been vacuumed. Yet the tragedy of 1989 also marked the end of the healthy, "primitive" carnival. The nativist imaginary of a nonofficial version of the "Chinese folk" in the myth-making 1980s was soon to be reappropriated into expanded cultural nationalism for a new round of ideological legitimation. The native-soil writer himself, offering his heart to heal the wounds of the bleeding native land thus runs the risk of becoming a heart of loyalty to that ideology of cultural nationalism. Meanwhile, the return to the lost community actually took place at a time when mass consumerism finally began to invade the postrevolutionary society of the People's Republic. Under these circumstances, the "heart," like the people prior to it, was up for grabs.

If 1989 marks a point of changing tide in contemporary Chinese consciousness, it is inevitably reflected in Mo Yan's shift from celebrating the folk heroism of the past to exposing the heart-wrenching conditions of the present. After the film *Red Sorghum* put him in the national spotlight, Mo Yan became more openly critical of official corruption and abuse. But the deeper his critique cuts to the "bottom line" of humanity, the more "obscene" his language becomes, utterly doing away with the idealized image of victims central to the construction of "the people." The carnivalesque celebration of the "primitive" body in *Red Sorghum* has been gradually replaced by lurid images in his more recent writings.[7] In this new social environment, it would be just too pathetic to invoke the romantic image of the folk and reinscribe it around the carnival.

Theoretically, any anachronic reinscription of the carnival in modern literature would amount to nothing more than a symptom of historical displacement and imaginary nostalgia. Even the Bakhtinian version of the carnival is in itself tinged with a sense of nostalgia for an immanent totality and an organic cultural practice that are irretrievably lost. To him, grotesque realism is unique precisely because of its distinction from "the purely formalist literary parody of modern times." Instead of conceiving and regenerating, the modern genre of parody and other forms of degradation have "a solely negative character" (Bakhtin 1984, 21). Therefore, the carnival as it is restaged in a modern scene has two characters. It either reaffirms the body's positive degradation or reveals its negative decadence. Once removed from the kind of utopian totality found in Bakhtin's theory, the grotesque images are literalized as well, evoking instead a sense of repulsion and abjection. What used to be grotesque realism now stands for a realism of the absurd, much as the once romanticized body now stands for a mere piece of meat.

The carnival thus must be redefined in accordance with the negative principle of modern parody and laughter in Mo Yan's more recent works. In other words, the changing cultural politics around 1989 has also transformed the healthy body of the folk for cultural redemption into the diseased body of human meat for social condemnation. Not a purely formalist literary parody, *Liquorland* still contains the material bodily principle of his early writing, but such a bodily principle obtains now only in its semantic reversal. As the meaning of carnivorism is expanded and modified for a new entry into the writing of cannibalism, so is the notion of carnivalesque writing. The linguistic connection for my reading already exists: the term *carnival* shares the same etymological root as *carnal* and *carnivore*. Although it originated from a culture-specific practice (prior to the fasting and penitence of Lent) and has no equivalent in the Chinese language, its translation as *kuanghuanjie* nevertheless evokes the imagery of "carousal" to Chinese salivary glands, known as *dachidahe* (big eating and big drinking). Historically, the revelry in carousal signifies defiance of the imperial order and elitist decorum. In the Ming novel *Water Margin*, for example, the rebels' utopian ideal of brotherhood is expressed in their commensal feasting, called *dawanhejiu, dakuaichirou* (drinking liquor in big bowls [and] eating meat in big chunks). The uninhibited drinking and feasting of the folk depicted in *Red Sorghum* is traceable to that disruptive function of the carousal. However, *dachidahe* also signals moral corruption and social decadence when it involves parasitic officials and the wealthy elite (since the masses can rarely afford it). In post-Mao China, extravagant squandering of public funds for feasting has reached such an unprecedented extent that even the Party has issued a series of directives to ban it. In the Party directives as well as in popular discourse, *dachidahe* often serves as a synonym for corruption and decadence. Like these alimentary expressions of *jiuchi roulin* ([drink] pond of liquor and [eat] forest of meat) and *zuochi shankong* (sit idly and eat up all one's fortune), *dachidahe* as a contemporary Chinese version of the carousal, then, is doubly removed from the carnival as theorized by Bakhtin.

On the formal level, the discursive and generic hybridity of the carnival still pertains to the mode of writing in *Liquorland*. But it follows the same negative principle whereby the semantic meaning is inverted from the healthy to the diseased cultural body. This corresponds to the heteroglossia of *rou* and its textual embodiment. If the magic of brewing a beautiful wine out of urine in *Red Sorghum* is meant to reaffirm a positive degradation of the body for its renewal, feasting and drinking in *Liquorland* are literalized through the carnivoristic tropes to show the corrupt cycle of *rou*. If the lighter sorghum wine could release all the demons from beneath the thin veneer of high civilization, the stronger liquor in *Liquorland* turns the laughter into a chilling outburst that shatters the cultural body into pieces of wasteland—a wasteland literalized as the latrine pit. The two substances that are fermented in Ding Gou's "drink"—meat and liquor—return us to the symbolic network of carnivorism in which the body is circulated, dispersed, and eliminated.

The earlier folk humor that fermented the red sorghum wine has now brewed a far more wicked brand of folly in *Liquorland*. What remains is Mo Yan's persistent push of his carnivalesque writing to the new horizon of the diseased "spirit(s)." The novel then can be read as a parody of his own past, à la his own "unfilial" heart. Once the urine-turned-wine outlives its magic, Mo Yan reformulates the liquid, turns it into the gruel-like stuff in the latrine pit, and shoves it down our throats as a poisonous food for thought. A writer who once offered his heart for the health of the collective body now puts his body to an infernal trial so that he can paint the most awful scenes of madness and death all the while insisting on its fictional truth.

In the end, though, how can one assimilate these things? It may be a long time before another writer can surpass Mo Yan, in thought, in style, and, most importantly, in offering wicked insight into the human condition.

IV

Sampling of Variety: Gender and Cross-Cultural Perspectives

Cannibalism and hunger are invested with gendered desires as well as thematic concerns and generic attributes. Lu Xun's configuration of the father with the national allegory of modern China sets off Shen Congwen's appeal to the nurturing mother and the native soil. In Freudian-Lacanian psychoanalysis, they embody, respectively, the symbolic and the imaginary, or, in the Chinese tradition, the language of *yang* and the writing of *yin*. This engendered difference is important to bear in mind when we consider women's alimentary narratives.

That some male writers display feminine traits indicates that gender sensibilities are not solely invested in female authorship. A further distinction, however, can be made in terms of the presence or absence of the mother when eating and cooking are involved. The image of the mother and its association with the child's oral pleasure are a recurrent leitmotiv in the works of male writers in modern China. Although not all male writers follow the same model—and those who do vary in their individual flavors—there is a clear pattern of incorporating the mother as a source of symbolic nourishment. The mother and the child do not have to be literal or biological: any woman who feeds and nurtures can occupy that space as a sort of a surrogate mother. What is more interesting is that the father or the family man is often absent from the world of the male narrator. A further pursuit along this Freudian line would suggest a modern Chinese version of the Oedipus complex, one centered more around food than sexuality. Freudianism is not strictly applicable here paradoxically because it can be used to open some possibility of revision. Regardless of their differing connotations, the narrative of the physical or spatial relationship often evokes a poignant sentiment of nostalgia and entails the temporal return to "home." The spatial theme and its temporal form are thus entwined as a trademark for the discursive practice around the personal experience of lack. If "in time things part, and in space things touch"—just to play with E. M. Forster's famous epigram—there is a reconfiguration of time and space in writings of hunger: in time, things are reconnected that no longer touch in space.

This part of the book, which examines six women writers from the China of the 1930s to contemporary America, also constitutes a time-space that samples a variety of alimentary writings. As such, the sampling is meant to come *after* the preceding saga. This positioning of women's writing signifies the order in which God created woman after man, though Chinese mythology does not contain the same order—what created humans are said to be a brother and a sister (with no incest taboo implied in the legend). Nevertheless, after feminism we have come to recognize how women have had to create "a room of their own" in the grand edifice of men's language. An immediate twist can be applied to that symbolic order by raising this question: if male writers in modern China tend to associate food with the imaginary of the "mother," where does that leave women, themselves supposed to be or to become the "sources" of nurturing?

This question, however, cannot be addressed by means of a simplistic bifurcation along gender lines. As the following pages will demonstrate, the selected women writers occupy radically different positions. For practical purposes, they are grouped together here only because they all write about food, eating, and consumption from a broadly descriptive Chinese perspective. With Xiao Hong's personal essays, collected in *Shangshijie* (Market street, 1936), we are thrown into an empty space suspended on the author's empty stomach. Yet on the empty site of material and social lack stands a female hunger artist whose poetic sensibility is so original that we are unable to locate it in any particular thematic or generic convention. This is a story hitherto untold precisely because it does not belong to any well-trod path of literary history: it is a tragic tale of a Nora who has left the "mother" and the hearth only to find herself stranded in the historical exile of modern China. "Hitherto untold" also characterizes the secrets of the stove presented in Wang Anyi's 1996 novel, *Changhenge* (Melody of everlasting regret). But Wang Anyi begins where Xiao Hong and the two generations of "new women" writers left off, and her poetic treatment of the pleasure of double orality comes in sharp contrast to her female predecessors and contemporaries, reminiscent of Shen Congwen and Ah Cheng yet short of reinscribing the "motherly." Wang's is a postrevolutionary reconstruction of the "minor" from within the tiny gaps and cracks left by the pounding footsteps of the major history. At the same time, this reconstructive project is carried out through a brilliant deconstruction of an age-old male fantasy about the "short-lived beauty," shifting the female body from the visual spectrum of objectification to the oral interiority of subjectivity. Set apart by six decades and opposite in themes of eating, Xiao Hong and Wang Anyi share a remarkably feminine sensitivity to the corporeal and carnal details of food and words and their ritualistic power in shaping the everyday.

The same sensitivity is found in Li Ang's *The Butcher's Wife* (1983), now a monumental text of feminist literature in the Chinese language. But her probing into the everyday is launched in a direction opposite that of the poetic treatment of "normal" eating under unusual circumstances, as in Xiao Hong's and Wang Anyi's works. By juxtaposing animal slaughter and the oppression of women in the rather "normal" state of traditional society, the novel shows the destructive forces inherent in the human conquest of nature and male domination of women. The bloody penetration of the knife into the throat of the pig parallels the violation of the most inviolate major orifices of the female body, the mouth and the vagina. The images of animal meat and female flesh are inscribed in the rhetoric of *rou* similar to Mo Yan's rewriting of cannibalism through carnivorism. But short of the kind of pastiche found in Mo Yan's work, Li Ang's text displays a revised version of the allegorical. It replaces the national body with the female body and reveals a similar schizophrenic position of the Westernized third-world intellectual.

The schizophrenic position turns out to be the very site of liminality for my personal encounters with ethnicized food images. As the next chapter turns to Chinese American writers, I will first relate three episodes. The story of the "banana" marks my American initiation in the metaphor of "yellow outside, white inside." This position is turned around in my classroom encounter with the monkey brain feast from Kingston's *The Woman Warrior* (1975), which defines my split status as a native informant and an ethnographer at the same time. In the end, a series of twists and turns around the fortune cookie restore some sense of sanity and allow me to reread two "fortune cookie–like" texts, Jade Snow Wong's *Fifth Chinese Daughter* (1945) and Amy Tan's *The Joy Luck Club* (1989). Using the fortune cookie as the organizing trope for my reading, I argue that the orientalist packaging of this cultural tidbit conceals the desire of the cookie. By recovering the absent in what has been presented, a hungry self emerges from "behind the scenes" in Wong's text and a "double-tongued" discourse returns the "Chinese cannibal" from Amy Tan to the "motherland."

To return to where we started, the valorized symbiosis of food and the "motherly" in Chinese American women's writings points to the ethnicized structure of their affective ambivalence about a feminized China, the mirror of the "mother" in which they find themselves. The differences between Chinese and Chinese American women writers would not be comprehensible unless we accounted for the dissimilar ways in which the gendered subject is defined in relation to different domestic arrangements, roles of women writers, socioeconomic classes, ethnic divisions of labor, and symbolic resources available to individual authors. Since there is no fixed set of gender attributes shared cross-culturally by Chinese and Chinese American women writers, this disparity perhaps reaffirms the very paradox of feminism. If women are different from men, their intergender alterity is no less embodied in their intragender difference across cultures.

8. Embodied Spaces of Home

Xiao Hong, Wang Anyi, and Li Ang

Xiao Hong's Art of Hunger

Published in the heyday of national crisis and social revolution, Xiao Hong's personal essays relate her own stories of intense hunger in an amazingly poetic fashion. I characterize her alimentary writing as an "art of hunger" first to illustrate what it is not. In our bifurcating scheme, her art of hunger would belong to the poetic realm of eating—though poetics and politics are always entwined to a varying degree in the larger social context. But her art of hunger does not deploy the "motherly" image as a symbolic fulfillment, on the one hand, and is thematically opposite to Zhou Zuoren's art of the gourmet on the other. If we were to locate her art of hunger in the traditions of ancient China or elsewhere, we might also be disappointed with our inability to find a familiar model. She is neither a Daoist who cultivates wisdom and seeks immortality by enduring hardship, nor a Buddhist who chooses not to eat in order to deny her flesh and transcend the domain of carnality, nor in the least a political loyalist like the two fasting brothers Bo Yi and Shu Qi. The "hunger artist" à la Kafka may come to mind. But Xiao Hong insists on her redemption in the everyday of this world, absurd as it is, rather than separating the existential world of absurdity from a transcendental world of art. Her fundamental difference from these ancient and foreign artists of hunger is that she does not choose hunger; rather, it is imposed upon her by an economy of lack. Instead of seeking her salvation in an imagined paradise, Xiao Hong suspends her empty stomach in the present, turns it into a spatial trope, lets it assimilate and eliminate whatever is offered in the everyday, and confirms that which survives.

Empty Stomach as Spatial Trope

The storyteller was sitting in the dark, wide awake. She felt the weight of gravity "almost as though [she] had been transported to the depths of a coal mine." The law of gravity may release the soul from the body and propel it into lightness of being. Enclosed in a small room and cut off from the outside world, she had the strange sensation of "being in the middle of a vast deserted public square" where the "walls seemed farther away than the heavens themselves." How, then, could the body, locked in the compressed space of reality, launch the soul into the vast open emptiness? "It all boiled down to this: I had an empty stomach." So begins the story of Xiao Hong on a snowy day in the early 1930s of Harbin (20; 7).[1]

The empty room has a window open to the outside, but it only creates a spatial illusion when she imagines her escape to the heavens. In "Hunger," the author details how intense hunger releases her mind, only to pull it back to the solid ground of emptiness: "I ascended up, up through the window, utterly naked, immersed in the sunlight." How more blissful could the soaring soul feel—if and only if there were a sufficient supply of calories to keep the blood circulating. So her flight landed her "standing on a cold mountaintop, without a single soul in sight." Engulfed there by snow and ice, she "began to merge with the ice" (47–48; 25). The openness of the window is deceptive, reinforcing its physical emptiness when the signifying chain of the spatial imagination is anchored on the empty stomach. These physical spaces of emptiness are recurrent images of melancholia in Xiao Hong's *Market Street*. It is a different kind of poetic melancholia, however, because the objective correlative of the isolated soul is its own deprived body. The flesh is not what the soul can manage to transcend. To ease the melancholia, then, the hungry storyteller had to reconnect her stomach with the material world of food.

So the young woman decided to follow the law of gravity and move her depleted body to the window after her imaginary flight ended in ice. Once she redirected her eye down to the material world, the open space of the window could no longer create an illusion. Instead, the window frames her social and emotional exchange and circumscribes her writing. Looking out from behind the window, the narrator's eyes roamed down the bustling street until they fixed upon a woman. She was "begging for some coins," "holding one child by the hand and cradling an even smaller one in the front part of her coat." Ignored by the well fed as though a penniless soul only deserved starvation, she nevertheless kept pleading for pity, if only for her hungry children perhaps. It suddenly occurred to the spectator that the beggar "was exactly like me" (48; 26). As she could not but feel "like a duck that had fallen down a well, forlorn and completely isolated," her searching eye bounced back to her own rumbling innards and protesting intestines. Once again, her inward look found what had existed for a prolonged period of time: "only my aching stomach, hunger, and cold kept me company." "This was a home?" she asked herself. "This was a public square at night, totally devoid of light and warmth" (56; 31). Although one woman is ensnared in a desolate room and the other is begging in a crowd, their ill-fated bellies connect the two women in an existential void.

Prolonged hunger can reduce humans to helpless creatures. The form of incarnation can be "a duck forlorn and isolated down a well" or "a hungry caged chicken," as she found herself vis-à-vis the beggar woman in the street. The most miserable of all is the image of a silkworm. When she was watching her lover buying Russian black bread, or *khleb*, the narrator relates, "I stayed prone in bed and raised my head, looking like a silkworm that has just seen some mulberry leaves." The "silkworm," unfortunately, "only licked [her] lips with [her] wet tongue" when the vendor not only refused to sell bread on credit but took their money to write off a portion of their debts (43; 22). From the angle of these creatures there seems to emerge a different circuit between visuality and orality, one canceling out the other in a cyclical return to the state of nothing.

Caged within the flesh that cries for food, the hungry creature may follow its animal instinct. Nature might even lead the creature to ponder the limits of edibility. Looking around the forlorn room, the narrator asked herself: "With what was I going to fill my belly? The table? The straw mat?" (48; 26). When food is within reach yet cannot be taken, such an excruciating temptation and despair can drive one truly crazy. On hearing the bread peddler's voice in the hallway, Xiao Hong recalls, "I began to be frightened by the bread. It wasn't that I wanted to eat any. I was afraid that the bread would swallow me up" (43; 22). The inverted order between the eater and the food is no longer structured in the allegory of cannibalism; it is the material lack that threatens the function of the most basic instinct. The madness of history à la Lu Xun has continued in

Xiao Hong's embodiment of the world, but its site of social anatomy is relocated from the diseased national head to the depleted personal torso.

Interestingly, the human-eating "Confucian virtue and morality" also plays into Xiao Hong's poetics of hunger in a way that supplements and revises the Madman's original version. She recalls how she found herself trying twice to steal her neighbors' bread and milk and how she failed both times. In the middle of her struggle with herself, the author writes:

> Stealthily, I turned the key in the lock, not making a sound. I poked my head out to take a look. Some khleb hung on the door directly opposite and on the doors on either side [of the hallway]. *It's almost light outside!* The milky whiteness of the bottles nearly dazzled me. The khleb seemed larger than usual. But I took nothing—nothing. My heart was on fire, my ears were burning. *Stealing!* Words from my childhood flashed back into my mind: *A child who steals pears is most shameful of all.* I stood there for the longest time flattened up against the now closed door. I must have looked like a soulless paper doll stuck to the door. . . . I hugged myself tightly; my head drooped onto my chest. *I'm hungry!* I said to myself. *I'm not stealing!* (46; 24).

In the heated struggle with hunger, tender memory of the mother and the hearth could flash back to assuage the pains, as it often does in the work of Shen Congwen and other male writers. But Xiao Hong's mother only appears once, like her superego checking on her animal instinct. In describing her fear of being caught stealing by her lover, she considered the lover an "enemy," and went on confessing that "had I had a mother, she, too, would have been my enemy" (47; 24).

Her inner outcry "I'm hungry! I'm not stealing" could have moved the destitute being out of dark emptiness into the textual world of a "hunger artist," à la Kafka or otherwise. To be sure, Xiao Hong was to become a hunger artist of eternal exile, twice abandoned in the middle of the war and dead in poverty at the age of thirty-one. Yet this female Chinese hunger artist would insist on redeeming herself in the realm of the everyday, however abject its poverty, rather than in some metaphysical form of artistic transcendence. In the everyday, her stomach rumbles in echo to other empty bellies; her heart aches in response to other bleeding hearts. When it comes to other little creatures like herself, she would rather choose not to eat.

Unlike some of the leading social realist writers of her time, Xiao Hong tends to treat her encounter with the downtrodden in personalized details rather than brushing them into a footnote to the narrative of class struggle and social rebellion. Often her reaction to social disparity seems to suggest a spontaneous, childlike naïveté. Yet her thematic simplicity works hand in hand with her stylistic sophistication, with the latter's artistic subtlety quietly polishing the former's political edge. The visual movement from the empty room to the deserted square to her own stomach is a case in point—a signifying move that is more poetic than narrative. As she holds back her sadness while looking at the beggar pleading for pity in the street, Xiao Hong adds a beautiful detail: "The window frosted up as soon as I closed it. Before long, tears were dripping down the pane of glass. At first there were only a few streaks, but then these streaks burst into torrents! Tears were running all over the face, just like the face of the beggar-woman on the street below" (48; 26).

Following this scene of window "crying" is the "caged chicken" remark. Here we no longer know who is crying for whom. If the two women are both crying, one outside and the other inside, their tears are "reflected" upon the thawing frost on the window pane. It is this little warmth of tears, almost as if it were sprayed directly from the narrator's heart, that defrosts the icy glass and melts the little streaks into running torrents. The circulation of tears blurs the visual boundary between the viewing subject and her object and adds more nuances to the allegorical spectacle of social misery since the time of Lu Xun. And it captures the sadness of the social condition with an even more acute poignancy.

It is through this kind of poetic "simplification" or complication of suffering that we must read Xiao Hong's naïveté. It would appear to be nothing extraordinary that she went out of her way to help those even more unfortunate than herself. For example, the moment she left a pawnshop where she exchanged her only coat for a meager sum of money to buy food, she saw an old man begging on the street and handed him a copper coin. The reason is simple: "since I had food to eat, he should have some, too" (81; 47). Likewise, she would burst into tears of embarrassment and grief as two old laborers thanked her for her kindness in giving them some bread. "They were my grandfather's age," Xiao Hong recalls, "how could they feel gratitude over a little bread?" (141; 88). Indeed, these little acts of sympathy and decency would be anything but extraordinary if she had enough food to survive herself.

Much as the "crying" window mediates the writing of tears, a "like-fated fish" furnishes Xiao Hong's probing into the destructive environment of social cruelty. A scene of cooking and eating unfolds like this:

> I didn't know what to do [with a fish just gutted yet still flapping on the chopping board a moment before]. I hadn't the heart to look at that miserable thing, so I tried to hide in the doorway. *We won't eat that one*, I thought to myself. But its innards were gone. How could it be still alive? Tears welled up in my eyes, and I simply couldn't look any longer. I turned and looked out the window. The puppy was chasing the chicken with the red feathers, and the landlord's maid Xiao Ju was crying at the base of the wall, having suffered a beating.
>
> *What a cruel world! A world devoid of human feelings! A violent world bent on destruction! All these things that have lost their human feelings deserve to be destroyed!*
>
> We served up the fish for dinner that night, but it had such a fishy taste that we ate little of it. We threw most of it into the garbage. (116; 71)

With her rare outburst of rage and condemnation, this scene reminds us of the fish eyes in Lu Xun's works. But their different construction of the specular is made even clearer in this instance. It bears repeating that, unlike the Madman, who links the fish with cannibals and thus turns it into an image of the Other, Xiao Hong identifies herself with the "like-fated" fish and other brutalized creatures, human and nonhuman alike. The oral theme is blended with her visual move to the crying maid, once again framed by her view outside the window. It is not just the diseased national head under decapitation that threatens the political body. It is the "gutted belly"—the fish, the beggar on the street, and the maid crying in the courtyard—that foregrounds the critical thrust of Xiao Hong's art of hunger. Although Shen Congwen's "critical lyricism" has already revised the national allegory, Xiao Hong expands that *episteme* by directing our attention beyond the human domain. The fish is no longer just a textual image to be played with in words but a "substance" that ritualizes the tangible meaning of the everyday. It may be too much of a luxury to advocate "animal rights" when a large portion of the human population is suffering under perennial starvation. Xiao Hong of course was not protecting the fish's right to life exactly as it is articulated by ancient Buddhist vegetarians or contemporary animal rights activists. Her empathy with the fish and all other "like-fated" creatures is crystallized in her detailed depiction of what we might call "social ecology." This poetic assimilation and elimination of the everyday and its cruelty insists on a more material, and indeed corporeal, tie to the social body. That is why the narrative voice shifts to a more controlled mood in her characteristic "dialogue" with other fish after that rare outburst of indignation. Later in the same essay, all the little fish have died one after another, and all the time she expresses her tender feeling through the daily ritual of caring, cleaning, and disposing.

It must be pointed out that Xiao Hong, like any omnivore of the human species, enjoyed eating and would rather eat her fill without any sense of guilt. There are ample examples detailing the young couple's "feasting" at the stalls of street vendors and common eateries—usually after her lover has earned some money to end a few days of starvation. As the two young writers later find their way into the local circle of arts and letters, they become acquainted with some well-to-do individuals and are invited to their homes. Yet every time she was enjoying the food, her pleasure would be spoiled when she saw some rude diners mistreating beggars at an eatery or when she found the party at a friend's home too extravagant. She could not feel at home as long as the table was not equally shared.

By contrast, when the young couple shared whatever they had, poverty strengthened their love. In "Black Khleb and White Salt," Xiao Hong depicts how they spent their "honeymoon" in their empty room, eating only black bread and salt. The coarse tissue and the biting taste could only be sweetened with humor. A table scene unfolds like this:

> He twisted off another piece of black bread and added a pinch of salt. He acted like someone from a honeymoon scene in the movies, offering it up to my mouth. I took a bite and handed it back to him. He swallowed it. It must have stung his tongue—too much salt, I suppose—and he gulped down some water. "This is no good, no good at all. This sort of honeymoon'll get us both pickled!" [he shouted]. . . . I sat off to the side and laughed. (63–64; 36)

About their malnutrition and deteriorating health, Xiao Hong continues to joke: "We were like legendary people awaiting our metamorphosis into [Daoist] immortals, cultivating and nurturing our spirits by enduring hardships. . . . We accomplished quite a lot: our faces were turning yellow, our frames were growing thin; my eyes seemed to be getting larger, his cheekbones were jutting out like pieces of wood. . . . But we still hadn't become immortals" (63–64; 36).

Obviously, this female Chinese hunger artist is different from her ancient Chinese or Western counterparts—whether it is the Kafka version or the medieval Buddhist or Christian nuns engaged in ritual fasting. The comparison is perhaps not very relevant since Xiao Hong's hunger was not self-imposed for religious or artistic transcendence, but it is heuristic to our understanding of their "cultural" difference as one fundamentally rooted in historical and material experiences.

A Motherless Child

Xiao Hong's relationship with men has been one of the most frequently discussed topics in biographical and scholarly works (see, e.g., Xie 1972; and Goldblatt 1976). Critics have attributed much of her tragedy to her mistreatment at the hands of selfish men. What has been largely unexamined, however, is how we may deepen our understanding of Xiao Hong's tragedy from the angle of her everyday life, especially as it is looked upon in her autobiographical accounts of eating and cooking. A feminist approach may shed some insight, but this must be complemented by a detailed analysis of her situation. Just as Xiao Hong's art of hunger does not neatly fit into any existing model of alimentary writing, her relationship with men as it revolves around the "table" must be understood in its variety of flavors.

Like other "new women" writers (and male writers as well) from wealthy families, Xiao Hong did not know how to cook until after she was married. As depicted in *Market Street*, she had to take care of the kitchen since Xiao Jun (named Lang Hua in the text) was gone most of the day trying to sell his labor. In describing her first cooking experience, Xiao Hong writes: "Standing there alongside the stove, I suddenly found myself preparing a meal, just like a little housewife (*xiaozhufu*). I burned the vegetable and failed to cook the rice completely—it was too tough to be called gruel and too sticky to be called steamed rice." She went on to comment on her entry into this domestic space as making herself a *furen*, placed in quotation marks in the text to refer to the traditional type of (usually married) woman, as opposed to the modern term *funü* or simply "woman" (regardless of marital status) (56–57; 31–32). With her upbringing in a traditional wealthy household, which had maids and other domestic laborers to attend to the daily chores, her entry into the kitchen must be understood literally as a social descent that came with her domestic role change from a *funü* to a *furen*.

Although it is a trying and tiring task, cooking may also generate moments of sensual pleasure, especially for a writer so meticulously sensitive to aesthetic details. At one point, Xiao Hong describes her cooking with a kind of enthusiasm rarely found among other women writers of her time. In the short piece entitled "Getting By," a cheerful morning comes to life, as a slice of life:

> When the iron plates of the stove were heated, I stood close to the stove and made breakfast. The cleaver and the spoons rang. The burning firewood inside the stove popped and sizzled. Steam rose from the pot, and the onions frying in the oil smelt nice—I watched the onions dancing in the boiling oil, gradually turning yellow. With my little paring knife I peeled the skins of potatoes just as I would peel the skins of pears. The light meat of the potatoes looked so clean, so pretty, a sort of off-white, soft but springy. I spread a piece of newspaper out over the counter board and cut the potatoes in thin slices. By the time the rice was cooked, the potato slices were fried and ready. I opened the window and looked outside. Some puppies were playing in the courtyard. (65–66; 37)

A well-cooked meal can bring much pleasure when the author activates all her senses. Blended with the sensuous beauty is an epiphany of the little joy. But the fleeting joy is bound to be ruined by the daily routine. "After the breakfast my time was spent washing the dishes, scrubbing the pot, cleaning off the stove top, and tidying up the shelf." Then comes the time to prepare the supper. "I began to pace around the stove. Everyday it was the same: eat, sleep, worry about firewood, fret over food. . . . *I was no longer a child.* I was a married woman now, and the time for getting by had begun" (66; 38; emphasis added). Here, we can almost hear Xiao Hong sighing for her loss of innocence.

Indeed, the author would rather stay a child, in the way Long Hua calls her "baby" (*xiaohaizi*, which has a more generational connotation than the English term). But Xiao Hong was no longer a child, and it hurt her to see her lover bear the duty of being their sole breadwinner. Thus, when he said to her "Baby, you must be terribly hungry," she responded by saying "Not really." "How could I tell him the truth?" asked she. "His clothing was frozen stiff from his search for something to eat" (28; 12).

Another scene is even more heart-wrenching: " 'Hungry?' he asked me, as he lay there stiffly, sort of like a simpleton. I was nearly in tears. 'No,' I said, keeping my head so low that my face nearly touched the soles of his frozen feet" (23; 9). Conversely, Lang Hua is also viewed as a miserable creature, despite the fact that he would rather act like a real man. The reminiscence, "He Goes Job Hunting," begins with a single line as its first paragraph: "He was a freezing, starving dog!" (25; 10). "The fact that both of us had shared nearly identical feelings surprised me at first," Xiao Hong later reflects on the best moment of their marriage. "For both of us, the same hunger had forged our feelings" (108; 65). For a couple that went through thick and thin, the lack of food reinforced their bond of love, just as hunger heightened her social consciousness.

When Lang Hua is gone her hunger and cold become all the more unbearable. In fact, the absent Lang Hua is always present in Xiao Hong's mind. Underlying these episodic pieces is a narrative of double presence: time is frozen in the empty space of the present, yet the frozen and freezing "now" are somehow made less frightening by the presence of a loving man, often recalled when he is away. In a simplistic way, I would contend that the mother is, in Shen Congwen's nostalgic imagination, what the husband is in Xiao Hong's art of hunger.

A question that would inevitably arise is anticipated: how can one characterize a writer with all the tendencies of dependence a "new woman"? I anticipate this question mindful of the familiar narrative of women's liberation—a historical narrative that describes women's liberation from the shackles of the domestic space (the kitchen being a major fixture of it) and entry into the public arena of social equality and economic independence. This narrative is nothing new in modern China, even though it is still far from complete in reality. It began with Lu Xun, Zhou Zuoren, and others from the May Fourth period and culminated in Mao's famous proposition that "women hold up half the sky." With this grand narrative in mind, Xiao Hong's self-portrait would no doubt belong to the "minor" but definitely not the "traditional" (i.e., those female characters found, say, in the stories of Ling Shuhua or Zhang Ailing). Yet precisely because of her "minor" place in the grand narrative (and hence in our saga) it allows us to revisit history with an enhanced sense of ambivalence about the revolution.

A brief biographical detour might help. The events related in *Market Street* took place when Xiao Hong was suffering from physical illness and emotional trauma, though this only surfaces in bits and pieces between the lines and is glossed over by the poetic beauty of the text. The immediate cause for her misery was her first but failed romance with a man who impregnated and then abandoned her. Still a teenage secondary school student, Xiao Hong had been deeply attracted to her first lover, then a "progressive" college student. In order to escape from her father's arrangement for her marriage, she broke with her family and eloped with him. Thus, she met her second lover, Xiao Jun, while she was suffering all the bitter consequences of her failed rebellion and romance. Cut off from the support of her family and relatives, penniless, sick, and wounded, the young Xiao Hong had no economic and social capital whatsoever. This is a major subtext for her isolated condition as a "helpless creature," suspended in the empty space of the "now" except for the love and support from Xiao Jun. The ghost of her recent past is an "absent presence" in these personal essays, haunting her all the time alongside the abject poverty of her present condition. The image of a wounded child to be nursed and nurtured clearly is incomprehensible apart from these devastating experiences.

It would take many more years of healing for Xiao Hong to distance herself from her past and call back the memory of her childhood. Her childhood stories are recorded in the autobiographical novel, *Tales of Hulan River* (1942; see especially chapter 3 for her memories of the family). What is most touching in the novel is Xiao Hong's tender feelings toward her grandfather. Here we are told that her father was cold and cruel; her mother was stern, unloving, and often chided her. The grandmother would be an ideal substitute for the parents in a typical family drama. The author does remember the grandmother giving her candies and other fine food—a familiar episode evoked repeatedly by Shen Congwen, Zhou Zuoren, and Jade Snow Wong. But Xiao Hong never forgave her grandmother, who once poked a needle at her fingers to prevent her from damaging her window paper. Only the beloved grandfather remained a cherished image. He taught her ancient poems while both were enjoying their food. This episode of poetic-cum-gastronomic acculturation is found in many other autobiographical stories, though it is usually a loving mother or grandmother who feeds and nurtures a young boy.

The grandfather, together with many cherished stories about Xiao Hong's childhood, is another subtext in *Market Street*. Like the bitter memory of her failed romance, the memory of her childhood is also "hidden" between the lines and disseminated around the image of the "child" and her sympathetic overtures to some poor old-timers of "my grandfather's age" (141; 88). Perhaps the grandfather, who would play the role of the authoritarian patriarch in the typical family melodrama (e.g., in Ba Jin's seminal novel *Family*), was out of the ordinary because he was often shouted at by his wife and ignored by his son. Perhaps the rarely explored association of the little girl's oral pleasure with a nurturing and caring grandpa in a traditional society would have to take more time to develop into a clear image in the mind of a modern woman writer. For whatever reasons, the spiritual food of the familiar is not evoked to ease the pain of the isolated, hungry narrator. This absence is particularly intriguing, given that both the theme of hunger and the genre of the personal essay would otherwise beg for such an imaginary fulfillment.

In the stories of *Market Street*, we seem to see a child who does not want to grow up and yet must face the daily challenge of living in poverty. With her failed rebellion and her desperate condition in mind, Xiao Hong's entry into the domestic space is marked with a rite of passage twice over. It is at once an emotional passage backward to the lost childhood and a social journey forward to the needed shelter in reality. This rite of passage, already ambiguous, is further complicated by the disparity between the past abundance of food and the present lack of it. What happens at the joining node seems to be a symbolic substitution and displacement. Regret for a bygone past is embedded in an inactivated memory of the grandfather, a nurturing and loving man that happens to overlap with the caring and supporting husband. The "content" remains the same while the "form" has changed. Thus, the image of the wounded, dependant child is simultaneously a textual figure for the narrator's "personal history" and a social position of necessity for survival.

Even if we dovetail this "minor" position into the major history, Xiao Hong's is not a typical Nora's story: she is ahead of Nora in her rebellion and yet has come back to look for a new home because the historical condition has failed her. This home is new not just because she finds a new loving man. It is an empty room in which she has to start from scratch, leaving behind all the burdens and legacies that have shaped her life up to this point. For better or for worse, this utter truncation of the present from the past is symbolic of many "like-fated" women (and men, too) in modern China. Xiao Hong is one of the few who has passed to us such a puzzle with which to digest the sweet bitterness of modern Chinese history. From this broad historical perspective, Xiao Hong's story of eating can also be read as a social parable, if not a "national allegory," told from a hungry "child's" point of view. The "child" is perhaps not consciously aware of the historical burden placed on her. She scribbles her dream and nightmare around "random" alimentary and bodily images, and thereby turns her own body into a material embodiment of a minor tradition in modern Chinese literature.

Commenting on *Market Street*, Goldblatt (1976, 57) has noted that "[t]rying as that period in the author's life had been, there is a notable lack of self-pity in her account; contrariwise, the dominant mood . . . is one of stoic resignation fortified by dogged optimism." Elsewhere in his book, Goldblatt also notes that "[b]y temperament an autobiographical and personal writer, there is an almost inverse relationship between her degree of detachment and the success of her works. The greater the element of fiction in her stories, the less convincing they become" (1976, 124). How could it be that an autobiographical writer by temperament displays little self-pity in her most convincing personal stories? How should we read her attitude toward personal hunger, written in a most fitting genre of self-construction, which nevertheless reveals little self-pity? Since her wounded self and her empty stomach were not prepared to join the ongoing hungry revolution, a personal account of hunger without self-pity would logically turn out to be a piece of the absurd. All the signs of emptiness that imbricate bodily existence and its social meaning are available to the pen of a Kafkaesque hunger artist. The moment she cries out to herself "I'm not stealing! I'm hungry," one might well expect a modernist turn to the absurd: even the form of her desperate scream could be readily developed into a modernist interior monologue. Yet none of these things happened.

Her sanity could be explained in terms of "stoic resignation" and "dogged optimism," though these phrases should be qualified by detailed analysis, not used for ethnographical typology.[2] But taken for granted these personal traits can be understood only in light of her spontaneous, childlike naïveté and the poetic beauty of her writing, contradictory as this may sound. The child is by nature a "narcissus" fixed upon her own image reflected in a pool or mirror. The "child" in Xiao Hong could be the same were it not for the "crying window," which disperses her tears and defocuses her self-fixation. It is her seemingly casual glance outside the window—the beggar woman, the weeping maid, the playing puppies, and so forth—that has redeemed her from erosive self-pity and transformed her childlike self-love into a beautiful flower, a small violet perhaps, not a showy narcissus.

In summary, Xiao Hong's *Market Street* depicts a world devoid of meaning, gutted of its innards, that nonetheless comes to life in her artistic rendering of that which survives. Revolving around the spatial trope of an empty stomach, the carnal logic of her self-embodiment defies the circulation of the blood and flesh in ideology and politics. It would be too facile to treat her feelings and position as reflecting some abstract humanist decency and sympathy; few decent and sympathetic human beings may possess such nuanced sensitivity. She may not have read about Kafka and his hunger artist, but modernism was by her time no longer an oddity in Chinese literature. Her personal essays share generic attributes with Zhou Zuoren's, but hunger and gourmandism are opposite in experience and theme. As a young writer from rural China, Xiao Hong's urban experience had much in common with Shen Congwen's, but she could not alleviate her misery through an imaginary trip to the homeland because "home" had rejected her—and would continue to do so. She did not join Xiao Jun in the revolution, and her ideals may not have been as lofty. Where she belongs not, she has a bit of everything that makes her stand out as one of the few truly self-exiled writers in modern China.

Secrets of the Stove in Wang Anyi's Urban Folklore

Wang Anyi's *Melody of Lasting Regret* features a former Shanghai beauty named Wang Qiyao and the legendary ups and downs of her romances over four decades. Book 1 of the novel is centered on her ascent in a 1946 beauty contest and her consequent fall into concubinage to a high-ranking KMT official. Book 2 revolves around her post-1949 survival and her entangled relationships with three men. Book 3 leaps over the Cultural Revolution into the post-Mao era and depicts how she becomes "fashionable" again, is seduced by a man about half her age, and finally is murdered by another young man who admires her fame and covets her wealth. The trilogy largely runs parallel to the narrative of the three historical phases from the old society to liberation, through the 1957–77 setback, to the final triumph in the reform era. A revised version of that history would inject more melodramatic scenes of suffering into the second phase, as represented in the hunger stories from the early 1980s. Furthermore, if we take account of the time of the novel's writing in the 1990s, the materials would provide ample sensational fodder for the renewed hunger for tabloid fiction of romance/murder.

But these ideological, thematic, and generic features are quietly attenuated as cultural asides, presented in the text only to set off a social alterity absent in more familiar accounts of contemporary China. The author often likens herself to a beachcomber, collecting little shells left by ebbing tide, unwilling and unable to ride on the frontal waves of history.[3] Once again, in her nearly two decades of fiction writing, she has demonstrated her artistic vision to look elsewhere, not obsessed with the hot and the pop. As her smooth and nonjudgmental storytelling leads us to crisscross the narrow alleys of a forgotten Shanghai and traverse the maze of an untold history, there emerges a masterpiece of urban folklore. By folklore I not only refer to the stylistic interplay with the oral transmission of sociocultural (mis)information, which is depicted in minute details around the backstreet labyrinth of Shanghai and its spatial structuration of social relations through rumor production and circulation. By folklore, I also emphasize the hitherto unexplored experience of a marginal female figure, a woman of no political significance. Specifically, I will show that the protagonist's extraordinary story reveals a rather ordinary way of life crucial to her survival—until, of course, she becomes "refashioned" in the post-Mao era. Central to the urban folklore is the simultaneous deconstruction of an age-old male fantasy and the reconstruction of a gender-specific, alternative social history. In this section, I will focus on these two interrelated issues by examining how the author dissects the male fantasy and reconstitutes the female body around orality.

An "Over-aged" Imperial Concubine

That the author names her novel after the classical masterpiece by the Tang poet Bai Juyi (a.k.a. Po Chü-i) demands that we read it first as a parody. Bai's narrative poem, let us recall, is an artistic revision of realpolitik on its own terms. Through an exquisite rendering of the human side of the emperor and his most favored concubine, Yang Yuhuan, and by juxtaposing Yang's radiant charm with the emperor's heartbroken regret over her death, the poet redeems her from the evil image of a femme fatale held responsible for the loss of the empire. Even since the time of Bai Juyi, the image of Yang Yuhuan has provided an inexhaustible fountain to soothe the insatiable thirst for sentimental romance. Underlying this male imaginary is the eternal fascination with her embodiment, along with a few other legendary belles, of the beautiful young woman doomed to early and tragic death because of her "fatal attraction." This is an ever-present theme known as *hongyan boming. Hongyan* or "beautiful face" continues to nourish refined poetic tastes paradoxically because the woman is *boming* or "short-lived." Thus, the survival of the "beautiful face" as a cultural signifier requires that its physical referent not survive its youth. The premature death of the woman is the precondition for the immortality of the beauty effigy.

Wang Anyi quietly unravels this age-old myth and lays bare its hidden violence. Her textual strategy hinges on a narrative reversal carefully designed to upset the face-body bifurcation. The protagonist's burgeoning rise from the beauty pageant sets into motion male fascination and female objectification over three generations of admirers. In the end, because her withered body has "outlived" her legendary charm, it must be destroyed to unveil the violent history ingrained in her bodily designation. The intertextual subversion of Bai's urtext is explicitly laid out early in the novel. When Wang Qiyao fled Shanghai after the liberation and was hiding in the countryside, the author plants for her a secret admirer, a sentimental lad named Ah Er, and lets him quote from Bai Juyi in a dreamy fashion. "All these beauties he conjured up in his mind [from Bai's poems], Ah Er thought to himself, ended in tragedy, proving the truth of *hongyan boming*. . . . He sensed the tragic aura of that Shanghai woman. But how beautiful that aura was! . . . Ah Er's imagination took off" (141).[4] Yet this young man never reappears in the novel after he sets out for Shanghai, determined to make a fortune so that he can realize his fantasy. Likewise, all the men romantically involved with the young Wang Qiyao are "short-lived" in the narratological sense, either dying or vanishing when the narrative moves to the next chapter of Wang's life. Only Wang herself has weathered three decades of storms to the point where her body has existed too long to perform the role assigned to her face. But the discovery of this simple truth takes another ironic twist, as Ah Er is "reincarnated" in a young man, nicknamed Old Color. The latter is so enamoured of the old ways of preliberation Shanghai that he becomes entranced with the nostalgic aura he projects upon Wang. After a series of unspeakable attempts of seduction, he eventually wins her over and stirs up her own unfulfilled passion, only to wake up to his self-created nightmare and leave her sinking into despair. As if such persistent cruelty were not enough to smash the male fantasy, the author deals the fatal blow by describing her death from her murderer's viewpoint: "His huge hands encircled her neck. There was only a tiny stick covered with a thin layer of dry skin; the feel of her neck made him sick. Wang Qiyao struggled to curse the bastard. He tightened the grip a bit. Then he saw her face: how ugly and dried up it was! Her hair was dry, too. It looked quite funny, though, jetblack on the top and greyish white at the bottom" (383). The former Shanghai beauty was strangled to death in a manner similar to the death of Yang Yuhuan. But Wang Qiyao's death comes too late for her face to stand the test of immortality, hence, the end of the novel and the sentimental tradition of "lasting regret."

Wang Anyi's mild blasphemy reminds us of Yu Hua's wicked pastiche of the classical romance (introduced at the beginning of part three). The heightened critical consciousness toward intertextual production of meaning is manifest in both texts. But Wang's novel is not a piece of avant-garde experiment, as is Yu's story. The latter's burlesque mockery is solely based on a negative interplay with the illusive fantasy of the male subject, which leaves the female part of the drama largely unexplored. Wang Anyi has a different agenda beyond intertextual subversion. The novel's deconstructive mode is constantly crisscrossed with a parallel narrative aimed at reconstructing the woman's physical survival from her own viewpoint. If the "beautiful face" survives at the expense of the "short-lived body" in the traditional romance, Wang's novel turns it upside-down, not just to expose the hidden violence but to show how the woman manages to survive. Her lived experience thus must be located in the realm of social history rather than be reduced to a purely literary exercise. Physical survival, a gender-specific point of view, and social history constitute the site of postrevolutionary reconstruction. And eating and cooking are centrally figured in the material experience of Wang Qiyao as a living subject.

I devote much space to discussing a romance apparently irrelevant to our topic not simply to introduce the basic story line of the novel and its intertextual implications. The image of the "short-lived beauty" is also encoded in a cultural metaphor that turns her into an object of visual-oral consumption, known as *xiuse kecan* (beauty is edible). This metaphoric expression is not limited to the discourse of eroticism, as it often signifies the aesthetic perception and incorporation of the beautiful in nature and works of art, especially in visual forms such as painting. The sensuous circuit of the "palatable" between visual and oral "tastes," however, is implicitly inscribed around Wang Qiyao's passage from a displayed object on a magazine cover to her bodily exhibition at the beauty contest. The author then evokes the idiom to describe the carnal desire of the KMT official, one of the judges of the pageant. To him, female beauty is "only part of the landscape of his life" to be "consumed" (86). As he gets older, his taste changes somewhat, switching from the voluptuous type to the less glamorous but more refined aura embodied in Wang Qiyao. Intended or not, this metaphorical transformation of the female body into a palatable object is narrativized, as the man courts the young woman four times, always in fancy restaurants. In fact, book 1 makes little reference to eating and food other than in these restaurant courting scenes (with one exception, when, by contrast, a leftist filmmaker invites Wang to a dinner and asks her to withdraw her name from the pageant, a scene of "backstaging" in which the visual relationship between a male spectator and a female object is consequently reversed). Since the KMT official invites Wang to dine with him only to add another "dainty" to his gastronomic landscape, the reconstructive narrative can also be viewed from her narrative reversal, this time, to a subject of eating and cooking. And alongside her shifting position is her symbolic and narrative relocation from the visually organized magazine cover, beauty show, and restaurant courting scenes to the interior space of her home and its orally centered activities.

Spatial Interiorization of History

The most extensive descriptions of eating and cooking are presented in book 2. The majority of the hunger stories in post-Mao fiction are set in the same period of time. I highlight this historical period in order to foreground the social alterity not represented in other works. For one thing, the author reflects on the 1959–62 famine with a certain degree of comic detachment. In urban centers such as Shanghai, the food shortage was relatively benign and generated not so much real hunger as the fear of hunger stirred up a "passionate craving for food" (221). Above all, there is little to write about the famine after Zhang Xianliang and Ah Cheng. Instead, the author delves into the realm of the libidinal economy and foregrounds the domestic space as a locus of self-invention and self-fulfillment. At the same time, although Wang Qiyao figures as an image of redemption and entertains a couple of male characters at her home, her cooking and eating are not brushed under the rubric of female sacrifice to save a hungry man, as the "motherly" love of Mimosa is portrayed in Zhang's novella. Indeed, the nurturing image of the "mother" is as utterly debunked as is the image of the "short-lived beauty": the protagonist's mother appears only briefly, at intervals, exhibiting a grudging resentment of her dishonored daughter. With these familiar signposts sidelined, the symbolic source of food and its alimentation of life are relocated in the room of her own and the folklore overlaps food lore around the diegetic centerpiece of the stove.

Let me cite a few passages at some length to delineate the contour of this interior space:

> In the winter of 1957, something big was taking place in the world. But what was happening outside didn't disturb this little corner of life around the stove (in the middle of Wang Qiyao's small bedroom). The latter existed on the fringe of the former, or in a little crack of it, and each ignored the other to the benefit of both. How much cozier it is when you sit at the fireside while snow is falling outside! They [Wang Qiyao and her three regular guests] put their creative minds to work and made the best of the stove. Over the lively flames they roasted Korean fish and crispy slices of New Year cake, and then they set a tin to make instant boiled tender mutton and noodles. Before lunchtime, as soon as the visitors dropped in, they found their seats around the stove, and a day's chatting, eating, and drinking began. With no interruption, lunch slid into afternoon snack, snack slipped into dinner. . . . And time passed by as if it had just drawn a deep breath. (179–80)

Three of the characters were suspicious figures in the furious time of the Anti-Rightist Campaign. Wang Qiyao's past left little room for social and economic advancement in the new society. So she had to open up a small nursing service to feed herself. A fortune left by the dead man—a box of gold bars—is quite a liability until the official ban on the trade of precious metals is lifted three decades later (which ironically sows the seeds of her murder). Wang's neighbor, middle-aged Mrs. Yan, is the wife of a former capitalist. Yan's relative, Mr. Kang, who later falls in love with and impregnates Wang but cowers away from marriage, is the sole heir of a large capitalist family. Only Sasha, half-Chinese and half-Russian, is a "red" youth fathered by a revolutionary martyr. Having spent his early years in the Soviet Union and depending on a small sum of government aid for his living, he is handicapped in the larger society and a lonesome ghost fitting only into Wang's little shelter. The hostess meets them on separate occasions while playing mah jong and bridge, and gradually they form a kind of "joy luck club." It is through this spontaneous act of getting together to get by that they create a tiny spatial crack for survival.

Wang Qiyao's questionable past is complicated by her no less suspicious social or marital status. A former concubine and now a single woman, the last thing she would reject is the legal protection and economic security promised by wedlock. But she is acutely self-conscious of her "devalued" body as she is evaluated in public opinion. This awkward position is further aggravated by her isolated social life and her unwillingness, as we learn later, to compromise herself for the practical needs of matrimony. As a result, a shared life in one's own home has to be negotiated beyond the legal framework and social customs. It is thus a creative process of reinventing a new definition of "family life." The first time Wang Qiyao invites Yan and Kang over, "a big flower leapt off the curtain as she drew it up and turned on the light." An interior space thus created, this is followed by series of acts that captured her rekindled embrace of life. As "she found herself in tears," the author calls attention to what has brought her back to life: "After such a long time, the cold kitchen and the lonesome stove finally became full of life and energy, as if they had recovered from death. . . . The sizzling of the frying pan came back to life, too, echoing the voices of the guests in the bedroom" (168).

If food conjoins the lonely souls, oral pleasure is doubled when shared eating fosters "table" talk. Commensality eventually generates a sense of consummation—not bluntly sexual but intimately carnal. As their friendship developed, writes the author,

> A homey atmosphere emerged, too. When Wang Qiyao and Aunt Yan were doing their needlework, Kang Mingxun and Sasha helped them straighten out the knitting wool. While the two women were making egg rolls, the two men arranged the rolls into a floral pattern or pagoda shape. They also became quite casual as they joked along. The three teased Sasha and asked

him if he had made up his mind to eat Russian bread for his entire life, referring to the [round-figured] Soviet woman [Sasha was dating]. He told them that Russian bread was all right to eat, but Russian onions and potatoes would be pretty hard to take. The three laughed and shouted at the [wicked sexual] implication. He put on a thick face and went on: if they were interested, he could provide Russian bread on the condition that they also take Russian onions and potatoes. They pounded him with words, and he pretended to be hurt and accused them of a bourgeois attack on a member of the proletariat. (180)

As much as food and words are circulated in the unnoticed passage of time around a double orality, the images of food and sex blend with the textual reconfiguration of carnality. In contrast to the refined taste of "edible beauty," the "eatable" images of bodily parts are equally allocated to both sexes with a distinct folksy flavor. For a writer known for her graceful prose, Wang's little stove-side joke quietly tickles the male tradition of "pillow talk." Although these metaphors have become naturalized into near invisibility (hence my translation does not highlight "bread," "onions," "potatoes," and "hard to take" with quotation marks), in our eavesdropping we can almost hear the author's hearty laughter.

The gastronomic-erotic joke should be noted for its ethnic reference as well. The author seems to be interested in creating a "Russian" perspective so that she can probe their cultural attitudes, a perspective we might dub "stoic hedonism," contradictory as this may sound. Here is how the text presents this ethnic angle:

As the New Year was drawing near, Wang Qiyao placed a small set of millstones by the stove and began to grind glutinous rice. . . . The fragrance of sesame permeated the room and sharpened one's appetite. Sasha felt in the festive ambience an exquisite air of pleasure. These people approached life from within a shell; they saw the sky as a frog sees it from the bottom of a well. Such an attitude is near-sighted, for sure, but it breaks time up into tiny pieces so that they can prolong the transient life. Sasha was somewhat touched and turned quite serious. He asked them why the rice had to be water-ground. . . . The two women explained it to him patiently, as if he suddenly had become a good little boy. . . . They promised him everything a Chinese child would have for the New Year: sweet cake made of glutinous rice flour, egg rolls, walnut meats, pine-nut candies, and so forth—enumerating them as if they were counting their family treasures. Sasha thought to himself: eating is really just about everything in their world. (183)

One is tempted to read some cultural essence into all the eating and cooking scenes from the prerevolutionary world of Shen Congwen and Zhou Zuoren to this postrevolutionary corner of Shanghai. There is certainly a shared attitude no matter how we characterize it. But Wang Anyi adds to this legacy a more nuanced touch of feminine sensibility at the same time that she carves this "woman's space" out of the weighty block of political history. On a more abstract and theoretical level, her "ethnographical" probing into the way these women break time into tiny pieces seems to suggest a culture-specific version of what Kristeva calls "women's time." In a philosophical mode, the author comments:

Matter, space, sound, and smell—all became jittery, blurry, and uncertain. Only the flames in the stove brightened, generating heartfelt warmth and excitement. In this most intimate moment, all their desires were transformed into the need for a mutual bond. What could they do even if the sky were to fall and the ground were to sink? So let go of yesterday, let tomorrow come. . . . As they peeled off the skin of fried chestnuts, the sweet smell pervaded their bodies; as they chatted leisurely about the least significant things, every word came out of the bottom of their hearts as though the word carried palpable warmth from their innards. . . . [After a while] they would lose track of the conversation and forget one another's casual remarks. . . . Words came with no trace, yet went on and on with no end. What they talked about was all but the sweet rice flour mixed with chestnuts, the balmy scent of sunflower seeds, the bitter taste of almonds, the soft and smooth texture of rice-flour dumplings, the rich fragrance of rice-wine soup, and the tenderness of the eggs in it. . . . The sounds and scents of so many little dainties over the stove quietly filled up the little gaps and cracks in the world. (184–85)

These are the secrets of the stove in Wang Anyi's urban folklore. In the sense that the folklore is made up in large part of food talk, shared eating and speech can sustain the body and redeem the isolated soul because food provides a material basis for community and communication. The soothing flame and the bubbling water blend with aimless chat and laughter, orchestrated like the harmonious tunes of a fireside lullaby. It is sung to one's own heart when the mother is gone, the father is absent, and the outside world is frozen in the scorching heat of political fervor. The cumulative, symbolic effect of the little details is produced through a careful assembly of fragments to ritualize the footsteps of contingent time. The meaning of survival does not have to be staged in the political arena, significant as it is in the great saga of hunger and cannibalism. As the dust of the political storm settles, many forgotten corners are bound to resurface to estrange our perception of the historical landscape. The trace of a minor social history can even be discerned in the heart of urban Shanghai, in the calm eye of many sweeping political hurricanes. We do not know how Wang Qiyao survives the Cultural Revolution, but we can make a guess based on her attitude. The political myopia of the frog in the bottom of the well preserves a degree of sanity when the grandiose vision of totality has generated so much madness. Once again, the orality-centered existence of the physical body furnishes a counterpoint to the excruciating spectacle of the body politic.

Within the existing alimentary discourse, Wang Anyi restores the redeeming power of orality to the realm of the existential present, an approach similarly manifested in Ah Cheng's "The Chess King." But the latter's lapse or transcendence into the mysterious Dao and the idealized mother also indicates a gender-specific difference within the shared heritage. Most remarkable of all is Wang Anyi's introduction, for the first time in our study, of a female protagonist as a creative cook. There are no male protagonists in our modern saga who actually cook; at best they are imaginative gourmets. It is primarily the act of cooking that breaks time up and anchors the fleeting present on the solid interior space. Eating and chatting are secondary to cooking in that the cook is the one who initiates the sequence and creates the atmosphere of home. I am aware of the risk of gender reductionism here. The cook does not have to be a woman; the mythical chef Yi Yin is a man. Although Wang Anyi's insistence on the material present has much in common with Xiao Hong's spatial trope, their texts differ in theme, genre, and historical backdrop. If Xiao Hong at one point reluctantly allowed herself to be incorporated into the domestic space of the kitchen—and if other major women writers of her time did not even write much about cooking, six decades of drastic social change have made it possible for a reflective hindsight to emerge, now from Wang Anyi's celebration of the stove. What interests me at this juncture are the implications of her positive rewriting of the domestic space for our rethinking of social history. And the author seems to have the same question in mind when we read the stories of Jiang Lili.

Jiang serves as a kind of alter ego for Wang Qiyao. She was born into a wealthy capitalist family, self-indulgent yet conscientious, and always managed to be ahead of her time. As best friends in their teenage years, Jiang backed, with her family fortune and connections, Wang's passage from humble girlhood to the glamour of uppity Shanghai. They parted after Wang fell into the hands of the KMT official, "a life of self-destruction" in Jiang's view (106). After the liberation, Jiang chose the opposite direction, disowned her bourgeois family, married a Communist cadre from a northern village, and worked laboriously for the new society. Well versed in the revolutionary lexicon, she often put up a stern face and cited political slogans to show how serious she was in her ideological self-reformation. In the end, however, she still failed to convince the Party to accept her into its ranks because of her family background.

While the novelist portrays Jiang's unsuccessful public life with a mild touch of caricature, she is more sympathetic to Jiang's tragic fate as a woman. At bottom, Jiang remains a bourgeois urbanite with a deep-seated disdain for her husband, his relatives, and even her own children. Honest and caring as he is, the man is irreducibly a country bumpkin. His provincial lifestyle and peasant habits even infect their three boys. In the mother's view, her sons are "copies of their father, as they all talk in half-baked Mandarin, always smell of raw onion and garlic mixed with the stinking odor of their feet." She is "disgusted with her children and never talks to them except to shout at their rude speech and crude manner." Worst of all, she cannot stand sharing the table with them and often chooses to isolate herself and eat alone (243–44). Beyond the irreducible gulf of lifestyle, Jiang's tragedy is rooted in a fatal triangular romance: she fails to compete with Wang Qiyao for a gentleman of old bourgeois Shanghai—a brokenhearted man who in turn tries fruitlessly to win Wang's heart. In the end, Jiang leaves the world still young, a lone spirit disillusioned with her public as well as her private life.

By presenting Jiang's tragic path as stemming from a misguided conflict between her private life and her public ambition, the author adds a more ambiguous layer to the existing narrative of women's liberation. A character foil, Jiang has everything Wang does not have in terms of her liberated political vision and its duplication in her domestic arrangement. Conversely, her life is deprived of the intimate relationships found in Wang's otherwise derailed family life. From this angle, one is tempted to argue that Wang is able to preserve a room of her own because of her unmarried status, whereas it is the empty content of the family that makes Jiang's life so miserable. To further pursue this line of interpretation, one would have to repudiate the repressive institution of marriage and the family.

But the author is no radical feminist in this sense. A conventional critique of the family in Chinese state socialism would focus on the double burden of exploitation placed on working-class women when they are called upon to "hold up half the sky" and attend to the bulk of domestic groundwork at the same time. It reveals a deep-seated contradiction between the ideological insistence on women's nondifference in the public sphere and the continuous assignment of them to the traditional role of housewife. Because this feminist critique is based on a value theory of labor, the institution of the family must take the blunt of the charge for its complicity in the patriarchal production and reproduction of labor. Such a feminist critique is not applicable to Wang's novel. For one thing, these two women characters are not typical members of the working class. As a matter of fact, the novel largely leaves the question of production out of the picture. Jiang Lili actually refuses to perform her duties as a mother, reflected in the way her sons are brought up in the image of their father. It is her peasant mother-in-law and other relatives from the country who take care of their residence. Instead, the text is very much about consumption—and a peculiar "bourgeois" mode of consumption at that—as the author explores a broad range of issues concerned with the two women's bodily needs, erotic desires, and aesthetic tastes. Although eating is not the whole story, it provides a crucial entry point to the libidinal economy. The contrast between the two women is manifested by whether or not there is a shared table, meaningful table talk, and mutual acceptance in terms of gesture, taste, and smell. It should be noted that even the homey atmosphere that gives rise to the erotic joke about "Russian onions and potatoes" provides a counterpoint to the alienating odor of onions and garlic emanating from Jiang's husband and children.

The focus on the personal and bodily dimension of life allows the author to move the narrative of marriage and family into a more carnal and experiential arena. A thick historical subtext behind the shift, one might well argue, is the saturated discourse of a Marxist-inspired political-economic and labor theory, with the degendered revolutionary heroines and "iron girls" at the center of cultural signification. The novel clearly does not confront this revolutionary tradition head on and thus avoids the inevitable reinscription of its rhetoric. The changed social conditions and cultural dynamics in the 1990s have opened up other possibilities for reconstructing historical memory. Just as the author deconstructs the beauty effigy so that Wang Qiyao is able to tell her own stories of the stove, she situates Jiang Lili's tragic family life in the libidinal realm in order to chart another course of critical reflection on the untold stories of revolutionary women. She is more interested in filling up the little cracks of history than in repudiating socialism—now a "tradition" that has inspired generations of revolutionary women writers, including her own mother, Ru Zhijuan.

Wang Anyi's nuanced treatment of the recent past is also echoed in her ambivalence toward the rising consumerism of the post-Mao era. While the reforms have created some economic prosperity and a certain degree of cultural pluralism, the public taste has become increasingly crude and vulgar. In the name of revitalizing the glorious culture of old Shanghai, the popular imagination only produces fake chic. Commenting on the cosmopolitan flavor of old Shanghai, Wang Qiyao reminds her young friends that "the menu forty years ago looked very much like what makes up the United Nations, open to all kinds of scenery throughout the whole world." Of course, since "landscape is something one sees outside the window," she turns to the interior space to insist on its more authentic nature. "The crux of the matter is what we did inside in the old days, not contrived or advertised, like the way you wash each grain of rice and each piece of vegetable, clean and simple." By contrast, today's fads have become "not only showy and superficial but muddle-mouthed, just like the crass hodgepodge dished out in the big kitchens." In the end, she returns to her philosophy of life, recalling that "forty years ago, do you know, the noodles were cooked one small bowl after another," orderly and with no rush (335). Her nostalgia for the old Shanghai reflects not so much the extravagant cultural surface as the refined interior space that has preserved a way of life. This is a way of life Wang Qiyao embodies, and her tragic death seems to be a haunting witness to the new storm of mass consumerism, which is proving more forceful perhaps than the revolution in changing Chinese society. Above all, the author can dream of nothing more than collecting some little shells when the tide of revolution has receded, only to lament the coming disappearance of interiority under the sweeping waves of mass consumerism. In this sense, the stove is also a symbolic site where one can pause to cope with the dizzy phantasmagoria of time-space compression that is today's China.

Wang Anyi's keen observation and reflection leaves us with more questions than she probably intends to raise, not to mention answers. Her hindsight and insight challenge us to foster multiple viewpoints upon the private home we probably will never let go. From Xiao Hong to Wang Anyi, there is an implicit resistance to reproducing the clear-cut dichotomy between the public and private domains. If domestic space in the old order is repressive of women, the task is to negotiate an alternative means of survival from within rather than tearing down the walls altogether. Conversely, if the traditional kitchen has mainly confined women, its spatial form, which interiorizes transient life, can also be mobilized for a revised self-empowerment and self-reinvention, for women and men alike.

The Subject of/to Carnivorism: *The Butcher's Wife*

With Mo Yan's *Liquorland*, we come across a semiotic of *rou* that crisscrosses between "flesh" and "meat" and provides an entry point to the configuration of "carnivorism," "carnality," and "carnivalism." The linguistic inscription of these bodily tropes happen to approximate the morphology and semantics of "meat/flesh" in European traditions. At the same time, linking flesh eating to meat consumption implies an epistemological shift from the human-centered discourse of cannibalism to a critical scrutiny of human carnivores at the top of the food chain. With Li Ang's *The Butcher's Wife*, our attention is directed to the violent circuits between the consumption of animal meat and the torture of female flesh. As in the chapter on Mo Yan's novel, I will use the Chinese term *rou* unless a distinction must be made between "meat" and "flesh," between carnivorism and carnality.

This approach seeks a linguistic and cultural interpretation, but it is not meant to dehistoricize a landmark work of feminism in the literature of post-1949 Taiwan. While the two texts share the same "anatomy" in enacting social allegories of dismemberment, an important point of departure for laying out their contextual differences is that Mo Yan has behind him a more established canonical tradition, developed since May Fourth, from which he can draw artistic inspiration and undertake ideological deviation at the same time. The alimentary discourse of that tradition in particular is so saturated that any breakthrough from within requires the magic of genus, like the Monkey King defeating the Ox Demon from inside the latter's belly depicted in *The Journey to the West*. On the other hand, the younger generation of writers in Taiwan were basically cut off from that tradition and what became of it on the post-1949 mainland until recently, while they were widely exposed to contemporary Western intellectual trends and artistic experiments. As Sung-sheng Chang (1993, 183) has pointed out, Li Ang "has embodied a typical 'schizophrenic' position that characterizes Westernized third-world intellectuals." In *The Butcher's Wife*, that subject position turns out to be rather typical of the Madman's, bifurcated between a Westernized authorial viewpoint and the nativized world of darkness. It is ironic that, thanks to the official sanction on a more "authentic" Chinese tradition before May Fourth at the expense of what comes after it, cosmopolitan writers of Li Ang's generation have embodied the split consciousness of their May Fourth predecessors. By contrast, Mo Yan, a writer of peasant stock whose "splitness" is grounded in the emptiness of the stomach, has succeeded in crafting a brilliant pastiche of that "schizophrenic" position. As a result, the sense of irony inherent in exploiting the trope of *rou* is as absent in Li Ang's novel as it is present in Mo Yan's. For the former, the exchange of *rou*, though no longer figured in cannibalism, constitutes the very material and symbolic texture of the nativized society and allows her to "engender" a no less carnivoristic narrative in the name of an undifferentiated womanhood.

The creating process of *The Butcher's Wife* indicates a fascinating parallel with the historical route many young writers in Taiwan have taken with regard to pre-1949 China. The novel is based on a real story that broke in Shanghai toward the end of the Japanese occupation in World War II. The case involved a woman who killed her abusive, hog-butchering husband for revenge, although the police suspected that she must have had a lover—a familiar tale repeatedly told in such popular fiction as *Water Margins*. The media coverage of the case only made it more sensational. Li Ang came across the story at the Southern California home of author Bai Xianyong in the summer of 1977, when she just earned her M.A. in dramatic arts from an American university. She used the murder case for the novel but kept the manuscript unpublished until after she rewrote it several years later. The most significant change in the published version is her transplanting of the Shanghai story to a Taiwanese fishing port named after her hometown. According to the author, what motivated her to make the change was her writing and thinking, over those years, on the cause of women in Taiwanese society. This heightened awareness of women's conditions "provided a clear and new focus" for her rewriting of the novel, which she considered a "feminist novel" at the time of its publication. Moreover, she chose the new setting in order to examine "women's role and status in a traditional society" (1983, viii–ix). Thus, the creative process began with the author's "accidental" discovery, abroad, of an old Shanghai story about a "sensational murder" (1986, author's preface) that caught her attention. Thanks to the author's second thoughts on publishing the first draft, the latent theme of female oppression and rebellion is made manifest. But the novel was also produced through the condensed reconstruction of historical memory created by, and glossed over with, the contemporary intellectual trends of the West. As such, the text embodies the clash and conflict between polarized forces, between a cosmopolitan writer armed with all the symbolic capital of progress and the distorted society of her backward "hometown." Such a "schizophrenic" position is reflective of the author's extratextual migration through geographical locations of different historical times.

The reception of the novel was as multifaceted as its creative process. Some established writers and scholars in Taiwan and overseas praised the controversial young author for her fabulous yet unrelenting exposure of primitive and destructive "human nature" (see Li Ang 1983, ii–iii; also see Goldblatt 1990 for other sources). The fact that they emphasize the dark side of the human condition more than gender relations probably reflects other women's blind complicity in perpetuating the misery of the protagonist. Above all, except for the novel's ending, the "killing of the husband" (*shafu*), Li Ang expresses her views more often by means of controlling the narrative of the "enunciated subject" according to the cultural logic of the unenlightened characters. As a result, the novel's feminist tenor may have been overshadowed by its artistic success, especially at a time when the term *feminism* was yet to establish its theoretical authority in the critical discourse (as signified by her use of the term in quotation marks in the preface). In contrast to these Chinese scholars' literary explication of "human nature," some American reviewers voiced moralistic outrage, reacting to a third-world text as if it were a sociological, if not outright ethnographical, document. A *Los Angeles Times* reviewer, for instance, found the novel "the meanest, most frightening book ever written about women oppressed by men, or any helpless victim snuffed out by an uncaring society" (qtd. in Goldblatt 1990, 158). Meanwhile, the sensationalism of the original story is not lost in the novel. Sung-sheng Chang (1993, 181) has detected "the influence of the modernist aesthetic in its highly sensational treatment of such primitive instincts as hunger and lust," thus pointing her finger at the *amalgamated* effects of the novel's aesthetic principle, its stylistic and rhetorical attributes, and its subject matter. It must be noted here that sensational treatment of animal instincts is a topic perhaps as old as "world literature," and certainly it has fascinated as wide a spectrum of modernist writers and artists as, say, Joseph Conrad, the existentialists, the theater of the absurd, and William Golding. What exactly is it, then, that makes the novel qualify as "the meanest, most frightening book"?

Circulation of Rou

The linguistic and cultural hermeneutic I propose may help us zero in on some particular features of this "sensational treatment," though the use of the term *sensational* here is meant to be as descriptive as it is evaluative. Sensational as it already may be, the phrase "sex for food" still does not quite capture the novel's peculiarity because it sounds universal or naturalized in literary representation. What happens in the novel is that the theme of "sex for food" is "fleshed out" through extremely gruesome details about the interchange between female and animal *rou*. When Butcher Chen was "courting" Lin Shi by delivering free pork to her uncle's door, for example, the text reads: "During times of need, food . . . was the best betrothal gift of all. No wonder the neighbors all remarked enviously that Li Shi was able to exchange a body with no more than a few ounces of *rou* for pig-*rou* by the pound" (83; 12).[5] Here a remark on the economy of female "lack" is "carnalized" through the rhetorical economy of *rou* in the equation of her flesh with pork. As always, the site of the personal is where female sexuality comes into play with domestic and social institutions. But the personal in the novel is no longer simply a human person; it is a piece of *rou* caught up with the brute machine of producing and consuming *rou* centered on the story of the butcher.

Consequently, unlike the author's other stories, which explore the psychological subtlety and libidinal depth experienced by urban, educated women, *The Butcher's Wife* largely bypasses what can be defined as the "self" in the modern sense of the word and cuts to the bottom line of the human animal. As social interchange is centered on the butcher, the narrative revolves around his daily routine in the slaughterhouse and the bedroom. In this spatial configuration of the everyday, the butcher's forceful thrust of the knife into the pig's throat is tied to his violent penetration of the woman's body. As pigs are expected to squeal at the thrust of the knife, the woman is forced to scream with the piercing pain. As blood bursts with the release of the knife to mark another triumphant kill, the crimson fluids of virginity and menstruation gush out to signal one fresh conquest after another.

On their wedding night, "drunk though the groom was when he came to bed, he insisted on fulfilling his conjugal obligation, causing Li Shi to exhaust with pitiful screams what little energy she had left. Her screams of pain were so loud and lasted so long . . . that some people who heard them above the whistling night winds took them to be the bleating of ghostly pigs." To dramatize the trope of *rou* for maximum effect, the violent penetration into the lower body is followed immediately by one into the mouth:

> When it was over, Lin Shi was nearly in a dead faint. Chen Jiangshui . . . quickly forced some wine down her throat, and she came around at once, choking hard. Still groggy, she complained that she was hungry. Chen Jiangshui went into the living room and came back with a big piece of pork, dripping with fat, which he stuffed into her mouth, skin and all. With bloated cheeks, she chewed on the pork, making squishing noises as fat oozed out the corners of her mouth and dribbled down in rivulets to her chin and neck, all greasy and wet. (84; 13)

The man's sadistic thrust and thrill are painted with sensational imagery of the most abnormal perversion and cruelty:

> As soon as Chen Jiangshui's hand moved away [from the throat of the pig], the pig's head slumped sideways and a geyser of blood shot forth

in a column some seven or eight inches high. There was a great deal of blood, all foamy and frothy. . . . This was Chen Jiangshui's moment. As the knife was withdrawn and the blood spurted forth, he was infused with an incomparable sense of satisfaction. It was as though the hot stream coursing through his body was converted into a thick, sticky white fluid spurting into the shadowy depths of a woman at the climax of a series of high-speed thrusts. To Chen Jiangshui, the spurting blood and ejaculation of semen had the same orgasmic effect. (139; 74–75)

These passages include only a few samples of the sensational effects of "action," "sound," and "color." Numerous portraits like these show the author's daunting boldness as to how deep down the abyss she dares launch her imagination.

One might expect that the like-fated woman and animals would be indicative of oppressed nature to be redeemed—a central thesis in feminism that seeks to undo the metaphysical dichotomy in Western thought. That is true only to the extent that it involves the tender image of ducklings. Li Shi raised these ducklings initially to produce eggs and meat but became attached to them as pets only to see Chen Jiangshui slaughter them for no reason other than maintaining his absolute authority. When it comes to pigs, however, it is an entirely different story. After all, the pig is raised to produce the favorite and most frequently consumed of all animal meats in the Chinese diet. It therefore serves in the novel as the organizing metaphor for "animal instincts" (albeit an insulting cliché to animal rights activists). Specifically, the image of the slaughtered pig, though analogous to the abused woman, is also inscribed in the evil image of the butcher himself. With a "short, stocky body and a prominent paunch," he "walked with a sort of waddle . . . and had such a sloping crown that the back of his skull seemed to be missing altogether. . . . [H]is small beady eyes were sunk deep into a swelling of flesh around the sockets," "known as pig-eyes" and "belonging to people whose fate was tied to pigs" (83; 12). So it comes as no surprise that, faithful to the original report of the murder, the woman in the end stabs him with the same knife with which he has slaughtered hogs and threatened her life. Then she carves his body into pieces exactly the way he cuts pork. The symbolic principle of interchange thus overdetermines the image of the pig as a signifier for the circulation and dispersal of *rou*.

Apart from the text's conventional view toward irredeemable "animal instincts," the reading process also generates so much repulsion and horror because the modernist aesthetic prevents the narrative from developing into a conventional tragedy or from presenting any chance of conscious resistance (the murder is depicted as a rather "crazy" act). Combined with the sensational portrayal of the most nefarious vice, this narrative constraint leaves little room for cathartic or illusional outlet. Even worse, the woman's most instinctive reaction to pain is stifled, too. Later, when Lin Shi learns that other women take her screaming as a shameless expression of her sexual ecstasy, she has to struggle to hold back no matter how much pain she feels. Imposed on her for just the opposite reason, her silence can only magnify her misery because the butcher is so thrilled at the squealing and screaming that he would double the torture to make her shriek.

Such a situation of total absurdity, however, did not lead the author to turn to the absurd. Given her modernist leaning, a Kafkaesque or Sartrean solution would seem natural and inevitable. Yet nowhere in the text do we even sense the kind of irony found in the Baudelairian *dédoublement*. Here we seem to deal with a rather unlikely example of how modernism is "resisted" in a "native" setting. This is not because the author chooses "nativist resistance" but because the cultural logic of the nativized world overrides the modernist aesthetic. Above all, modernism assumes the existence of a psychologically defined self even though that self occupies the position of negativity in textual and social realities. In traditional society as it is construed in the novel, the formation of the self is only subject to the "primitive" rules that govern the brute power relations of the "mere" physical body. Short of the psychologized, "ironic self" in the world-in-text and obligated to the proactive politics inherent in feminist intervention at the same time, the author simply cannot allow the dazzling sense of absurdity to degenerate or transcend itself into Baudelairian laughter or Kafkaesque despair. Instead, she continues to punctuate the narrative of cruelty with imagery of bodily pain and physical repulsion.

This latent, textualized "native resistance" is manifest in the development of the victim's "subjective" experience regardless of the author's pronounced position. The absence of a narrowly defined bourgeois "self" does not mean that the protagonist only exists as a "pound of flesh." Critical moments in her life are revealed through her fantasies, dreams, and nightmares. These psychodramas, however, are staged with the same concrete images of animal instincts as they appear in her objective experience. This "subject of enunciation" (which of course stands for the "enunciated subject" from the author's point of view) also reduplicates her "self." Yet the reduplication does not occur between the empirical and the ironical positions of the modernist self. Rather, her "*dédoublement*" follows the very empirical logic of her material existence in accordance with the sensational principle of the interchangeable *rou*. Some of her psycho-stories anticipate what will happen in her empirical experience while some others mirror it, but both are derivative reinscriptions of the slaughterhouse on the symbolic level.

The pig's feet episode provides a good example of her distorted "subject." It starts out with a surreal flavor, only to develop a haunting reality. These pig's feet, along with a bundle of noodles, are used in a domestic ritual to dispel the "hanging ghost" of a neighbor who committed suicide. The temptation to eat the pig's feet combined with the fear of touching the ghost's food launch Lin Shi into a nightmare:

Her dreams that summer afternoon were disturbing and confusing: She went over, took down the pig's feet, and cooked them with the noodles. But when she picked them up with her chopsticks, every one of those long, skinny noodles turned into a protruding purple tongue. Dark red blood oozed from the cuts she made in the pig's feet, but she kept stuffing the meat and noodles into her mouth until her eyes bulged and her throat was squeezed tighter and tighter" (134; 69–70).

While the stuffed mouth recalls the horrifying abuse she suffered on her wedding night, it also anticipates what will happen to her that evening when the butcher forces her to finish the pig's feet:

"Eat, eat, eat!" he commanded her. "No one can accuse me of being stingy. Not after I let my wife eat an entire pig's leg."

The section where the foot was connected to the leg had only been partially cooked, and layers of flesh beneath the skin were still nearly raw. Bright red blood seeped out from the center, giving off a rank odor. Lin Shi took one look at the big hunk of bloody meat in her hands and noisily threw up everything she had eaten. When her stomach was nearly empty, she had the dry heaves, then vomited yellow bile." (136–37; 71–72)

Here dream is no longer a "text" that constructs the "self" through its metaphoric working out of the repressed unconscious. Lin Shi's dream that summer afternoon is a condensation, with no trace of displacement, of the very material reality of her body, continuously caught in the most tortured experience of food and sex. It is this kind of pathetic reduplication of the lived cruelty that characterizes the woman's psychodrama. In this sense, the novel can be read as an allegorical tale of the "lower body" without the "head."

Reduplication of Revenge

With no exit through tragic catharsis or modernist formalism, the only solution has to be real. *Shafu* (killing [the] husband) is based on a real event, of course. But missing from the title is the "subject": *furen* ([a] woman). *Furen shafu* (a woman killing her husband) was the intended title according to Li Ang, who still insists, in the preface to the Chinese edition, on her preference for it over the abbreviated, published title. For whatever reasons, the publisher's removal of the "subject" of a woman is paradoxically more truthful to the "subject position" she occupies in the text. In the narrative, this position is determined by her forced witness, on site, to the bloody slaughter of pigs. In other words, her "subject position" is derived from *shazhu* (killing pigs), which is none other than the butcher's profession. It comes as no surprise that the final scene of "killing the husband" reinscribes the very language of "slaughtering pigs," recalling almost every scene of *rou* to invert the gender opposites.

The author describes the killing scene: "The broad-backed, thin-edged knife was extraordinarily heavy. Lin Shi gripped it with both hands and stabbed downwards. . . . Then it was a squealing, struggling pig with a butcher knife buried at an angle in its gullet, buckets of dark red blood gushing from the wound, the animal's body wracked with convulsions." She thrust the knife into the man's body in a fashion that resembled his double penetration into the bodies of the pig and the woman, thus symbolically inverting male-female power relations in "man's language." As if the heavy knife were sucking her into the abyss to probe at the deepest truth, she opened up the man's belly, reached in, and

> scooped out a handful of intestines, all warm and long and tangled together. She scooped out more and more, finally coming up with a tangled mass of noodles. Countless bright red tongues noisily jabbered on and on. She raised the knife and hacked and hacked until the tongues went away.

I must be dreaming, she thought. I should cut off the head next. As she hacked away with the knife, she kept thinking, I must be dreaming. Why else would there be so much blood? . . . Hacking, hacking, she reached the feet. Parts close to the body still had big chunks of meat on them. The pig's feet must not be done yet, that's why the center is still red, with all that strong-smelling bloody liquid draining from it. She chopped a few more times until it was all reduced to a pulpy mound of flesh and blood. (199; 139)

Shazhu and *shafu*, the butcher and the butcher's wife, are thus incorporated into the same drama of killing, with the second term in each pair copying its role in the first term and deriving its meaning from it. In the end, the entire world-in-text becomes a slaughterhouse. Flesh and meat, sex and food, squealing pigs and screaming human animals, blood from the killed and from the raped—all these bits and pieces of the dismembered social body are inseparably amassed in a social allegory about the contagious recycling of butchered *rou* and the butchering hatred.

On the rhetorical level, these outrageous images spawn extraordinary sensations of horror and repulsion. While they are translatable as textual signs, their underlying system of signification may be elusive to readers of the Chinese text and can be completely alien to those who do not read it. The signifying system of *rou* can be mobilized to stage an allegorical farce for Mo Yan's ingenious pastiche of cannibalism; it can also be activated to provide the sensational fodder for Li Ang's furious enactment of revenge. As a novelist, Li Ang has succeeded in following the narrative logic in overriding her preconceived social agendas. For her political advocacy, however, the novel has succeeded in a way opposite to her insistence on the "subject" of the woman, showing instead the very vacancy of a feminist subject position. The most significant success of the novel lies in its implication, that is, in its symptomatic revelation of the deep-seated contagiousness of butchering and torture inherent in the broadly defined "consumption" of *rou*. For better or worse, *Shafu* paints a horrific picture of women's oppression and rebellion, not a story of a truly feminist reconstruction. And it should therefore be read as a text without a true subject, a nightmarish tale of a "headless" ghost that waddles over the ruins of the slaughterhouse on pig's feet.

The linguistic-cultural reinterpretation is not intended to diminish the novel's theme of women's rebellion. Given the perverse nature of the "subject" (the butcher) and the subject matter (animal slaughter and female torture), there is nothing pitiful about the butchered man himself. Situated in the modern literature of the Chinese language, and especially compared with its development on the mainland up to the 1980s, the significance of *The Butcher's Wife* lies not so much in its advocacy for women's rebellion as in its unabashed refusal to subsume the oppression of women under the existing ideologies of emancipation, humanist and Marxist alike. There are ample examples of rebellious women in modern Chinese literature and art. The absence of a positive force of liberation is epitomized by the protagonist's social isolation and her embodiment of that disconnection in her final dissection of the husband's body. The only connection she has is with her mother—a motif notably absent in Xiao Hong and Wang Anyi's works. However, their connection only shows up in "the face of a man in a soldier's uniform," an image that overlaps with the butcher in the final scene in which she is carving him up. This is a memory from her early childhood, when her widowed and penniless mother was caught in the clan shrine having sex with a soldier. The mother was selling her sex for food and, lying under the soldier, her mouth was making "low moaning sounds" and was "stuffed with food." The daughter's final revenge is also undertaken for the mother and fulfills a generational (dis)connection textualized around the image of the double penetration of *rou*. Such an economy of female "lack," however, is conditioned at least in part on their abject poverty, which has left them nothing to eat but pig slop (79; 8). There is a clear tension between Marx and Freud at work, but the author chooses to develop the narrative only on the personal front, reflecting perhaps both the influence of liberal feminism and the author's uneasy relationship with the cultural politics of the basically class-oriented nativist literature of Taiwan in the 1970s.

This gendered inscription of the oppression of women is important. As Meng Yue (1993) has pointed out, in the revolutionary narrative of class struggle and liberation there is a persistent ideological short-circuiting of gender by class. The class-based "nondifference," as opposed to the gender-based equality that recognizes difference, has turned women into a degendered signifier of the revolutionary hero(~~ine~~). In tracing the historical revisions of *The White-Haired Girl*, Meng Yue foregrounds the process in which Xi'er's liberation has left "behind the scenes" the story of her rape by the landlord, so that a victim of sexual violence returns only as a liberated slave of class oppression. *The Butcher's*

Wife does not share the same ideological burden of *The White-Haired Girl*, and Li Ang is applauded for bringing to the fore the engendered nature of rape and torture. Paradoxically, this could only happen in a political environment in which the articulation of class struggle and liberation was muted by the official discourse of anticommunism.

Such a paradox can be turned around as well, as I have done in pointing out that the novel's potential tension between Marx and Freud is tilted entirely toward the latter. Political constraint and ideological difference (from nativist literature) notwithstanding, such a bias also indicates the ideological blind spot of liberal feminism when it is applied to a "native" background. This was disturbing at a time when the economy of Taiwan was taking off partly on the back of the "smokeless industry" of tourist prostitution; it was particularly disturbing because the exchange and "consumption" of women's *rou* is not only the focal point in the story of Lin Shi but also involves an older "sex worker" (with whom the butcher has a longtime relationship). Moreover, the erasure of the political economy goes hand in hand with the authorial ridicule of nativized culture. The novel incorporates a number of ritual scenes appropriated from folk religion and food practice, only to let these religious-alimentary motifs reinforce the author's mockery of the "superstition" of the unenlightened "natives." This elitist prejudice closes the door on further examination of the human ecology in a traditional setting—a phenomenon scattered all over the text but left to the state of "cultural unconscious." All of this suggests to me the old story of the problematic relationship between Westernized intellectuals and their native other. That relationship must be further problematized in an increasingly globalized cultural and economic environment. It is sad enough to see the early Lu Xun try to rescue the beheaded nation from its diseased body in the heyday of modernity. But it is even more painful that in the alleged era of postmodernity Li Ang has returned to the dismembered body that still lacks a "subject." The only difference is that the headless nation now takes a backseat, replaced with some classless womanhood. With Lu Xun and Li Ang placed side by side, the disease of the traditional society is told as a never-ending allegorical tale about the consumptive circulation of *rou*, human and animal alike.

9. Blending Chinese in America

Maxine Hong Kingston, Jade Snow Wong, and Amy Tan

"Banana," Monkey Brain Feast, and Fortune Cookie

As a group of "strangers from a different shore" (Takaki 1989), Chinese immigrants were the first Asians to see their "entry denied" and be targeted for legalized exclusion from American citizenship (Chan 1991). Their exclusion was only part of the ongoing process of racializing the body politic based on the discriminatory principle of assimilation and elimination. These metaphors central to the formation of the American body politic have also shaped modes of self-embodiment for many Americans of Chinese descent. The shift in terminology from "Chinese immigrants" to "Americans of Chinese descent" indicates the process of incorporation more than any "generation gap." For those who are American born and bred, who feel more comfortable with the English language and American expressive culture, the question is no longer whether they really "belong here," already assimilated as they are. The matter is the degree to which they struggle to convince the body politic of their "Americanness" out of the anger and fear that they are treated as "inscrutable" Chinese. The narrative of their self-embodiment is described as moving "from necessity to extravagance" (S. Wong 1993). The underlying ideology of incorporation is modeled on the familiar but expanded melting pot: it promises to dish out extravagance as much as it insists on assimilating different ingredients. This is a tale about the American feast, a utopian vision that necessitates a bodily transformation of the personal into the political.

Much ink has been expended on the American part of the Asian American story, and a new generation of Asian American scholars have further negotiated a multidisciplinary framework for examining Asian American sociocultural practice in the global context of capitalist expansion and hegemony (see, e.g., Lowe 1996). Sau-ling Wong's groundbreaking work on alimentary discourse in Asian American literature (1993, chap. 1) set the terms for further studies on this topic. What follows can only offer a moment of rumination from the perspective of "the mouth that begs."

"Eating" Episodes

Three episodes, on "banana," the monkey brain feast, and the fortune cookie, punctuate a "personal" history and metaphorize the way I read Chinese American texts. In the late 1970s and early 1980s, *banana* was used as a mildly disparaging epithet for those visitors who were of Chinese descent but spoke little or no Chinese (any of its dialect, that is) or had barely any knowledge of the People's Republic after its three decades of international isolation. A small minority of such visitors, from North America especially, were rather condescending toward the "natives." A few individuals even carried a lingering missionary mind set of ignorance and arrogance. Insisting that they were "Americans" (without the ethnic adjective attached) rather than "overseas Chinese" (the customary category for ethnic Chinese from outside of the PRC, Taiwan, Hong Kong, and Macao), their anxiety to distance themselves was underscored by the geopolitical relations and ideological prejudices of the time. But the fact that some of these individuals had an attitude of superiority gave rise to the sad background in which the term *banana* was used to indicate that they were "yellow outside" and "white inside." This is just a small example of how geopolitical differences and socioeconomic disparities were played out on the cultural axis of national and ethnic identities. Because any public expression of disrespect toward "overseas Chinese" would contradict the state policy of an international "united front" of anti-imperialism, the epithet had a very limited circulation in private circles. It appears to have disappeared since the late 1980s.

When I came to the United States as a graduate student in the late 1980s, I first worked as a teaching assistant of Chinese. In my first year of teaching, I once remarked jokingly to a student of mine that her Chinese was so good that it would disqualify her from being a "banana." This student had never been to China or Taiwan, nor had she heard of this epithet before. As soon as she understood its meaning, she became very upset, not by my comment on her language proficiency but by the implication of the term. With increased exposure to the then rising tides of post-structuralist theory and postcolonial discourse, I came to realize that the implication of a Chinese national using the ethnic epithet reached far beyond a mere "speech act." Although *banana* has never been circulated nearly as widely and its "cultural grammar" is not as politicized as *oreo*, it captures in a nutshell the politics of inclusion and exclusion, inside and outside, acceptance and rejection, all based on the assumption of one's authentic identity. In hindsight, what is disturbing about this episode is that it happened at a time when I was trying to rid myself of Communist ideology, a historical memory that was informed, among many other things, by the Maoist version of the third-world revolution. One page of that memory was filled with the stories of the Opium War, the coolie trade, and the euphemized "indentured laborers" and their bloody persecution in the western United States. I was trying to forget all these so that I could "enlighten" myself from the weighty baggage of history and pursue the American dream.

But the lessons that our students teach us are seldom as simple as this one—even though it took me quite some time to learn how to theorize about the image. A few years later, in an introductory literature class, I used the monkey brain feast from Maxine Hong Kingston's *The Woman Warrior* to illustrate the painful process of the narrator's identity formation with a simplified Freudian-Lacanian twist. I was aware of the furious reaction this image had generated among some ethnic Chinese when Kingston's "memoir" was published (which she wrote as fiction but was labeled nonfiction by the publisher).[1] Yet I was still caught off guard when a non-Asian student asked me whether the Chinese ate monkeys alive like that. Out of either a knee-jerk or divine inspiration, I found myself asking him instead: how many monkeys do you think there are in the entire world for the billion-plus Chinese each to have just a small spoon of the brain? The class nodded, and many laughed. Released, I went on to explain that I was from northern China and had traveled extensively from the eastern seaboard to Tibet. I had only seen a few monkeys in zoos and circus shows. The same is true of the vast majority of the Chinese population. Then I added that northern Chinese often teased southerners for their daring food habits, mostly those from Guangdong Province, from which Kingston's parents and the majority of early Chinese immigrants came. I tried to drive the point home that China was an extremely diverse country and that a few individuals' gastronomic adventures must not be exploited to perpetuate the stereotype of so-called Chinese cruelty.

When I look back on this incident, however, I am still troubled by the way I dismissed the question. Innocent as it sounded, the student's interest in referential truth could have allowed me to address a series of critical issues such as the epistemological assumptions of reading on the part of Kingston's editor and the student, the poetics of self-imagination in the text, and the politics of representation illustrated by the publisher's marketing strategy and the exchange between the author and her critics. But I missed this opportunity in which ethnographical clarification—though useful to some extent—functioned much the way ideology conceals contradiction. It distracted our critical attention away from examining these important issues by a facile shortcut to referential truth and cultural authority. With Sau-ling Wong (1993, 24–44), we come to understand that the image of the "big eaters"—a predominant image of immigrant parents in many literary works by their American-born children—is rooted in their experience of poverty in China and reinforced by the necessity of survival in the harsh socioeconomic environment of the United States. As their "dietary fortitude" works its way onto the symbolic level, it becomes a gesture of their "omnivorousness toward experience." By telling their children real and hyperbolic tales like the monkey brain feast, the parents expect them to develop the same "guts" and face tough challenges in their lives. But the rugged foodway of the immigrant generation is incompatible with the American-born children's "finicky palate." The "Rabelaisian list of animals and birds" served on the dining table and in food lore has generated a milieu of "quasi-cannibalism." The "children often have reservations about the parents' food choices; they identify with the creatures slaughtered for food; . . . and most distinctively . . . they frequently feel themselves sacrificed—made into [a] food source—for their parents." By situating it in the history of injustice, Wong suggests that quasi-cannibalism should be read as an apt metaphor for the social condition in which "a subjugated group powerless to change the larger society would turn on itself." In tracing how material and symbolic forces crisscross one another in the making and reading of an alimentary image, Wong's exemplary work allows us to connect the libidinal economy of the narrative subject with the political economy of social injustice. In this way, the fixed boundary between authenticity and simulation, between reality and fiction, is blurred to open up other possibilities for our discussion of cultural translation.

The "hidden" meanings of these two episodes, however, were to resurface around the least offensive image of "Chinese food," that is, the fortune cookie. The May 24, 1995, issue of the *University Gazette*, a campus publication for faculty and staff at the University of North Carolina at Chapel Hill, featured the newly elected chancellor, Michael K. Hooker ('69), and his triumphant return to his undergraduate alma mater. Before Hooker accepted the new position, he had been president of the University of Massachusetts system, a job he held for only three years. His wife, Carmen Hooker, was a Massachusetts state legislator with another year to serve in her current term. Understandably, it must have been very difficult for them to decide to move to Chapel Hill. In his formal acceptance remarks, the new chancellor described what had nailed their final decision:

> So Carmen and I labored for a weekend over the question whether we should really go forward with this career move. And at the end of a day's discussion, we went to our favorite Chinese restaurant. And at the end of the meal we were given our customary fortune cookies, and our conversation was still heavy. I opened my fortune cookie, and I will read you the message it contained:
>
> *You are offered the dream of a lifetime.*
> *Say yes!*
>
> Mr. Chairman [of the UNC Board of Governors], it is the dream of a lifetime, I have said yes. (original format)

The same fortune-cookie message was cited toward the end of the feature story and reprinted as part of the caption of a photograph in which Hooker, surrounded by his wife and the retiring chancellor and his wife, holds the tiny piece of paper, posing for the camera. Printed beneath the photograph is Hooker's abbreviated curriculum vitae. It shows that he holds a doctorate in philosophy; has served in some leadership positions in national and regional educational, scientific, and technological organizations; and has edited books on Descartes and Leibniz.

I was amused to see such a display of irony. One might well stretch it out to construct an "accidental" history in the Western imagination of China. It would run from Leibniz, the seventeenth-century master, to one of his late-twentieth-century disciples, with Hegel serving the "second term" in the middle (see Saussy 1993 for the imagined China in Leibniz and Hegel). Although Hooker at that moment was not a philosopher deep in deliberation on the first principles, the "China" he had at hand did help him solve a dilemma of the first order in reality. Nevertheless, I was touched by the sincere playfulness expressed toward a solemn ritual of uppity America. The next spring, when I was preparing a presentation of my work in progress on "Chinese eating" to other fellows at the Institute of Arts and Humanities, I realized that, since mine would be the last of all the presentations, I might as well serve a "Chinese dessert" to give the program a final touch. So I put together a packet that began with Hooker's acceptance remarks and the photograph, followed by a short excerpt from Amy Tan's *The Joy Luck Club* and some other materials.

The passage from Tan's novel features a group of Chinese immigrants laboring in a fortune-cookie factory and describes two women's conversation about the faked Chineseness of the cookie and the silly nonsense of the inserted messages. A newcomer, one of the four mothers, insists that the messages "are not fortunes" but "bad instructions." A younger woman, who appears to have lived in the United States a bit longer, jokes about how powerful they could be to "determine someone else's fortune." Through the latter's voice, the author teases the reading public by asserting that "American people think Chinese people write these sayings," that "it is our bad fortune to be here making these and somebody else's bad fortune to pay to get them" (299–300). The week before my talk, coincidentally, Chancellor Hooker visited the Institute and joined the fellows in the weekly luncheon. I happened to sit next to him, so I handed him a packet and brought up the topic. He took a quick glance at what I described as the "menu"—the list of readings—and was a little embarrassed that I was welcoming him to the luncheon with such a bad joke. But he was candid in confirming the story and added that they were already leaning toward making the move to Chapel Hill when the little message arrived. I was not sure how he would respond if he were to read Tan's women's conversation. I was afraid to ask because I thought it would be, well, "un-Chinese" to be so disrespectful. As expected of such a comic subject, the presentation went well the next week. What I did not expect was yet another surprise.

Shortly after the fall semester began, I ran into one of the institute fellows. On his way to teach a class on U.S. labor history, he told me that at the first class meeting he had handed out the Hooker story and the two pages from Tan's novel, adding emphatically that the students loved it. As he hastened away, I was left speechless. In the highly compartmentalized world of American research universities, academics usually feel rewarded when anything we do is of some use to colleagues in other disciplines. The fellowship program was designed to bridge the gulf between disciplines, as it did in this case, but I was unprepared when what I had intended as a farcical tidbit ended up with such a serious flavor. It was not that I was blind to the sweatshop conditions in which unskilled immigrants like the two women in the fortune-cookie factory labor; I had my own short acquaintance from washing dishes in a Chinese restaurant in my early American experience. It is the highly ethnicized social arenas and discursive fields that often reduce a complex phenomenon to a simplistic, predominantly culturalist mode of interpretation (this is one of the central points in Lowe 1996). The juxtaposition of a white, male, academic CEO with two Chinese women workers readily calls critical attention to race, gender, and class. Yet the "transcendental signifier" (to the philosopher Hooker) of the cookie and the way I had put it tended to smooth out these edges and leave only a slightly blasphemous comedy for our intellectual self-entertainment.

So I felt very grateful to this colleague of mine. I imagined that alongside the production and consumption of the fortune cookie he also mentioned the role played by the white workers' union in the legislation of the Chinese Exclusion Act, the subsequent persecution of all workers of Asian ancestry, and the more recent murder of Vincent Chin by two laid-off white workers and the judge's racist treatment of the case. Above all, organized labor in the United States historically has contributed more injury than support to Asian American workers. This tragic history cannot be explained away by the theory of "divide and conquer." No wonder Cornel West, despite his Marxist tenor, continues to insist that "race matters" (1993). Soon after that, I learned that this respected scholar of labor history was undertaking a major study of Latino workers and their struggle in North Carolina—the home state, I should mention, of Jesse Helms.

Being Episodic

As a student of literature, I struggle to keep a balance between a text-centered approach to values and forms and a contextual approach to the sociohistorical production of these values and forms. What the fortune-cookie episode has illustrated to me, once again, is the complex network in which meaning is created and circulated in contingency, enriched or attenuated according to one's taste, determined in a specific setting yet open to negotiation in its dissemination across different terrains. The above accounts are therefore more heuristic than I can thematize. But because these stories are open to interpretation, they delineate a multi-layered social and semantic field in which the meaning of being Chinese is defined for an educated Chinese immigrant by his encounters with things Chinese in the United States. If the syntax of the preceding sentence is confusing, let me say that this is because I as a person am often so confused.

But that is not the whole story. I hasten to add another footnote: my self-understanding is always already ethnicized. I am constantly reminded that I am a member of a minority group in the United States, and yet the memory stays with me that I am also a member of the Han Chinese—not only the majority in China but the largest population in the entire world. For two decades before I came to the United States, I lived in western China and had extensive contact with various ethnic groups in that vast region. The differences between the Han and its other and among these "others" were palpable in the mores and rituals of the everyday. These differences were contained within the ideological parameters of a multiethnic and multicultural history of the old Middle Kingdom, now unified in the modern nation-state of the People's Republic. The sinified practice of Marxism-Leninism was more emancipatory in the early years of the PRC and became increasingly repressive as the overall political environment went awry in the frenzy of the "class struggle." As a result, ethnic consciousness was managed in service of state-sanctioned "class" interest. In the areas of economic and cultural policies, however, I would be hard put to support the argument that there has been a state-sponsored "internal colonialism" at work in the PRC. Beginning in the early 1950s, the Chinese government put in place a series of "affirmative action" programs. These include economic aid to destitute minority regions, quota systems favoring minority enrollment in institutions of higher education and increasing their representation in the People's Congress and other official bodies, and special support for cultural projects aimed at reconstructing the "lost histories" of ethnic groups and salvaging their heritages. What distinguishes this Chinese "multiculturalism" from its American counterpart is the former's class-based universalism.

That is one of the main reasons that in the Chinese political arena oppression and persecution of those perceived to threaten the socialist revolution intensified in the late 1950s. The oppressive measures became "ethnicized" once they were applied to non-Han peoples in the name of maintaining China's national unity. The 1959 Tibetan rebellion is a case in point. It began largely as a social-religious movement for theocratic self-determination against the socialist land reform and other secular social agendas imposed by the Communist Party, but it ended up crushed for an alleged conspiracy of political separatism. Yet the regime often justifies its harsh policies on the basis of China's sufferings at the hands of Western imperialism. That historical experience has in fact helped shape the modern Chinese nation, and the memory of that history has been reinforced in recent years by the breakup of the former Soviet bloc and the bloodbaths that have followed.

These issues are so complex that even a brief scholarly account is beyond the scope of this book. I bring them up only to highlight my historical memory of such an ambivalent nature and the difficulty of maintaining coherence for a "personal" narrative already "episodic," as it is in the early accounts. It seems no longer possible to articulate a coherent sense of myself in good faith, as my "subjectivity" has been fragmented by all the "border crossings" of times and places. Yet I cannot simply join in the often self-congratulatory celebration of intellectual "homelessness" or postmodern cosmopolitanism when the real homeless people and refugees of the world make me realize that the gesture is a cheap shot. To return to those "eating" episodes, I find them illustrative of the maddening condition in which some of us have to live. If the "banana" story figures my "subject position" vis-à-vis Chinese Americans, the monkey brain feast re-turns that position to its reverse in the public imagination of China, forcing me to play the role of an ethnographer and a native informant at once. A native informant trained in an American graduate school and now acting as an ethnographer—this is precisely the bottom line if I am to make a living and get this book published. But such cynicism cannot spare me the schizophrenic condition. It only intensifies the madness—unless one naively assumes a return to the state, say, of Kingston's mother and ignores the rules of both the human and the ghost world, or unless one accepts that schizophrenia is the normal state of mind in the postmodern era so that one can happily allow oneself to be borne along the free play of the signifier. The problem remains, however, that I am dealing with "eating"—yet a signifier of irreducible materiality.

The fortune cookie is such a signifier, and the fortune-cookie syndrome may well offer a fortune-cookie solution. This little goody was invented in the 1930s with the development of tourism in San Francisco's Chinatown (see Takaki 1989, 248), which "promised an 'Oriental experience' in the Occident" (Cao and Novas 1996, 68). The question of origin does not matter to me in that newcomers from China find it as much a curiosity as perhaps anyone who first sees it. Of all things Chinese, originated in China, or invented overseas, the fortune cookie is perhaps the tamest image packaged as an exotic commodity for sale. Its inside contains the kind of pidginized "fortune cookie wisdom" that dates back to Charlie Chan of early Hollywood, though it has lost some of its exotic quality in recent years because of the quantity of its more standardized mass production and consumption. The outside is literally sugar coated and signifies the sweetness of a feminized China. Put together, the exotic message and the tamed form play perfectly into the mainstream taste for the quaint readily brought home.

Such an ideological critique of the China-imaginary crystallized in a goody is no doubt necessary, but it must also take account of the economic history of survival figured therein. Much as the fortune cookie tops off a cheap but palatable meal, it functions as a synecdoche for the economics of Chinese food service. Those of us who obtain a steady stream of income by producing words should not diminish the economic importance the fortune cookie holds for tens of thousands of workers. A so-called industry built on the backs of the industrious workers (including the proprietors and their families, who cook and serve in addition to running the business), the restaurant industry nevertheless provides a major venue of livelihood for many immigrants who would otherwise find themselves totally stranded. With as little financial and social capital as they possess, these immigrants have succeeded in establishing a niche in the saturated market of food service, now found even in small rural communities. Whatever is coated and coded in the orientalist packaging of the cookie, there are things untold about those who produce it as a food. The materiality of the fortune cookie exists as an "absent presence": it is absent from Hooker's world but can and must be "presented."

On the symbolic level, the cookie is an ingenious invention of cultural hybridity paradoxically because it feeds on the orientalist fantasy through playful simulation. The person or persons who invented the cookie knew that this tiny treat was faked to feed the orientalist palate for the authentic. This very knowledge applied to the exploitation of the orientalist *episteme* requires us to read the act of invention as a parody. To echo Tan's joke, the cookie is symbolic of how the powerless manage to extract some surplus meaning of self-control where they are subject to control by those they serve. Extreme and fortuitous as it may sound, the Hooker story is indicative of the ritualistic power of the "superstitious" in our highly rationalized calculation and mechanical routine. It is true that the underlying logic of the parody is not confrontation or even subversion. For those busy with their daily struggle for survival, the "desire" of the parody is marked with the principle of maximum efficacy. This principle determines a self-conscious position of the *yin*, or the "feminine," already given to the feminized China, which attempts to turn that given to its own advantage.

Even if we were to assume that the desire of the fortune cookie reveals nothing but some "false consciousness" at work, the question I would ask is this: what fortune would lie ahead for those with "false consciousness" if the mere form of their desire were to be written off? This is a major reason that I choose to write about Jade Snow Wong's autobiography and Amy Tan's novel—beyond the fact that they offer plenty of material on "Chinese eating." Along with Kingston, Wong and Tan have been the most popular writers of Chinese ancestry in their respective times. Their popularity places them together more than anyone else in a *sugar-sisterhood*, a nonexistent Chinese term that Tan concocted in her misreading but is captured by Sau-ling Wong (1995) for dissecting the "Amy Tan phenomenon" created by her *The Joy Luck Club* and *The Kitchen God's Wife*. With Sau-ling Wong and other scholars of Asian American literature, the two "sweet sisters" are, in the realm of American cultural politics, what the fortune cookie is in the orientalist palate of the exotic. There is little one can add to the impressive body of critical literature produced in the past that critiques the two authors. What I offer in the following is aimed at reappropriating the hungry desire of Wong's autobiography and the "double-tongued" discursive practice of Tan's novel. This approach is deliberately underscored by a twist of the notion of authenticity, an appeal to sanity, and a hope for education and self-education.

I bear the burden of authenticity and authority not only as someone who is China born and bred but also because of my professional affiliation with Chinese studies. Still called sinology by some scholars, Chinese studies has long excluded Chinese Americans and other diasporic Chinese groups around the world because they are not considered authentic representatives of Chinese culture. This issue is not limited to the field of Chinese studies; there is a history of controversy over the real or fake representation of Chinese culture among Chinese American writers (see Chin 1991 for a recent example). On the other hand, in an academic environment in which one's demonstrated familiarity with theory has become the symbolic capital par excellence in legitimating one's own authority, what used to be a self-reflective and skeptical stance has turned to feed on itself for the sake of being critical (of which I am guilty, too). Under these circumstances, it would be more appropriate for me to read the "sugar sisters" with a "sweet tooth."

This stance—tactical as it may appear—is marked by a desperate appeal to sanity. Once I have told my stories of "episodic" self-fragmentation, I still have to live with some sense of coherence. Eating provides a mundane, earthy anchor. Finally, because the three episodes all took place in academic settings and have outlined my own learning experience at the same time, my reading of the "sugar sisters" also is intended to be educational and self-educational, that is, about the values of food, art, and life.

The Hungry Self in *Fifth Chinese Daughter: The Making of a Chinese American Ingredient*

Oral experience is one of the basic areas of human life through which individual consciousness is formed and a culture makes sense of itself. In *Fifth Chinese Daughter*, orality figures in three textual aspects. First, the use of food and cooking plays into the book's central theme of blending different ingredients in the American melting pot. Reminiscent of the Chinese mythological chef/prime minister Yi Yin and his cooking/governing ideal of harmony, Wong's descriptions of eating and cooking project a utopian desire in responding to a different social reality. In this cross-cultural translation, the ancient Chinese model of blending for harmony corresponds to the ideal of America as "a teeming nation of nations" represented by writers such as Walt Whitman and Herman Melville.

The ideas of harmony and peace imply as their opposites social conflict and historical contradiction, which can be found in the narrator's inability to conjure up a fixed identity according to the fixed ideal. Wong's identity is constructed, deconstructed, and reconstructed in a dynamic and ever-changing process in that the meaning of food is never fixed but mutable, multilayered and even contradictory—just like our appetites. It is true that when other "native" symbolic resources are not readily accessible to her American readers Wong has utilized the simplest signs generated by food and cooking as an index to her identity, seasoning the book's exotic flavor for the appetite of the reading public. As a result, the cook, through her "self-cooking," is symbolically appropriated as an item for public consumption. The tensions between what she tries to identify with and how she is defined and circumscribed by society can be seen in terms of different meanings of food and in whether the reader perceives her as a desiring/speaking subject or an object for consumption.

The third aspect of Wong's alimentary discourse is concerned with the textual structuration of orality at several levels of signification. The trope central to orality operates on the model of hunger (and sometimes appetite) and fulfillment. Hunger fulfillment figures the relationship between the eater and food at the existential level, between a Chinese American woman and the social environment that defines the meaning of her presence on the sociocultural plane, and between the narrator and the narrative world to which she addresses herself on the stage of communication. Thus understood, hunger fulfillment is the pivotal metaphor that unifies the acts of eating and speaking and sets the terms for a "double-tongued" discourse. Corresponding to the melting pot and the narrator's identity formation in it, hunger fulfillment is as much the mode of signification as the theme of the text. As hunger desires fulfillment, it motivates writing-as-desiring. It is through locating and bringing to the fore the dramatic working out of personal desire that we can recapture what has been appropriated in history.

Wong begins her story by telling the reader that her book includes "the significant episodes which . . . shaped [her] life" (vii). Food lore and alimentary practice play a major role in shaping her childhood memories. In the section "Lucky to be Born Chinese," Wong describes one feast after another held by the community to celebrate the Chinese New Year and the Moon Festival. "The Americans, Jade Snow heard, did not have a Moon Festival nor a seven-day New Year celebration with delicious accompaniments" (43). The narrator's memory of her grandmother is filled with the early taste of food. The grandma had an ancestor worship table in her room on which were offered a variety of dainties. She was also very generous to her grandchildren and whenever they came to see her offered them various goodies they rarely tasted. After an incident in which Jade Snow was punished for a minor mistake, the grandma comforted her with some fantastic food and immersed her in ancestral memory (9). When she was scared by a ferocious turkey, the grandma acted like a sorceress, made a pot of herbal tea with the magic of her jade pendant and pearl brooch, and exorcised the fear. "Although it was difficult to understand such things, Jade Snow remembered them" (11). What she remembered was the panacea of food for healing, curing, ritualizing the everyday, and constructing a cultural memory of Chinese ancestry. Not fully differentiated, sensual images of food symbolize immanent totality, in which food is the world and her act of eating and drinking constitutes her connection with it.

The textual configuration of food and the grandmother calls back many of the familial episodes in the works of modern Chinese writers. As noted previously, the association of food with the "motherly" imaginary is absent in works by "new women" writers in revolutionary China, highlighting once again the problematic of the notion of cultural authenticity. To Wong, the traditional family is not a problematic institution to be dismantled by revolutionary means. Rather, the family problem is a domestic issue to be solved within that institution. In catering to public curiosity about the "Chinese family" yet producing a readable memoir with enough narrative tension, Wong manages to stage a family drama in which generational, gender, and cultural conflicts are simultaneously enacted and contained. Central to this drama is her relationship with her father.

The father's view of life is summed up in two words: eating and thinking. According to him, "one was not supposed to talk when one was either eating or thinking, and when one was not eating, one should be thinking. Only when in bed did one neither eat or think" (4). Likewise, the little girl's childhood is characterized by the way she is taught to "ruminate" over food—the meaning of eating and cooking—and ruminate over the meaning of life, both provided and defined by the father. Correspondingly, the episodes that shaped Wong's life unfold along two interlaced narrative lines: eating or earning a living, thinking or reflecting upon the meaning of life. Her significant episodes are staged in two intermerged cultural spaces where eating and education take place: the table, the kitchen, grocery stores, festivities, schools, and the church.

From a family that owned a rice store in China, the father views rice as central to their experience and identity: "What is more important than the rice we eat twice a day and which is our main food? It is what we are, or we are what it is" (60). As such, the daughter's relationship with rice defines a crucial moment of her entry into culture: "To wash rice correctly is the first step in cooking rice correctly, and it is considered one of the principal accomplishments or requirements of any Chinese female. When Jade Snow was six, Daddy had stood her on a stool at the kitchen sink in order to teach her himself this most important step, so that he could be personally satisfied that she had a sure foundation" (57). Unlike the typical Chinese patriarch, the father "intrudes" into the "feminine" space of the kitchen to lay a sure foundation, not of a cook but of a Chinese female. This anecdote corresponds to the social and semantic space in which Asian men have been defined in American popular culture.

If rice nurtures, it also disciplines, and it does so as a whip. The rice sacks imported from China were "sewn with strong hemp twine" reinforced with "double strips of flexible cane about three-eighths of an inch wide." The father, who "wasted nothing, carefully untied the cane, straightened it out, and saved it to make switches for whipping disobedient or improper children" (60). And the Wong children did suffer occasional flogging to remind them of the key words of life: "respect and order" (2). "So it was no wonder," the daughter later reflects, "that the Wong children always watched a delivery of new rice with sad eyes and heavy hearts" (60).

Wong's entry into culture is an entrance into a world of differences, and these differences are already coded in folklore as food of different colors. When she was asking her mother where babies came from, the mother evaded this question, embarrassing to a traditional Chinese mother, by telling her that they were "roasted in hospital ovens." "There are three kinds of babies," the mother explains. "When they are nearly done, they are white foreign babies. When they bake a little longer, they become golden Chinese babies. Sometimes they are left in too long, and they become black babies!" (24) Racial difference thus defined, visual images of food function as an epistemological category in the formation of consciousness and interpretation of the world. These colored images are later reinscribed in the narrator's discovery of different attitudes toward food.

At the age of six, Jade Snow was sent to an American public school. The American world opened up new horizons for her. "One of the most memorable events occurred" one day when Wong and her classmates were asked to make butter. "After the cream had been churned for some time, sure enough, yellow flecks appeared, and then joined and thickened into a lump of butter. Jade Snow experienced a wonderful new feeling—the pride of personal creation. And when she smeared her own butter made with her own hands on the crackers . . . she thought that she had never tasted anything more delicious in all her life" (13). Washing rice and making butter, trivial as they may appear, season distinct flavors of two cultures. This cognitive process blends fragments of her experience and blurs the boundary between school and kitchen.

Accompanying her entry into American culture is a growing sense of discomfort with the borders of the two worlds she straddles. This is also marked with her growing awareness of the value of food. In the American world, food has lost its magic power. A crucial moment occurred one day in school when she was hurt by the careless fling of a baseball bat. The teacher, a Miss Mullohand, came to comfort her. Miss Mullohand "was quite the loveliest person that Jade Snow had ever known," "with wavy, blond hair, fair skin, and blue eyes." "Held to a grown-up foreign lady's bosom," she was suddenly stricken with "undefined confusion." It suddenly occurred to the girl that her Mama and Daddy had "never embraced her impulsively when she required consolation" (20). In her teacher's bosom, the memory of a past incident swelled up in her mind. She and her little sister were left locked in a dark room in their parents' basement factory. Clinging to the only window they cried for "an unbearably long time." When their parents returned,

> Daddy took a bag of fried soybean curds he had just bought to cook with deep-sea bass and green onions, split them and sprinkled them with white sugar, and gave the two children as many as they wanted as an unusual treat to "mend the hurt."
>
> But Mama and Daddy had not caught them up in their arms in comfort, Jade Snow remembered at first, finding it wonderful comfort to be embraced by Miss Mullohand.
>
> . . . [S]he was now conscious that "foreign" American ways were not only generally and vaguely different from their Chinese ways, but that they were specifically different, and the specific differences would involve a choice of action. Jade Snow had begun to compare American ways with those of her mother and father, and the comparison made her uncomfortable. (21)

The absolute value of food in Chinese culture had melted away in the warmth of her teacher's embrace. A different kind of hunger has been aroused, and the desire to fulfill it is expressed through the "choice of action." Such a choice of action is also what has awakened the girl to the choice of consciousness she has to make. Her changing consciousness is shown, in addition to the obvious statement she has made, by whether quotation marks are attached to the word "foreign." When she was held in the teacher's arms, Miss Mullohand was still a "foreign lady" without quotation marks. But quotation marks are added to " 'foreign' American ways" after she has completed her comparison. It is a different voice that is speaking in the latter moment, a subject whose hunger can no longer be satisfied by the remote and perhaps "foreign" Chinese food.

Wong's reading of cultural difference not only hinges on whether affection is expressed through direct bodily contact or mediated through food; it must be visualized as a facial feature: her teacher had "wavy, blond hair, fair skin, and blue eyes." America is what makes her feel comfortable, and this America is white. Yet this moment of her consciousness formation is at variance with the established dichotomy between the "feminine China" and the "masculine America." Between washing rice and making butter, between the father's food and the teacher's embrace, there arises a reversal of the stereotypical imagery of Chineseness and Americanness. This reversal not only describes her assimilation but does so by replacing "Uncle Sam" with "Aunt Samantha." Thus, this America is not just white but ultimately feminine. This white, feminine America will open her warm arms to welcome Wong to Mills College.

The reality, of course, is not always as warm as Miss Mullohand's bosom. Wong's experience in the expanding world outside Chinatown has forced her to see another face of America. Transferring to a junior high school outside Chinatown, she found herself the only Chinese student in a small neighborhood school, a situation in which she was "introduced for the first time to racial discrimination." Her first bitter taste of America came from a white boy's racist slurs and insults. She protested by invoking ancient China's "superior culture" and its contributions to world civilization, a silent invocation because it was made to the reader only (68). Although Wong's generation of Chinese Americans was the first to be legally permitted to attend public schools and her life was not representative of the majority of Chinese immigrants of her time, her response is characteristic of the Chinese image as it is perceived in the United States. In fact, she did not respond in the sense that she kept silent to the boy. The reason she gave for her silence is found in her "silent" charge of the "foreigners" who "were simply unwise in the ways of human nature, and unaware of the importance of giving the other person 'face' " (69). The agony caused by repressing the voice thus is balanced with an inner voice that invokes ancient China. Elaine Kim, quoting Gerald Haslam (1970), describes how this works psychologically: "[T]he Chinese in America were sustained through their travails by this notion: 'the knowledge that their ancestors had created a great and complex civilization when the inhabitants of the British Isles still painted their fannies blue' enabled them to rationalize and endure rejection without significant anger or injury" (1982, 69). This reminds us of how religion functions as "opium" (Marx) or "illusion" (Freud) and how "opium" or "illusion" is consumed as symbolic food and medicine.

Wong's sense of cultural superiority actually disguises a deep inferiority complex imposed by the social reality, and the psychological tension will surface again and again to sharpen her desire for ascending the social hierarchy. To pay for her college education, Wong worked as a kitchen servant for "a political middle-aged couple." Resentful of being treated like "merely another kitchen fixture," she worked stoically in the hope that her college education would lift her out of such a fate (106).

One day she found a new meaning of Chinese food in another affluent white woman's kitchen. Failing to make a proper meringue cake for an ongoing party, she was ordered by her hostess to make another. "That afternoon was a tortuous nightmare and a fever of activity," she recalls. "By the time she was at last washing the dishes and tidying the dining room she felt strangely vague. She hadn't taken time to eat her dinner; she was too tired anyway. How she wished that she had been asked to cook a Chinese dinner instead of this interminable American meal, especially that cake!" (124) These instances have compelled Wong to recognize the problems of being a Chinese American woman. Above all, the experience of a child making butter and being held in her teacher's bosom did not help much the lot of a woman of color, who was to be denied employment and housing solely due to her skin color. Alongside her attempt to climb the social ladder, food images are gradually reinvested with more abstract meanings.

Faced with more and more social and familial discordance, Wong began to seek answers in the Confucian tradition of ancestral worship and scientific rationalism and individualism. To reconcile the two attitudes and work out "her own personally applicable combination," she "studied her neighbor in class, Stella Green, for clues":

> Stella had grown up reading Robert Louis Stevenson, learning to swim and play tennis, developing a taste for roast beef, mashed potatoes, sweets, aspirin tablets and soda pop, and she looked upon her mother and father as friends. But it was very unlikely that she knew where her great-grandfather was born, or whether or not she was related to another strange Green she might chance to meet. Jade Snow had grown up reading Confucius, learning to embroider and cook rice, developing a taste for steamed fish and bean sprouts, tea, and herbs, and she thought of her parents as people to be obeyed. She not only knew where her ancestors were born but where they were buried, and how many chickens and roast pigs should be brought annually to their graves to feast their spirits.

"In such a scheme," she concludes, "the individual counted for little weighed against the family, after sixteen years it was not easy to sever roots" (131–32).

For a Chinese American who was yet to visit China, her sense of origin was basically rooted in two interlaced cultural icons: the Chinese Book (Confucianism and its core doctrine of the family) and Chinese food.

Just as ancestral worship inscribed in the Confucian Book is staged as a feast for the spirits, these spirits are reinscribed in the teaching of that book and dispersed through the familial tree of symbolic nourishment. This two-way nurturing connects in imagination the subject to her ancestry and at the same time accommodates a sensible space for the split self. In the same way the Christian joins the divine in Holy Communion, the narrator (re)joins the ancestral spirits in sacred Chinese food. Her experience with food is thus transcribed into a transcendental narrative. Along her path in the increasingly complex world is the overcoding of food to an ever higher symbolic realm. Nevertheless, between the two principles the father dictates for her life, eating figures thinking and governs the way she thinks. She thinks of her ancestry in terms of food, and her mental digestion of both shapes the way she thinks. Food-for-thought and thoughts-of-food become two sides of the same coin.

In this process, Wong has found a common ground on which people can share, if nothing else, a table. Not questioning what social forces circumscribe her role as a kitchen servant—a role many Chinese immigrants and their American-born children had to perform, she exploits Chinese cooking to her best advantage. It culminated in her acceptance by Mills College. At Mills, she lived in the dean's residence and was affiliated with a residential hall whose "kitchen staff was entirely Chinese, some of them descendants of the first Chinese kitchen help who worked for the founder of the college" (157). Unlike these Chinese kitchen staff, she is a talented student in a selective women's college; unlike other students, she has a point of distinction. Eating and education finally reach the dramatic climax in the "first kitchen" of Mills.

After a Chinese meal she cooked to entertain a few friends at Mills, she found again that "the girls were perpetually curious about her Chinese background and Chinese ideologies, and for the first time she began to formulate in her mind the constructive and delightful aspects of the Chinese culture" (161). Having learned about her cooking skills, the dean of Mills requested that she prepare a party honoring a group of musicians. With help from her family, the party was a great success. The guests so marvelled at the food that in the end the kitchen became the central scene of the party. "That was a wonderful evening," Wong writes, "which Jade Snow thoroughly enjoyed. . . . Because of everyone's interest in the kitchen preparations, she soon lost her shyness in the presence of celebrities and acted naturally. There was no talk about music, only about Chinese food. And Jade Snow ceased thinking of famous people as 'those' in a world apart. She had a glimpse of the truth, that the great people of any race are unpretentious, genuinely honest, and nonpatronizing in their interest in other human beings" (173). As the ancient chef/prime minister Yi Yin advocates, harmony represented by the ideal cook should also serve as the highest principle of human society. Although there is no specific reference to that mythological sage in the text, its language and motifs translate that ideal into the context of the melting pot. Throughout the book, Wong's uses of food symbolism are consistent with the theme of blending for harmony.

However, her successful assimilation has made her a curious object. The last episode of Wong's autobiography serves as an apt metaphor for the role in which the society at large defines this successful Chinese American woman. During World War II, she was an office worker in a military shipyard. She attained national fame by winning a prize for an essay on absenteeism. As a result, Wong was given the honor of christening a Liberty Ship. After the war ended, she returned to Chinatown and established her pottery business, an art she learned at Mills and was inspired to pursue through her introduction to ancient Chinese ceramics. To save space and help attract customers to the store where she was to operate the clay splatter (wheel), she offered the store owner a deal: she would work in one of the two store windows. This did attract curious crowds, which bet on whether she was making bricks, a model kitchen, or even a rice-threshing machine. An oriental woman playing with mud in a store window on the edge of Chinatown became "a wonder in the eyes of the Western world." The morning paper reported it with "a picture and two-column story of the new enterprise" and even "declared that she had invented a new mousetrap" (243–44).

Critics of Jade Snow Wong have pointed out that "through the blending of the 'Chinese' and 'American' qualities, Wong becomes mere curiosity to both cultures" (E. Kim 1982, 71) and that "the consciousness at work . . . is fundamentally a limited one as it is a vision of life that insists on totalities" (Blinde 1979, 55). In this sense, Wong succeeded by offering herself up for the American feast. The desire to assume the role of a cultural ambassador is dispersed in her narrative development from an innocent eater to a curious item palatable for cultural consumption. This becomes particularly disturbing when we note that the narrator is fully aware of the irony between ideal and real yet does not present it as such. That is why Wong readily invites criticism for ideological complicity.

The Totality of Orality

The critique of Wong's ideological complicity, however, needs to be supplemented with a different kind of reading of what ideology effaces in the last scene. This is meant to uncover the absent in the present, to retrieve the voice of the personal from behind the scenes rather than rescue a cultural hero from her self-exhibition. There is no question that Wong's desire for assimilation is rather pathetic by today's standards. The question is: is there anything in the self-exhibition that eludes the public gaze? We only need to trace the "pot" to the real life of the author and its symbolic significance to her. To Wong, pottery is an art form, analogous to her writing, and is not entirely for sale. In 1951, a Chicago corporation proposed to use her designs and reputation for the mass production of cookware and offered her a generous contract. Uncertain how to deal with it, she consulted some friends and their colleagues. Their opinions were contradictory: she should either avoid potential damage to her reputation or use her "million-dollar reputation" as an "asset." "Reluctant to reject what appeared to be 'easy money,' " she finally went to her father for advice. Her "old-fashioned Chinese father taught her a lesson in moderation" and "warned her to beware of limitless self-created material desires." Wong turned down the offer and has since led a moderate life.[2]

Looked upon from this angle, the artist is not just a passive object in the melting pot; she is also a participant in the making of a dynamically "meltable pot." She did this in her own way, which was not aggressive enough and thus easily mistaken for timidity. Wong's choice may be politically conservative, but it is also based on the ethical principle of nonaggression and modesty. Her dilemma has been forced upon her, a modest private person who has been judged by the standard of a public figure, that is, a spokesperson for Chinese Americans. By the same token, if we were to continue to read her autobiography simply as a transparent document of ethnography, we would perpetuate the same anthropological fallacy applied to the editing process of her book.[3]

In light of her striving for harmony and moderation, I want to demonstrate that the text at various points defies its own tendency toward totality or aims at a different kind of totality, one that is not purely for ideological self-exhibition. While acts of eating and cooking function in the ways culture defines them, they are rooted in human desire and disseminated in the narrative from hunger toward fulfillment. At the deepest or the most "primitive" level, hunger fulfillment is presymbolic, "felt" in the nonintentional psycho-dynamic process. Food signs become transcendental signifiers only when they signify abstract ideas, when the corporeality of food is submerged under a higher level of signification. Precisely at this point, linguistic signs become signifiers of myth. But even when food signs become transcendental signifiers food images still embed in their abstraction immanent and sensual elements that undermine their complete ideological closure. This can be shown even in a "recipe" like this:

> For the egg foo young, everything was shredded for quick cooking. So two onions were sliced thin, and a cup of celery slivered on a bias. The ham was cut into long shreds about one-eighth inch thick. Proceeding with the precooking, Jade Snow fried the onions slightly in the frying pan, and added the ham until both were barely cooked through. Lifting out this mixture, she put in the celery with a little water and covered it until that was barely cooked through, but still crisp. Two or three minutes only were given each vegetable. Then these ingredients were beaten up with enough eggs—about six—to bind them together. A little soy sauce and chopped green onions were added for flavor and color, and the dish was ready for final cooking later on. Any firm meat could have been used in place of the ham—shredded or leftover chicken, roast pork, shrimp, or crab, but never beef, which would have been too juicy. A few cooked peas or bean sprouts could have been added to or substituted for the celery and onions. There were no specific proportions to Chinese cooking; just imagination according to personal preference, common sense, and knowledge of basic principles were necessary. (159–60)

There is no doubt that this piece can be *used* as a recipe—which may well be intended by the author through her mechanical explanations of certain details. Yet it is not a recipe as such. With a beginning and an end, the narrative conjures up a series of actions in a sensual scene with a wide array of colors and scents. There is a mood of performance that teases the explicit utilitarian function, a performative desire that not only transgresses generic rules of recipe writing but in the end undermines the authority on which any authentic cookbook hinges. We seem to hear two voices competing in the same passage: one responds to cultural demands, claims cultural essence, and plays into the established model of Chineseness; the other is more personal, appeals to the sensual and the aesthetic, and emphasizes open-ended imagination and creativity. If the "recipe" within the overall context is designed to satisfy a cultural appetite, it projects in the meantime a deeper desire because hunger exists prior to culture and its cultural production must operate in terms that correspond to "nature."

In a way, this "recipe" even has its own theme. For a dish as simple as egg foo young, the cooking procedure requires the "common sense" and "basic principles" of blending different ingredients into a whole without erasing the distinctiveness of the composing elements. Furthermore, imagination is embedded in the cooking process in figural terms such as *mixture* or *condensation* and *substitution*. Even though *substitution* is intended to explain what other materials can be used, it allows for a moment of freedom that, once unleashed, metonymically "spills" over in the end. In this way, the boundary disappears between the cook who is a stereotypical servant and the writer who is capable of imagination and creation. What makes all these possible in a conceivably documentary passage is the "literariness" of language, the self-reflexive capacity that transgresses the grammar imposed by systematic referentiality. This example shows that the sign system always carries within itself the seeds of its transgression—especially when language deals with things as amorphous as desire or when desire is dispersed in the sensuality of eating and cooking.

If the desire of the personal is only latent in the narrative of the "recipe," the voice hungry for connection and communication is manifest in the textual configuration of eating and speech. It is at this conjunction that a crucial episode in the text unveils a different vision of totality. Returning to Chinatown in the wake of the war with her honor and fame, Wong was hospitalized for orthopedic surgery. The day after her operation her father came to visit her.

He carried a pot of nutritious Chinese chicken-and-herb soup, which he had made himself, and a porcelain spoon and bowl. He knelt by her bed, said a prayer for her recovery, and had her turn her head so that he could spoon-feed her. With his bamboo chopsticks, he fed her mushrooms and red dates from the soup. It was one of the few times when father and daughter had been alone together, and Jade Snow felt warmly grateful for this brief and affectionate companionship.

She tried to be light. "I haven't been such a baby since I had my tonsils out, and you waited with me until I woke up. I guess I haven't been fed like this since then."

Daddy's response was unexpectedly tender, although he tried to sound matter-of-fact. "I didn't personally feed you enough as a baby, and now I am patching up the hurt!" (204)

This moment reminds us of two early scenes: her rice washing under the father's gaze and its association with the whip, and the food the father fed her to "mend the hurt." In terms of characterization, this scene portrays the father as a complicated figure. But the father has not changed much in that he is doing the same feeding to "mend" and "patch up the hurt." What is different is the semantic space in which he is recast. The image of the father undergoes a kind of cross-dressing and reemerges no longer the harsh father who threatened to whip the children but a benign "motherly father" who literally nurses her. This "feminine" space in which the father is re-placed is established on the narrative principle of hunger fulfillment and is explicitly grounded on the desire of the "baby."

Equally important in this scene is the temporal structure of hunger fulfillment. The father's feeding fulfills the daughter's hunger at two interconnected moments. It satisfies the daughter's present hunger and awakens a deeper emotional thirst. It is her desire for communication that the father has long neglected and suppressed and the daughter has displaced on other people (her schoolteacher, for example). The moment she remembers the last time her father fed her, she "re-members" herself as a baby of the past *and* into a baby of the "now." This "baby," told in direct speech referring to the speaker herself, signifies the eternal need for warmth and love. Acted out around oral experience, the yearning for totality is as nostalgic as it is futuristic. Sensual, corporeal, and aesthetic, eating and feeding have preserved her nostalgic memory of an eternal desire that can only be called back and reenacted for its fulfillment.

What makes this feeding scene one of the text's most touching moments is the symbiosis of eating and speech. As hunger generates the desire for food, silence engenders the motivation for speech. To the extent that the act of eating appeases hunger and connects the self with the world, the act of speech reduces the distance between the speaker and his or her community and produces the feeling of proximity and sharing. This casts the narrative mode of a third-person autobiography in a different light. *Fifth Chinese Daughter* is an autobiography, the author tells us in her note, "written in the third person from the Chinese habit" that silences the voice of "I." She makes this submissive gesture specifically toward the father. This double play between telling about oneself and doing so in third-person indirect speech defines the text as autobiography and fiction at the same time. There is a latent narrative irony created by the double gesture to at once breach and obey the rule of silence. As a result, the narrative irony is spatialized as "distance" and "self-distancing": the former exists between the daughter and the father, the latter between the author and the narrator. But the text is not based on an authorial irony at all; its authorial discourse is "heroic" in style, theme, and characterization. What bridges this gap and overrides the logic of silence and distance is a simple act: she talks with the father in first-person direct speech. It is in this moment that the communicative distance is dramatically erased. When the "motherly father" feeds the daughter like a "baby" and the daughter reciprocates his nursing in a kind of "baby talk," her hunger is appeased by words as well as by food, words as food. Symbolic of Wong's return to Chinatown is her "return" to an oral totality where food and words are blended to nurture the eternal dream of harmony.

It is true that the text insists on a vision of totality, blending utopian ingredients into a harmonizing melting pot. But this vision is not simply "visual" in the sense of "illusion." It is also "oral" in that even transcendental signifiers such as the ancestral-spiritual feast and the melting pot are themselves sensuous correlatives of materiality. Despite historical constraints, Wong's text offers us a brief taste of totality: oral in ontology, nostalgic and futuristic in temporality, feminine in semantics, and dialogic and communicative in social practice.

The Carnal Texture of the "Double Tongued":

The "Double-Tongued" Storyteller

I never thought my mother's Kweilin story was anything but a Chinese fairy tale. The endings always changed. Sometimes she said she used that worthless thousand-yuan note to buy a half-cup of rice. She turned that rice into a pot of porridge. She traded that gruel for two feet from a pig. These two feet became six eggs, those eggs six chickens. The story always grew and grew. (Tan 1989, 12)

Jing-mei, the primary narrator in Amy Tan's *The Joy Luck Club*, reads her mother's story in a way that also serves as the narrative model for her own storytelling. This mode of storytelling highlights the materiality of food and language and the reciprocity between them. At various points, I have referred to it as "double-tongued discourse." It is traceable to the ancient chef-orator Yi Yin and resurfaces in Shen Congwen's imaginary nostalgia, the story of Mao's braised-pork feast, Zhang Yonglin's bibliophagy of Marx, Wang Qiyao's stove-side folklore, and Jade Snow Wong's "baby talk." Just as eating is ineluctably connected with speech and the former's materiality figures the latter's, alimentary discourse does not simply represent human experience with food; it furnishes social communication and artistic expression. This twofold function of the mouth weaves eating and speech around the tongue that tastes and talks.

By locating it in an age-old Chinese tradition, the term *double tongued* is also meant to distinguish Chinese American writing from that of other ethnic groups so that we can lay bare its corporeal root in the "motherly." This is not to suggest that Chinese American literature, as a "hyphenated" textual body, is not "double voiced"—a term I borrowed from Henry Louis Gates (1988) that inspired my coinage of *double tongued*.[4] As Bakhtin (1981) has suggested, discourse is by definition always double- and multivoiced. The distinction I emphasize here is between the tongue and the voice. The tongue is an organ, a piece of flesh, and thus closely tied to the "lower," carnal body. This carnal connection is often lost in favor of the "upper" body in our current conceptualization of "voice," even after its logocentrism has been deconstructed. Thus defined, the talking tongue always talks, in reality or imagination, with its "other," who feeds it. Because of its association with the carnal body, the "double-tongued" mode structurally depends on the relationship between the "mother" who tells and feeds and the "baby" who listens and eats. Shen Congwen's hungry nostalgia, the peasant woman Mimosa, Wang Yisheng's mother in "The Chess King," Jade Snow Wong's final return to Chinatown and the "motherly father"—all these images locate the narrative desire in the "oral stage," where eating, feeding, and communication are not yet rationalized into different realms of experience.

The comparison between Chinese and Chinese American writers runs the risk of simplifying their relationship as a one-way cultural inheritance. This risk is further compounded by gender difference. If the narrative trope of the tongue reveals some timeless fascination with the "motherly" in male Chinese writers, revolutionary women writers in China would belong to a different "time zone" of history. But interculturally speaking we must look at the process of cultural transformation as well as historical context. As a result, while I maintain that Chinese and Chinese American writers share common (but not universal) features of "double-tongued" syntax and semantics, these features are always subject to revisions determined by contextual pragmatics. When Chinese immigrants bring with them the "double-tongued" legacy from China, it is inevitably put to a different use and encoded with new layers of social and symbolic meaning.

In Kingston's *The Woman Warrior* (190), for example, a "tongue twist" is played out around a linguistic and cultural misreading that takes place between the immigrant mother and the American-born child. Maxine recalls how her mother cut her tongue, "pushed [it] up and sliced the frenum." The young Maxine could not in the least comprehend the rationale of the mother's act, not to mention stand the pain. But the mother hoped that, as she explained, "[y]our tongue would be able to move in any language. You'll be able to speak languages that are completely different from one another." The mother's act may be based on some Chinese practice (she was trained as a doctor in China), but the meaning is entirely (mis)translated because the context is anything but Chinese: to speak English is the prerequisite for survival. Because the immigrant mother is "tongue-tied" in the land of the "ghost," she wants her daughter to have a free tongue. It is the transcultural practice of the "double-tongued" that simultaneously connects Chinese and Chinese American writers in the oralized tradition and separates them in the pragmatics of circumstances.

For Chinese American writers of Tan's generation, socioeconomic change has brought a favorable environment for bilingualism and biculturalism. Reconnection with the mother and the "mother tongue" is the first step toward reconciling the American born with her "roots" (which is acted out in a rather melodramatic fashion toward the end of Tan's novel).[5] The "double-tongued" mode of storytelling provides a formal receptacle that the daughter can fill with her American stories. Since Chinese immigrant mothers and their American-born daughters have their own "motherland" to identify with emotionally, their difference is often thematized in their emotional ties to their different mother tongues and tastes for food. Telling a story about such a relationship is an action that symbolically works out their conflicts. Tan's novel complicates cross-cultural misunderstanding by situating the problem of the "female Oedipalization" in the intercultural experience of food and language.[6]

Walter Benjamin (1969, 86) has noted that storytelling depends on "the communicability of experiences"—experiences that are or can be shared between the storyteller and the audience in order to be emotionally "communicable." "Double-tongued" storytelling does not differentiate the function of food from that of words insofar as "commensality," "community," and "communication" are configured. This narrative configuration is centered on the dining table, braiding the threads of the communal memory and communicable experience around eating and "saying stories" (Tan 1989, 11). The ungrammatical expression of "saying stories" is very much in line with Kingston's "talk-story," and situates Tan's storytelling in that intertextual tradition as well.

For heuristic purposes, then, materiality, maternity, and community constitute the three aspects of the "double-tongued" discourse, blending oral experiences with the texture of the tongue in a community-oriented mode of communication and interpreting life through the ways that eating and speaking incorporate the world. I do not intend to propose a matriarchal theory, as the three concepts might suggest. In ancient China, Yi Yin's principle of blending for harmony was not gendered even though he and his audience were male figures. In *Fifth Chinese Daughter*, the father's nursing of the daughter does not change his gender as much as his act of nursing is circumscribed in a feminine semantic that is very much a modern construct (i.e., why is it that a father nursing and feeding his adult daughter makes the act "feminine," if not "womanly"?). Thus, the proposal of the "double-tongued" discourse is also a matter of reading and rereading. This is epitomized in the passage cited at the beginning of this section: it is not the mother's story that grows as much as the mother's telling and retelling that grows her life-story into her daughter's own.

This dynamic telling and retelling was recognized before Amy Tan. In *The Woman Warrior*, Kingston retells a story her mother told her. The story is neither about her mother nor about herself but an intertextual and intercultural transcription of "Song for a Barbarian Reed Pipe" by the ancient Chinese woman poet Ts'ai Yen. "Here is a story my mother told me," writes Kingston, "when I told her I also talk-story. The beginning is hers, the ending, mine" (240). Through her mother's telling and the daughter's retelling, Ts'ai Yen's poem reconnects them in a dynamic and ever-changing narrative. The making of "hyphenated" female identity thus is an effect of rewriting the collective memory. When Kingston finishes her story with "It translates well," she recognizes the power of "translation" as that which transforms. In *The Joy Luck Club*, it is the generative and transformative capacity of the mother's storytelling that generates Jing-mei's narrative and transforms her mother's story into her own. "Over the years," Jing-mei says of her mother, "she told me the same story, except for the ending, which grew darker, casting long shadows into her life, and eventually into mine" (7).

When Jing-mei makes that remark about her mother's ever-growing story, her mother's story grows into another cycle in which she finds herself the successor. Suyuan Woo, Jing-mei's mother, founded the Joy Luck Club in China during World War II. Stranded in Kweilin on her way to join her husband, she found refuge in sharing with other women three things: playing the mah jong game, feasting, and "saying stories." In the San Francisco version of the club, their talk is "the same game, everybody talking in circles" (28). Talking-playing the "game" follows the same rule of cooking: "Auntie Lin cooked red bean soup for Joy Luck," the mother told Jing-mei, "I am going to cook black sesame-seed soup" (5). However, her American-born daughter harbors a deep suspicion that the club "was a shameful Chinese custom, like the secret gathering of the Ku Klux Klan or the tom-tom dances of TV Indians preparing for war" (16). Her suspicion is reinforced by her mother's story about the earlier club in China, a story that is "anything but a Chinese fairy tale." Even the first time Jing-mei is called upon to substitute for her mother at a member's home, she notices that the "house feels heavy with greasy odors. Too many Chinese meals cooked in a too small kitchen, too many once fragrant smells compressed onto a thin layer of invisible grease" (15). The mother's original story is also "greased" over by the repeated storytelling, where lived history and myth converge. When the daughter learns how to tell the Joy Luck Club stories, she begins to remove the grease of myth created by the visual images of Hollywood.

But eventually Jing-mei must take the empty seat left by her mother. When the tongue that fed and talked to her has ceased to eat and talk, she is called upon to carry on that tradition. She takes her mother's seat on the East, "where the things began, the direction from which the sun rises, where the wind comes from" (22). She is to discover the secret, not of a Chinese secret society but of the meaning of the two characters that make up her mother's given name. *Suyuan*, a pun in Chinese that can be read as either "long-cherished wish" or "long-held grudge," is symbolic of the relationship between all four mothers and their daughters. The mothers' long-cherished wish for the daughters' joy and luck has been mistaken by the daughters for long-held grudges against themselves. Sitting on the East, Jing-mei is going to reconstruct the past from "where things began" to honor, for the first time in her life, the truth of the mother's stories and fulfill her "long-cherished wish." She is to realize that her mother's Kweilin story "had been true all along" (14), that she did have two half-sisters lost during the war, and that she was invited to the club not to play a game but to be sent to China to meet her sisters.

That is why the story can never end. Just as the mother's wish would not fade away with her death, the daughter must continue to tell the stories in such a way that storytelling itself becomes a way of life, the remembrance of life. Similar to the narrator in *The Woman Warrior*, who grows up on her mother's talk-stories of ghosts, the truth of the Joy Luck mothers' stories is the truth of their lives as stories. *Suyuan* does not stop at death, nor will the story. Storytelling is thus not a mere choice of genre for writing a novel. It connects mothers and their daughters, orchestrates their dialogues across the boundaries of cultures and generations, heals the wounds inflicted by ignorance and misunderstanding, and restores orality as the primal site of bonding. When Jing-mei sits at the eastern corner of the table telling her mother's and her own tales, she is to be joined by her aunts and their daughters. To read *The Joy Luck Club* this way is to join a feast of words, to understand the limit and possibility of joy and luck offered by life.

The novel not only "tells" the themes of materiality, maternity, and communication; it also "shows" them through its formal structure. Interweaving the sixteen individual stories into an intricate, multivoiced text, the novel demonstrates that the formal is the material: the material form of collective storytelling valorizes the communal sense of cultural identity without erasing the individual voice. If the internal structure hinges on the table, with each member following the rules of the game in cooking and storytelling, on this table there seems to have emerged a "salad bowl" in place of the "melting pot." While these master tropes of American historical narrative may sound too facile or even hackneyed in current studies of ethnic literatures, these metaphors are material "containers" from the standpoint of alimentary discourse in the Chinese American tradition. Jade Snow Wong appealed to the ideal "pot" and sincerely "cooked" her way into it. She was exhibited as a curiosity yet refused to hand herself over for a lucrative sale. Kingston wanted to "see the world logically" and "enjoy simplicity," while ironically the simple logic is made logical and simple by "TV dinners with vegetables no more complex than peas mixed with diced carrots" (1975, 237). In both cases, the melting pot plays havoc with the hyphenated subjects despite their distinct subject positions in this model of assimilation.

For Tan, to remember things past in another cycle of life-as-story is to "re-member" a physical body that was painfully "dismembered" by the body politic. This is not simple wordplay. Tan certainly remembers the pain inflicted upon her body when it was caught in the "beauty system." She has related how she wanted to "Americanize" her features in her adolescent years through plastic surgery or by sleeping with clothespins on her nose.[7] This case reflects how the discourse of the melting pot has worked upon women in general, but for Tan it epitomizes what racial integration in the United States meant until very recently for many Asian American women. "There was shame and self-hate," Tan recalls of the price she paid for assimilation. "There is this myth that America is a melting pot, but what happens in assimilation is that we end up deliberately choosing the American things—hot dogs and apple pie—and ignoring the Chinese offerings."[8] In order to be assimilated, she must internalize the features circumscribed by the dominant "beauty system" and reinscribe them on her face. Assimilation thus not only operates at the symbolic level but cuts into the physical body and "melts" it on the standard(izing) model. To remember the mother's past is thus a task of rewriting her emotional and physical ties to what has been "eliminated" in the process of "assimilation." And the changing narrative of integration readily offers the historical context.

While the multicultural "salad bowl" may be subject to ideological cooption to serve the gluttony of transnational capitalism, the "salads" may well turn the "bowl" to some other use. One of the effects of the social change unleashed by multiculturalism is the way in which individual consciousness or identity is reconstituted. Sharing with her predecessors the "double-tongued" narrative, Tan goes beyond the early generations' struggle for individual identity. By structuring her text around the table, whose four sides signify what makes up the world, identity is shown as a matter of relationality. The "salad bowl" is as much a metaphor for the peaceful coexistence of different ingredients as for the relationality of the body, individual and national alike. It is the relationality figured in the "bowl" that "contains" the speaking subject in a posthumanist understanding of self, voice, and collectivity.

When the narrative subject is constituted in a reconfiguration of the "salad bowl" of American multiculturalism with the "double-tongued" discourse of Chinese tradition, the oral nature of such a cross-cultural fertilization generates some unexpected implications. The central theme of mother-daughter reconnection literalizes an ancient Chinese ritual of bodily exchange to stand the master metaphor of Chinese modernity on its head. This is the story of an uncanny return of the Chinese "cannibal."

The Recycling of Rou *and the Remembrance of Life*

I saw my mother on the other side of the room. Quiet and sad. She was cooking a soup, pouring herbs and medicines into the steaming pot. And then I saw her pull up her sleeves and pull out a sharp knife. She put this knife on the softest part of her arm. I tried to close my eyes, but could not.

And then my mother cut a piece of meat from her arm. Tears poured from her face and blood spilled to the floor.

My mother took her flesh and put it in the soup. She cooked magic in the ancient tradition to try to cure her mother this one last time. She opened Popo's mouth, already too tight from trying to keep her spirit in. She fed her this soup, but that night Popo flew away with her illness.

Even though I was young, I could see the pain of the flesh and the worth of the pain. (Tan 1989, 40–41)

This scene is from the short chapter entitled "Scar" in *The Joy Luck Club* and is highly dramatized in the namesake film. It vividly details the act of *geguliaoqin*, one of the five allusions in Lu Xun's "Diary of a Madman" to cannibalism in ancient China. But the ghost of history returns as an ethnographical imagination of self-love, not a metaphoric image of self-hatred. Previously I have put Tan's reenactment of this ancient ritual in juxtaposition with Lu Xun and some other Chinese writers mainly as an interpretative tactic. When it returns to the American end of our transcultural spectrum, we can no longer ignore the controversy surrounding this "sugar sister" herself. At the same time, Tan's ignorance of modern Chinese cultural politics paradoxically enables us to revaluate Chinese modernity as well.

As noted before, *gegu* originated from a legend of the Buddha sacrificing his flesh to save the hungry. It was domesticated into a practice of filial piety (*liaoqin*) when Buddhism was adopted in ancient China. That long process of cross-cultural transplantation shifted the noble sacrifice of the Buddha saving the masses to the folk-religious act of children redeeming parents. Underlying that domestication of a foreign legend was the inscription of medicinal meaning in human flesh. Although the practice was banned by the imperial court later because of the physical injury it entailed, its symbolic meaning continues to surface in a variety of forms in modern Chinese literature. In light of its postrevolutionary resurgence in Mo Yan's novel, Tan's use of *geguliaoqin* coincides with Mo Yan's playful parody of cannibalism in that both texts activate the rhetoric of *rou* (flesh/meat) for their distinct embodiment of social interconnectedness and reciprocity. But Mo Yan deploys the trope with self-conscious irony, whereas Tan exploits it as a piece of ethnographic information to flesh out her imaginary reconstruction of the mother's past. So Tan is first guilty—I take an exception to the rule of authenticity—for digging up, if not faking, an obsolete ritual without having the slightest idea of its significance in modern China.

The issue of authenticity or historical accuracy, however, is secondary in importance to her narrative mode. The way Sau-ling Wong (via Elliot Butler-Evans) differentiates the "interrogative modality" in Kingston's presentation from the "declarative modality" in Tan's provides a theoretical point of departure for analyzing this episode. With interrogative modality, *The Woman Warrior* "ceaselessly deconstructs its own narrative authority and overtly thematizes the epistemological difficulties of the

American-born Chinese." With declarative modality, "*The Joy Luck Club* is epistemologically unproblematized. . . . The mothers' narratives about their Chinese life are displayed as im-mediate [and] are valorized as correctives to the daughters' unenlightened or biased outlook" (1995, 195). In other words, Tan is also guilty of an unmediated presentation of old China. This prompts us to ask: how could the author simultaneously fantasize (the question of authenticity) *and* realistically present (declarative modality) her China?

To address this question we need to first distinguish the bodily zones and tropes in the two modalities. As I have shown in the chapter on Lu Xun, the modern discourse of cannibalism is established on a specular relationship between the viewing subject and the other. The same epistemic structure also applies to Kingston's "interrogative modality." The monkey brain feast points to the textual logic of "quasi-cannibalism," which puts the young Maxine in the same position Lu Xun occupied when he was a child reading and hearing all the grotesque tales. Their identification with the "devoured" also results in a remarkably similar break from the scene of cannibalism. Maxine had to find a place remote from home so that she could "sort out what's just [her] childhood, just [her] imagination, just [her] family, just the village, just movies, just living" (1975, 293). To sort things out means to put them in a simple order. That is precisely the reason why the young Maxine, who was fed up with the Rabelaisian list of animals and birds, yearned for "TV dinners with vegetables no more complex than peas mixed with diced carrots." Television ads are not food to eat but food images to see. Kingston is more fortunate than Lu Xun because she can leave home without crossing the national border and does not have to bear the burden of national salvation. But she has to sustain the same pain inflicted by quasi-cannibalism, and interrogative writing enables her to sort things out and heal the wounds. "Interrogative modality" thus implies epistemological distance and requires visualized (physical and mental alike) distancing. As such, let's call it the "interrogative modality of specularity."

In comparison, Tan's narrative mode in depicting the scene of *geguliaoqin* may be characterized as "declarative modality of orality." It can be further differentiated from Mo Yan's "ironic modality of orality." Because Tan does not live in the shadow of the "father," she is in no position to see, nor has the need to ironize, the master trope of modern China. Her China is a remote land of mothers and sisters, a distant entity of the past to be bridged by means of "double-tongued" discourse. Once we shift our reading from the visual distance to the oral proximity, how Tan came to know this ritual no longer matters. What is important is her literal use of a ritual she believes to be authentic and real. As we sort out these formal and structural ramifications, the remaining issue then is a matter of locating this episode in the intertextual and international context of this study. It is significant that Tan's narrative operates in the same rhetoric of *rou* found in Mo Yan's *Liquorland* and, in a more modified fashion, Li Ang's *The Butcher's Wife*. In this sense, we can further narrow it down to a "declarative modality of carnivorism" (note even the English terms *meat* and *flesh* in the scene become interchangeable). So I will focus on the orality of *rou* in my analysis.

It should be clear that we do not "see" the ghost of cannibalism in Tan's depiction of *geguliaoqin* because the ritual is enacted within the parameters of orality rather than visuality. Central to the story "Scar" is the image of soup—two soups both tied to *rou*. The story is told by An-mei Hsu, one of the four mothers in the club. She was three years old when her father died of an illness. A year later her widowed mother fell into concubinage to a merchant. The man had raped her, and his second wife spread the rumor that it was the widowed woman who had seduced her husband. This dealt a great blow to her family's honor. An-mei's grandmother and uncle threw her mother out without allowing her to take the two children. At her departure, An-mei recalls another soup:

> I could see my mother's face across the table. Between us stood the soup pot on its heavy chimney-pot stand—rocking slowly back and forth. And with one shout this dark boiling soup spilled forward and fell all over my neck. It was as though everyone's anger were pouring all over me.
>
> This was the kind of pain so terrible that a little child should never remember it. But it is still in my skin's memory. (38–39)

Now compare this soup with the one made for *geguliaoqin* (which appears later in the narrative) and the twin theme of pain and memory immediately comes to light. In this way, An-mei's story crystallizes the Chinese ecological attitude toward, and its cultural rhetoric about, the recycling of *rou* in the remembrance of life. This rhetorical feature is consistently inscribed through a number of variations on the body. After An-mei's mother was forced to leave alone, her Popo [grandmother] "would use her sharp fingernails like tweezers and peel off the dead membranes" (40). Not only would she try to peel off her memory of her daughter; Popo wanted her granddaughter to forget her mother, too. "In two years' time," An-mei recalls, "my scar became pale and shiny and I had no memory of my mother. That is the way it is with a wound. . . . And once it is closed, you no longer see what is underneath, what started the pain" (40). What she remembered was the stories her Popo told her.

Once Popo told the girl that she and her brother "had fallen out of the bowels of a stupid goose, two eggs that nobody wanted, not even good enough to crack over rice porridge." If Popo "said this so that the ghosts would not steal [them] away" (33), "Auntie had a tongue like hungry scissors eating silk cloth" (35). Five years later, when Popo grew sick, she "had swollen up like an overripe squash." Before her death, she told the granddaughter two more stories:

> One was about a greedy girl whose belly grew fatter and fatter. This girl poisoned herself after refusing to say whose child she carried. When the monks cut open her body, they found inside a large white winter melon.
>
> "If you are greedy, what is inside you is what makes you always hungry," said Popo.
>
> Another time, Popo told me about a girl who refused to listen to her elders. One day this bad girl shook her head so vigorously to refuse her auntie's simple request that a little white ball fell from her ear and out poured all her brains, as clear as chicken broth. (34)

When Popo was about to leave the world, her outcast daughter came back to bid her a last farewell. An-mei remembered nothing of her mother. But when she met her, An-mei describes it, "I saw my own face looking back at me." "I saw that she had a long white neck, just like the goose that had laid me." The mother asked: "An-mei, you have been a good daughter?" An-mei felt she "was the girl whose belly held a colorless winter melon" (37). Although these alimentary metaphors are not necessarily authentic in Chinese, they are consistent with the spirit of "double-tongued" storytelling.

Popo passes away before her daughter can feed her the soup that contains her flesh and blood. But the narrative continues to play out the theme of the oral-carnal bond between An-mei's mother and herself. The mother took her to Tientsin, where she would kill herself by swallowing poison, as Popo's story had predicted. She killed herself not because she was afraid to tell the name of the "winter melon's" father. She did it as a last resort to get even with the man who had ruined her life: "Three days before the lunar new year, she had eaten *ywansyau*, the sticky sweet dumpling that everybody eats to celebrate. And I remember her strange remark. 'You see how this life is. You cannot eat enough of this bitterness.' And what she had done was eat *ywansyau* filled with a kind of bitter poison" (271). Her mother finally ate enough bitterness and turned the New Year into a curse. As a vengeful ghost, she would be able to watch over the man to secure a safe future for her daughter. Her life ended in bitterness, but bitterness that was encoded in a food symbol that, with its roundness and sweetness, usually stands for the renewal of life.

If we read these alimentary images from the angle of cannibalism—as Lu Xun did in the story "Medicine," the entire narrative of "Scar" is strung with tropes of "self-eating" or autophagy. These food signs are not just used to represent human misery; they are part and parcel of the discourse of revenge. In fact, all three of the stories Popo told Anmei have the vengeful effect of warning: if the little girl fails to follow the rules, she will fall from human grace and turn into an egg. To make things even worse, she will become a "bad egg," not fit for human consumption. Popo's intent is even clearer in the other two stories. The worst "sin" a woman could commit in the traditional society was to have a child out of wedlock yet refuse to show remorse by revealing the father's name. For this, Kingston's "No-Name" aunt had to jump into the village well, taking revenge by "polluting" the source of life. Tan's depiction resonates with Kingston's but strikes the theme of human eating in an even more literal fashion. The woman's belly must be cut open to show what is inside: "a large white winter melon." This winter melon, moreover, is as much a food to be eaten as a source of hunger or greed. The violence of the everyday is graphically manifested in the violence of language, in auntie's "tongue like hungry scissors eating silk cloth." If the little girl were to protest against such violence, her brains would pour out "as clear as chicken broth." Even Popo herself, the "cannibal," has "swollen up like an overripe squash." The whole world, the whole life cycle, looks like an endless web of autophagy.

How can one reconcile this picture of self-eating with the tear-jerking scene of the woman offering her flesh and blood, which is not described with any sense of irony? If the repressive world in Tan's text is not fundamentally different from the one in Lu Xun's, there is a clear distinction in the ways these two authors "see" and "report." This difference is determined by their differing subject positions. Because the imagery of cannibalism in Tan's text is contained within the "double-tongued" discourse, the reading subject has to negotiate her position, her survival, from inside the "minor" world of orality rather than attempting, as Lu Xun does, to transcend it into the totality of history and the comforts of evolutionism.

It is the two soups, one severing the mother from her daughter and the other reconnecting the mother with the grandmother, that contain and blend the pain and its memory in an ambivalent narrative of recycling and remembrance. Without this second soup, which signifies bonding, the first soup that left the scar on the child would simply be wasted. Melting her flesh in soup for her mother, who once peeled her off like a disgraceful membrane from her own body, is the only way the outcast woman can redeem her honor. She shows no grudge, no shame, no repentance, even "the pain of the flesh is nothing."

An-mei's mother is no revolutionary woman, certainly. Tan's parents, like many Chinese immigrants of their generation, were refugees of the wars and revolutions. American-born writers of Chinese ancestry were often confused about the chaos and misery in modern China, and their confusion was further compounded by the reality and the propaganda of the Cold War. As a result, the mother in precommunist China had no other choice but to endure the suffering by swallowing bitterness, or to protest by swallowing poison. While I am fascinated with Chinese American women writers' interest in writing about food and eating, the sharp contrast with modern Chinese women writers' lack of such interest points to a central question about women's liberation. Revolutionary women writers such as Ding Ling clearly had more symbolic capital on which to draw. Yet once the symbolic resources were emptied out as the ideology of revolution came to feed on itself they had little left to enable them to reconstitute their relationship with materiality. So it is no surprise that the postrevolutionary woman writer Wang Anyi looks into the domestic space of a nonrevolutionary woman in her reconstruction of material history.

Moreover, cross-cultural gender comparison needs to take account of class differences as well. I have already pointed out that the "new women" writers of the May Fourth generation were among the privileged few to receive a modern education. Domestic labor was not part of their daily lives. The negative attitude toward cooking is reflected also in the middle-aged women writers active in the 1980s. A distinction can also be made along this line in comparing quasi-cannibalism in Chinese American literature with Lu Xun's treatment of the old cannibalistic feast. In Chinese American women's writings, the theme of quasi-cannibalism is intimately tied to a concrete *oral* experience with *food* (in the literal sense of these words) and thus immanently grounded in the carnal body. Whereas Lu Xun and his generation of Chinese intellectuals did not have to bother to cook, much less write, about actual cooking and eating, American women writers of Chinese descent grew up in kitchens and at dining tables listening to their parents', mostly their mothers', "talk-stories" about China. The effect of quasi-cannibalism is part of the cultural menu the children digest, a process of acculturation inseparable from their experience with the overall foodways and food lore of their parents. It is from this oral, often "feminized," memory that quasi-cannibalism derives its specific cultural meaning.

The relationship of the writer with food in the everyday thus has much to do with the subject position of the narrator in the narrated field of eating. In the story "Scar," the narrative is anchored on the granddaughter's point of view; she would otherwise be an outsider watching a spectacle of cannibalism. But she was *in* it: her "other" was her mother and her mother's mother. Not only did she see her own face reflected back from the mother's, but underneath the surface of the scar she felt the pain of the soup that at once severs and ties the female bodies. The soup that once severed her from her mother now flows into the soup her mother feeds her grandmother. Echoing the authorial dedication of the novel to her remembrance is An-mei's voice: "You must peel off your skin, and that of your mother, and her mother before her. Until there is nothing. No scar, no skin, no flesh" (41). In this way, the narrative voice is intimately assimilated into the metaphor of the soup, and her position becomes as fluid as the soup. The first soup, which severs the daughter from the mother, smooths the images of cannibalism. The second soup, which reconnects the mother with the grandmother, saturates the narrative of bonding and sutures the scar. Unlike Lu Xun's Madman, An-mei is so "soaked" in the sticky language of soup that there is no way for her to exit the spectacle. Through this shift of perspective, even the "cannibal" herself, the grandmother, is seen as a victim. The recognition that it is one's fate to be caught in endless misery is incorporated into an unquenchable desire for love and life. In the narrative ambivalence and reconcilliation over the two soups, a long-established mode of representing cannibalism is decentered. It collapses the very spectacle of revenge that can only perpetuate hatred. Between Tan and Lu Xun, the difference is between oral reciprocity and specular opposition, the former operating on the principle of mutability and relationality whereas the latter seeks authority and totality.

Popo's stories, the mother's ritual performance, and An-mei's remembrance of them can all be traced back to an old Chinese interpretation of the world as a dangerous monster that devours the bodies of *rou*. The truth of the myth is the truth of human existence: it is the fate of the individual body to decay in the natural cycle of things. Yet life in its collective recycling and remembrance must go on forever. This reveals a philosophical paradox with regard to eating and being eaten, death and memory, fate and faith—all graphically presented in the paradox of the scar and the soup, pain and remembrance. The continuation of life is not to repeat the cycle of hatred but to rely upon a fundamental decency and sympathy ingrained in the warmth of orality. What all these boil down to is an *attitude* toward life, an attitude that has faith in life but does not rationalize it in absolute terms. This paradoxical attitude recognizes the complexity and ambiguity of the human condition and in this way allows room for healing and bonding. This is precisely what An-mei, herself a mother now, tells her American-born daughter.

Conclusion

Several years ago, when this work was in the initial stage of conception, I was quite naive. I thought that because "eating" in modern Chinese literature appeared to be a simple yet unexplored topic I might work out an original thesis to finish up my graduate work. The idea may sound a bit too pragmatic, if not cynical, but behind it lay my intellectual confusion about what I perceived to be an increasing gap between humanistic scholarship and the real world. My confusion could be attributed in part to the theory boom in the field of comparative literature. The big-time comparatists and theorists then included de Man, Jameson, Said, and Spivak, among others, not to mention their predecessors and contemporaries in continental Europe. More trouble came from the fact that I came from the "other shore." Humble as my personal journey was, it had a local history that went through "deconstruction" three times over before the term became popular jargon here.

There was the continuous impact of violent hatred toward, and cultural rupture with, a three-thousand-year "dinosaur"—the weighty legacy of Chinese history as viewed by my generation of mainland Chinese. The sense of historical displacement was doubled when the utopian experiments of Maoism dramatically collapsed, followed by an intense disillusionment. The post-Mao reform and opening up to the outside world ushered in all kinds of mutually discordant Western ideas from Enlightenment humanism to Nietzsche to high modernism. Contradictory as these bodies of thought may be in the Western context, they were received in good faith in China as a coherent system that reaffirms humanist values. This meaningful cultural misreading enabled many of my generation to recuperate from post–Cultural Revolution disillusionment and reestablish confidence in the "spirit of man." Yet my "reeducation" in American graduate school has been almost a "deeducation" in the sense that the truth and values I embraced in the post-Mao years have been radically destabilized. The personal is thus a fragmented history of ideological learning, unlearning, relearning, and delearning. And if one visits post-Deng China one will surely understand what time-space compression really means: what took two hundred years to evolve in the West has been compressed in China in bits and pieces in just two decades. This local history is prefixed with a series of "posts" that seems endless in the postponement of telos.

It is against this background that I found in "eating" something I could reaffirm, a solid ground on which to start over, a path that is as futuristic and open-ended as hunger, as diverse and ambiguous as taste, and as rich and colorful as the mystery of life. But this idealistic yearning, preconceived in a dream of returning to coherence and simplicity, points to the very paradox of alimentary *writing*. Whenever food is depicted in words, it already has lost its (presumed) simplicity and entered the web of competing tastes (even the cooking section of local papers suggests that). The more we strive to uncover some uncontaminated site of the body, the more mediated and fragmented the forms of embodiment become. This dialectic interplay between materiality and discourse stages disturbing dramas of social dismemberment, especially when it is acted out around hunger and cannibalism, twice removed from the utopian state of fulfillment in peace and harmony. In our alienation from nature (if nature ever existed outside of culture), words of food are food for thought. There is just no escape from theoretical discourse and fragmentation.

The alimentary saga of modern China highlights a historical experience that has more than its share of fragmentation and alienation. Deposited in the oral space are traces of ecological disaster, political catastrophe, social disintegration, and cultural displacement. Some of the works contain a certain documentary value for historians and social scientists, especially those written in response to real problems of hunger and famine. Much of the revolutionary literature falls into that category. But it cannot be overstated that literary writing generates meanings far richer than reflected realities. The more distanced the text is from the effects of reality and ideological dogma, the more complex and ambiguous alimentary signs become. Even though this book stresses the politics of eating, we cannot afford to give up the aesthetic value of literary imagination.

In the more realistic genre of hunger writing, it is the artistic imagination of fulfillment in words-as-food that sharpens our appetite for more reading and imagination. It captures a saga of desire articulated in voices of decency and compassion. Shen Congwen's hungry nostalgia for the native soil not only nurtures a sense of sanity in a time of madness but provides an intimate explanation for his "modest proposal" because it is based on a stomach-centered social body as opposed to the valorized head of the nation. Xiao Hong's art of hunger becomes all the more fascinating when we consider her poetic reconfiguration of aesthetic and ethic values on the empty belly. Within the revolutionary narrative of hunger, the peasant story of Mao's braised pork puts revolution on holiday; in Zhang Xianliang's "Mimosa," the bibliophagy of Marx delivers a feast of words, standing asceto-Marxism on its head. And Ah Cheng's appeal to zero-degree eating and chess playing paradoxically crystallizes the true essence of Dao. Words of hunger are inseparable from real experience, for sure, but they feed off a void to open other possibilities for critical inquiry and artistic expression.

It is no surprise that the more surrealist genre of cannibalism has carved out a more fertile ground for imagination, regardless of whether the writer treats it as fact or fiction and what moral judgment is passed to the subject. Except for Mo Yan, however, the fantastic nature of writing cannibalism is tied to the search for absolute truth outside textuality. Lu Xun's childhood fascination with ancient writings of the fantastic and the grotesque, especially the frightening yet alluring human-eating image of the unknown world, is a major force behind his visual enactment of the devoured body. This imaginary force becomes all the more powerful in driving Zheng Yi's journey in a direction opposite that of his proclaimed search for historical truth. In both writers, the utmost horizon of imagination marks the very limit of knowledge, both condensed in a synecdoche for what lies between the human world and its beyond. Only through the differentiating system of colonial modernity is a social-evolutionist *episteme* established that legitimates its ideological authority on the back of the cannibalistic other. The ambivalence inherent in the mutual encoding of ancient mythos and modern ethos cannot but give rise to a racking sense of madness. Intellectual trauma thus is contained by the very articulation of madness. In the end, it is the author's imagined totality that captures the fantastic nature of writing cannibalism.

That is why the modern myth of cannibalism can be dispelled by a simple flip of the coin. In the feast of words, is it really crazy to just add a piece of flesh? In our modern world, in which flesh-eating has become economically unnecessary and culturally tabooed, unbridled power and gluttonous capital continue to cannibalize the powerless. Let's just unleash the monster of cannibalism and lay bare the essence of truth. The lingering flavor of Mo Yan's devilish pastiche compels us to digest such unthinkable yet imaginable food for thought. A well-wrought piece of words is like a well-cooked meal. It does not have to be a delicacy suitable only for the finicky palate. To assimilate the meaning of hunger and cannibalism in particular requires a rugged stomach and a bold gallbladder.

Unlike hunger and cannibalism, the politics of orality is not treated just as a theme in this study. For one thing, alimentary discourse always operates in a mode of double orality, which is cross-cultural and transhistorical. What is distinctly Chinese is a self-conscious configuration of food and words, body and embodiment, crystallized in the single verb *chi*—a "mouth [that] begs [food and words]." The tradition of blending five flavors for harmony, dating to the legend of the master chef-orator Yi Yin, plays out a variety of "double-tongued" narratives. In male Chinese writers, alimentary imagination signifies the desire to bond with the "motherly" and reveals an economy of the libido apart from the Freudian thesis. Conversely, the absence of such "motherly" references in the work of modern Chinese woman writers indicates the centrality of their own bodies in articulating selfhood and reconstructing the alterity of culture and history. But in this gender dichotomy Chinese American woman writers do not fit—to them the meaning of the "motherly," inscribed in food and speech alike, is revised and reinvested in their cross-cultural experience. Gender and cultural dissimilarities are further complicated by generic attributes and thematic concerns. If the madness of hunger and cannibalism signifies a more individuated state of disconnection and isolation, double orality is underscored by the desire for commensality and communication. Eating and speaking (the baby's crying included) are what ritualize the activities of life from birth to death. In this broad sense, food and words are the most basic materials that enact the drama of life, and the politics of orality stands for the politics of survival.

This book is heavily tilted toward the writing of desire under colonial modernity and asceto-Marxism. In this process, the notion of desire has received little critical scrutiny. This theoretical bias, though basically determined by texts and their historical contexts, must be historicized as well. If the historical memory of twentieth-century China is fraught with images of "lack," the last decade of the century is likely to be remembered for its explosive leap toward "excess." The haunting prospect of China surpassing the United States to become the world's largest consumer society has prompted Lester Brown's "wake-up call" on the question of "who will feed China?" The shock waves Brown sent across the world have generated such panicky responses as the *Washington Post* headline "How China Could Starve the World." To shift the metaphor from starvation to cannibalism, one might well ask how China could "eat up" the world. The fear of a "Chinese environmental threat" cannot but play into the rising nationalism of China and the geopolitics of the post–Cold War era. To many Chinese, the United States is in no position to point its finger because its energy consumption and pollution in per capita terms surpass those of China by as much as eight to ten times.[1] This global politics is a topic beyond any systematic treatment here. But it is against the broad backdrop of our collective survival that I conclude this book with some notes on overconsumption and indigestion.

Strictly speaking, China did not set out on the long march to a modern consumer society until the late 1970s, and the emphasis on consumption came even later. Only with the rise of consumerism has the critique of consumption switched from hunger to gluttony, epitomized by Mo Yan's *Liquorland.* The almost overnight arrival of a mass consumer culture in a still poor country has created a number of time-space compressions, which neither fit any existing model of socioeconomic development nor cohere with any established conceptual framework. Within China's national borders, booming coastal regions are undergoing a face-lift of postmodern extravagance while the vast interior countryside is still struggling to meet the basic needs of the people. The same generation that suffered malnutrition in the early 1960s is now at its peak as consumers. Jianying Zha's depiction allows us to get a glimpse of this compressed cultural landscape:

> "[T]he Whopper effect:" there is an impure, junky, hybrid quality in nearly all spheres of the present Chinese life. . . . This is not romantic, not a picturesque scene for the camera. It's too blurry, too slippery, often shamelessly vulgar. Who can blame the CBS, ABC, and NBC anchors for not having rushed back since Tiananmen? To some, it might be akin to filming a merry, grotesque banquet on the ruins of a slaughterhouse. (1995, 11)

Among the many blurry, hybrid scenes depicted by Zha is a big art exhibit that was held in the spring of 1993 at the McDonald's in downtown Beijing—the first branch of the multinational giant to have a Communist Party chief on its staff. Some of the participants were former artists on the cutting edge before they "jumped into the sea" for a quick buck. One greeting card in the exhibit, Zha reports, "showed a bizarre creature—with the body of a dragon, the head of Donald Duck, a foot in a Nike sneaker, and claws clutching a stack of dollar bills." Her observation is playfully illuminating: "what other place could better highlight the idea of 'art as fast food, ready to serve the people'? Push things to an extreme, and, with a bit of luck, you may end up at the cutting-edge all over again" (1995, 111–12).

Zha's observation is limited, as her book is, to the postrevolutionary cultural collage of the urban centers. But it does capture the tip of a totality rapidly melting down to fragmentary decomposition and hybrid recomposition. If international capital cannot destroy the "superstructure" of China as it toppled the Soviet Union, it has done an even better job in subverting it from the belly up. If absolute power corrupts absolutely, nothing could be more powerful than the mighty greenback in seducing and taming the ferocious dragon. No where can the much acclaimed idea of hybridity be better realized than through the "art as fast food," served to "red China" along with imported red meat (beef is not a common item in China except in the far northern and western minority regions). One might want to celebrate this peaceful transformation from the "slaughterhouse" to the "merry, grotesque banquet," and I hesitate to make a judgment that this process of depoliticization is merely a symptom of postmodern schizophrenia given that the political system responsible for the "slaughterhouse" is still in place. But we must also pause to question whether the vast majority of the population will withstand the rapid changes, just as Brown questions whether China's food carrying capacity can sustain its climb to the full-fledged order of *carnivora*. In spite of the alluring creation of "art as fast food," the majority of the Chinese population (mostly the Hans) may have trouble developing the new dietary habits and digestive capacities, especially lactose tolerance, that will enable them to swallow double cheeseburgers and Whoppers.

Because the cultural appetite of contemporary China is being increasingly shaped by the desire to catch up with the level of consumption of late capitalist societies, the alimentary discourse is saturated with a number of competing narratives either celebratory or critical of that cultural fantasy. As Jameson (1983; 1984a) has pointed out, erasure of historical trace and memory is a key component in the cultural logic of the postmodern consumer society. In contemporary China, some of the young artists on the "cutting edge" may be driven by the desire to leap ahead of the rest of society to "get rich first" (which is deemed "glorious" in the Dengist era), but other writers keep reminding society of the danger of forgetting the past. Now that the "Whopper effect" has become symbolic of the "grotesque banquet" taking over the "slaughterhouse," the memory of socialist scarcity and simplicity is becoming endowed with a new layer of critical meaning.

Lu Wenfu, the author of "The Gourmet," adds some satirical spice to the grotesque banquet of social gluttony. He characterizes the new fashion of wasteful banqueting as *chikongqi*: "eating empty air." In the newly constructed fancy restaurants that have flourished with rising affluence and official corruption since the 1980s, the diners now have to pay many times more for extravagant furnishings and glamorous decor than they pay for food. To make the dining experience even more superficial, many dishes are designed to stimulate visual illusion rather than satisfy oral voracity. The system that ranks chefs is based on whether or not they have won awards at international culinary contests and festivals, where judges evaluate primarily the dish's "visual beauty." Chinese cuisine has thus assumed another function to please the exotica-hungry gaze of some Westerners while the real China is becoming too blurry to attract the camera. As in other areas, turning global here means transforming Chinese food into a spectacle, one that creates new fashions for domestic consumption as well. One well-known chef, for example, spent three hours creating one piece of "visual pleasure" by carving a pumpkin in the shape of a phoenix so that the nouveau riche could show off their fat pockets and "cosmopolitan" tastes. What Lu laments, however, is not the kind of asceto-Marxist practice he criticized earlier in "The Gourmet." Rather, he fears that the immanence of simple dining and the intimacy of "sharing a table" will disappear from the cultural landscape. Symptomatic of a decadent consumer desire, "eating empty air" epitomizes, as he puts it, "the alienation of eating itself" (1994, 349).

The rush to consume perceived foreign fads without the capacity to digest them, known in Chinese as *shiyang buhua*, may cause real digestive troubles, personal and political. Wang Meng's 1989 short story, "Jianying de xizhou" (Crusted congee), is a little parable that gave rise to a political tempest in a teapot. Blending witty parody of propagandist pomposity with calculated street vulgarity, "Crusted Congee" dramatizes the historical clash of values around a family's dietary reform. For forty years, an extended family, now numbering fourteen members, has lived together in peace, content with the simple menu that always includes plain congee for the breakfast. A sudden urge to reform the diet erupts one day when the benign patriarch encourages the younger members to recommend changes. His great-grandson, a high school student, takes the lead to attack their miserable lack of animal protein. In his eloquent speech on modernization, he contends that the age-old congee has produced the *petit physique* of the Chinese race, which in turn embodies the backwardness of the Chinese political and economic system. In the end, he concludes that a diet mainly composed of congee and pickled vegetable was "the root for the super-stability of our feudal system, for our underdevelopment and lack of historical progress. Unless we eliminate congee and pickled vegetable there will be no hope for China" (Wang Meng 1993, 101).

After the family decides to let the teenager undertake the dietary reform, he introduces a brand new menu to modernize the breakfast: buttered toast, fried eggs, milk, and coffee. In order to enlist the elders' support, he sinicized the Western menu by adding spices to reduce the alien odor of milk. But in just three days he has strained the family's monthly budget for food. Even more disastrous is the physical resistance to such an abrupt reform: the whole family except the boy reacts to the reformed breakfast with severe constipation and diarrhea. Some members are hospitalized while others have to ease the hardened lumps of undigested food out of the grandfather's anus. The failure of his dietary experiment leads to the family's decision to split up into their constituent nuclear units, each cooking its own meals. This modern arrangement cannot last long, either, because all the nuclear units still have to share the same kitchen and line up for the stove. Because of this inefficient arrangement, the rationed cooking gas runs out well ahead of schedule. Later, with more housing becoming available and the younger units able to move out, they finally settle for a balanced diet. Now that income has gone up and meat and eggs are no longer a luxury, they keep the rice congee, curiously because it always induces feelings of simplicity, warmth, grace, and nostalgia. Most of all, congee is easy to digest, providing the best protection against stomach cancer. In the end, as the narrator reflects upon that chaotic period, "ideas come and go; only food habits stay." In light of the larger cultural milieu in the late 1980s, when the story was written, the narrator's comment highlights the tale's rather Daoist theme: "theoretical concepts and methods may constantly change, but the order [of things] is constant" (1993, 114).

It is interesting to note that Wang Meng once called Ah Cheng's "The Chess King" a strange tale incompatible with the spirit of the age. The reception of "Crusted Congee" was even stranger, however, reflecting a phantasmagoric cultural politics of consumption at the time. Published just a few months before the massacre of 1989, the story drew little attention until it won two national prizes in the early 1990s. But it was also grossly misinterpreted by some hard-liners as a parabolic attack at the gerontocracy because the term *jianyingde* in the story's title could mean "ossified" as well as "crusted." After a major mouthpiece of the Party's propaganda machine launched an attack, Wang Meng, a former minister of culture who had been sidelined after June Fourth but still held the nominal title of a formal member in the Central Committee of the CCP, filed a civil lawsuit against his slanderers. Being a longtime political insider, he should have known that the legal action would lead nowhere, and it was in fact dismissed later by the court. But the fact that a senior Party official had taken a Party organ to court was an unprecedented event, even though the political show itself ended up much like a farce. What is buried in this political farce is the story's "hidden message." It is as much a satirical exposé of the ossified political system as a lament for the vanishing of a time-tested culinary culture together with a domestic economy of survival.

If "Crusted Congee" highlights the cultural value of thrift and simplicity developed throughout China's long past in response to limited resources, the cultural construction of desire is no longer governed by the principle of necessity when globalization of mass consumerism takes over to manufacture desire for nothing but profit. The sweeping change from the old economy of hunger to the new "grotesque banquet" of gluttony has been completed in less than two decades. Alimentary writing once again has detected the symptoms of the changing cultural appetite. Faced with the overwhelming force of mass consumerism, however, the words of serious writers can only dish out a pitiful dose of protest, lost in the clamor of feasting in the new karaoke bars.

The Rabelaisian list of food in Kingston's *The Woman Warrior* is as indicative of our dietary capacity as it is frightening to the finicky palate. What Brave Orchid, the mother, cooks for her American-born children includes "raccoons, skunks, hawks, city pigeons, wild ducks, wild geese, black-skinned bantams, snakes, garden snails, turtles that crawled about the pantry floor and escaped under refrigerator or stove, catfish that swam in the bathtub" (1975, 106). This list points to a horrifying scenario in which poverty and environmental destruction are caught in a vicious cycle of mutual perpetuation. Brave Orchid is compelled to adhere to the principle of Necessity because overpopulation, along with other human-induced catastrophes in modern China, has made such a rugged stomach a necessity for survival. Placed side by side, Wang Meng's parable of indigestion and Brave Orchid's list of devoured animals seem to wrap up a tragicomedy of the stomach: it is vulnerable even to a cup of milk when good times have finally arrived, yet it marks the ferocious capacity of human omnivorousness in the drama of climbing the food chain.

On a more optimistic note, the Rabelaisian list may add a less correct twist by opening our eyes to the ever-receding horizon of what is edible. Not long ago, many Americans had trouble digesting tofu, a very rich source of protein far more economically efficient and environmentally sound than meat and dairy products. Yet, is not tofu becoming a "politically correct" food for more and more Americans? As to China, Brown's wake-up call may be a bit far-fetched. The latest trend for well-to-do Chinese is actually moving away from the consumption of red meat. Of the few with fat pockets, some bold souls are trying the new fashion of eating exotic bugs and worms. For the vast majority, grain and vegetables remain the staple.

Notes

Introduction

1. I have in mind Zhang Ailing (a.k.a. Eileen Chang) and Nie Hualing (Hualing Nieh). Zhang's 1954 novel *Yangge* depicts the famished experience of peasants during the early years of the People's Republic and is considered by Hu Shih to be "a book that can be entitled 'hunger' " (see Wang Dewei 1997, 30). Nie's 1977 novel *Sangqing yu Taohong* contains many episodes of hunger suffered by the main character in China, Taiwan, and the United States over three decades. But the most intriguing aspect is her treatment of the 1846 Donner Lake incident of cannibalism during the American Gold Rush. The thematic configuration of cannibalism and madness (played out around the "divided personality" of Sangqing and Taohong, who are the same person) breaks away from the Lu Xun model of national allegory and ties her tragic experience to the madness of international politics and U.S. immigration policies.

2. Lester Brown's recent publications in this area provide some food for thought, and the controversy over "Chinese environmental threat," stirred up around his "wake-up call" over "who will feed China," will be briefly dealt with in the conclusion. See D. Goodman and M. Redcliff, *Refashioning Nature: Food, Ecology and Culture* (1991), for a well-researched work that combines political economics, cultural critique, and environmental studies.

3. The relationship between Marxism and environmentalism is a complex one. On the one hand, some environmentalist scholars, especially those affiliated with deep ecology, attribute the environmental crisis in existing socialist economies to the productivist model of Marxism itself, which they deem part of the legacy of modern instrumental rationalism. This view is represented by some of the authors in George Session's edited volume *Deep Ecology for the 21st Century* (1995). On the other hand, Marxist-inspired environmentalists insist on the critique of capitalism as an integral program of environmental thought and action (see, e.g., Gare 1995).

4. The term was coined by Fiona Burns. For a brief discussion, see Ryan 1989, chap. 4.

5. A similar use of the wooden fish can be found in the film *The Yellow Earth* (1984), directed by Chen Kaige, in which a wedding banquet is served.

6. "Laoxue'an biji," in Zhou Zuoren 1983, 360–66. For Zhou's poetics of gourmandism, see Qian Liqun 1990, 82–85.

7. Many of his sources on China, however, would not be considered authentic by contemporary standards (see nn. 27–34 on p. 196, some of which are based on secondhand or even thirdhand reports of hearsay published in nineteenth-century European texts); the same might be true of his sources on European cannibalism.

Chapter 1. Discoursing Food: Some Notes toward a Semiotic of Eating in Ancient China

1. By *agri/culture,* I mean the interrelation between *agriculture,* understood as human activities involved in food production, distribution, preparation, and consumption, and *culture,* understood as the discursive and symbolic system that reflects and defines beliefs and values developed from agricultural activities. It needs to be emphasized that *culture* does not mean mere "reflection" of the "base," as defined in classical Marxism, nor has it absolute autonomy above the "base." Rather, it is a dynamic system of symbolic response to material conditions in which meaning not only is produced according to these conditions but also actively shapes the perception and conception of them.

2. In *Zhoushu,* it is said that "the Yellow Emperor initiated the roasting of meat on the fire" (Gao 1983, 12). Since there are few sources available today about the relationship of the Yellow Emperor with agriculture, food production, and preparation, I will focus on the Red Emperor in the following discussion. As for the translation of Yandi as "Red Emperor," I borrow *red* from Sarah Allan's rendering of the Red Lord while maintaining the conventional title *emperor* to emphasize his position in the mythological-imperial genealogy. Shen Nong is translated as the "Noble Farmer" largely according to its ideological function in the popular version of the myth rather than the imperial genealogy, where even he did not belong before he was mixed up with Yandi.

3. The Red Emperor initially only occupied the marginal seat of the god of the south while the Yellow Emperor was the god of the center. In the mythological-imperial genealogy, such as that of "Wudi benji" in Sima Qian's *Shiji,* the Red Emperor is not included as one of the major ancestral gods. It is in *Shiben,* a text dated to the years around 200 B.C.E., that Yandi and Shen Nong become identical (Yuan 1979, 86). The source and reason for this have never been given, probably due to a lack of documentation resulting from the burning of books under the First Qin Emperor. Its implication, however, is more than trivial, be-

cause the coming-into-one of the sun/time and agri/culture opened up a much more powerful symbolic space that would eventually place the Red Emperor before the Yellow Emperor as the two ancestral gods in the popular version of the Chinese mythological pantheon as well as in modern nationalist discourse, which is epitomized by the appellation *yanhuang zisun* (sons and grandsons of the Red and the Yellow Emperors) for the "Chinese race."

4. There are three versions about how Shen Nong came to introduce the five grains. In *Zhoushu*, as quoted in *Yishi*, "Shen Nong saw grain [seeds] fall from heaven, so he planted and grew these seeds in the field. He cultivated the land with various farming tools he made himself. Hence large yield of the five grains and abundance of fruits" (Yuan 1979, 79; 1960, 74, n. 8). This could be called Heaven-blessing myth. The second version is recorded in *Baihutong*: "In ancient times people ate only meat of wild birds and animals. But this source of food supply had been exhausted by the time of Shen Nong due to the growth of the population. Shen Nong thus introduced the magic of farming to the populace. That is why he is called the Noble Farmer" (Yuan 1979, 74, n. 5). This could simply be called magic theory. The third version is recorded in a local gazette, quoting a lost source about Shen Nong's discovery of grain seeds. This should be termed the discovery theory. Tao Yang and Zhong Xiu, in their *The Creation Myth of China* (1989), contest the above three versions and argue that the discovery theory appears reasonable because it agrees with both the myth of the discovery of herbal medicine and the actual evolution of agriculture (287–88).

5. Among various legends and folktales about the Red Emperor/Noble Farmer, his image as the god of medicine is the most popular. For instance, one of the classical texts of Chinese medicine, *Shennong bencao jing*, is named for him. In *Huainanzi*, it is said that in his trial tasting of herbs he was "poisoned seventy times in a single day" (Yuan 1960, 74, n. 11; 1979, 80). Another folktale goes even farther, claiming that he made a martyr of himself by tasting an extremely poisonous herb (1960, 71). What is interesting here is not so much the "truth" of these stories as his dual popularity as a god and a martyr. As for the relationship between food and medicine, it is impossible to separate one from the other in the sign system (e.g., *chiyao*: medicine is "eaten" instead of "taken"). Whether food is medicine or medicine is related to general bodily balance affected by food intake is not important here. It is more important to note that the "origin" of grain-food and medicine were attributed to one single cultural icon in his act of eating.

6. In *Qianfulun*, for example, it is said that "Shen Nong set the time for the market by noon so that timely trading was conducted and goods exchanged to the benefit of all" (Yuan 1960, 75, n. 14).

7. I follow the sinological convention in the documentation of sources from

classical works such as *The Analects*. References are to, and in the order of, book, chapter or section, and sentence (or whatever form is used in the cited text) separated by periods.

8. Lin's point is even more interesting when we note that he has been accused by contemporary leftist writers and the Communists of being elitist and callous about the sufferings of the common people. Lin treats food as an absolute value, however, in a way that echoes the literati-gourmet theme in ancient China—the Song poet Su Shi being his model (see Lin 1935, 335–44). I quote Lin's remark here to show how food is treated as an absolute value in China even though different people approach it from their different socioeconomic experiences.

9. My awkward translation is only meant to highlight the etymological and cultural difference found in the notion of governance. "Shepherd" certainly would be a better translation of *mu*.

10. Rickett (1985) renders *mumin* as "shepherd(ing) (the) people." Again, my awkward alteration is merely meant to highlight the etymology of the word and the subsequent symbolic and semiotic significance in analyzing Chinese political discourse according to the metaphor *mu*.

11. There seem to be two interrelated but somewhat different versions of Yi Yin's ascent to power in classical sources, depending on what central argument is made. One version, found in *Hanfeizi* and *Huainanzi*, emphasizes Yi Yin as a committed and persistent *shuike*, the shuttling persuader-mediator between states. The other leans more toward the king's efforts in seeking advice from the virtuous man in spite of his inferior social status, centering on a Chinese brand of meritocracy. This is represented by *Taiping yulan*, which I will discuss in some detail later in this section (see Yuan 1979, 391–95; also see "Yinbenji" in *Shiji*, which briefly mentions the two versions with some alterations).

12. Knechtges renders *benwei* as "perfect flavors" (1986, 53). My translation indicates my emphasis on the discursive function of the trope that mediates between the act of tasting and knowing, cooking and governing, and the "essence" of the physical and the political.

13. For a more detailed description of this "personnel roaster," see Knechtges 1986 (49–50), where he points out that "[a]lthough the kitchen bureaucracy . . . probably never existed, the fact that a classical ritual text establishes it as an ideal demonstrates the importance ancient Chinese ritualists attached to culinary functions."

14. The two sources are referenced to *Gushikao*, a lost text attributed to Qiao Zhou of the Three Kingdom period, and *Lieshizhuan*, also lost but attributed to Liu Xiang of the Former Han. Both are collected in Yuan 1979 (438–39). In the latter text, the story even sounds like a fairy tale: "A week after Bo Yi and Shu Qi stopped eating ferns, Heaven sent a doe to provide them with milk. The two

thought that the doe would certainly become delicious meat for them. But the doe sensed their intention, never came back, and the two brothers died of hunger."

15. Mao Zedong once described Bo Yi as "a man with quite a few 'democratic individualist' ideas" (1961, 4: 1499; 1975, 437). In Mao's vocabulary, "democratic individualist" is a coded reference to the political "middle roader," who stands between the imperialist and the counterrevolutionary on the right and the Marxist revolutionary on the left. Mahatma Gandhi would fall into this category. The "nonviolent" theme of the historical myth did not survive, it appears, partly because the authenticity of the poem in which it is expressed was discredited by Confucius and Sima Qian.

16. We have no way of knowing whether this particular song is authentic or not. All that seems clear and relevant here is that some early version(s) of the myth might cast Bo Yi and Shu Qi as "feeling rancor" about their situation. This not only can be deduced from the fact that out of the four places where the two brothers appear in *The Analects* twice Confucius emphasizes that they did not "feel rancor"; in one of the cases, he is actually asked by a disciple whether the two "felt rancor," with no specific reason given (7.15).

17. The English translation includes a note: "Zhu Ziqing (1898–1948), Chinese man of letters and university professor. After the War of Resistance (1937–45), he actively supported the student movement against the Chiang Kai-shek regime. In June 1948 he signed a declaration protesting against the revival of Japanese militarism, which was being fostered by the United States, and rejecting 'U.S. Relief' flour. He was then living in great poverty. He died in Peiping on August 12, 1948, from poverty and illness, but even on his death-bed he enjoined his family not to buy the U.S. flour rationed by the Kuomintang government."

18. See Freud's *Civilization and Its Discontents* (1961). While Freud discusses "oceanic feeling" mainly as a religious experience in terms of his theory of the ego and ego formation, the Chinese version of it, due to the secular nature of its elite culture and official ideology, seems more a moral-psychological experience underlined by worldly politics than the kind of religious experience Freud describes. In other words, I use the Freudian terms as metaphors that describe a historical-ideological—that is, fundamentally discursive—process in which the body and its bodily functions are caught and rendered "meaningful."

19. I follow the year-numbering system, which corresponds to the Western calendar, provided by Burton Watson in his selection and translation of the *Tso Chuan*. In some early Chinese versions, the "Duke Xiang 21st Year" is dated 550 B.C.E.

20. I have retained the page references provided by Schafer in the 1892 Ḥobunkan (Tokyo) edition of this eleventh-century text.

21. A note referring to Xu and his execution is given in the 1981 edition of the text, part of which says that "his heart and liver were cut out, cooked and eaten after he was executed" (Lu Xun 1981, 1:432).

22. I altered Legge's translation of *zi* in *yizi ershi* to read "sons" instead of "children" because I believe *zi* is gender specific in this case, as in *Zuozhuan* as a whole. The English translators of Lu Xun's "Diary of a Madman" also rendered it "sons." This does not suggest that daughters enjoyed the privilege of being free from such an atrocity. Rather, their flesh was probably "unclean" or "unsuitable" to the highly organized public business of war. But again the case may simply be hyperbole representing a remembered cannibalism of desperation.

23. It could be argued just the other way around: we know the existence of the *Guanzi* first through the *Hanfeizi* (see Rickett 1985, 5). This might help to explain the Confucian "humanist" element in the former text—even though it is basically a legalist document in content. These Confucianist elements were probably added by early Han Confucian scholars, whereas the *Hanfeizi* could not possibly have been altered in that way.

24. There are numerous examples of mystical food and eating in the Buddhist-inspired fictional writings of *chuanqi* (classical tales). In the Buddhist canon, eating is as fascinating as in fiction. For example, in his preface to *The Sutra of Hui Neng*, a text attributed to the legendary Sixth Patriarch of Chan, the Tang monk Fa Hai describes the birth of Hui Neng: "The master did not suck milk [from his mother]; instead he drank sweet dew (cf. nectar) offered to him by a magic man he met at the night" (Hui Neng 1982, 1).

25. There have been some institutionalized exceptions to this prohibition plus, of course, numerous individual transgressions of the rule. The famous example of the monks at the Shaolin Temple in Henan Province illustrates the configuration of eating and politics. Historically, the Shaolin monks came to the rescue of Li Shimin, who, after ascending the throne as the Taizong Emperor (627–83) of the Tang, granted the Shaolin monks the privilege of consuming animal meat. In the golden years of the state-sponsored propagation of Buddhism in the early Tang, the Buddhist consumption of meat is rather symbolic of the power relations between the state and religion. See *Shaolinsi ziliaoji*, 14.

26. See his introduction to the American edition of *Monkey* (Wu 1943).

Part I The Social Embodiment of Modernity

1. Fredric Jameson's allegorical reading of Lu Xun is now the most familiar example, to which I will return later. But cross-cultural misreading can generate as much insight as it shows the ignorance of the uninformed reader. Alice

Walker's reaction to "The True Story of Ah Q" is a case in point: "Lu Xun has condescended to his character, in precisely the way white Southern writers have condescended to their characters who are black, and as male writers have condescended to characters who are women. He can't, in fact, believe a peasant capable of understanding his own oppression, his own life. Since the story is also exceedingly dull, we wonder what the Chinese value in it, beyond the fact that it is perhaps the first attempt to portray a Chinese peasant in fiction" ("China," *Ms.*, March 1985, 52).

2. In her translator's note, Tani Barlow points out that the phrase *reniunai* (boiling milk) is a "reference to masturbation" (see Ding Ling 1989, 354, n. 1). If that is the case, my literalization of this metaphor is meant to use it for a larger metaphoric purpose in describing most May Fourth authors' lack of interest in writing about eating. It is intriguing to note, though, that masturbation as a form of self-gratification structurally parallels the act of heating milk without drinking it, both being symptomatic of incompleteness in relation to the larger world. The rhetorical cross-reference between eating and sexuality certainly has a long history, as they constitute the basic activities of the carnal body and are configured in the vocabulary of *rou* (flesh/meat).

3. All citations of Lu Xun's works refer to the 1981 *Quanji* and, if noted otherwise, to the 1980 English edition of Lu's *Selected Works*. I have made certain changes to the English translations. When both are referred to, the first reference is to the Chinese edition.

4. See Lu Xun, "Suiganlu 42" (1: 327–28), which was published in January 1919, eight months after the publication of "Diary of a Madman." The author indicated that it had been some time since he read Grey's book (probably its Japanese translation). *Polynesian Mythology* was published first in Maori in 1854, with its first English translation dated to 1855. In this book Grey records—in a "disinterested" fashion—a few incidents of "human sacrifice" as told by some Maori priests and chiefs. Because of this "documentary" mode of writing, the familiar narrative of cannibalism is absent in his book. This is markedly different from, say, Captain Cook's accounts (see Sanborn 1998, chap. 1, for a recent analysis of Cook's accounts and his role in establishing the post-Enlightenment discourse on cannibalism). Grey's intention was to facilitate a better understanding of the native culture so that he and his fellow settlers could manage their conflicts with the natives in a more effective way. This apparently innocent interest in native knowledge for political purpose did not elude Lu Xun and the authors of Grey's biography (Rees and Rees 1892). But Lu Xun took for granted the unequal power relations in the construction of ethnographical knowledge and directed his bitterness toward the natives, Chinese and Polynesian alike. In this process, the dispassionate depictions provided by Grey of the Polynesian practice of flesh eating became encoded in the colonial

discourse of cannibalism. The gap of meanings between Grey and Lu Xun can be accounted for only by their distinct modes of reading. The global production and circulation of colonial knowledge would be incomplete without the "native" intellectual's reinterpretation and contribution.

Chapter 2. Lu Xun and Cannibalism

1. The original name for the practice was *gegu*. It dates back to the "iatric (i.e., medicinal) cannibalism" in the stories of the previous lives of the Buddha. The Buddhist legend and practice were transmitted during the Tang and Sung dynasties through the ideals of compassion and sacrifice, which were figured in the bodhisattva of Guan Yin and her various human incarnations. *Liaoqin* (to cure the dying parent[s]) was a later addition that indicates the Chinese adaptation of a Buddhist idea to Confucian filial piety. Because of the physical injury inflicted on the body, it was discouraged and sometimes prohibited by officialdom. See Chün-fang Yü 1995.

2. See Lee 1987, chap. 1, for sources and a brief analysis of Lu Xun's childhood experience of the "fantastic" and its impact on his life and writing.

3. This italicized sentence is translated by William Lyell (1976, 74); the rest of the citation is from the Yangs' version. The former seems more accurate than the latter ("it was not necessarily deplorable if many of them died of illness") because the original emphasizes, not "many," but "uselessness" of their physical health without a strong and healthy spirit.

4. From a historian's point of view, this question would confirm what Leo Lee has suggested: "Lu Xun may have fabricated the incident" (1987, 203, n. 61). Lee's exhaustive research, which includes a large amount of information from original Japanese sources and takes account of some eighty years of vain attempts to find this slide, has led him to this conjecture. It also has been pointed out that the execution scene may well be a fiction created by Lu Xun to hide his poor performance in his medical studies and offer a "public-spirited explanation as to why he changed from medical studies to literature" (Lyell 1976, 75; also see Larson 1991, 185, n. 16, for more sources on this topic).

5. Leo Lee's translation of the Chinese term *qunzhong* as "crowd" (1987, 211, n. 1) seems more accurate than the established Marxist-Maoist designation of it as (potential revolutionary) "masses." In "Random Thoughts (38)," published in 1918, Lu Xun even uses the term *mob* in its original English form to describe the crowd or the masses (1:311).

6. Since the completion of his last book on photography just after (and because of) his mother's death and just before his own, the name of Roland Barthes has itself become a kind of specter that haunts our reading of photography. While this whole myth cannot go unheeded, some of his points are curi-

ously pertinent to Lu Xun's early works. For one thing, the connection he made of the photographic spectacle with "spectrum" rightly locates Lu Xun, the narrator-observer, in his relationship with death. This relationship is staged as a spectacle in terms that Barthes uses to describe the kinship of photography with theater (in its Greek origin) rather than with painting: spectacle-as-spectrum stages a sort of necromantic interplay between the specter and its spectator (see Barthes 1981, 31). But photography also differs from theater or any other visual representation such as film, which is at the same time immersed in a stream of temporality to simulate life. This difference, according to the film critic Christian Metz, highlights the "importance of immobility and silence to photographic *authority*." "Immobility and silence are not only two objective aspects of death, they are also its main symbols, they *figure* it" (Metz 1990, 157; original emphasis).

7. Lydia Liu (1995, chap. 2) has made a thorough analysis of the translated notions of "face" and "Chinese characteristics" embodied in Ah Q, both drawn from Arthur Smith's *Chinese Characteristics* (1894).

8. The earliest reference to Baudelaire in Lu Xun's works is dated 1924, when he was translating *Symbols of Mental Anguish* by the Japanese literary critic Kuriyagawa Hakuson. In the process, he also translated Baudelaire's prose poem "Windows" (Les fenêtres), cited in that work. About the same time, Lu Xun started writing prose poems, to be collected later in *Wild Grass* (Yecao). But Lu Xun was introduced to Baudelaire and French symbolism as early as 1922. Baudelaire's "influence" on Lu Xun, mainly found in *Wild Grass*, has been detected by several scholars (see Prusek 1980, 56; also see Sun 1982, chap. 7, for the reception of Baudelaire and the import of the genre of prose poetry in the Chinese literature of that period). After he turned to Marxism in the last years of the decade, Lu Xun basically followed the Soviet line and treated Baudelaire as displaying fin de siècle bourgeois decadence. In his "Preface to the Second Collection of Fiction for *A Comprehensive Anthology of the New Literature of China*" (1935), Lu Xun reflects upon the "negative influence" of Western fin de siècle artists and thinkers, such as Oscar Wilde, Nietzsche, Baudelaire, and L. Andreev, on Chinese literature in the early 1920s (6:243). But when he was writing about art in ways not directly related to politics his understanding of Baudelaire seems close to Walter Benjamin's. In his "Preface to *Selected Paintings by Aubrey Beardsley*" (1929), Lu Xun senses a dialectic (i.e., "allegorical" in Benjamin's terms) relationship between "hell" and "paradise," "beauty" and "ugliness," in Beardsley's paintings as in Baudelaire's poems (7:338). Although Lu Xun may not have been exposed to Baudelaire as early as the time when he was writing "Diary," he seems to have a lot in common with Baudelaire in terms of artistic predisposition. Leo Lee's reading of Lu Xun's story "In the Tavern," citing Ralph Freedman, seems quite resonant of de Man's reading of Baude-

laire: "In a sense both men [the narrator and the protagonist] are projections of Lu Xun's self; their dialogue a fictional dramatization of inner monologue conducted by the author. What Ralph Freedman (in *The Lyric Novel*) has detected in the prose poetry of Baudelaire proves amazingly apt in this regard: 'The poet detaches himself from the scene; one part of himself enacts the moral point in symbolic gestures, while the other part of himself functions as an observer who is detached at the very time that he is drawn into the scene' " (1987, 64).

9. Opinions on the call are too numerous to reference here. For a summary of major differences in evaluating the character of the Madman in the PRC, see Beijing shifan daixue 1981, 139–53. Also see Lee 1985, 8, and Huters 1984, 75, n. 3.

10. The term *demigod* is borrowed from Thomas Metzger's *Escape from Predicament* (1977). While I agree with other critics that Lu Xun, taken as a whole, is more complicated in his understanding of modern China and his own role in it than the majority of his contemporary "demigods," I would suggest that his self-understanding not only "oscillate[s] erratically between the status of a victim and that of a demigod" (Huters 1984, 49) but embodies the split world between the two. Unlike the Song Neo-Confucians, Lu Xun is equipped with modernity's "escape from the (traditional Neo-Confucian) predicament," yet at the same time he perceives himself also as the victim not of modernity itself but of the modern condition wrought by forces unknown to his predecessors.

11. For a lucid introduction to the theory of allegory in Western classical and medieval traditions, see MacQueen 1970.

12. See Plaks 1976; 1977. For a "deconstructive" review of Plaks's theory, see J. Wang 1989.

13. Hillis Miller has delineated a trajectory of the interplay between two kinds of allegory that he designates as "Hegelian" and "Benjaminian." The Benjaminian, or "deconstructive," one has been "present as a shadow in the use of [the Hegelian or constructive] allegory" from Dante to Yeats (1981, 363). According to Lloyd Spencer, Benjamin "wishes to give prominence . . . to modes of allegory which register the *dissolution* of the stable, hierarchised and meaningful existence which allegory seems to imply. This is because Benjamin sees the evocation of that 'framework' of meaning for allegory—and especially the forced, deliberate or ostentatious evocation of such a framework—is itself symptomatic of a significant loss of a sense of genuine, immediately accessible, *immanent* meaning. Allegories . . . can thus be seen as deconstructing themselves, as revealing the opposite of that which they seek to imply" (1985, 63; original emphasis).

14. I render *feng* as "mad" (translated "crazy" by the Yangs) to highlight the author's, rather than the other characters', point of view. In his "Changmingdeng" (The lamp kept alight, 1925), a story about another "madman," Lu Xun

uses *feng* throughout for the same effect. For a detailed reading of the two terms, see X. Tang 1992.

15. See Zhou 1974, 24–31, and Lee 1987, 8. It is interesting to note that sixty years later Zhou still remembered that his ailing father told him ghost stories, especially one that details a monster with dog's head and a human body eating the brains of the dead. On another note, Zhou Zuoren grew up often feeling sick and hungry while Lu Xun suffered little from starvation. Yet the physically weak Zhou, only four years younger than his brother, outlived him by twenty-seven years and died at the advanced age of eighty-three (were it not for his miserable lot in the last two decades of his life he might have lived even longer). If one were to assume that Zhou's longevity was due to his good appetite, it would be difficult to explain why Lu Xun, who was also a good eater but was never enthusiastic about writing about it, did not last that long. The "pleasure of the text" exhibited in Zhou's poetics of eating seems to be a major factor for his longevity.

16. The use of the Freudian notion of fetishism might sound preposterous here because Lu Xun's "death drive" has nothing to do with "sexuality." Freud himself is acutely aware of some "cultural difference" toward the end of his "Fetishism" (1975), though the bound feet of Chinese women still work for his theory of sexuality rather than death. Yet, curiously enough, in that short essay Freud compares the fetishist with the obsessional neurotic, who oscillates between the death of his father and his denial of it in the same way that the fetishist oscillates between the "castration" of the woman and his denial of it. Both share a double attitude toward the object: loss (death or "castration") and protection against loss. Metz's explanation with respect to the snapshot, the third character that photography has in common with death, clarifies Freud's point lucidly: "The photographic *take* is immediate and definitive, like death and like the constitution of the fetish in the unconscious, fixed by a glance in childhood, unchanged and always active later" (1990, 158; original emphasis).

Chapter 3. Shen Congwen's "Modest Proposal"

1. Unless noted, all citations of Shen Congwen's works are referenced to the 1984 twelve-volume *Shen Congwen wenji*, and all translations are mine.

2. Among numerous biographical studies of the author, the most informative and comprehensive works include, in English, Jeffery Kinkley's *The Odyssey of Shen Congwen* (1987); and, in Chinese, Ling Yu's *Biography of Shen Congwen* (1988) and Miaozi's *Biography of Shen Congwen* (1991). Also see Wang Jizhi's *On Shen Congwen* (1992).

3. The "rediscovery" of Shen Congwen in post-Mao China was influenced in part by scholarship published overseas before the 1980s. Among early Anglo-

American scholarly studies, the representative works are C. T. Hsia's *A History of Modern Chinese Fiction* (1961), William Lewis MacDonald's *Characters and Themes in Shen Ts'ung-wen's Fiction* (1970), and Hua-ling Nieh's *Shen Ts'ung-wen* (1972). Portions of these works were translated into Chinese or introduced to mainland readers at various points. Because PRC scholars then had limited access to publications in foreign languages, writings by Hsia, Nieh, and others that were originally published in the Chinese language in Taiwan and Hong Kong had a much broader appeal to mainland readers. In 1991, the publication of the Chinese version of Kinkley's *The Odyssey of Shen Congwen* perhaps marked the peak of the decade-long effort to reestablish Shen's canonical position in modern Chinese literature through the work of prominent scholars abroad. See Wang Jizhi 1992, 144–66, for a summary of the mainland reception of overseas studies on Shen (which includes useful references to Japanese and European sources).

4. See Benjamin's "Central Park" (1985). For his extensive study of Baudelaire, see *Charles Baudelaire: A Poet in the Era of High Capitalism* (1983).

5. I have consulted Chi-chen Wang's English translation (C. Wang 1944, 95–107). Several things need to be noted about this story's republication and translation. According to Kinkley (1987, 401), this piece is the first story by the title "Ye." It was republished in *Shen Congwen xiaoshuo xuan* (1982) edited by Ling Yu, and in the end of the text the editor notes that "Ye" appeared first in the 1930 edition of *Shizihe*. Curiously, in the twelve-volume *Shen Congwen wenji* (1984) coedited by Ling Yu, this particular text is not included. Another story, which is also entitled "Ye" but does not contain any reference to cannibalism, is selected under the anthology title *Shizihe*, in volume 3. It is difficult to determine whether the editors of *Shen Congwen wenji* replaced the "Ye" about cannibalism with another story of the same title because of the former's graphic depictions or whether they made an editorial mistake. Meanwhile, it is revealing that the "Ye" about cannibalism is the only story by Shen Congwen that was included in Chi-chen Wang's *Contemporary Chinese Stories* (1944), which is one of the earliest anthologies of modern Chinese fiction published in any Western language. In his preface Wang writes that he chose these stories to show the dark side of modern Chinese society.

6. Although I have translated the passages that follow, I have benefited from Kai-yu Hsu's English version in Lau et al. 1981, 253–65.

7. Translated by Eugene Eoyang, in Lau et al. 1981, 108.

Part II Writing Hunger: From Mao to the Dao

1. A recent essay by Wang Dewei (1997) draws attention to the topic of hunger in Zhang Ailing's novel *Yangge* (1954) as well as in a number of earlier works

written by Jiang Guangci, Wu Zuxiang, Rou Shi, and Lu Ling, writers of diverse ideological alliances and artistic tastes. Jiang Guangci, Rou Shi, and Lu Ling were involved to varying degrees with the leftist movement of social realism in the 1930s. As in the case of Shen Congwen, these writers have had a limited influence on the formation of the metanarrative of hunger in revolutionary and postrevolutionary literature, which is strictly a discourse of Chinese Communism. But it is important to note that outside Yan'an literature many others have also written about hunger.

2. I have in mind Gunder Frank's recent thesis in "Re-ORIENT" (1998) in addition to the systematic critique of orientalism undertaken since the publication of Edward Said's namesake book. Though I am not very enthusiastic about Frank's predictions for the future China, his meticulous revision of world history is based on solid research and presented convincingly.

Chapter 4. Hungry Revolution and Revolutionary Hunger

1. The first reference is to *Mao Zedong xuanji* (1961) and the second, if given, is to *Selected Works* (1965).

2. See Mei Lin, "Lun budui wenyi gongzuo" (Literature and art in the military) (1940) reprinted in *Wenyi lilun juan* 1984, 272–77.

3. Ai Qing, "Zhankai jietoushi yundong" (Promoting the movement of poetry in the street) (1942), reprinted in *Wenyi lilun juan* 1984, 450–55.

4. Tian Lan, "Wo, Yan'anshi Qiaoergouqu de gongmin" (I, a citizen of Qiaoergou District, Yan'an City), (1941; publisher unknown) and reprinted in *Shige juan* 1984, 29.

5. *Baimaonü* was "collectively composed" by the Lu Xun Academy of the Arts, with He Jingzhi and Ding Yi being the "actual writers" (He and Ding 1946). It was first staged as a "new opera," an eclectic form evolved from *yangge* (a popular form of musical in northern China), local opera, and Western opera. The political theme of the play was so effective that during its performance spectators sometimes could not distinguish the theatrical from the real, and some soldiers even rushed to the stage attempting to kill Huang Shiren in the scene where Huang comes to grab Xi'er away from her father's body. This effect has been praised as a model for literature and art as a powerful educational weapon. While Brecht was trying to create a new political theater by drawing on certain aspects of traditional Chinese theater, he could never have dreamed that the "familiar" could also tear down the so-called fourth wall. In addition to Yang Bailao's suicide, many other changes have been made in the play, some by Mao himself. During the Seventh Congress of the CCP in 1945, Mao and other members of the Central Committee watched the performance. After the show, Mao stated that "Huang Shiren should be executed" in the end, reflect-

ing the CCP's policy change in land reform from its relatively lenient approach during the War of Resistance against Japan to its reemphasis on "internal class struggle" after that war. For all these changes, the opera was nevertheless criticized for "reconciling class struggle" and failing to glorify the Party's leadership by ultraleftist Party officials and critics in the 1960s. See Wang and Zhang 1982 for various accounts and sources of the play's history and its reception and revisions; also see Meng 1993 for an analysis of the erasure of gender by class in the history of the play.

6. The original source of publication is not given. It was reprinted in *Xiaoshuo juan* 1984, 2:390–410. It is interesting to note that Wang was born into a well-to-do family. His father was a country school principal and later served in the government bureaucracy. Starvation was not part of his own experience until he joined the revolution at the age of sixteen in Shanghai. But hunger is a persistent motif in his *Autobiography* (1991b).

7. The original source of publication is not given. It was reprinted in *Shige juan* 1984, 369–70.

8. *Wenyi zhanxian* (Front Line of literature and art) 1.1 (February 26, 1939); reprinted in *Xiaoshuo juan* 1984, 1:68–82.

9. This story is another popular myth about Mao and other Communist leaders. It is true that Mao and his government during the revolutionary era and the early years of the PRC were relatively clean, probably one of the least corrupted ruling groups in Chinese history. But this does not suggest, as popular wishful thinking would have it, that high-ranking Party officials did not enjoy certain privileges. For one thing, even in the most idealistic years of the Yan'an period, Mao and other members of the Central Committee did have a special food service. Called *zhongzao* (medium-sized kitchen), it was distinguished in terms of material supply, diet, preparation, and service from *dazao* (big kitchen), where his bodyguards and other staff members were served. For a recent firsthand account of Mao's life in this period, see Quan Yanchi, *Zouxia shentan de Mao Zedong* (1990), a memoir of Mao told by Li Yinqao, his chief bodyguard from 1947 to 1962, and penned by Quan. The book describes from Li's point of view his beloved leader as an ordinary person with human feelings and flaws. It is different from the vast body of anticommunist literature produced overseas that heaps the most evil traits imaginable on Mao.

10. The original source of publication is not given. It was reprinted in *Xiaoshuo juan* 1984, 2:431–36.

11. It is interesting to note that braised pork was in fact Mao's favorite dish, which he tied to the palate of Chinese peasants. According to his chief bodyguard, Li Yinqiao, during the Communist-Nationalist Civil War (1946–49) Mao always wanted to eat braised pork to celebrate battlefield victories. After the founding of the PRC, even though living conditions improved, Mao did not

change his food habits. He often defied his dietician's advice against him eating too much fat pork and was ridiculed by his wife Jiang Qing as a *tubaozi* (country bumpkin). After he learned of this, Mao became angry and told Li: "No doubt she is right. I am a *tubaozi*! I am a peasant's son with the peasants' lifestyle. She is a *yangbaozi* (Westernized). So let's split it up. She will have her dishes and I mine. One won't meddle in the other's business. This is fixed." Subsequently, Mao never touched Jiang's food when they ate at the same table (Quan 1990, 107–16).

12. The original source of publication is unknown. It was reprinted in *Xiaoshuo juan* 1984, 1:452–68.

13. From the literary historian's point of view, there is a great need to uncover—if that could possibly be achieved—what has been erased in the name of, say, "vulgarity" in the way the narrator corrects the "comic flaw" of what he deems a tragic story. Given the fact that this text was reprinted nearly forty years later under the auspices of the Party's central propaganda apparatus, the reader can still gain a glimpse into the actual process of ideological reification.

14. The first page reference is to "Ji'e sanbuqu," originally published in *Shouhuo* (1980); the second is to Kyna Rubin's English translation (1991a) with occasional minor changes.

15. The first reference is to "Meishijia," originally published in *Shouhuo* (1983); the second, if given, refers to an abridged English edition published by Readers International (1987), which does not name its translator(s). At various points, I have altered the translation.

Chapter 5. Postrevolutionary Leftovers: Zhang Xianliang and Ah Cheng

1. Official estimates put the death toll during the famine at more than twenty million. Overseas estimates vary from twenty to fifty million. For a recent source in Chinese, see chapter 1 of Chen Yizi's *China's Ten-Year Reform and the Democratic Movement of 1989* (1990). For a comprehensive analysis in English, see Penny Kane's *Famine in China, 1959–61* (1988). As to the death toll from hunger during the Cultural Revolution, there is no official estimate, and it may forever remain a mystery because of the paralysis of government civil functions and the complication of other factors such as massive violence among regional and political factions. Chen Yizi, a former official in a leading government think tank and a policy adviser to Zhao Ziyang, the ousted general secretary of the CCP, gives in his book graphic accounts of devastated rural life during the Cultural Revolution, including certain occurrences of "hunger cannibalism." Meanwhile, the tragedies must also be understood in the larger international environment of hostility toward the PRC, exemplified by the Soviet withdrawal

of aid, the demand for repayment of debts incurred during the Korean War, and international economic embargoes.

2. Numerous articles and commentaries have been published on "Mimosa." *Wenyibao* (Literature and the arts) and *Dangdai zuojia pinglun* (Contemporary writers and criticism), which published more than a dozen articles each on the novella in their 1984 issues, are two of the major journals encouraging discussion. For a brief summary of the critical literature, see *Wenyibao* 1984.

3. As the critic Ji Hongzhen (1985, 54) has noted, Zhang Xianliang's rethinking of history has two focal points: contemporary China's sociohistorical contradictions and the intellectual's subjective inner conflicts. Ji argues that Zhang "internalizes political catastrophe" as "the intellectual's inner conflict."

4. For a recent analysis of the debates over the young "humanist" Marx and the implications of socialist alienation, see Jing Wang 1996, chap. 1.

5. In citations to "Mimosa," the first page number refers to the Chinese text, "Lühuashu" (1985a), and the second to Gladys Yang's English translation (Zhang Xianliang 1985b). At various points, I have altered the translation or reinserted text that was omitted.

6. See Wang Xiaoming 1986; Ji Hongzhen 1985; and Huang Ziping 1984. This masculinist narrative becomes even more explicit in Zhang's next novel in the series: *Half of Man Is Woman* (1986), where Zhang Yonglin transcends his material existence in the end by deserting the heroine Huang Xiangjiu, whose sexuality has rescued and restored his masculinity from impotence. Wang Xiaoming has pointed out a pattern in Zhang's fiction of reverence and abandonment of women and argues that this shows a deeply rooted pathetic male anxiety and arrogance (1986, 94–96).

7. Chen Yizi (1990) provides a full account of the post-Mao reform, its historical background, and the policy debates involved. The references to food and speech in two subtitles in the book are illuminating. Chapter 2 describes the Party's rural policies in the first thirty years. The first section is entitled "The Peasants Say: 'For Thirty Years the Communist Party Neither Allowed Us to Fill Our Stomachs Nor Let Us Speak Out.' " The fifth section's title is "Chinese Peasants' Great Creation: 'Filling the Stomach Is [China's Political] Top Priority.' " The debates on reform in the late 1970s were characterized by this kind of rhetorical mixture of ideological jargon and down-to-earth sayings.

8. While Louie's critique of Duke and others offers many cogent points, it must be noted at the same time that his reading is underlined by "truly Marxist concerns" against "a reactionary Confucianist ideology whose material social base is fast disappearing." In accusing Ah Cheng and Daoism of escapism, he echoes the Minister of Culture Wang Meng's reservation by citing the latter's comment on "certain passive traits" in the text.

9. *The Tao of Physics* (1975) was translated into Chinese and published in 1983

with the title *Xiandai wulixue yu dongfang shenmi zhuyi*, meaning literally "modern physics and oriental mysticism."

10. For an account and analysis of Chinese writers' and critics' drive for international fame, see Wendy Larson and Richard Krauss (1989).

11. The other major force was officials from the "liberal" wing of the Party. They were not so much concerned with culture per se as with taking advantage of the situation to advance their reform agenda (see Chen Kuide 1992).

12. Li Zehou's authority as a leading thinker was well established before the cultural fever. Among his earliest critics was Liu Xiaobo (1989), who was known for his radical thought and polemical rhetoric. For comprehensive presentations of Li's thought and its impact on the cultural movement, see Jing Wang (1996, chap. 2) and Xudong Zhang (1997, pt. 1).

13. Although both *shenghuo* and *shengming* are conventionally translated as "life," their connotations in the text are different. For the lack of a better word, my rendition of *shenghuo* as "living" emphasizes the process of material subsistence, whereas *shengming* as "life" implies the established abstract meaning of human existence.

14. Wang Xiaoming (1988, 35, n. 14) points out that this erased ending is in fact "more consistent with the story's overall structure." Also see Huters 1985, 417, n. 4.

15. All citations of the novella refer to the 1992 Taipei edition, which is slightly different from the original version published in *Shanghai wenxue* (1984), and to Jenner's English translation (1985). I have also consulted McDougall's translation (1990).

16. Wang Xiaoming (1988, 33) points out that Wang Yisheng's talk about the Dao of chess in terms of philosophical Daoism and the *Yijing* is incompatible with the narrative development and reveals a contrived attempt on the part of the author to reconnect contemporary China with its ancient tradition.

17. There is another instance of the "always already" at work in this process. In his influential *Essays on Ancient Chinese Thought* (1985, 198), Li Zehou begins the section on Chan with this statement: "As recognized worldwide, Chan is a product of China," invoking Suzuki, Jung, and Erich Fromm to support his point.

Part III The Return (of) Cannibalism after Tiananmen, or Red Monument in a Latrine Pit

1. In his translator's postscript to Yu Hua's *The Past and the Punishments* (which includes the story "Classical Love"), Andrew Jones has noted that "the horrific scenes of cannibalism are recycled from a Tang dynasty anecdote (which later

became a notorious Ming dynasty story called 'A Filial Woman Sells Herself to a Butcher at the Yangzhou Market.' " Jones emphasizes that "Yu Hua gives us the story in the absence of the moral imperative (filial piety) that made the original tick" (Yu Hua 1996, 265). The absence of moralism, ancient and modern alike, points to the fundamental distinction between the experimental fiction of the late 1980s and the allegorical mode of writing cannibalism from Lu Xun to Zheng Yi and Liu Zhenyun.

2. For a summary of this cultural consumption and Mao fever in the context of rising consumerism, see Dai Jinhua's "Redemption and Consumption: Depicting Culture in the 1990s" (1996).

Chapter 6. Monument Revisited: Zheng Yi and Liu Zhenyun

1. All page references are to *Hongse jinianbei* (Zheng Yi 1993), and all translations are mine.

2. All page references are to "Wengu yijiusier" (Liu Zhenyun 1994), and all translations are mine.

3. The narrator indicates in the opening paragraph that a friend introduced him to White's memoir and other historical sources and assigned him the task of revisiting history. The fictional friend does not play an important role in the story except that he occupies a mysterious position of authority. Whether Liu Zhenyun was introduced to the book or came across it some other way is not important here. Nor is it important whether he read the English version or the Chinese translation (my understanding is that he did not read the English edition).

Chapter 7. From Cannibalism to Carnivorism: Mo Yan's *Liquorland*

1. The author explains that so many people died in a very short period of time that the region ran out of wood for making coffins for the burial of the dead. He adds that those still alive were often too feeble to resist the dogs' attack (1997, 95).

2. All page references are to *Jiuguo* (1992) and all translations are mine.

3. While the English word *carnal* is still tied to its root in *flesh*, it has been curiously dissociated from the meat-eating practices of the carnivore. The reason perhaps lies partly in the older differentiation of human flesh from animal meat but more so in the historical reconfiguration of the flesh with the increasingly sexualized body (hence "carnal pleasure," "carnal lust," "carnal abuse," and "carnal knowledge"). Behind the linguistic change is the larger cultural history, dating at least to the dusk of the European medieval age. The drive to free the flesh from religious asceticism may have much to do with it. Food, on

the other hand, has never been as rigidly codified as sex. Thus, the gastronomic aspect of the flesh did not have to be reinvigorated in the fashion of its sexual counterpart, though one still has to make a deal with God when it comes to heavy drinking and feasting. See Bakhtin's *Rabelais and His World* (1984) for detailed discussions.

4. The multiple meaning of *rou* and the "decarnalization" of the sexual body under asceto-Marxism in the PRC has resulted in some tragicomic instances that are anything but laughable. An extreme case reported by Jianying Zha is illuminating. A Beijing doctor of "abnormal sexual psychology" once treated a couple who had "tried to conceive by putting a piece of lean pork into the wife's anus every time they had sex." This couple was misled, Zha quotes the doctor as saying, "because they'd read somewhere in an old Chinese book about *rurou*, 'enter the meat.' It happens to be one of those very graphic characters, but they took it literally" (1995, 151–52).

5. The last sentence, read *fengjing neibian zuicha* in Chinese, is a parody of *fengjing neibian duhao* (The scenery on the other side is the best), a line from a well-known poem by Mao.

6. At least two critics of the film *Red Sorghum* use the Bakhtinian concept in their analyses. See Yingjin Zhang 1990 and Yuejin Wang 1991.

7. I do not suggest that Mo Yan's style went through a radical change in the late 1980s and early 1990s. The 1986 story entitled "Fuqin zai minfulianli" (Father in the food-shipping company), for example, depicts one of the most hellish scenes we find in his fiction. Set in the wartime of late 1948, the story focuses on the desperation and cruelty of the human creature under conditions of extreme hunger. A team of paramilitary peasants, who were shipping food to the Communist troops, had to kill one of their cart-hauling donkeys to ease their severe hunger. As they were cooking the donkey in a local village close to the frontline, a crowd of villagers starved to the brink of death crawled to the cooking site, begging for a share. Some of the villagers suffered from such edema that the body looked "like a fat, huge maggot." As a bullet shot open the chest of a balloon-bellyed woman villager, "out from her body spilled a shot of yellow fluid, with a few traces of red" (1991, 46–47). In the controversial novella "Huanle" (Joy), published in 1989, the withering body of the narrator's mother is traversed by rats and other creatures, including a detail of fleas crawling into her vagina (1989b, 315).

Chapter 8. Embodied Spaces of Home: Xiao Hong, Wang Anyi, and Li Ang

1. All page references are to *Xiao Hong de Shangshijie* (Market street, 1987) and, with occasional changes, to Goldblatt's translation (Xiao Hong 1986).

2. These phrases are traceable to the early Western construction of "Chinese characteristics," whereby the alleged Chinese tolerance of pain and endurance of hardship were admired as a sign of their stoic optimism (as in Pearl Buck's works) or despised for a reflection of their passive resignation and cruelty (as in many missionary writings and travelogues about Chinese "coolies").

3. See, for example, her portrait of the autobiographical narrator in the 1990 novella, "A Singing Star from Japan" (1996b, 187–256).

4. All page references are to *Changhenge* (1996a), and all translations are mine.

5. All page references are to *Shafu* (1983) and, with minor changes, to *The Butcher's Wife* (Li Ang 1986), translated by Goldblatt and Yeung.

Chapter 9. Blending Chinese in America: Maxine Hong Kingston, Jade Snow Wong, and Amy Tan

1. Note how the narrator (the young girl Maxine) reacts to the tale: "Did she say, 'You should have seen the faces the monkey made'? Did she say, 'The people laughed at the monkey screaming'? It was alive? The curtain flaps closed like merciful black wings. 'Eat! Eat!' my mother would shout at our heads bent over bowls, the blood pudding awobble in the middle of the table" (1975, 108). While the author is less concerned about the factuality of the tale than its effect on the girl, in her response to some readers' negative reactions she tried to defend the tale's authenticity by insisting that she had heard it from many Chinese immigrants (Kingston 1982). In my view, it is very likely that some self-imagined "big eaters" told such tall tales simply to show off their rugged "guts" and perhaps fat pockets. Assuming that the tale is true, Kingston's justification nevertheless contradicts her pronounced intent to undo the rigid boundary between fiction and reality in the book.

2. See J. Wong 1975, 46–47. On a different note, Wong's belief in modesty and moderation is also reflected in her reluctance to become involved in Asian American political movements, whether during the civil rights movement or in the recent controversy surrounding multicultural curricular reform at Mills College. In 1993, she was invited to be the convocation speaker at Mills but refused to endorse Asian American students' request for the establishment of a curriculum in Asian American studies (see K. Su 1994 for a detailed analysis of her recent activities in public life).

3. According to the author, her English teachers and the book's editors cut two-thirds of her original manuscript. Wong admits that she would have liked to keep some of the things that were eliminated, some aspects of which were deemed "too personal." But she understands that "[e]verybody has a purpose in mind in what they're carrying out. So . . . you kind of have to work with them" (see Chin et al. 1972, 39; also see E. Kim 1982, 69–71). In other words,

her assimilation entails the elimination of things "too personal" for her autobiography, an oxymoron symptomatic of the anthropological fallacy applied to "ethnic writings." Henry Louis Gates Jr. (1984; 1986) has emphasized that studies of African American literature, while repudiating the "post-colonial legacy," should also avoid what he calls the "anthropology fallacy." The anthropology fallacy reduces black texts to the status of collective and functional documentation and concerns them "in 'non-literary' arenas rather than with their internal structures as acts of language or their formal status as works of art." "Because of this curious valorization of the social and polemical functions of black literature, the structure of the black text has been *repressed* and treated as if it were *transparent*." Reducing black literary texts to anthropological documents, Gates argues, perpetuates the status of black subjectivity as the "transcendental signified of absence" constituted on a binary paradigm that begins with Plato (1984, 5–6). It should be noted that there is a paradox in his theory, which emphasizes the literariness of black texts not for mere formalistic reasons. Hence my reappropriation of Wong's ethnographical text.

4. According to Gates (1988), black subjectivity is constituted in its "double-voiced discourse." As such, "blackness" is a metaphor with three specific meanings. First, black literature cannot be "whitewashed" or interpreted solely in Western theoretical terms. If the black text is clothed in "blackness" by the black writer, it must be unpacked by the critic in a theory of criticism indigenous to it. Second, "blackness" signifies the opacity of the formal language; thus, black texts are not transparent anthropological documents. Third, as a metaphor "blackness" does not denote "essence," which has been posited in the white-black dichotomy as negative essence or lack. The "double-voiced" means "Signifyin(g)," as opposed to "signification," in our normal language use. Its power rests on its self-conscious use as a political act by black speakers in order to "mislead," pointing at one thing while suggesting and commenting on his or her subjective attitude toward that "pointing." Signifyin(g), or the double-voiced signification, is the principle of the open-ended, indirect use of language and the textual figures that speak in that language. The relevance of black literary theory to my study of a Chinese American text is its emphasis on language use and literary form as material shaping forces of cultural consciousness. Frank Chin's reading of Louis Chu's *Eat a Bowl of Tea* and especially John Okada's *No-No Boy* twenty years ago suggested such a critical consciousness in Asian American literary studies (Chin et al. 1972, 42–46). Unfortunately, the exclusion of living Chinese American women writers from the two *Aiiieeeee* anthologies also indicates how cultural politics could limit Chin's vision.

5. Tan elaborates on this issue in her essay "Mother Tongue" (1991b).

6. Many feminist scholars have pointed out the "lack" of a female version in Freud's theoretical analysis, a metaphor that fully plays into Freud's phallo-

centrism and reduces women to the status of "lack." In *The Hungry Self* (1985), Cherin Kim proposes the notion of the "Cinderella complex" as an alternative to Freud's "Oedipus complex" for examining mother-daughter relationships. In parallel to the male fear of incest and castration, she defines *Cinderella complex* as "the fear of independence," which "is in reality a pervasive worry about our mothers' lives" (43). Her notion of the "Cinderella complex" bases the mother-daughter relationship on orality and emphasizes the mouth, instead of the penis or the lack of it, as the ontological site of female experience and discourse. "The child who lives through and loves with the mouth is already constructing that hunger knot in which identity, the beginnings of the mother-separation struggle, love, rage, food, and female body are entangled" (99). Revising Freudian theory on male guilt, she argues that "our most fruitful understanding of female psychology will come from the exploration of the dual-unity, mother and child, mouth-to-breast dyad of earliest childhood, which implies that for a woman to develop into her full womanhood she must surmount the guilt that arises from her fantasy of having damaged the mother through the force of her oral aggression and rage" (120). The ultimate concern of her theory is to "liberate an anger that indicts not the mothers but a social system that has never ceased to suppress women" and "finally to set free from the tangled knot of self-destruction and obsession the radical and healing knowledge that eating disorder is a profoundly political act" (92). Although Kim's study focuses on contemporary American women's eating disorders, her analysis extends beyond clinical experience and offers many theoretical insights into the interactions between the symbolic and the symptomatic systems of eating. I find some of Kim's points relevant to Tan's novel, as much as Tan's text problematizes Kim's theory from a cross-cultural perspective.

7. Dorothy Wang has reported that Tan, while growing up in California, "dreamed of getting plastic surgery to Westernize her features" (*Newsweek*, April 17, 1989, 69). An article (author unknown) published in *Current Biography* (February 1992) provides another version: "For a week Tan even slept with a clothespin on her nose, hoping to alter her Asian appearance" (56).

8. Quoted by Dorothy Wang in *Newsweek*, April 17, 1989, 69.

Conclusion

1. For a summary of Western media reactions to Brown's thesis, see Ayres 1995 and L. Brown 1995. Chinese responses are more complex, ranging from serious consideration of Brown's proposal to outright attacks on the concept of a "Chinese environmental threat" allegedly provoked by his wake-up call. The ambivalence toward Brown is best reflected by Li Xiguang's essay "Will

China Become the 'Demon' that Eats Up the Food of the World?" (1996). In this piece, the author is candid about his personal friendship with Brown and positive about his environmental concerns, adding a most ironic twist to the fact that the essay was published in *Behind Demonizing China*, a book coedited by Li himself.

Glossary

Ah Cheng 阿城
  Qiwang 棋王
Ai Qing 艾青

Ba Jin 巴金
Bai Juyi 白居易
Baihutong 白虎通
Baimaonü 白毛女
benti 本體
Benwei 本味
bianxi quan shiren 編戲勸世人
Bing Xin 冰心
bubai 補白
bushi renjian yanhuo 不食人間煙火
bushi ziwei 不是滋味

canwu rendao 殘無人道
chan 饞
Chen Kuide 陳奎德
Chen Pingyuan 陳平原
Chen Sihe 陳思和
Chen Yizi 陳一咨
chibao 吃飽
chicu 吃醋
chifan 吃飯

chijing 吃驚
chiku 吃苦
chilaoben 吃老本
chili 吃力
chinai 吃奶
chiren 吃人
chirende jiushehui 吃人的舊社會
chirou 吃肉
chirou yidun, buru jinrou yicun 吃肉一頓, 不如進肉一寸
chixiang hela 吃香喝辣
chiyabakui 吃啞巴虧
chiyao 吃藥
chiyikufan 吃憶苦飯
choudoufu 臭豆腐
chuantong minzu wenhua 傳統民族文化
chui'niu 吹牛

dachidahe 大吃大喝
Dai Jinhua 戴錦華
dajiuxing 大救星
dawanhejiu, dakuaichirou 大碗喝酒, 大塊吃肉
dazao 大灶
dianxing(hua) 典型 (化)
ding 鼎
Ding Gou 丁鉤
Ding Ling 丁玲
dingwei hewei, zuzhe gecai tianxia 鼎為和味, 俎者割裁天下
dixia fandian 地下飯店
Du Maike 杜邁可
Du Shengxiu 杜聖修
duanqiwan chirou, fangxiawan maniang 端起碗吃肉, 放下碗罵娘
Dukang 杜康

Fa Hai 法海
fengjing neibian duhao 風景那邊獨好

fengjing neibian zuicha 風景那邊最差
fengkuang 瘋狂
fengzi 瘋子
fudingzu, yiziwei shuitang, zhiyu wangdao 負鼎俎, 以滋味說湯, 至於王道

Gao Xingjian 高行健
Gao Yang 高陽
geguliaoqin 割股療親
gewenhuaming 革文化命
gewu zhizhi 格物至知
Guan Zhong 管仲
Gushikao 古史考

Han Fei 韓非
  Shiguo 十過
Han Yu 韓愈
  Bo Yi song 伯夷頌
haochi lanzuo 好吃懶做
haorang 好讓
He Jingzhi 賀敬之
  Taiyang zai xintou 太陽在心頭
henbude bani chile 恨不得把你吃了
Heshang 河殤
hongyan boming 紅顏薄命
Hu Heqing 胡河清
Hu Pan 胡畔
Hu Yepin 胡也頻
huaidan 壞蛋
Huainanzi 淮南子
Huang Fangzhu 黃鳳祝
Huang Ziping 黃子平
Huangdi 黃帝
huangdi shi fanrouweizhi 黃帝始燔肉為炙
Huapian zazhi 話片雜誌

Hui Neng 惠能
  Liuzu tanjing 六祖壇經

Ji Hongzhen 季紅真
Jia Yi 賈誼
Jiang Guangci 蔣光慈
Jiang Yuanlun 蔣原倫
Jin Gangzuan 金剛鑽
jingshen 精神
jingshen shiliang 精神食糧
jiu se cai qi 酒色財氣
jiuchi roulin 酒池肉林
Jiushehui baren biancheng gui; xinshehui bagui biancheng ren
  舊社會把人變成鬼, 新社會把鬼變成人

Kongzi 孔子
  Lunyu 論語
kouchi 口吃
kuanghuanjie 狂歡節
kuangren 狂人
Kunan de licheng 苦難的歷程
Kuriyagawa Hakuson 廚川白村

laihama xiangchi tian'e'rou 癩蛤蟆想吃天鵝肉
Laozi 老子
  Daodejing 道德經
Li Ang 李昂
  殺夫
Li Ji 李季
  Wang Gui he Li Xiangxiang 王貴和李香香
Li Oufan 李歐梵
Li Tuo 李砣
Li Yi 李怡
Li Youyuan 李有源
Li Zehou 李澤厚

Lieshizhuan 列士傳
Lin Yutang 林語堂
Ling Shuhua 凌淑華
Ling Yu 凌宇
Liu Qing 柳青
  Tudi de erzi 土地的兒子
Liu Xiaobo 劉曉波
Liu Zhenyun 劉震云
  Wengu yijiusier 溫故一九四二
Lü Buwei 呂不韋
  Lüshi chunqiu 呂氏春秋
Lu Ling 路翎
Lu Wenfu 陸文夫
  Chi kongqi 吃空氣
  Meishijia 美食家
Lu Xun 魯迅
  Changmingdeng 長明燈
  Dengxia manbi 燈下漫筆
  Kuangren riji 狂人日記
  Lunzhaoxiang zhilei 論照相之類
  Nahan 吶喊
  Shidiao de haodiyu 失掉的好地獄
  Yao 藥
  Yecao 野草
  Zhaohua xishi 朝花夕拾
Lu Yin 盧隱
Lu You 陸游
  Laoxue'an biji 老學菴筆記
Luo Guanzhong 羅貫中
  Sanguo yanyi 三國演義

Ma Feng 馬烽
mamu de shenqing 麻木的神情
mantou 饅頭
Mao Dun 茅盾

Mao Zedong 毛澤東
Mei Cheng 枚乘
  Qifa 七發
Mengzi 孟子
Miaozi 苗子
minyishi weitian 民以食為天
minzu chuantong wenhua 民族傳統文化
minzu wenhua chuantong 民族文化傳統
minzu yishi 民族意識
minzude dazhongde wenyi 民族的, 大眾的文藝
Mo Yan 莫言
  Baimianhua 白棉花
  Fennu de suantai 憤怒的蒜薹
  Fuqin zai minfulian 父親在民兵連
  Honggaoliang jiazu 紅高粱家族
  Huanle 歡樂
  Huanle shisanzhang 歡樂十三章
  Jiuguo 酒國 (Mingdingguo 酩酊國)
  Shicao jiazu 食草家族
  Tiantang suantai zhige 天堂蒜薹之歌
  Touming de hongluobo 透明的紅蘿蔔
  wangbuliao chi 忘不了吃
  Wode guxiang he tongnian 我的故鄉和童年
momo 饃饃
Mozi 墨子
  Guiyi 貴義
mu 牧
mumin 牧民

Nanyanpian 難言篇
Ni Bin 倪彬
niannian youyu 年年有余 (魚)
Nie Hualing 聶華苓
  Sangqing yu Taohong 桑青与桃紅

paima 拍馬

Quan Yanchi 權延赤
Qian Liqun 錢理群
qianchengde 虔誠的
Qianfulun 錢賦論
qianghua minzu wenhua yishi 強化民族文化意識
qidaizi 棋呆子
Qin Zhaoyang 秦兆陽
Anmen Maozhuxi youbanfa 俺們毛主席有辦法
Qiujin 秋瑾
qunzhong 群眾
quwei 趣味

Re'ai shengming 熱愛生命
renben zhuyi 人本主義
reniunai 熱牛奶
renmin neibu 人民內部
renrou 人肉
renxiangshi 人相食
Rou Shi 柔石
rougan 肉感
Rouputuan 肉蒲團
roushen 肉身
roushi 肉食
roushizhe 肉食者
routi 肉體
rouyan 肉眼
rouyu 肉慾
ruci eryi 如此而以
rurou 入肉 (肏)

sancun bulan zhishe 三寸不爛之舌
se, xiang, wei 色, 香, 味
Shanhaijing 山海經

shangjian 賞鑒
shanyaodanpai 山藥蛋派
Shao Yanxiang 邵燕翔
Shaolinsi ziliaoji 少林寺資料集
Shen Congwen 沈從文
  Ailisi Zhongguo youji 愛麗思中國遊記
  Chuzi 廚子
  Labazhou 腊八粥
  Lansheng tong Lanshengtaitai 嵐生同嵐生太太
  Lubian 爐邊
  Qige yeren yu zuihou yige yingchunjie 七個野人與最後一個迎春節
  Sange nanren he yige nüren 三個男人與一個女人
  Shangui 山鬼
  Songzijun 松子君
  Wangshi 往事
  Yeyu 夜雨
  Ye 夜
  Yisheng 醫生
  Xue 雪
  Zaisishu 在私塾
Shen Nong 神農
Shen Nong bencao jing 神農本草經
Shen Rong 諶容
shenghuo 生活
shengming 生命
shenti 身體
Shi Nai'an 施耐庵
  Shuihuzhuan 水滸傳
Shi Shuqing 施叔青
Shiben 世本
shice xingye 食色性也
shijie yanguang 世界眼光
shikesi er bukeru 士可死而不可辱
shiren 食人
shirou qinpi 食肉寢皮

shiyang buhua 食洋不化
shizhong de shengju 示眾的盛舉
Shu Qi 叔齊
shuike 說客
shuitang yizhiwei 說湯以至味
Sima Qian 司馬遷
  Bo Yi liezhuan 伯夷列傳
  Shiji 史記
  Wudi benji 五帝本紀
  Yinbenji 殷本紀
sixiang gaizao 思想改造
Su Ding 蘇丁
Sun Yushi 孫雨石

Taiping yulan 太平御覽
Taizupian 泰族篇
Tan yanhua 歎煙花
Tao Yang 陶陽
tiaohe wuwei 調和五味
titian xingdao 替天行道
tubaozi 土包子

Wang Anyi 王安憶
  Changhenge 長恨歌
  Gexing Riben lai 歌星日本來
Wang Dewei 王德威
Wang Jizhi 王繼志
Wang Meng 王蒙
  Jianyingde xizhou 堅硬的稀粥
Wang Ruowang 王若望
  Ji'e sanbuqu 飢餓三部曲
  Lüzhanzhang 呂站長
Wang Xiaoming 王曉明
Wang Yisheng 王一生
Wang Zengqi 汪曾祺

wanzhong ziwei 萬種滋味
weidao 味道
weitong jiaola 味同嚼蠟
weiwulunzhe de qishilu 唯物論者的啟示錄
wenbao jieduan 溫飽階段
wenbao sheng yinyu 溫飽生淫慾
wenhua duanlie 文化斷裂
wenhua jiaodu 文化角度
wenhua shiliang 文化食糧
wenhuare 文化熱
wenhuaxinli jiegou 文化心理結構
wenyi zaidao 文以載道
Wenyibao 文藝報
wode youyu jiushi wode yule 我的憂鬱就是我的娛樂
Wu Cheng'en 吳承恩
  Xiyouji 西遊記
Wu Zuxiang 吳組緗
wukong 悟空

Xia Gaizun 夏丐尊
Xiandai wulixue yu dongfang shenmi zhuyi 現代物理學與東方神秘主義
xiangshi 相食
Xiao Hong 蕭紅
  Hulanhe zhuan 呼蘭河傳
  Shangshijie 商市街
Xiao Jun 蕭軍
xiaokang jieduan 小康階段
xiaozhufu 小主婦
Xie Shuangtian 謝霜天
xinggan 性感
xingyu 性慾
xinshang 欣賞
xintianyou 信天遊
Xinyue 新月

xiuse kecan 秀色可餐
Xu Xilin 徐錫麟

Yan Hui 顏回
Yan'an wenyi congshu 延安文藝叢書
Yandi 炎帝
yangbaozi 洋包子
yanhuang zisun 炎黃子孫
yaoyan miaodao 要言妙道
ye buguo shi 也不過是
Ye Hong 野蕻
  Xinkendi 新墾地
Ye Shengtao 葉聖陶
Yi Yin 伊尹
yiku sitian 憶苦思甜
yishi fumu 衣食父母
Yishijuan 繹史卷
yishizu zezhi rongru 衣食足則知榮辱
yishu siwei 藝術思維
yisi 意思
yiwei 意味
yiwei shenchang 意味深長
yiya xianzi 易牙獻子
yiyi 意義
yizi ershi 易子而食
Yu Dafu 郁達夫
Yu Hua 余華
  Gudian aiqing 古典愛情
Yuan Ke 袁珂
  Gushenhua xuanshi 古神話選釋
  Zhongguo gudai shenhua 中國古代神話
yuanxiao 元宵

zaifu 宰夫
zazhong 雜種

Zhang Ailing 張愛玲
Yangge 秧歌
Zhang Xianliang 張賢亮
Lühuashu 綠化樹
Zhao Shuli 趙樹理
Zhen Yi 鄭義
Hongse jinianbei 紅色紀念碑
zhiwei 至味
Zhong Chengxiang 仲呈祥
zhongguo chuantong wenhua 中國傳統文化
zhongguo chuantong yishu renge 中國傳統藝術人格
zhongguo minzu qizhi 中國民族氣質
zhongguo minzu wenhua 中國民族文化
zhongguo wenhua jingshen 中國文化精神
zhongguo wenhua tese 中國文化特色
Zhonghua qidao bijing butui 中華棋道畢竟不頹
Zhonghua zhidao bijing butui 中華之道畢竟不頹
zhongzao 中灶
Zhou Libo 周立波
Zhou Zuoren 周作人
Zhoushu 周書
Zhu Ziqing 朱自清
Zhuangzi 莊子
yangsheng 養生
ziwei 滋味
Zizhitongjian 資治通鑒
zu 俎
Zuo Qiuming 左丘明
Zuozhuan 左傳
zuochi shankong 坐吃山空

Bibliography

Ah Cheng. 1984. "Yixie hua" (A few words). *Zhongpian xiaoshuo xuankan* 6:237.

———. 1985. "The Chess Master." Trans. W. J. F. Jenner. *Chinese Literature* (Beijing) 2:84–131.

———. 1990. *Three Kings: Three Stories from Today's China*. Trans. Bonnie S. McDougall. London: Collins Harvill.

———. 1992. "Qiwang" (The chess king). In *Qiwang shuwang haiziwang* (The chess king, the king of trees, the king of children). Taipei: Haifeng chuban youxiangongsi. Originally published in *Shanghai wenxue* 1984.7: 15–35.

Ahmad, Aijaz. 1987. "Jameson's Rhetoric of Otherness and the 'National Allegory.'" *Social Text* 17:3–25.

———. 1992. *In Theory*. London: Verso.

Ai Qing. 1984. "Zhankai jietoushi yundong" (Promoting the movement of poetry in the street). In *Wenyi lilun juan*. Changsha: Hunan renmin chubanshe. Originally published in *Jiefang ribao* (Liberation daily), Sept. 27, 1942.

Allan, Sarah. 1991. *The Shape of the Turtle: Myth, Art, and Cosmos in Early China*. Albany: SUNY Press.

Anderson, Benedict. 1983. *Imagined Communities: Reflections on the Origin and Spread of Nationalism*. London: Verso.

Anderson, E. N. 1988. *The Food of China*. New Haven: Yale University Press.

Ayres, Ed. 1995. "Note to Readers." *World Watch*, January-February, 3.

Bakhtin, M. M. 1981. *The Dialogic Imagination*. Ed. Michael Holquist. Trans. Caryl Emerson and Michael Holquist. Austin: University of Texas Press.

———. 1984. *Rabelais and His World*. Trans. Helene Iswolsky. Bloomington: Indiana University Press.

Barthes, Roland. 1978. *A Lover's Discourse: Fragments*. Trans. Richard Howard. New York: Hill and Wang.

———. 1981. *Camera Lucida*. Trans. Richard Howard. New York: Hill and Wang.

Beijing shifan daxue zhongwenxi (Beijing Normal University Department of Chinese), ed. 1981. *Jinian Lu Xun danchen baizhounian: Wenxue lunwenji ji Lu Xun zhencang youguan beishida shiliao* (Collection of essays in commemoration of the hundredth anniversary of Lu Xun's birth and historical materials preserved by Lu Xun concerning Beijing Normal University). Beijing: Beijing shifan daxue chubanshe.

Benjamin, Walter. 1969. *Illuminations*. Ed. Hannah Arendt. Trans. Harry Zohn. New York: Shocken.

———. 1977. *The Origin of German Tragic Drama*. Trans. John Osborne. London: New Left Books.

———. 1983. *Charles Baudelaire: A Poet in the Era of High Capitalism*. Trans. Quintin Hoare. London: Verso.

———. 1985. "Central Park." Trans. Lloyd Spencer. *New German Critique* 34:32–55.

Bhabha, Homi K., ed. 1990. *Nation and Narration*. London: Routledge.

Blinde, Patricia Lin. 1979. "The Icicle in the Desert: Perspective and Form in the Works of Two Chinese-American Women Writers." MELUS 6.3: 51–71.

Brenkman, John. 1983. "Theses on Cultural Marxism." *Social Text* 7:19–33.

Brown, James W. 1984. *Fictional Meals and Their Function in the French Novel, 1798–1848*. Toronto: University of Toronto Press.

Brown, Lester R. 1995. *Who Will Feed China? Wake-Up Call for a Small Planet*. New York: Norton.

Brown, Paula, and Donald Tuzin, eds. 1983. *The Ethnography of Cannibalism*. Washington, D.C.: Society for Psychological Anthropology.

Cao, Lan, and Himilce Novas. 1996. *Everything You Need to Know About Asian-American History*. New York: Plume/Penguin.

Capra, Fritjof. 1975. *The Tao of Physics*. Berkeley: Shambhala.

———. 1983. *Xiandai wulixue yu dongfang shenmi zhuyi* (Modern physics and oriental mysticism). Ed. and trans. Guan Geng. Chengdu: Sichuan renmin chubanshe.

Chan, Sucheng, ed. 1991. *Entry Denied: Exclusion and the Chinese Community in America, 1882–1943*. Philadelphia: Temple University Press.

Chang, K. C., ed. 1977. *Food in Chinese Culture: Anthropological and Historical Perspectives*. New Haven: Yale University Press.

Chang, Sung-sheng Yvonne. 1993. *Modernism and the Native Resistance: Contemporary Chinese Fiction from Taiwan*. Durham: Duke University Press.

Chen Kuide. 1992. " 'Wenhuare' de zhuyao sixiangyuanyuan ji liangzhong qingxiang" (Major intellectual origins and two trends in the "cultural fever"). In *Cong Wuci dao Heshang* (From May Fourth to River Elegy), ed. Su Xiaokang et al. Taipei: Fengyunshidai chubangongsi.

Chen Pingyuan. 1986. "Wenhua xungen yuma" (Culture, searching for roots, and linguistic code). *Dushu* 1:40–43.

Chen Pingyuan, Qian Liqun, and Huang Ziping. 1985–86. " 'Ershi shiji zhongguo wenxue' sanrentan" (Discussions of the essay" on twentieth-century

Chinese literature"). *Dushu* 10 (1985): 3–11; 11 (1985): 79–87; 12 (1985): 68–76; 1 (1986): 83–93; 2 (1986): 74–82; 3 (1986): 86–94.

Chen Sihe. 1986. "Dangdai wenxuezhong de wenhua xungen yishi" (Cultural consciousness of searching for roots in contemporary literature). *Wenxue pinglun* 6:24–33.

Chen Yizi. 1990. *Zhongguo: shinian gaige yu bajiu minyun* (China's ten-year reform and the democracy movement of 1989). Taipei: Lianjing chuban shiye gongci.

Chin, Frank. 1991. "Come All Ye Asian American Writers of the Real and the Fake." In *The Big Aiiieeeee! An Anthology of Chinese and Japanese American Literature*, ed. Jeffery Paul Chen et al. New York: Meridian.

Chin, Frank, et al. 1972. "Aiiieeeee! An Introduction to Asian-American Writing." *Bulletin of Concerned Asian Scholars* 4.3: 34–46.

Chow, Rey. 1991. *Woman and Chinese Modernity*. Minneapolis: University of Minnesota Press.

———. 1995. *Primitive Passions: Visuality, Sexuality, Ethnography, and Contemporary Chinese Cinema*. New York: Columbia University Press.

Chu, Louis. 1961. *Eat a Bowl of Tea*. Seattle: University of Washington Press.

Conrad, Joseph. 1988. *Heart of Darkness*. Ed. Robert Kimbrough. New York: Norton.

Dai Jinhua. 1996. "Redemption and Consumption: Depicting Culture in the 1990s." Trans. Edward Gunn. *positions: east asian cultures critique* 4.1: 127–43.

de Man, Paul. 1983. *Blindness and Insight*. 2d ed., rev. Minneapolis: University of Minnesota Press.

Delezelova-Velingerova, Milena. 1977. "Lu Xun's 'Medicine.' " In *Modern Chinese Literature in the May Fourth Era*, ed. Merle Goldman. Cambridge: Harvard University Press.

Denton, Kirk A., ed. 1996. *Modern Chinese Literary Thought: Writings on Literature, 1893–1945*. Stanford: Stanford University Press.

Derrida, Jacques. 1981. *Dissemination*. Chicago: University of Chicago Press.

Ding Ling. 1983. *Ding Ling wenji* (Writings of Ding Ling). 2 vols. Changsha: Hunan renmin chubanshe.

———. 1989. *I Myself Am a Woman: Selected Writings of Ding Ling*. Ed. Tani E. Barlow with Gary J. Bjorge. Boston: Beacon.

Dirlik, Arif. 1983. "The Predicament of Marxist Revolutionary Consciousness: Mao Zedong, Antonio Gramsci, and the Reformulation of Marxist Revolutionary Theory." *Modern China* 9.2: 182–211.

Douglas, Mary. 1972. "Deciphering a Meal." *Daedalus* 101.1: 61–81.

Du Maike [Michael S. Duke]. 1985. "Zhonghua zhidao bijing butui" (The Chinese way has not declined after all). *Jiushi niandai* 8:82–85.

Du Shengxiu. 1989. " 'Shangshi shirenminzu' de xianjuezhe de beiju" (The tragedy of the enlightened in "a cannibalistic nation"). In *Lu Xun yanju* (Studies of Lu Xun), vol. 14. Beijing: Zhongguo shehuikexue chubanshe.

Duke, Michael S. 1987. "Two Chess Masters, One Chinese Way: A Comparison of Chang Hsi-kuo's and Chung Ah-ch'eng's Ch'i wang. *Asian Culture Quarterly* (Winter): 41–63.

Eagleton, Terry. 1987. "Estrangement and Irony." *Salmagundi* 73:25–32.

Eco, Umberto. 1979. *A Theory of Semiotics.* Bloomington: Indiana University Press.

Ellmann, Maud. 1993. *The Hunger Artists: Starving, Writing, and Imprisonment.* Cambridge: Harvard University Press.

Farquhar, Judith. 1994. "Eating Chinese Medicine." *Cultural Anthropology* 9.4: 471–97.

Frank, Andre Gunder. 1998. *ReORIENT: Global Economy in the Asian Age.* Berkeley: University of California Press.

Freud, Sigmund. 1957. "Fetishism." In *Collected Papers,* ed. James Strachey. Vol. 5. London: Hogarth.

———. 1961. *Civilization and Its Discontents.* Trans. James Strachey. New York: Norton.

Gao Yang. 1983. *Gujin shishi* (Food past and present). Taipei: Huangguan chubanshe.

Gare, Arran E. 1995. *Postmodernism and the Environmental Crisis.* London: Routledge.

Gates, Henry Louis, Jr., ed. 1984. *Black Literature and Literary Theory.* New York: Methuen.

———, ed. 1986. *"Race," Writing, and Difference.* Chicago: University of Chicago Press.

———. 1988. *The Signifying Monkey: A Theory of African-American Literary Criticism.* New York: Oxford University Press.

Goldblatt, Howard. 1976. *Hsiao Hung.* Boston: Twayne.

———. 1990. "Sex and Society: The Fiction of Li Ang." In *Worlds Apart: Recent Chinese Writing and Its Audiences,* ed. Howard Goldblatt. Armonk, N.Y.: M. E. Sharpe.

Goodman, David, and Michael Redcliff. 1991. *Refashioning Nature: Food, Ecology, and Culture.* London: Routledge.

Grey, George. 1956. *Polynesian Mythology and Ancient Traditional History of the Maori as Told by Their Priests and Chiefs.* Ed. W. W. Bird. Auckland: Whitcombe and Tombs LTD.

Han Fei. 1963. *Han Feizi jishi* (Collected writings of Han Feizi). Annot. Chen Qiyou. 2 vols. Taipei: Shijie shuju.

Han Yu. 1957. "Bo Yi song" (Eulogy of Bo Yi). In *Han Changli wenji jiaozhu* (Collected essays of Han Cangli), annot. Ma Tongbo. Shanghai: Zhonghua shuju.

———. 1979. "Eulogy of Bo Yi." Trans. Shih Shun Liu. In *Chinese Classical Prose.* Hong Kong: Chinese University Press.

Harris, Marvin. 1985. *Good to Eat.* New York: Simon and Schuster.

Haslam, Gerald W. 1970. *Forgotten Pages of American Literature.* Boston: Houghton Mifflin.

He Jingzhi. 1984. "Taiyang zai xintou" (The sun shines in our hearts). In *Shige juan.* Changsha: Hunan renmin chubanshe.

He Jingzhi and Ding Yi. 1946. *Baimaonü* (White-haired girl). Zhangjiakou: Xinhua shoudian.

Hsia, C. T. 1961. *A History of Modern Chinese Fiction.* New Haven: Yale University Press.

Hu Heqing. 1989. "Lun Ah Cheng, Ma Yuan, Zhang Wei: Daojia wenhua zhihuide yange" (Continuation and development of Daoist cultural wisdom in Ah Cheng, Ma Yuan, and Zhang Wei). *Wenxue pinglun* 2:71–80.

Hu Shih. 1953. "Ch'an (Zen) Buddhism in China: Its History and Method." *Philosophy East and West* 3:3–24.

Huang Fengzhu. 1987. "Shilun 'Qiwang'" (A commentary on "The Chess King"). *Wenyi lilun yanjiu* 2:54–56.

Huang Ziping. 1984. "Wodu 'Lühuashu'" (Reading "Mimosa"). *Wenyibao* 11: 22–25.

Huang Ziping, Chen Pingyuan, and Qian Liqun. 1985. "Lun 'ershi shiji zhongguo wenxue'" (On "Twentieth-century Chinese literature"). *Wenxue pinglun* 5:3–13.

Hui Neng. 1982. *Sutra of Hui Neng (Liuzu tanjing).* Bilingual ed. Hong Kong: H. K. Buddhist Book Distributor.

Hulme, Peter. 1986. *Colonial Encounters: Europe and the Native Caribbean, 1492–1797.* London and New York: Methuen.

Huters, Theodore. 1984. "Blossoms in the Snow: Lu Xun and the Dilemma of Modern Chinese Literature." *Modern China* 10.1: 49–77.

———. 1985. "Speaking of Many Things: Food, Kings, and the National Tradition in Ah Cheng's 'The Chess King.'" *Modern China* 14.4: 388–418.

———. 1993. "Lives in Profile." In *From May Fourth to June Fourth: Fiction and Film in Twentieth-Century China,* ed. David Derwei Wang. Cambridge: Harvard University Press.

Jameson, Fredric. 1981. *The Political Unconscious.* Ithaca: Cornell University Press.

———. 1983. "Postmodernism and the Consumer Society." In *The Anti-Aesthetic,* ed. Hal Foster. Port Townsend, Wash.: Bay Press.

———. 1984a. "Postmodernism, or the Cultural Logic of Late Capitalism." *New Left Review* 146:53–92.

———. 1984b. "Literary Innovation and Modes of Production: A Commentary." *Modern Chinese Literature* 1.1: 67–77.

———. 1986. "Third-World Literature in the Era of Multinational Capitalism." *Social Text* 15:65–88.

———. 1987a. "A Brief Response." *Social Text* 17:26–27.

———. 1987b. "The State of the Subject." *Critical Quarterly* 29.4: 16–25.

Jeanneret, Michel. 1991. *A Feast of Words: Banquets and Table Talk in the Renaissance.* Chicago: University of Chicago Press.

Ji Hongzhen. 1985. "Liangge bici canzhao de shijie: lun Zhang Xianliang de chuangzuo" (Two mutually contrasting worlds: on Zhang Xianliang's fiction). *Dushu* 5:53–60.

———. 1986. "Yuzhou, ziran, shengming, ren: Ah Cheng bixia de 'gushi' " (Cosmos, nature, life, and humans: Ah Cheng's "stories"). *Dushu* 1:49–57.

Jiang Yuanlun. 1986. "Chubi: dangdai xiaoshuo chuangzuo zhongde yizhong wenhua xianxiang" (Crudeness and vulgarity: a cultural phenomenon in contemporary fiction). *Dushu* 10:82–87.

Kane, Penny. 1988. *Famine in China, 1959–61: Demographic and Social Implications.* New York: St. Martin's.

Kilgour, Maggie. 1990. *From Communion to Cannibalism: An Anatomy of Metaphors of Incorporation.* Princeton: Princeton University Press.

Kim, Chernin. 1985. *The Hungry Self: Women, Eating, and Identity.* New York: Times Books.

Kim, Elaine H. 1982. *Asian American Literature: An Introduction to the Writings and Their Social Context.* Philadelphia: Temple University Press.

Kingston, Maxine Hong. 1975. *The Woman Warrior.* New York: Vintage.

———. 1982. "Cultural Mis-readings by American Reviewers." In *Asian and Western Writers in Dialogue: New Cultural Identities*, ed. Guy Amirthanayagam. London: Macmillan.

Kinkley, Jeffery. 1987. *The Odyssey of Shen Congwen.* Stanford: Stanford University Press.

Knechtges, David R. 1986. "A Literary Feast: Food in Early Chinese Literature." *Journal of the American Oriental Society* 106.1: 49–63.

Kongzi [Confucius]. 1979. *The Analects (Lun yü).* Trans. D. C. Lau. Hong Kong: Chinese University Press.

Laozi [Lao Tzu]. 1963. *Lao Tzu: Tao Te Ching.* Trans., with introduction, D. C. Lau. Penguin.

———. 1987. *Laozi xinyi* (A modern translation of Laozi. Trans. and annot. Ren Jiyu. Hong Kong: Zhonghua shuju.

Larson, Wendy. 1991. *Literary Authority and the Modern Chinese Writer.* Durham: Duke University Press.

Larson, Wendy, and Richard Krauss. 1989. "China's Writers, The Nobel Prize, and the International Politics of Literature." *Australian Journal of Chinese Affairs* 21:143–60.

Lau, Joseph, et al., eds. 1981. *Modern Chinese Stories and Novellas, 1919–1949*. New York: Columbia University Press.

Lee, Leo Ou-fan [Li Oufan], ed. 1985. *Lu Xun and His Legacy*. Berkeley: University of California Press.

Lee, Leo Ou-fan [Li Oufan]. 1987. *Voices from the Iron House: A Study of Lu Xun*. Bloomington: Indiana University Press.

Lévi-Strauss, Claude. 1966. "The Culinary Triangle." *Partisan Review* 7.6: 586–95.

Li Ang. 1983. *Shafu—Lucheng Gushi* (The butcher's wife). Taipei: Lianhebaoshe.

———. 1986. *The Butcher's Wife*. Trans. Howard Goldblatt and Ellen Yeung. San Francisco: North Point.

Li Ji (Li Chi). 1990. "Wang Gui he Li Xiangxiang" (Wang Gui and Li Xiangxiang). In *Zhongguo xinwenxue daxi—1937–1949* (A comprehensive anthology of new Chinese literature—1937–1949). Vol. 14. Shanghai: Shanghai wenyi chubanshe. Originally published in *Jiefang ribao* (Liberation daily), Sept. 22–24, 1946.

———. 1954. *Wang Kuei and Li Hsiang-hsiang*. Trans. Yang Hsien-yi and Gladys Yang. Beijing: Foreign Language Press.

Li Oufan [Leo Ou-fan Lee], et al. 1991. "Wenxue: haiwai yu zhongguo" (Literature: overseas and in China). In *Zhongguo dangdai zuojia mianmianguan* (A panorama of contemporary Chinese writers), ed. Lin Jianfa and Wang Jingtao. Changchun: shidai wenyi chubanshe.

Li Xiguang. 1996. "Zhongguo huichengwei chiguang shijieliangshide 'ermo' ma?" (Will China become the 'demon' that eats up the food of the world?" In *Yaomohua Zhongguo de beihou* (Behind demonizing China), ed. Li Xiguang and Liu Kang. Beijing: Zhongguo shehuikexue chubanshe.

Li Yi et al. 1992. "Yu Ah Cheng Donglaxiche" (Chatting with Ah Cheng). In Ah Cheng, *Qiwang shuwang haiziwang* (The chess king, the king of trees, the king of children). Taipei: Haifeng chuban youxiangongsi.

Li Zehou. 1979. *Zhongguo jindai sixiangshi lun* (Essays on early modern Chinese thought). Beijing: Renmin chubanshe.

———. 1985. *Zhongguo gudai sixiangshi lun* (Essays on ancient Chinese thought). Beijing: Renmin chubanshe.

———. 1987. *Zhongguo xiandai sixiangshi lun* (Essays on modern Chinese thought). Beijing: Dongfang chubanshe.

Lin Yutang. 1935. *My Country and My People*. New York: John Day.

Ling Yu. 1988. *Shen Congwen zhuan* (Biography of Shen Congwen). Beijing: Shiyue wenyi chubanshe.

Liu, Lydia H. 1995. *Translingual Practice: Literature, National Culture, and Translated Modernity—China, 1900–1937*. Stanford: Stanford University Press.

Liu Qing. 1984. "Tudide erzi" (Son of the earth). In *Xiaoshuo juan*. Vol. 1. Changsha: Hunan renmin chubanshe.

Liu Xiaobo. 1989. *Xuanze de pipan: yusixianglingxiu Li Zehou duihua* (My choice of critique: the leading intellectual Li Zehou). Taipei: Fengyunshidai chubangongsi.

Liu Zhenyun. 1994. "Wengu yijiusier" (Revisiting 1942). In *1993 Zhongpian xiaoshuoxuan* (Selected novellas of 1993). Beijing: Renmin wenxue chubanshe.

Louie, Kam. 1987. "Short Stories of Ah Cheng: Daoism, Confucianism, and Life." *Australian Journal of Chinese Affairs* 18:1–13.

Lowe, Lisa. 1996. *Immigrant Acts: On Asian American Cultural Politics*. Durham: Duke University Press.

Lü Buwei. 1962. *Lüshi chunqiu jishi* (The annals of Master Lü). Annot. Xu Weiyu. 2 vols. Taipei: Shijie shuju.

Lu Wenfu. 1983. "Meishijia." *Shouhuo* 1:4–45.

———. 1987. *The Gourmet and Other Stories*. London: Reader's International.

———. 1994. "Chi kongqi" (Eating empty air). In *Shijian manbi* (Random notes of time), ed. Bai Hua and Lei Da. Changchun: Shidai wenyi chubanshe.

Lu Xun. 1980. *Selected Works*. Trans. Yang Xianyi and Gladys Yang. 4 vols. Beijing: Foreign Language Press.

———. 1981. *Lu Xun quanji* (Collected writings of Lu Xun). 16 vols. Beijing: Renmin wenxue chubanshe.

Luo Guanzhong. 1959. *Romance of the Three Kingdoms*. Trans. C. H. Brewitt-Taylor. Rutland, Vt.: Tuttle.

———. 1972. *Sanguo yanyi* (Romance of the three kingdoms). Beijing: Remin wenxue chubanshe.

Lyell, William A., Jr. 1976. *Lu Hsün's Vision of Reality*. Berkeley: University of California Press.

MacDonald, William Lewis. 1970. *Characters and Themes in Shen Ts'ung-wen's Fiction*. Ph.D. diss., University of Washington.

MacQueen, John. 1970. *Allegory*. London: Methuen.

Mair, Victor H. 1988. *Mei Cherng's "Seven Stimuli" and Wang Bor's "Pavilion of King Terng": Chinese Poems for Princes*. Queenston, Ont.: Edwin Mellen.

Mao Zedong [Mao Tse-tung]. 1961. *Mao Zedong xuanji* (Selected works of Mao Zedong). 4 vols. Beijing: Renmin chubanshe.

———. 1965. *Selected Works*. Vols. 1–3. Beijing: Foreign Languages Press.

———. 1975. *Selected Works*. Vol. 4. Beijing: Foreign Languages Press.

Mei Lin. 1984. "Lun budui wenyi gongzuo" (Literature and art in the military). In *Wenyi lilun juan*. Changsha: Hunan renmin chubanshe. Originally published in *Dazhong wenyi* (Mass literature and art), June 15, 1941.

Meng, Yue. 1993. "Female Images and National Myth." In *Gender Politics in Modern China*, ed. Tani E. Barlow. Durham: Duke University Press.

Mengzi [Mencius]. 1970. *Mencius*. Trans., with an introduction, D. C. Lau. Penguin.

———. 1984. *Mengzi yizhu* (Mencius). Annot. Yang Bojun. Hong Kong: Zhonghua shuju.

Metz, Christian. 1990. "Photography and Fetish." In *The Critical Image: Essays on Contemporary Photography*, ed. Carol Squiers. Seattle: Bay Press.

Metzger, Thomas. 1977. *Escape from Predicament: Neo-Confucianism and China's Evolving Political Culture*. New York: Columbia University Press.

Miaozi. 1991. *Shen Congwen zhuan* (Biography of Shen Congwen). Beijing: Shishi chubanshe.

Miller, Hillis J. 1981. "The Two Allegories." In *Allegory, Myth, and Symbol*, ed. Morton W. Bloomfield. Cambridge: Harvard University Press.

Mo Yan. 1986. *Toumingde hongluobo* (Translucent turnip). Taipei: Xindi chubenshe.

———. 1988. *Honggaoliang jiazu* (The red sorghum family). Taipei: Hongfan shudian youxiangongsi.

———. 1989a. *Tiantang suantai zhige* (The garlic ballads). Taipei: Hongfan shudian youxiangongsi.

———. 1989b. *Huanle shisanzhang* (Thirteen chapters of joy). Beijing: Zuojia chubanshe.

———. 1991. *Baimianhua* (White cotton). Beijing: Huayi chubanshe.

———. 1992. *Jiuguo* (Liquorland). Taipei: Hongfan shudian youxiangongsi.

———. 1993a. *Fennude suantai* (The garlic of wrath). Beijing: Beijing shifandaxue chubanshe.

———. 1993b. *Shicao jiazu* (The herbivorous family). Beijing: Huayi chubanshe.

———. 1993c. *Red Sorghum*. Trans. Howard Goldblatt. New York: Penguin.

———. 1995. "Wode guxiang he tongnian" (My homeland and childhood). *Xinhua wenzai* 1:104–6.

———. 1997. "Wangbuliao chi" (Can't forget about eating). *Tianya* 5:92–96.

Mote, Frederick W. 1977. "Yüan and Ming." In *Food in Chinese Culture: Anthropological and Historical Perspectives*, ed. K. C. Chang. New Haven: Yale University Press.

Mozi [Motse]. 1929. *The Ethical and Political Works of Motse*. Trans. Yi-Pao Mei. London: Arthur Probsthain.

———. 1974. *Mozi jinzhu jinyi* (Works of Mozi). Annot. Li Yushu. Taipei: Taiwan shangwu yinshuguan.

Nie Hualing [Hua-ling Nieh]. 1976. *Sangqing yu Taohong* (Mulberry and peach). Hong Kong: Youliang chubanshe.

———. 1981. *Two Women of China—Mulberry and Peach*. Trans. Jane Parish Yang with Linda Lappin. Beijing: New World Press.

Nieh, Hua-ling [Nie Hua-ling]. 1972. *Shen Ts'ung-wen*. New York: Twayne.

Owen, Stephen. 1992. *Readings in Chinese Literary Thought*. Cambridge: Harvard University Press.

Plaks, Andrew. 1976. *Archetype and Allegory in the "Dream of the Red Chamber."* Princeton: Princeton University Press.

———. 1977. "Towards a Critical Theory of Chinese Narrative." In *Chinese Narrative: Critical and Theoretical Essays*, ed. Andrew Plaks. Princeton: Princeton University Press.

Prusek, Jaroslav. 1980. *The Lyrical and the Epic: Studies of Modern Chinese Literature*, ed. Leo Ou-fan Lee. Bloomington: Indiana University Press.

Qian Liqun. 1990. *Zhou Zuoren zhuan* (Biography of Zhou Zuoren). Beijing: Beijing shiyuewenyi chubanshe.

Qin Zhaoyang. 1984. "Anmen Maozhuxi youbanfa" (Our Chairman Mao has his ways). In *Xiaoshuo juan*. Vol. 2. Changsha: Hunan renmin chubanshe.

Quan Yanchi. 1990. *Zouxia shentan de Mao Zedong* (Mao Zedong: descending the temple of gods). Hong Kong: Nanyue chubanshe.

Rees, William Lee and L. Rees. 1892. *The Life and Times of Sir George Grey, K.C.B.* 2 vols. London: Hutchinson & Co.

Rickett, W. Allyn. 1985. *Guanzi: Political, Economic, and Philosophical Essays—A Study and Translation*. Princeton: Princeton University Press.

Ryan, Michael. 1989. *Politics and Culture: Working Hypotheses for a Post-Revolutionary Society*. Baltimore: Johns Hopkins University Press.

Said, Edward W. 1979. *Orientalism*. New York: Random.

Sanborn, Geoffrey. 1998. *The Sign of the Cannibal: Melville and the Making of a Postcolonial Reader*. Durham: Duke University Press.

Sanday, Peggy Reeves. 1986. *Divine Hunger*. Cambridge: Cambridge University Press.

Saussy, Haun. 1993. *The Problem of a Chinese Aesthetic*. Stanford: Stanford University Press.

Schafer, Edward H. 1977. "T'ang." In *Food in Chinese Culture: Anthropological and Historical Perspectives*, ed. K. C. Chang. New Haven: Yale University Press.

Sessions, George, ed. 1995. *Deep Ecology for the 21st Century: Readings on the Philosophy and Practice of the New Environmentalism*. Boston: Shambhala.

Shao Yanxiang. 1984. "Xingchunzhe, dan bushi gouhuozhe: Zhang Xianliang's 'Lühuashu' duhou" (A survivor, not a capitulator: reading Zhang Xianliang's "Mimosa"). *Wenyibao* 5:22–25.

Shaolinsi ziliaoji (Research materials on Shao Lin Temple). 1982. Beijing: Shumu wenxian chubanshe.

Shen Congwen. 1984. *Shen Congwen wenji* (Collected writings of Shen Congwen). Ed. Shao Huaqiang and Ling Yu. 12 vols. Hong Kong and Guangzhou: Sanlian shudian and Huacheng chubanshe.

Shen Rong. 1980. "Rendao zhongnian" (At middle age). *Shouhuo* 1:52–92.

———. 1984. "At Middle Age." Trans. Margaret Decker. In *Roses and Thorns*, ed. Perry Link. Berkeley: University of California Press.

Shi Nai'an. 1972. *Shuihuzhuan* (Water margin). Beijing: Renmin wenxue chubanshe.

Shi Shuqing. 1987. "Yu 'Qiwang' zuozhe Ah Cheng de duihua" (A conversation with Ah Cheng, the author of "The Chess King"). *Wenyi lilun yanjiu* 2:47–53.

Shige juan (Volume of poetry). 1984. *Yan'an wenyi congshu* (Series of literature and the arts of the Yan'an period). Changsha: Hunan renmin chubanshe.

Sima Qian [Ssu-ma Ch'ien]. 1959. *Shiji* (Records of the historian). Vol. 5. Beijing: Zhonghua shuju.

———. 1969. *Records of the Historian*. Trans. Burton Watson. New York: Columbia University Press.

Simmons, Frederick J. 1991. *Food in China: A Cultural and Historical Inquiry*. Boca Raton: CRC Press.

Smith, Authur H. 1894. *Chinese Characteristics*. New York: Revell.

Spence, Jonathan. 1977. "Ch'ing." In *Food in Chinese Culture: Anthropological and Historical Perspectives*, ed. K. C. Chang. New Haven: Yale University Press.

Spencer, Lloyd. 1985. "Allegory in the World of the Commodity: The Importance of 'Central Park.' " *New German Critique* 34:59–77.

Su Ding. 1986. "Ping 'Shuwang' de tianrenguan he beiju yishi" (On the anthropo-cosmic ideal and tragic consciousness in Ah Cheng's "The King of Trees"). *Dangdai zuojia pinglun* 4:90–93.

———. 1987a. "Jinnianlai xiaoshuozhong de sanzhong rensheng zhuti bijiao" (A comparative study of three thematic treatments of life in contemporary fiction). *Wenxue pinglun* 3:45–53.

———. 1987b. "Quedao tianliang haogeqiu: Ah Cheng de beiju yishi" (Ah Cheng's tragic consciousness). *Dushu* 5:49–53.

Su Ding and Zhong Chengxiang. 1985a. "Lun Ah Cheng de meixue zhuiqiu" (On Ah Cheng's aesthetic search). *Wenxue pinglun* 6:53–60.

———. 1985b. " 'Qiwang' yu daojia meixue" ("The Chess King" and Daoist aesthetics). *Dangdai zuojia pinglun* 3:20–26.

Su, Karen. 1994. "Jade Snow Wong's Badge of Distinction in the 1990s." *Critical Mass: A Journal of Asian American Criticism* 2.1: 3–52.

Sun Yushi. 1982. *'Yechao' yanjiu* (Studies of *Wild Grass*). Beijing: Zhongguo shehui kexue chubanshe.

Takaki, Ronald. 1989. *Strangers from a Different Shore: A History of Asian Americans*. New York: Penguin.

Tan, Amy. 1989. *The Joy Luck Club*. New York: Ivy Books.

———. 1991a. *The Kitchen God's Wife*. New York: Putnam.

———. 1991b. "Mother Tongue." In *The Best American Essays, 1991*. New York: Ticknor & Fields.

Tang, Xiaobing. 1992. "Lu Xun's 'Diary of a Madman' and a Chinese Modernism." *PMLA* 107.5: 1222–34.

Tannahill, Reay. 1975. *Flesh and Blood.* New York: Stein and Day.

Tao Yang and Zhong Xiu. 1989. *Zhongguo chuangshi shenhua* (The creation myth of China). Shanghai: Shanghai renmin chubanshe.

Tian Lan. 1984. "Wo, Yan'anshi Qiaoergouqu de gongmin" (I, a citizen of qiaoergou district, Yan'an city). In *Shige juan.* Changsha: Hunan renmin chubanshe.

Wang Anyi. 1996a. *Changhenge* (Melody of lasting regret). Beijing: Zuojia chubanshe.

———. 1996b. *Wang Anyi zixuanji* (Self-selected writings). 4 vols. Beijing: Zuojia chubanshe.

Wang, Chi-chen, trans. 1944. *Contemporary Chinese Stories.* New York: Columbia University Press.

Wang, David Derwei [Wang Dewei]. 1992. *Fictional Realism in 20th-Century China.* New York: Columbia University Press.

Wang Dewei [David Derwei Wang]. 1991. *Yuedu dangdai xiaoshuo* (Reading contemporary fiction). Taipei: Yuanliu chubangongsi.

———. 1997. "Chongdu Zhang Ailing de *Yangge* yu *Chidi zhilian*" (Rereading Zhang Ailing's *Yangge* and *Love of Scorched Land*). *Journal of Modern Literature in Chinese* (Hong Kong) 1.1: 27–45.

Wang, Jing. 1989. "The Poetics of Chinese Narrative: An Analysis of Andrew Plaks' *Archetype and Allegory in the 'Dream of the Red Chamber.'* " *Comparative Literature Studies* 25.3: 252–70.

———. 1996. *High Culture Fever: Politics, Aesthetics, and Ideology in Deng's China.* Berkeley: University of California Press.

Wang Jizhi. 1992. *Shen Congwen lun* (On Shen Congwen). Nanjing: Jiangsu jiaoyu chubanshe.

Wang Meng. 1984. "Qieshuo 'Qiwang' " (A commentary on "The Chess King"). *Wenyibao* 10:43–45.

———. 1993. *Jianying de xizhou* (Crusted congee). Hong Kong: Tiandi tushu youxiangongsi.

Wang Ruowang. 1980. "Ji'e sanbuqu" (Hunger trilogy). *Shouhuo* 1:116–73.

———. 1984. "Lüzhanzhang" (Director Lü). In *Xiaoshuo juan.* Vol. 2. Changsha: Hunan renmin chubanshe.

———. 1991a. *Hunger Trilogy.* Trans. Kyna Rubin with Ira Kasoff. Armonk and London: M. E. Sharpe.

———. 1991b. *Wang Ruowang zizhuan* (Autobiography of Wang Ruowang). Hong Kong: Mingbao chubanshe.

Wang Xiaoming. 1986. "Suluomen de pingzi: lun Zhang Xianliang de xiaoshuo chuangzuo" (Soloman's bottle: Zhang Xianliang's fiction). *Shanghai wenxue* 2:88–96.

———. 1988. "Buxiangxinde he buyuanyi xiangxinde" (I don't believe and I don't want to believe). *Wenxue pinglun* 4:24–35.

Wang, Yuejin. 1991. "*Red Sorghum*: Mixing Memory and Desire." In *Perspectives on Chinese Cinema*, ed. Chris Berry. London: British Film Institute.

Wang Zongfa and Zhang Qiyou, ed. 1982. *He Jingzhi zhuanji* (Research materials on He Jingzhi). Nanjing: Jiangsu renmin chubanshe.

Wenyi lilun juan (Volume of literary theory). 1984. *Yan'an wenyi congshu* (Series of literature and the arts of the Yan'an period). Changsha: Hunan renmin chubanshe.

Wenyibao. 1984. "Benkan zhaokai 'Lühuashu' taolunhui" (A symposium on "Mimosa"). *Wenyibao* 11:18.

West, Cornel. 1993. *Race Matters*. Boston: Beacon.

White, Theodore H. 1978. *In Search of History: A Personal Adventure*. New York: Harper & Row.

White, Theodore H. and Annalee Jacob. 1946. *Thunder Out of China*. New York: William Sloane.

Wong, Jade Snow. 1945. *Fifth Chinese Daughter*. New York: Harper & Brothers.

———. 1975. *No Chinese Strangers*. New York: Harper & Row.

Wong, Sau-ling Cynthia. 1993. *Reading Asian American Literature: From Necessity to Extravagance*. Princeton: Princeton University Press.

———. 1995. " 'Sugar-Sisterhood': Situating the Amy Tan Phenomenon." In *The Ethnic Canon: Histories, Institutions, and Interventions*, ed. David Palumbo-Liu. Minneapolis: University of Minnesota Press.

Wu Cheng'en. 1943. *Monkey*. Trans. Arthur Waley. New York: John Day.

———. 1975. *Xiyouji* (The journey to the west). Beijing: Renmin wenxue chubanshe.

———. 1977–83. *The Journey to the West*. Trans. Anthony C. Yu. Chicago: University of Chicago Press.

Xia Gaizun. 1992. "Tanchi" (About eating). In *Xianqing leshi* (Leisurely mood and pleasurable things), ed. Chen Pingyuan. Beijing: Renmin wenxue chubanshe.

Xiao Hong. 1986. *Market Street: A Chinese Woman in Harbin*. Trans., with an introduction, by Howard Goldblatt. Seattle and London: University of Washington Press.

———. 1987. *Xiao Hong de Shangshijie* (Market street). Ed. Ge Haowen [Howard Goldblatt]. Taipei: Libai chubanshi youxiangongsi.

———. 1991. *Xiao Hong quanji* (Collected writings of Xiao Hong). 2 vols. Harbin: Harbin chubanshe.

Xiaoshuo juan (Volumes of fiction). 1984. 2 vols. Yan'an wenyi congshu (Series of literature and the arts of the Yan'an period). Changsha: Hunan renmin chubanshe.

Xie Shuangtian. 1972. *Menghui Hulunhe* (Dreams of the Hulan River). Taipei: Erya chubanshe.

Ye Hong. 1984. "Xinkendi" (Reclaimed wasteland). In *Xiaoshuo juan*. Vol. 1. Changsha: Hunan renmin chubanshe. Originally published in *Wenyi zhanxian* (Front line of literature and art) 1.1 (February 26, 1939).

Yü, Chün-fang. 1995. "Filial Piety, Iatric Cannibalism, and the Cult of Kuanyin." Paper presented at the annual meeting of the Association for Asian Studies, April, Washington, D.C.

Yu Hua. 1991. "Gudian aiqing" (Classical love). In *Shishi ruyan* (Like smoke). Taipei: Yuanliu chubanshiye gufenyuoxiangongsi.

———. 1996. *The Past and the Punishments*. Trans. Andrew F. Jones. Honolulu: University of Hawai'i Press.

Yuan Ke. 1960. *Zhongguo gudai shenhua* (Ancient mythology of China). Rev. ed. Beijing: Zhonghua shuju.

———. 1979. *Gushenhua xuanshi* (Selected readings of ancient Chinese mythology). Beijing: Renmin wenxue chubanshe.

Zha, Jianying. 1995. *China Pop: How Soap Operas, Tabloids, and Bestsellers Are Transforming a Culture*. New York: New Press.

Zhang Ailing [Eileen Chang]. 1995. *Yangge: Zhang Ailing Quanji* (Collected writings of Zhang Ailing). Vol. 1. Taipei: Huangguan chubanshe.

Zhang Xianliang. 1985a. "Lühuashu" (Mimosa). In *1984 zhongpian xiaoshuo xuankan huojiang zuopinji* (Anthology of 1984 *Selected Novellas* prize-winning works). Vol. 2. Fuzhou: Haixia wenyi chubanshe.

———. 1985b. *Mimosa and Other Stories*. Trans. Gladys Yang. Beijing: *Chinese Literature*.

———. 1985c. "Guanyu 'Lühuashu' de yixie shuoming" (Some explanations about "Mimosa"). In *1984 zhongpian xiaoshuo xuankan huojiang zuopinji* (Anthology of 1984 *Selected Novellas* prize-winning works). Vol. 2. Fuzhou: Haixia wenyi chubanshe.

Zhang, Xudong. 1997. *Chinese Modernism in the Era of Reform: Cultural Fever, Avant-Garde Fiction, and the New Chinese Cinema*. Durham: Duke University Press.

Zhang, Yingjin. 1990. "Ideology of the Body in *Red Sorghum*: National Allegory, National Roots, and Third Cinema." *East-West Film Journal* 4.2: 38–53.

Zheng Yi. 1985. "Laojing" (Old well). *Dangdai* 2:4–73.

———. 1993. *Hongse jinianbei* (Red monument). Taipei: Huashi wenhua gongsi.

Zhou Zuoren. 1974. *Zhitang Huixianglu* (A memoir). Hong Kong: Sanyu tushuwenju gongsi.

———. 1983. *Zhou Zuoren Wenxuan* (Selected essays). Ed. Yang Mu. Taipei: Hongfanshudian youxiangongsi.

Zhuangzi [Chuang Tzu]. 1962. *Zhuangzi jie* (Exegesis of Zhuangzi). Annot. Wang Fuzhi. Beijing: Zhonghua shuju.

———. 1968. *The Complete Works of Chuang Tzu*. Trans. Burton Watson. New York: Columbia University Press.

Zuo Qiuming. 1960. *The Ch'un Ts'ew with the Tso Chuen*. Trans. James Legge. *The Chinese Classics*, vol. 5. Hong Kong: Hong Kong University Press.

———. 1973. *Chunqiu zuozhuan jinzhu jinyi* (The annals of the spring and autumn and the zuo commentary). Annot. Li Zongtong. 3 vols. Taipei: Taiwan shangwu yinshuguan.

———. 1989. *The Tso Chuan*. Trans. Burton Watson. New York: Columbia University Press.

Index

Gang Yue is Assistant Professor in the Curriculum in Asian Studies at the University of North Carolina, Chapel Hill.

Library of Congress Cataloging-in-Publication Data

Yue, Gang.
The mouth that begs : hunger, cannibalism, and the politics of eating in modern China / Gang Yue.
p. cm. — (Post-contemporary interventions)
Includes bibliographical references and index.
ISBN 0-8223-2308-7 (alk. paper). — ISBN 0-8223-2341-9 (paper : alk. paper)
1. Chinese literature—20th century—History and criticism. 2. Politics in literature. 3. Hunger in literature. 4. American literature—Chinese American authors—History and criticism. I. Title. II. Title: Hunger, cannibalism, and the politics of eating in modern China.
PL2303.Y83 1999
895.1'09358—dc21 98-45873